Stanley Kubrick

Stanley Kubrick

Essays on His Films and Legacy

Edited by Gary D. Rhodes

McFarland & Company, Inc., Publishers

Jefferson, North Carolina, and London

LIBRARY OF CONGRESS CATALOGUING-IN-PUBLICATION DATA

Stanley Kubrick : essays on his films
and legacy / edited by Gary D. Rhodes.
p.   cm.
Includes bibliographical references and index.

ISBN-13: 978-0-7864-3297-4
softcover : 50# alkaline paper ∞

1. Kubrick, Stanley — Criticism and interpretation.
I. Rhodes, Gary Don, 1972–
PN1998.3.K83S84   2008   791.4302'33092 — dc22   2007046243

British Library cataloguing data are available

On the cover: Stanley Kubrick shooting handheld with
an Arriflex camera (background image ©2007 Creatas)

Manufactured in the United States of America

*McFarland & Company, Inc., Publishers
Box 611, Jefferson, North Carolina 28640
www.mcfarlandpub.com*

For Joseph Turkel.
At age ten, I thought he was the scariest man alive,
thanks to his amazing performance in *The Shining* (1980).
Befriending him some fifteen years later,
I realized he is one of the kindest
and most talented gentlemen on this planet.

Table of Contents

Part III. *Eyes Wide Shut* (1999): A Case Study

Part IV. Kubrick's Legacy

Introduction

Gary D. Rhodes

My memories of high school are plentiful, but some of the first that enter my mind are the wonderful times I had watching films with my friend Devin Williams. Thanks to the wonders of the VCR, we scrutinized the important works of Chaplin, Dreyer, Murnau, Lang, and many others. But it was always Stanley Kubrick who captivated us the most. We pondered endlessly over what *2001: A Space Odyssey* (1968) "meant," and buckled over laughing at the dark comedy in *Dr. Strangelove* (1964). The 1921 photo of Jack Torrance at the conclusion of *The Shining* (1980) enthralled us. And our countless viewings of *A Clockwork Orange* (1971) were matched only by countless playbacks of its soundtrack album.

Along with our interest in Kubrick's filmography, we were enthralled by Kubrick the man. Perhaps it was the fact we felt his presence through his absence; after all, he was the man whom movie magazines had dubbed a "recluse." For example, Devin and I read somewhere that he refused to drive an automobile and that he required his chauffeur to drive exceedingly slowly. Elsewhere we read that he loved to burn down the road at top speed behind the wheel of his sports car. These contradictions only served to increase our fascination.

Soon we became aware of the groundbreaking work of Michel Ciment, as well as Thomas Allen Nelson's illuminating text *Kubrick: Inside a Film Artist's Maze* (Indiana UP, 1982). And of course we anxiously awaited any word of a new Kubrick film, ever hopeful that his filmography would continue to grow. Our long wait began with the release of *Full Metal Jacket* (1987).

In the many years since that time, my interest in Kubrick continued, and on more than one occasion I taught a course on his films (as well as a course devoted solely to *2001: A Space Odyssey*) at my alma mater, the University of Oklahoma. During that same period, I befriended Joseph Turkel, who worked in three of Kubrick's films and who kindly gave a wonderful speech on the filmmaker in Oklahoma. The passage of time has also allowed me to learn much from the ever-increasing body of Kubrick literature: the biographical work of John Baxter and Vincent LoBrutto, the theoretical inquiries of Michel Chion, Randy Rasmussen, and Alexander Walker, the photographic analysis of Rainer Crone, and the rather staggering collection of Kubrick's archival materials that Alison Castle edited for Taschen in 2005.

The goal of this current anthology is not to conclude any debates on Kubrick, but rather to participate in the ongoing — indeed, expanding — conversation about his life and work. Indeed, this book does not cover key films like *Lolita* (1962), *Dr. Strangelove or: How I Learned to Stop Worrying and Love the Bomb* (1964) and *Full Metal Jacket* (1987) in any depth. At the same time, a number of essays do examine issues that have previously received very limited coverage, such as Kubrick's photography and newsreels.

Collectively, the seventeen selected essays in this anthology represent analyses of the narratives, genres, themes, visuals, and soundtracks that mark much of Kubrick's work. Without necessarily wanting to force categorical judgment onto Kubrick's canon, I have structured these essays into four sections for the ease of the reader: EARLY WORKS, MAJOR WORKS, *Eyes Wide Shut* (1999): A CASE STUDY, and KUBRICK'S LEGACY.

EARLY WORKS opens with Philippe Mather's fascinating and monumental examination of Kubrick's photography for *Look* magazine, which is followed by Marina Burke's exploration of Kubrick's generally overlooked and rarely seen newsreels. Charles Bane discusses *Fear and Desire* (1953), connecting it to Kubrick's *Paths of Glory* (1957). Tony Williams offers a valuable examination of the dream landscape of *Killer's Kiss* (1955), a film that, along with *The Killing* (1956), is considered by Hugh Manon in his engaging analysis of Kubrick and film noir.

Eric Eaton's revelatory essay on *Paths of Glory* places the film truly at the vanguard of Kubrick's "MAJOR WORKS." Reynold Humphries offers an important analysis on the much-maligned *Spartacus* (1960). My own essay attempts to unravel and interpret layers of surveillance in *2001: A Space Odyssey* (1968), while Kate McQuiston investigates the music in *A Clockwork*

Jack Nicholson (center, bottom) in the photograph dated 1921 that appears at the conclusion of *The Shining* (1980).

Kubrick working on *Full Metal Jacket* in 1987.

Orange (1971) in great depth. Homay King offers a deft examination of spectatorship and the zoom lens in *Barry Lyndon* (1975), and Jarrell D. Wright reconsiders genre and fidelity in *The Shining* (1980).

With regard to *Eyes Wide Shut* (1999), I am reminded that Jan Harlan, Kubrick's executive producer and brother-in-law, told me in 2007 that Kubrick believed it was his greatest film. Some audiences and critics might well disagree with that assessment, though we are still at an early stage in the history of its reception. Certainly we can say that it has not received as much analysis as Kubrick's other major works, largely because of its relatively recent date of release. Our "case study" of the film offers four very different examinations of *Eyes Wide Shut*. Randolph Jordan addresses the issue of sound, while Lindiwe Dovey investigates its representation of gender. Using Bakhtin as a key paradigm, Miriam Jordan and Julian Jason Haladyn examine the film's use of the "carnivalesque." Phillip Sipiora's engaging phenomenological inquiry concludes the quartet of essays on a film that deserves continued analysis.

The final section of the book, KUBRICK'S LEGACY, offers two essays that investigate aspects of the filmmaker's ongoing impact. Scott Loren's essay on *2001: A Space Odyssey* connects his discussion of the "posthuman subject" to Spielberg's *Artificial Intelligence: A.I.* (2001), a film based on Kubrick's unproduced ideas and released two years after his death. Finally, Robert J. E. Simpson's essay "Whose Stanley Kubrick?" tackles the mythology and ownership of the Kubrick image as constructed during his lifetime and in the years since his demise.

That this volume contains such a wide variety of new perspectives on Kubrick has resulted not from myself, but from the tireless efforts of the contributors. I would wish to thank each of them greatly for allowing me to publish their work, as well as for the enthusiasm, suggestions, photographs, and other ideas they offered during the process.

My appreciation also extends to each of the following persons who have assisted on this project: Ryan Baker, Doug Bentin, Melissa Conroy, Jack Dowler, Tony Fitzmaurice, Michael Lee, Marina McDonnell, Kevin Mahoney, Blair Miller, Michael H. Price, Amy J. Ransom, Don and Phyllis Rhodes, Alexander Webb, Devin Williams, John Wooley, and Geoffrey Yetter.

I should also offer great thanks to the film studies faculty and staff at The Queen's University in Belfast, Northern Ireland: Raymond Armstrong, Desmond Bell, Sylvia Borda, Alan Gildea, Fiona Handyside, and Patricia McMurray. I would also like to mention my joy at working with undergraduate students like Peter McCaughan; masters students like Connor Clements, Stephen Ferrin, Seana Kane, Chris Legge, Alanna Riddell, and Robert Simpson; and doctoral students like Fran Apprich, Silvia Casini, and Peter Johnston. The fact that Queen's University has an onsite film theatre and maintains close ties to the Belfast Film Festival adds immensely to the vibrant film culture on campus and in the city at large. The influence of these persons and the Queen's University environment has been tremendously helpful for my own work and enthusiasm for film studies.

Additionally, I would draw particular attention to the help and encouragement of two more colleagues at Queen's University Film Studies Department: Desmond O'Rawe, who took time out of his busy schedule to provide important feedback on my own essay on *2001: A Space Odyssey*, and Marina Burke, who scrutinized various aspects of the manuscript shortly before its completion.

In terms of colleagues in the U.S., I want very much to show appreciation for the assistance of Edward "Eric" Eaton, one of my dearest friends. He truly is a fount of knowledge on Stanley Kubrick and film studies at large, and it has been an honor to work with him.

Last but not least, I would acknowledge the assistance of John Parris Springer at the Uni-

Kubrick on the set of *Full Metal Jacket* (1987).

versity of Central Oklahoma. He was heavily involved in the early stages of this project in many different respects, ranging from soliciting to reading submissions. I have been privileged to work with him for many years on various film productions, film books, and film coursework, and for that he has my endless gratitude.

It seems that the number of new books and essays on Kubrick continues to grow, while others—like the Ciment and the Nelson—appear in revised versions. With the help of my colleagues and contributors, I strongly believe this anthology has resulted in some new ideas and important voices that will interact effectively with other work in this area of inquiry.

Gary D. Rhodes
The Queen's University—Belfast, Northern Ireland

1 Stanley Kubrick and *Look* Magazine

Philippe Mather

While the critical literature on Stanley Kubrick's fiction films is fairly extensive, his photojournalistic production during his five-year tenure at *Look* magazine in the late forties remains relatively unknown. Studies on Kubrick's cinema generally make only passing comments on his training as a photographer. For instance, Norman Kagan briefly claims that Kubrick's career at *Look* merely allowed him to "experiment with the photographic aspects of the cinema," overlooking photojournalism's narrative and editorial aspects.[1] Thomas Allen Nelson provides a half-hearted rationale for ignoring Kubrick's *Look* output, suggesting that the documentary nature of photojournalism was somehow an impediment to the future filmmaker's creative self-expression.[2] By contrast, Michel Chion correctly identifies the importance of the documentary aesthetic in Kubrick's feature fiction films, although he declines to investigate the *Look* photographs.[3]

Until recently, Vincent LoBrutto's biography of Kubrick was one of the only detailed sources of information on the *Look* photographs.[4] This might have alerted scholars to the scope and importance of Kubrick's photojournalistic work, for a more thorough understanding of an influential filmmaker's artistic genesis. The publication of Rainer Crone's photography book *Drama and Shadows* in November 2005 may also serve as a tantalizing introduction to the late American filmmaker's career as photojournalist. However, in avoiding *Look* magazine's original layouts, Crone's art historical approach isolates the photographs from their narrative context and ignores the original decisions in selecting multiple images. One may legitimately speculate that the process of editing still images in accordance with a shooting script, in the collaborative environment of a general interest photo magazine, shaped Kubrick's emerging talent in combining words and images for storytelling purposes.

This essay will focus on the production contexts at *Look* magazine, considering Kubrick's work within a sociology of production. George Ritzer's sociological model will be used to map the relevant components of the collaborative process at *Look* magazine, as well as study the dialectical relationships among the various levels of social analysis. Rather than assume a conflictual relationship between the artist and the institutional context in which he worked, it should be productive to investigate areas of common interest and thus potential influence between *Look* magazine and Stanley Kubrick.

Any decision to examine the influence *Look* magazine had on Kubrick's later development as a filmmaker touches on the issue of authorship, specifically the debate opposing individual agency and structural determinations. This may be controversial to the extent that most critical approaches to Kubrick's oeuvre tend to adopt traditional conceptions of art based on various features of romantic aesthetics, including assumptions regarding the filmmaker's authorial control and creative independence, as well as his unique artistic identity which is felt to emerge in spite of, rather than as a result of, contextual factors. When critic Alexander Walker asks, "What is it that makes Kubrick the kind of director he is," the notion that the filmmaker's photojournalistic training may provide an answer is never explored, perhaps due to a lingering auteurist prejudice against the collaborative natures of filmmaking and photojournalism which undermine the assumption of a singular, self-contained voice, or indeed an artistic genius.[5]

Rainer Crone's *Drama and Shadows* is the end result of an important curatorial effort conducted since 1998 by the Iccarus group, based in Munich at Ludwig Maximilian University's Institute of Art History. Articles published by members of the Iccarus group on Kubrick's work tend to downplay contributions from the social and historical context in analyzing the artist's personal signature. For instance, they present Kubrick's work "outside the magazine context," including unpublished photographs, thus making curatorial decisions intended to retrieve a voice thought to be concealed by the commercial journalistic environment.[6] Also, when acknowledging influences, they focus on comparisons with established art photographers such as Henri-Cartier Bresson, Walker Evans and Robert Frank, rather than with Kubrick's colleagues at *Look*.[7] Michel Chion points out that this curatorial approach elides the fact that Kubrick himself never organized exhibits or published books based on his photographic work during his lifetime, and that these photos were designed to be published in a magazine where they interacted with a written text.[8]

In terms of social theory, such an art historical approach to Kubrick's photographs may lean towards the notion of "innate genius," and only acknowledge appropriate artistic mentorships, largely as a means of assigning value and legitimizing the analysis of photojournalistic work.[9] While it is important to recognize the enduring social relevance of auteurism to the interpretation of texts, there is also a need to broaden the frame of reference for scientific reasons. An approach to authorship which includes both the reader's activity and the discursive contexts in which artists work may shed light on semiotic processes which are publicly accessible or at least located in the social, not the private, sphere. This essay will therefore endeavor to place the issue of individual agency within a sociology of production, and also take into account relevant social, psychological and cultural discourses and practices.[10]

One advantage of a sociology of production is that it acknowledges the fact that both photojournalism and film production are collaborative efforts which take place within an industrial context. Focusing on less noble personal influences and broader social factors may, ironically, help to achieve a fuller understanding of Kubrick's creative output and its development. Scholarship on Kubrick's early films in particular could be enhanced by a thorough examination of his photo-essays, including the contexts in which they were made. Another essay argues elsewhere that a comparative textual analysis of Kubrick's photo-essays, documentary shorts and early fiction films highlights a consistent use of narrative, rhetorical and visual tropes which can be shown to originate in *Look* magazine's photojournalistic methods.[11]

While romantic and humanist critics are committed to an individualistic conception of the expressive artist, post-structuralists argue that the human subject is determined by a host of external and constraining factors which undermine his/her autonomy. Similarly, sociologist George Ritzer describes a polarized and sometimes acrimonious debate in his field. This debate opposes theorists who claim that sociology should only focus on large-scale phenomena, and those who favor analyses of individual behavior.[12] Ritzer proposes instead an integrative sociological model which combines two different methods of describing levels of social reality (*see* Figure 1). The first method is the macroscopic-microscopic continuum, which refers to the scale of the social phenomenon, ranging from an individual interacting with others, to larger groups, organizations and world systems such as capitalism. The second method is the objec-

	OBJECTIVE	SUBJECTIVE
MACROSCOPIC	I. <u>Macro-objective</u> Examples - society, law, bureaucracy, architecture, technology and language	III. <u>Macro-subjective</u> Examples - culture, norms, and values
MICROSCOPIC	II. <u>Micro-objective</u> Examples - patterns of behaviour, action, and interaction	IV. <u>Micro-subjective</u> Examples - perceptions, beliefs; the various facets of the social construction of reality

Figure 1: Ritzer's major levels of social analysis.

tive-subjective continuum, which concerns the distinction between social phenomena that have a material existence, and those that exist in the realm of ideas.[13]

Combining these two continua creates four levels of social reality. Ritzer is quick to add that "the real world is *not* divided into levels of social reality, but it can be understood better with the explicit utilization of these levels."[14] His model functions therefore as a heuristic device. In terms of scale, for instance, formal organizations such as *Look* magazine represent an intermediate level referred to as mesoscopic.[15] Also, a given social phenomenon may manifest itself in several levels of social reality: Ritzer mentions the family as an institution endowed with both objective and subjective dimensions.[16] Finally, the analyst is encouraged to examine the dialectical relationships among all four levels of social reality.[17]

We can now attempt to apply Ritzer's model to Stanley Kubrick's career as a photojournalist (*see* Figure 2). The macro-objective level would include the formal organization of *Look* magazine as a commercial institution, and the micro-objective level would focus on the work culture at *Look*. The photo-essay genre as conceived by *Look* magazine could constitute the macro-subjective level, and Kubrick's conception of the genre, as far as we can determine on the basis of his work, would make up the micro-subjective level. In terms of the relationships between these levels of social reality, we may ask ourselves: how is Kubrick's artistic identity affected by *Look* magazine's organizational structure and culture, and by the photo-essay genre, and how does Kubrick's work, in turn, reflect itself or impact on these three levels?

Macro-objectivity

This level of social reality concerns *Look* magazine's organizational structure. Ritzer lists the major components of the ideal-typical bureaucracy according to sociologist Max Weber: offices or departments are organized into a hierarchical system, with specific areas of expertise requiring participants to obtain appropriate training; the salaried staff does not own the means of production but is provided with the technology to do its job, and the organization is bound by rules recorded in writing.[18]

Look magazine was published by Cowles Magazines, Inc., and founded in 1937 by Gardner (Mike) Cowles, a successful newspaper publisher from Des Moines, Iowa. The top of *Look*'s hierarchy included Cowles as editor-in-chief, along with associate, executive and managing editors, an art director and a picture editor. This was followed by several departments, each

	OBJECTIVE	SUBJECTIVE
MACROSCOPIC	I. Macro-objective *Look* magazine: Organizational structure	III. Macro-subjective Photojournalism: Photo-essay genre at *Look* magazine
MICROSCOPIC	II. Micro-objective *Look* magazine: Organizational culture	IV. Micro-subjective Kubrick-genre in photography and film

Figure 2. Sociological analysis of Kubrick's career at *Look* magazine.

with its own head: ten writers and ten photographers, a women's department, art department, and picture and editorial research, which added up to over sixty permanent staff.

On a personal level, *Look* founder and editor Cowles's published memoirs include a Kubrick portrait of Rocky Graziano waiting before the call to the ring: "Stanley Kubrick, a filmdom great, in his teens was a *Look* photographer. Here he caught Rocky Graziano in pre-bout tension."[19] The only other reference to Kubrick is an indirect one, when Cowles complains about advertisers' reactions to nudity: "After a lengthy sales effort, for instance, we convinced Campbell Soup to become a *Look* advertiser. But just before its schedule of insertions was due to start, we published an issue containing a black and white photograph of artist Peter Arno in his studio sketching a nude model — not a frontal view, as later became common in *Playboy*, but a discreet, semi-back view. That was the end of the Campbell Soup business for some time to come."[20] The offending picture was a full-page photograph taken by Kubrick and published in the September 27, 1949, issue of *Look*, inaugurating his dealings with public controversy which continued with the European ban on *Paths of Glory* and the X-rating of *A Clockwork Orange*.

Vincent LoBrutto describes Cowles as "a lifelong Republican with liberal ideas," a characterization which might also apply to Kubrick's films, if we consider their tendency to combine a masculinist discourse with sharp criticisms of the political and military establishments.[21] But the clearest influence Cowles could have had on Kubrick, as founder and editor of *Look* magazine, concerns the identity of the photomagazine itself. If Kubrick had ended up selling his first photograph to the *New York Daily News*, as he considered doing in April 1945, or even *Life* magazine, his future development might have been different.[22] Indeed, the *New York Daily News* was a tabloid, and *Life* magazine was a weekly which covered the news, whereas *Look* was a bi-weekly focusing on feature articles. Had Kubrick worked for the other two publications, he might have been directed towards spot news photography, and not had the same opportunity to contribute to the longer photo-essay format, which shares a closer affinity with fiction film.

According to Cowles, *Look* defined itself partly in opposition to its main competitor, *Life* magazine, known as the "Big Red One."[23] Published by Time, Inc., *Life* enjoyed far superior resources to *Look* (250 staffers, 28 bureaus worldwide, etc.), which allowed it not only to publish on a weekly basis, but also to follow breaking news more closely. *Life* could therefore outspend any of its rivals, which led *Look* to develop its own forte in well-researched, photographed and edited feature stories.[24] In terms of their respective ideologies, scholar James Guimond has argued that the two photomagazines were similar in many respects, sharing a basic optimism in and commitment to "capitalist realism," and providing a showcase for the values of the American middle-class.[25] Among the differences, Guimond finds that *Life*'s photo-essays were often sensationalistic and showy, its editorial comments brash, even chauvinistic, whereas *Look*'s essays were visually subtler and editorially calmer, more liberal and willing to identify social problems in the United States: "By American standards of the time, *Look* had better taste and considerably more 'class' than *Life* did."[26]

Aside from Cowles, founder of *Look* magazine, the person most responsible for setting the tone and the organizational climate of *Look* would be the executive editor. Dan Mich served in this capacity from 1942 until his death in 1965, with a three-year hiatus in the early fifties. Cowles attributes much of *Look*'s success to Mich's editorial style, which he describes as flexible, not bound by a formula.[27] Mich seemingly wanted magazine stories to be "a personal dialogue between the writer, photographer and editor," and encouraged editors to create less didactic stories than had been produced during the war years, focusing instead on informing the reader with an entertaining twist.[28] In his advice to writers he emphasized the importance of researching a topic thoroughly, striving to "learn 10 times as much about it as would seem necessary for the space allotted."[29] This systematic approach sounds similar to Kubrick's modus operandi when researching projects such as the aborted film *Napoleon*.

Life magazine's executive editor Wilson Hicks favored a strict separation of powers, photographers seldom being granted editorial control.[30] By contrast, Dan Mich's editorial process was more fluid and informal.[31] The editorial board met once a week, and accepted input from everyone on the board, including the picture editor. Staff members were invited on occasion to pitch story ideas.

To what extent Kubrick himself initiated some of his assignments is hard to know, although we can speculate that he may have suggested a handful or so of the 230 "jobs" he worked on. A recent thesis points out that newspaper editors often use their photographers' areas of interest in determining assignments.[32] Given Kubrick's own interest in sports and jazz music (he was a drummer in high school), it is no surprise to discover that he photographed several boxing and baseball stories, as well as some nightclub jazz performances.

Look magazine's look, including the style of the photo-essay layouts, was the art director's responsibility. Merle Armitage held this position during Kubrick's tenure, and is described by Cowles as a talented and gregarious fellow.[33] Photography historian Beaumont Newhall compares a magazine editor's layout of photographs to movie editing, including the use of wide, establishing shots.[34] Similarly, senior *Life* editor Joseph Kastner argued that "the writer produces a kind of sound track to be played as an accompaniment to the visual track, pictures."[35] The connection between the photo-essay form and motion pictures would not have escaped Kubrick, who spent his high school years watching eight films a week.[36]

As a member of the photographic staff, Kubrick's immediate boss would have been his department head, Arthur Rothstein. The likely influence of Rothstein on Kubrick's development as a photojournalist cannot be easily dismissed. Photography directors have been known to assign experienced "photographers to serve as mentors to younger staff members."[37] Rothstein himself shared at least five different assignments with Kubrick, and the young photographer was certainly smart enough to know when he had an opportunity to learn. Rothstein was a former photographer for the Farm Security Administration, and achieved notoriety recording the plight of rural folk during the Depression. Rothstein staged his famous 1936 photograph of a bleached steer skull in the South Dakota Badlands by moving the skull ten feet for dramatic effect. He was accused by some of faking the photograph to make conditions look worse than they were.[38] The staged photograph is a staple of the photojournalistic medium, highlighting the relationship between documentary and fiction which would remain a central feature of Kubrick's film style. This willingness to stage a documentary photograph for the camera's benefit may thus have impressed Kubrick, who was compared to a sponge in terms of his ability to learn by a film editor that he consulted in the early fifties.[39] Rothstein also had an interest in motion pictures and owned a collection of film books which Kubrick borrowed and even annotated.[40]

A final macro-objective factor we might mention is architectural. Architectural forms both influence and react to sociocultural phenomena, thus the relevance of citing the relationship between the *Look* magazine organization and the building in which it resided. Until 1950, the *Look* offices were located at 511 Fifth Avenue, in the 17-story Postal Life Insurance Building built in 1916. It is a Renaissance revival design, which today houses the Israel Discount Bank of New York. The magazine occupied several floors of the building, including offices for the various departments, photographic studios as well as developing and printing facilities.[41] Photographs of the editorial boardroom, various offices and the research library are included in *Look*'s in-house textbook, *The Technique of the Picture Story*.[42] The layouts displayed on the boardroom's walls unmistakably bring to mind the film industry's storyboards, which Kubrick later used for projects such as *2001: A Space Odyssey*. The magazine moved its offices to the newly-erected Look Building in May 1950, where Kubrick was to work for another five months before retiring. Located at 488 Madison Avenue, the Look Building is a striking "wedding-cake" white brick building with rounded corners, which signaled the magazine's prosperity and progressive attitude. It looks appropriately glamorous in the 1953 MGM musical *I Love Melvin*, shot on location in New York City. The movie stars Donald O'Connor as a young *Look* photographer who falls in love with Debbie Reynolds and ultimately succeeds in getting her on the magazine's front cover, the actual April 7, 1953 issue of *Look*.

Micro-objectivity

This realm of social reality concerns *Look* magazine's organizational culture and how it impacts on the individual actor's socioeconomic status, social contacts, behavior and patterns of action and interaction.[43] Kubrick's professional status with *Look* evolved over the six-year period between 1945 and 1950. He was selling pictures on a freelance basis while he was still in high school, during the summer and fall of 1945. He graduated from high school in January 1946, and began hanging out with experienced freelancers in *Look* magazine's "bullpen," waiting for assignments outside the picture editor's office.[44] Due to a combination of poor grades in high school and preference being given to returning servicemen (under the GI Bill), Kubrick could not be admitted to college. Aware of his predicament, picture editor Helen O'Brian offered the 17-year-old a position as apprentice photographer in the spring of 1946, which allowed him to contribute more regularly to *Look* magazine. Then, in January 1947, he became a full-fledged staff member, his name appearing on the contents page for the first time. He remained in that position until September 1950, when he decided to quit his job to make documentary films. Photo-essays he had worked on during the summer continued to appear until the end of the year.

In terms of patterns of interaction, *Look* magazine employed a collaborative method which would have influenced the young Kubrick in a positive way: "Whereas the *Life* photographer utilized a researcher or researchers in a strictly secondary role as assistant, *Look* developed a system of photographer-writer teams for the production of major stories and essays."[45] One reason for this system was to avoid possible resentment by photographers when their work would later be edited by people who were not in the field. Photographer Douglas Kirkland, who worked for *Look* from 1960 until 1971, argued that a "very good thing at *Look* is that the editor who creates the story goes on location with the photographer."[46] Another reason for the collaborative concept was "to ensure the photographer had complete knowledge of the information that would be covered and the angle from which the story would be told."[47] *Look* magazine's modus operandi was to encourage photographers to establish relationships with writers in order to think in terms of the magazine's goal, which was to produce photo-essays, i.e. narrative sequences of shots as opposed to isolated expressive pictures. The discipline required to not only consider visual and thematic links but also include storytelling concerns when taking individual photographs is one that would undoubtedly serve Kubrick well when he later applied this skill to documentary and fiction filmmaking.

An average of one out of ten assignments was shared with another photographer, and it is reasonable to assume that Kubrick learned much from working with his colleagues. The most common method identified by photojournalists "for learning new techniques and better ways to perform their jobs ... [was] to observe and ask questions of fellow staff members."[48] In 1947, G. Warren Schloat Jr. was a newly hired writer who was paired with Kubrick, notably for the photo-essay "Life and Love on the New York Subway," which appeared in the March 4 issue of *Look*.[49] Schloat, who was 33 at the time, had been a story editor for Walt Disney Studios, contributing to films such as *Snow White and the Seven Dwarfs* and *Dumbo*. Kubrick was interested by Schloat's background in film, and told him about his own plans as a future filmmaker. Interviewed by LoBrutto, Schloat also described Kubrick's candid camera technique for the subway story, which involved a switch hidden in his pocket and a wire running up his sleeve.[50] He likely received advice on the use of this apparatus from his colleagues at *Look*. The relationship between words and images defines the photo-essay form, and despite the collaborative nature of the work process at *Look* magazine, a breakdown of tasks and specialization remained. This had important consequences for Kubrick's development as a visual storyteller. According to biographer John Baxter, "Kubrick learned early the habit of looking to others for his narratives, and devoting his energies to illuminating them."[51] Almost without exception, Kubrick would later work with a writer on his film projects.

In his book on photojournalism, Arthur Rothstein identified six stages in the process of producing a photo-essay, obviously based on his 24-year experience as *Look* magazine's technical director of photography.[52] Many of these stages involved teamwork between the photographer and his fellow staffers, and thus potential influence in the work routine. The first stage occurred at the weekly board meetings, when ideas for stories were discussed. The ideas could originate from a number of different sources, including staff photographers.[53] Once a story was chosen, the board decided to which editor to assign it. It was almost always assigned to the person who proposed it, a policy which turned out to be "a great impetus to submitting well-thought-out ideas."[54] The second stage concerned the background research which the editor conducted in concert with research assistants. On the basis of this research, the editor decided whether a story could be pursued.

The third stage was when the photographer entered the picture. The editor consulted with the managing editor to choose a photographer. The photographer went over the research with the editor, and they developed a shooting script.[55] The picture editor would also be consulted, and according to Rothstein, would hopefully inspire and stimulate his photographers. In addition, photographers would be expected to internalize the editor's style, or at least the publication's general approach, while simultaneously demonstrating initiative, creative thinking and an eye for the unusual, which could certainly apply to Kubrick.[56]

The fourth stage was location shooting. The writer and photographer would travel together to capture the required visual and verbal material (in the case of interviews, for instance), using the shooting script as a guide. Departures from the script could occur.[57] Rothstein mentions the importance of coverage, the notion that since film is cheap, one might as well shoot as much as possible from various angles, to provide the layout artist with a greater range of options.[58] This logic is virtually identical to Kubrick's practice during his film career, made infamous in particular by his numerous takes of certain scenes which drove some actors to exhaustion.[59] Rothstein also discusses the importance of reenactments in order to produce more effective photographs: he argues that "in order to make a scene more forceful it is sometimes desirable to distort or accentuate the effect by photographic means."[60] Moreover, the staging of photographs "forces the photographer to become not only a camera man but also a scenarist, dramatist, and director as well."[61] In addition to the dramaturgical and cinematic reference, Rothstein's willingness to enhance what might otherwise be considered documentary images must have impressed the young Kubrick, whose later film style would always seek to find the interesting or slightly surreal element embedded in a realistic situation.[62]

The fifth stage was the assembly, which included the selection of pictures and the layout. The photographer and writer would work with the editors and the art department to select perhaps a dozen pictures out of a thousand for the final essay.[63] The photographer's main job ends here as the art director and editor work together on the layout. Rothstein mentions some basic principles in photographic layouts which can be shown to have impacted on Kubrick's film editing practices. He mainly emphasizes the importance of creating various contrasts in order to avoid monotony: contrasts in scale, tone or subject can maintain reader interest.[64] Rothstein's reference to contrasts in lines (verticals, horizontals, diagonals) is reminiscent of Sergei Eisenstein's theories of montage, to which he would have been introduced in the late forties from reading Jay Leyda's translations of the Soviet filmmaker's essays.[65] Kubrick was also interested in Eisenstein's theories, an influence which is noticeable in his early documentary films, as well as in a scene from his first fiction film, *Fear and Desire*.[66] Ironic contrasts achieved through editing would become a staple of Kubrick's later work, indicative of his pessimistic worldview. The sixth and final stage was the writer's task, drafting the headlines, text and captions for the photo-essay.

Look's Douglas Kirkland relates the degree to which the photographer's contribution was valued: "After the art director has completed the layout, the photographer generally has another look.... Fortunately at *Look* there is great respect for the picture and the photographer. If you don't feel you have gotten a 'fair shake' on a story, you can present reasonable variations which are certainly considered and frequently followed."[67] The kind of work culture described by Kirkland suggests that Kubrick must have had opportunities to contribute at various stages of the editorial process, despite being the most junior member of *Look*'s staff.

Macro-subjectivity

This realm of social reality refers to *Look* magazine's conception of the photo-essay genre, as well as the norms and values which it expected its staffers to adopt and implement. It has been argued that "the socialization of news photographers to professional and organizational demands begins in journalism textbooks, which include detailed instructions on how to photograph news events."[68] In Kubrick's case, he did not have the opportunity to attend a journalism school, but *Look* magazine published its own textbook on photojournalism in 1945, entitled *The Technique of the Picture Story*. A copy of this book, written by *Look*'s executive editor and art director at the time, Dan Mich and Edwin Eberman, would most likely have been supplied to Kubrick to familiarize him with some of the requirements of his new job, especially in his capacity as apprentice photographer.

The first chapter of *The Technique of the Picture Story* describes a few major types of photo-essays in terms of the relationship between words and images, ranging from images being used for purely illustrative purposes, to picture stories which avoid words altogether. The intermediate case, a balanced combination of picture and text, is the most common type of photo-essay, and is defined as "an article in which the storytelling is done by related pictures, arranged in some form of continuity. The text in such an article is important, but subordinated to the pictures."[69] Kubrick produced all three types of photo-essays. For example, in the January 31, 1950, issue of *Look*, Kubrick illustrated an article entitled "Don't be Afraid of Middle Age," written by Jacques Bacal, a lawyer specializing in family relations. Kubrick staged some photographs with models portraying a married couple injecting romance in their life by dining and dancing the night away. Despite their purely illustrative function, the staged photographs are interesting in that they provided Kubrick with the opportunity to create a mise-en-scène and to direct actors, which brings us a step closer to fiction. The blissfully waltzing couple may be usefully contrasted with Alice Harford (Nicole Kidman) and the greasy Sandor Szavost (Sky Dumont) in *Eyes Wide Shut*, a film thematically focused on married life.

An example of the standard photo-essay would be the aforementioned "Life and Love on the New York Subway," which is analyzed below. As for the "pure picture story," it can take the form of series photographs which resemble still frames selected from a strip of motion picture film. The April 2, 1946, issue of *Look* includes a series of four pictures entitled "Teacher Puts 'Ham' in Hamlet," featuring Kubrick's high school English teacher. Aaron Traister would teach literature by doing readings of Shakespearian plays, and playing the various parts himself. A brief caption under each photo includes a quote from the play's text, indicating an attempt to recreate the images and sounds of an event that falls short of being a documentary film of the teacher's performance. Even if Kubrick did not own a copy of the *Look* textbook, the published photo-essays are evidence of the knowledge of journalistic genres he acquired by collaborating with his colleagues.

The textbook's second chapter identifies some aesthetic goals that photographers are required to aim for. According to Mich and Eberman, a magazine photograph's most important aesthetic property concerns storytelling: "Storytelling quality is virtually always an essential, because each picture must move the story along in relation to the picture preceding or following."[70] *Look* magazine clearly encouraged an approach to photography which emphasized narrative, as opposed to the timeless, self-contained quality of art photographs. Other qualities mentioned include simple, uncluttered compositions, emotional impact and the avoidance of clichés such as sunsets. Kubrick's meticulous and controlled film style may thus owe something to the photojournalistic discipline of pursuing a simple and direct expressive form.

Entitled "Picture Continuities," the third chapter of *The Technique of the Picture Story* outlines the various kinds of visual and thematic relationships between images in a photo-essay, effectively defining the photojournalistic version of "continuity editing." In fact, the chapter begins with a comparison with motion pictures: "Many of the problems involved in constructing picture articles are similar to those involved in making movies."[71] Seven types of continuities are identified, including a literal chronological series of pictures which requires no narrative structure per se, as well as a narrative chronology which uses the classic three-act structure. A person or object repeated in every image is a strictly visual link which helps to hold a personality story together, for instance. Kubrick's July 19, 1949, portrait of Montgomery Clift, entitled "Glamor Boy in Baggy Pants," is a five-page essay with 9 photographs, all of which feature the movie star, except for two in which he interacts with fellow actor Kevin McCarthy and his family. The "how-to" form of continuity is a precisely identified sequence of photographs designed for didactic, step-by-step self-help articles.

Parallel or contrast is a fairly common structuring device, since it can "put over editorial points simply, speedily and vividly."[72] Contrasts are explicitly used in Kubrick's essay "Chicago, City of Extremes," published in the April 12, 1949, issue of *Look*: a lake-front park is opposed to a garbage-cluttered slum area, a cheap market to a fancy shop, and a homeless person eating a sandwich to a wealthy couple dining at a fine restaurant. In Kubrick's filmic oeuvre, ironic contrasts will become a trademark, as mentioned previously, both within a shot (soldiers engaged in combat under a sign proclaiming "Peace is Our Profession," in *Dr. Strangelove*), and between shots (Alex fantasizing about a biblical orgy while the prison chaplain believes that the inmate is deep in prayer, in *A Clockwork Orange*). Continuity may also be based on the layout artist's design, an "arrangement of borders, boxes, panels or typography to give visual cohesion to an article which may or may not possess it otherwise."[73] The last structuring device mentioned by Mich and Eberman is thematic development, which will be illustrated in a photo-essay analysis below.

In terms of subject matter, *Look* magazine's evaluative criteria are discussed in the fourth chapter, entitled "Ideas for Picture Stories." The three main prized qualities are "an interest that transcends spot news," a "focus on people, as opposed to things," and a "universal interest."[74] All three qualities were determined by the economic realities of magazine photojournalism. *Look*'s frequency of publication did not allow it to pursue spot news that might be quickly dated. The focus on people was reflected in the popularity of personality stories, both celebrities and unknowns whose appeal might be based on eccentricities or other human qualities. Kubrick certainly photographed his share of personalities, ranging from composer-conductor Leonard Bernstein in the March 14, 1950, issue of *Look*, to a family of weightlifters in the August 18, 1947, issue. Universal interest was based on the fact that a mass-circulation magazine such as *Look* could only survive if it told stories that would register with a readership of over 17 million in 1948.[75] These facts must have impressed Kubrick, who did not attend an art school that promoted the value of an artist's private vision, but instead worked for a commercial, professional magazine that valued the idea of informing and entertaining its readers. It could be argued that Kubrick always maintained a strong sense of the importance of entertaining a wide audience, as well as marketing, perhaps not in the same way as a Steven Spielberg, but at least to the extent that it impacted on his choice and treatment of subject matter.

Micro-subjectivity

According to George Ritzer, this realm of social reality "involves the feelings and perceptions, the mental aspects of the of the actors' position in the stratification system."[76] Ritzer suggests that one way of considering the relationships between the actor and the larger society is through the notion of personal biography, which may focus on the objective and subjective aspects of career patterns, for instance.[77] In principle, we should consider Kubrick's personal conception of the photo-essay genre and its relation to the film medium. Since Kubrick himself has said very little about his photojournalistic career, we must look to secondary sources, including analyses of the photo-essays he co-authored with his *Look* magazine colleagues.

However, it is fair to begin with Kubrick's best known comments regarding his career as a photojournalist, which he made to French film scholar Michel Ciment in 1980. He begins by acknowledging his indebtedness to picture editor Helen O'Brian and managing editor Jack Guenther, who gave him a job at *Look*. Ironically, neither would remain with *Look* very long, as O'Brian left the magazine in May 1946, shortly after she had recommended Kubrick for an apprenticeship, and Guenther died tragically in a plane crash in December 1947.[78] During the summer of 1947, Kubrick was able to pursue his growing interest in aviation by being assigned to cover an air show in June, although the results were never published. Then, on August 15, he obtained a pilot's license, and it may be that Guenther's accident contributed to the young photographer's eventual fear of flying.[79] There also appears to have been a "jazz connection" at *Look* magazine: Executive Editor Dan Mich inherited Guenther's collection of Dixieland jazz recordings, and Kubrick, himself a jazz drummer, got an opportunity to photograph some jazz legends in New Orleans and New York City.[80] The results were published in the June 6, 1950, issue of *Look*, for a story entitled "Dixieland jazz is hot again."

Kubrick then goes on to comment on the practical aspects of his schooling at *Look* magazine, which this essay has attempted to highlight: "This experience was invaluable to me, not only because I learned a lot about photography, but also because it gave me a quick education in how things happened in the world."[81] The commercial exigencies of producing work for a mass audience established themselves early in Kubrick's career, providing a grounding which strictly artistic aspirations may have overlooked. There remained a tension in the fact that some of the stories assigned to him were less than inspiring. However, he appreciated the personality stories, and identifies the experience of working with Montgomery Clift as one which he found interesting.[82]

While Kubrick displayed a talent for staged photographs, suggesting a predilection for the fictional mode, he also developed candid camera techniques in keeping with *Look*'s journalistic nature. In a sense, Kubrick was exposed to, and applied the aesthetics of, direct cinema *avant la lettre*. He appears to have learned the lesson that verisimilitude in representation, regardless of any narrative genre's specific conventions, is a key to ensuring the viewer's identification to the diegesis. Even the most absurd (*Dr. Strangelove*), supernatural (*The Shining*) or otherwise estranged (*2001: A Space Odyssey*) fictional worlds in Kubrick's work are grounded in an accuracy of detail and documentary realism which characterize his film style, one which "lends an unfamiliarity to the real and an empirical life to the surreal."[83] In a 1971 interview, Kubrick claimed that he "always enjoyed dealing with a slightly surrealistic situation and presenting it in a realistic manner."[84]

A brief analysis of a March 4, 1947, photo-essay entitled "Life and Love on the New York Subway" illustrates how the collaborative work between the photographer, writer and layout artist can produce a creative slice-of-life photo-essay. This essay consists of three double-page spreads containing a total of 29 photographs. Each spread forms one unit of design.[85] The first spread opens with an eye-catching full page "establishing shot" of Grand Central Station, printed as a "bleed picture," i.e. extending to the edges of the page for added impact (*see* Figure 3). Underneath the opening photograph is the headline, which also serves as the title of the photo-essay. Next to it is the "body copy" which announces the theme of the first spread. Hugging the bottom edge of the picture is the caption, beginning with a short phrase in bold type, followed by a complete sentence in regular type which comments on the photograph and adds information.

Thematically, the first spread focuses on overcrowding in the New York City subway during rush hour. Statistics are provided on the number of fares collected daily. The headline for the second spread, which runs down the middle of the page this time, identifies a new theme: picking out interesting personalities on the subway (*see* Figure 4). The third spread is similar to the previous one in design, with a headline describing the closing theme, the subway as "flophouse" (*see* Figure 5). In terms of layout, the second and third spreads begin and end with a larger picture, which provides a formal frame. The picture in the top left corner is the reader's entry point, and the one in the bottom right corner acts as a transition in the second spread, and as a conclusion in the last spread. The second spread ends with a picture of a woman and a boy shot from behind, looking out the window at the head of the train. Visually it is a kind of off-screen glance inviting us to turn the page, which is likened to the train's next stop by the caption. The last picture features "two children slumber sprawled on their parents' laps,"

Figure 3. The first spread from Kubrick's *Look* magazine photograph essay from March 4, 1947.

ending with the credit "photographed by Stanley Kubrick."[86] Rainer Crone could not resist comparing Kubrick's work to Walker Evans's photographs in the New York subway, which were taken in 1942 but only published in 1966, after Kubrick had retired from *Look*. We might instead consider the photojournalistic practice as the most relevant influence, and also note that the candid quality of these photographs remained intact eight years later in the subway scene from the film *Killer's Kiss*, when boxer Davy Gordon reads a letter from his Uncle George.

Most of the pictures in this essay (23 out of 29) are cropped into a square format, in order to focus on the idea being expressed by the writer and photographer. A comparison with the fourteen reproductions in Crone's book *Drama and Shadows*, which includes photographs left on the "cutting room floor," gives an indication of the editorial decisions that were taken.[87] On the basis of this material, it is fair to say that Kubrick's work was not "manhandled," as critic Enrico Ghezzi feared.[88] According to Rothstein, the editorial process remains a collaborative one, ideally, and photographers "should be consulted when the photographs are cropped and layouts made."[89] As a practicing photographer himself, Rothstein was sensitive to the photographer's feelings concerning each photograph as "a sacred and profound statement," and so there is every reason to think that Kubrick was a willing participant in this process.[90]

Figure 4. The second spread Kubrick's *Look* magazine photograph essay from March 4, 1947.

The perception of Kubrick as a self-contained artist who is impervious to criticism is belied by reports that he wept during a preview screening of *Fear and Desire*, as the audience laughed at Paul Mazursky's performance.[91] It should be no surprise that photojournalists assess the quality of their work in some measure based on responses from their colleagues as well as readers.[92] Kubrick received a number of public or official kudos during his tenure at *Look*, which no doubt helped him to gauge his performance. For instance, the last photograph of the New York subway story elicited a letter to the editor published in the April 29, 1947, issue of *Look*, and included the following hyperbolic description of the tired father: "It seems unbelievable to me that a young man could possess such a weariness of the soul. In America, no one should be so burdened with despair. He has the look of Lincoln in his eyes, and a bit of the suffering Christ." In the August 30, 1949, *Look* issue, one reader was particularly effusive in her letter to the editor, regarding the

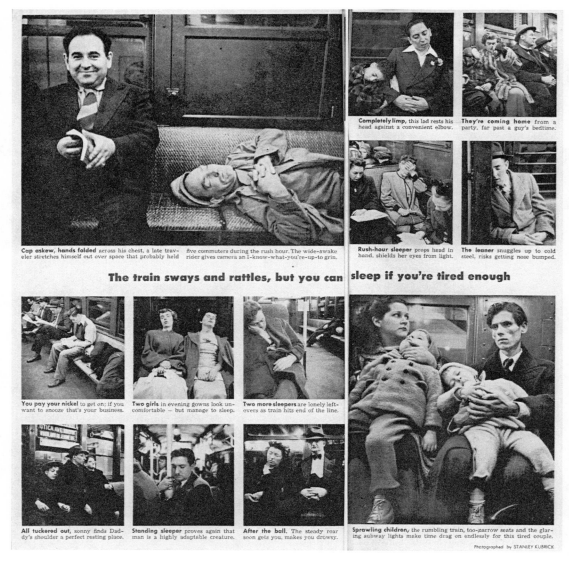

Cap askew, hands folded across his chest, a late traveler stretches himself out over space that probably held

five commuters during the rush hour. The wide-awake
rider gives camera an I-know-what-you're-up-to grin.

Completely limp, this lad rests his
head against a convenient elbow.

They're coming home from a
party, far past a guy's bedtime.

Rush-hour sleeper props head in
hand, shields her eyes from light.

The leaner snuggles up to cold
steel, risks getting nose bumped.

The train sways and rattles, but you can sleep if you're tired enough

You pay your nickel to get on; if you
want to snooze that's your business.

Two girls in evening gowns look uncomfortable — but manage to sleep.

Two more sleepers are lonely left-
overs as train hits end of the line.

All tuckered out, sonny finds Daddy's shoulder a perfect resting place.

Standing sleeper proves again that
man is a highly adaptable creature.

After the ball. The steady roar
soon gets you, makes you drowsy.

Sprawling children, the rumbling train, too-narrow seats and the glaring subway lights make time drag on endlessly for this tired couple.

Photographed by STANLEY KUBRICK

Figure 5. The third photograph spread from Kubrick's *Look* magazine photograph essay from March 4, 1947.

essay on Montgomery Clift which had appeared two months earlier: "Many thanks for giving us that wonderful story and picture spread on Monty Clift. Three cheers should go to Stanley Kubrick, the photographer, for taking the best natural pictures of the most natural actor on the stage."

Kubrick was obviously appreciated by his bosses at *Look*. For the May 11, 1948, edition, Kubrick spent two weeks providing photographic material for a 9-page article on Columbia University, including a portrait of the university's new president, Dwight Eisenhower. The editors of *Look* ran a short piece on their teenage photographer on the title page of the edition, including a small picture of Kubrick, pointing out that the photographic staff had formed a "Bringing Up Stanley Club," an advisory group to help him along. Kubrick also received an interoffice memo from Fleur Cowles, the associate editor of *Look* and wife of Editor Mike Cowles, after his full-page photograph of German expressionist painter George Grosz was published in the June 8, 1948, issue: "I think you just took the picture of the year.... George Grosz parked on a chair in the middle of Fifth Avenue traffic (with a NO PARKING sign alongside) is *IT!*"[93]

In assessing the emergence of the Kubrickian brand-name or signature, it is useful to examine relevant biographical issues, as well as the production context at *Look* magazine, the rivalry with *Life* magazine and other economic factors affecting photojournalistic practices. This should help to gauge the extent to which Kubrick's later work as a filmmaker remains indebted to this formative period in his life. Situating the discursive intent exclusively in an individual consciousness, the spirit of the age or a specific artistic tradition is less helpful than attempting to integrate these various influences into a broader explanatory scheme.[94] In other words, an agency-structure integration is more productive than positing a singular agent, whether this agent is free from influence, necessarily in conflict with the institutional contexts in which he worked, or a mindless robot reflecting society's concerns.[95] Studying areas of common interest and thus potential influence between *Look* magazine and Stanley Kubrick should remain the most constructive approach.

The proposed method of analysis may also prove useful in examining the works of other photographer-filmmakers, such as Ken Russell, who was a freelancer for *Picture Post* and *Illustrated*; Jerry Schatzberg, who contributed to *Vogue* and *McCall's*; and Gordon Parks, who was a staff photographer for *Life* magazine for 25 years. On the one hand, there are considerable differences between Parks and Kubrick. For instance, Parks was the only African American staff photographer at *Life* magazine. He had some previous experience as a professional photographer and was in his thirties when he was hired by *Life*. Moreover, he only began directing films in the mid-sixties. Given those and other differences, the parallels are perhaps even more striking.

They both started making short documentary films based on their most popular photo-essays: in Kubrick's case it was "The Prizefighter." Parks used a 1961 article about a destitute child from the slums of Rio, Flavio de Silva. Parks was then encouraged to direct his first feature-length fiction film in 1969, *The Learning Tree*, which was adapted from his own autobiographical novel. The critical response combined praise for the film's polished cinematography, and concern for the awkward and undramatic acting. This parallels the response to Kubrick's first feature, *Fear and Desire*. Parks went on to direct *Shaft!* in 1971, which includes some gritty New York City street scenes that recall similar moments in Kubrick's second film, *Killer's Kiss*.

Further research into the relationships between Kubrick's photographic and filmic work could begin by comparing the work culture at *Look* magazine with the teamwork required to produce a major motion picture. Also, a comparative textual analysis of the photo-essays and the films needs to develop a system of correspondences between the codes and conventions of the photojournalistic and cinematic media, based on knowledge of magazine genres on the one hand, and the Kubrick film genre on the other. This work should go some way to uncover the publicly accessible historical sources of the Kubrickian worldview, a worldview which has been identified by critics as a means of interpreting his later films, but whose origin has seldom been studied as such.

2 Kubrick's Early Non-Fiction Work

Marina Burke

While Stanley Kubrick has a well-established place in the pantheon of important film directors, what is often not remembered is that he was originally a cinematographer and photographer. Those pursuits had a substantial and long-lasting impact on his cinematic career, an impact evident as far back as the three short documentaries with which he began his film career, films which are seldom taken into account in discussions of Kubrick's work. This is not surprising, perhaps in view of the fact that Kubrick later removed these films from distribution, as well as his first short feature *Fear and Desire* (1953), subsequently dismissing the latter as "a bumbling amateur film exercise" and "a completely inept oddity, boring and pretentious."[96] We may presume that he did not look any more forgivingly on the documentaries, which as of 2007 have never been reissued and which are available for viewing only in badly-duped copies. However, the three documentaries—*Day of the Fight* (1950–51), *Flying Padre* (1950–51) and *The Seafarers* (1953)—are noteworthy for the glimpses they give of the future Kubrick and the evolution of his style, both through the influence of his early grounding in photographic practice and a devotion to film-viewing that spanned mainstream American to European arthouse and avant-garde production.

In addition to his early work as a photographer, Kubrick — unable to secure a college admission because of his poor grades— enrolled in classes at New York's City College, thus beginning a lifelong career as an autodidact. He also continued his lifelong career as a *cineaste*, begun when he was a boy when he religiously attended the local movie theaters twice a week for the double features. In a later interview he said:

> One of the important things about seeing run-of-the mill Hollywood films eight times a week was that many of them were so bad. Without even beginning to understand what the problems of making films were, I was taken with the impression that I could not do a film any worse than the ones I was seeing. I also felt I could, in fact, do them a lot better.[97]

His taste later expanded to the foreign art and avant-garde films of Greenwich Village art house cinemas and the film program of the Museum of Modern Art. The latter was influenced by the predilections of its curator Iris Barry, a left-wing film enthusiast whose radical taste was reinforced by another employee, Jay Leyda, documentary maker and Soviet film historian. The museum's collection reflected their unorthodox leanings, favoring Soviet cinema and the European avant-garde over Hollywood, and stressing the maverick tradition of the latter as exemplified by directors such as Erich von Stroheim, for whom Kubrick never lost his enthusiasm. With Alexander Singer, a high school friend who was similarly fascinated by photography and films, Kubrick discovered the work of Eisenstein, Pudovkin and the fruits of various French and German avant-garde movements. Of the European directors he particularly admired Max Ophüls, of whom at one stage he said: "Highest of all I would rate Max Ophüls, who for me possessed every possible quality. He has an exceptional flair for sniffing out good subjects, and he got the most out of them. He was also a marvelous director of actors."[98] Eisenstein's work, on the other hand, he dismissed as "all form and no content"; his films while "distinguished by the beautiful visual composition of his shots and his editing," as far as content was concerned "were silly, his actors are wooden and operatic."[99] Eisenstein's fellow director Vsevolod Pudovkin was more appealing, as is obvious from the homage paid to Soviet montage cinema in Kubrick's early films. Indeed in an echo of one of the earliest theorists of Soviet montage cinema, Lev Kuleshov, Kubrick said in an interview much later: "Everything else [in film] comes from something else. Writing, of course, is writing, acting comes from the theatre, and cinematography comes from photography. Editing is unique to film. You can see something from different points of view almost simultaneously, and it creates a new experience."[100] Kubrick adhered to this conception of film form throughout his career, shooting each scene from many angles and becoming infamous for his endless retakes.

While Kubrick continued taking photographs for *Look* magazine, Singer landed a job as an office boy at Time Inc., where the famous newsreel series *The March of Time*, inaugurated in 1935, was then being produced by Louis de Rochement. Singer discovered that the latter would spend up to $40,000 for an eight- or nine-minute film. With Singer as producer, Kubrick decided that he could easily do it for $1,500 and planned to use his *Look* magazine savings to supplement the film's budget. The subject of the documentary was to be the middleweight boxer Walter Cartier, on whom Kubrick had already done a photo-feature for *Look* entitled "Prizefighter Walter Cartier." Cartier was a photogenic, promising champion who had been boxing and giving exhibitions with his twin brother Vincent since youth. Over seven pages and in twenty-two black-and-white photographs, the photo-essay provided a glimpse of the young boxer's private life, showed him praying quietly in a church, visiting the beach with friends, and working out with the famous trainer Bobby Gleason, culminating in a fight with middleweight Tony D'Amico.

As Singer later pointed out, the concept of using this story was "inspired. Not only were the drama elements of it marvelously compressed, but the subject himself, Walter Cartier, was a textbook hero.... He surely looked good — and his brother, Vincent, looked good — and the two of them together were really quite marvelous figures."[101] The concept of the documentary would be to compress all of the action into a day-in-the-life format, observing a boxer as he prepared to face an opponent in the ring. Kubrick already had a good rapport with Walter and Vincent Cartier that dated to when he covered Walter for the story in *Look*. In addition to being the focus of the film, Walter would also act as technical advisor on the project, advising on what needed to be integral parts of the film — both he and Kubrick were keen for it to go down in the annals as a classic fight documentary. "I had no idea what I was doing, but I knew I could do better than most of the films that I was seeing at the time," he said with typical lack of modesty.[102] Kubrick approached the project with what was to become a trademark thoroughness. For the fight with black middleweight Bobby James, he spent time with Vincent Cartier, who was present for all of his brother's fights, and the trainer Gleason, observing the pre-fight rituals. He also spent time with the brothers and their aunt in their small Greenwich Village apartment, capturing the essentials of their daily routine. This classic observational stance was mediated by the addition of some human-interest touches familiar from Kubrick's years at *Look*, such as giving Walter a dog. On the other hand, Kubrick was seemingly open to direction from

Walter, with whom he worked closely while he organized the pre-fight sequence, incorporating the latter's suggestions into the construction of the shot sequence. "Walter would say, 'Stanley this would be a good shot, why don't you take this,'" his brother Vincent remembered. "Stanley would think about it and make a quick decision, he was amiable to suggestions."[103]

To shoot the film, Kubrick rented an Eyemo, a daylight loading camera that took 100-foot spools of 35mm black-and-white film. For the fight scene that is the film's climax, a second Eyemo was added, operated by Alexander Singer. *Day of the Fight* is shot in a style very much derived from the *March of Time* format, with shots accompanied by an authoritative voice-over by veteran CBS newsreader Douglas Edwards, punctuated by jaunty music. The beautiful cinematography and the vivid editing remove the film from the standard newsreel format, however. Shots are frequently punctuated by frequent changes of camera angle and by dissolves, an editing device used extensively by Kubrick in his early work despite his apparent later dislike of the technique.[104]

The film opens with a shot of the marquee of New York's boxing mecca, Madison Square Garden, and a close-up of the sign "Tonite Boxing" in bold letters. In a rapid montage of shots we are given a quick history of boxing, reinforced by the terse, film noir-style narration. We see images of boxers working out in the ring and in the gym.

Nat Fleischer, boxing historian and publisher of the fighters' bible, *Ring* magazine, is shown looking through a boxing record book. We see pictures of boxing heroes Joe Lewis and Jack Dempsey. Finally, a shot of a fight poster advertises the coming match: "Walter Cartier versus Bobby James" is displayed on a street pole in a deserted Manhattan street. It is 6 A.M., we are reminded, on the day of the Cartier-James fight — to be fought at 10 P.M. It's a long day for our protagonist — as the commentary repeatedly makes clear — and the patient detailing of the minutiae of the hours leading up to the fight is enthralling. It begins with Walter Cartier, who has just wakened in one of the bedrooms of the Greenwich apartment he shares with his aunt. His equally photogenic brother Vincent is also in the bedroom; we are told that he lives out of town but stays with Walter on the nights before a fight. The depiction of his devotion to his twin brother is touching. We see him making breakfast for Walter, then the two walk through the empty New York streets to go to church for an early service, their entrance to the church caught in an extreme high angle, the deserted church itself acting as a stylized backdrop to brotherly love and religious piety.

The day continues, with the advancing hours and the familiar rituals of a fight day punctuated by allusions to the passing time, time that "has a way of staring you in the face when you want it to pass." In relaxed and intimate vérité style, we see scenes of Walter playing with his dog, eating, submitting to a final check from the boxing commission doctor, and eating a second meal at his usual restaurant, Steak Joint, its owner smoking a cigarette and prophesizing proudly that one day Walter will be the champ. The day drags on; finally it is 4 P.M., and Cartier begins to assume his fighter persona. He lays out the tools of this trade on the bed: the camera pans over a towel, shoes, ice bag, Vaseline, a robe with his name outlined in script on the back. He takes a long last look in the mirror, dispassionately feeling his nose and jaw; the dramatic tension rises as the music takes on a bombastic tone and the voice-over tells us that, "Before a fight there's always that last look in the mirror. Time to wonder what it will reflect tomorrow." The mirror effect of the double reflection and the dramatic framing of this shot are an echo of some of Kubrick's photo essays for *Look* exploring the threshold between private life and public image, and give a sense of how, for public performers, even the most intimate moments can be consciously staged events.[105] It also calls into question the seeming vérité style transparency of the earlier scenes.

But time is moving on. The brothers, inseparable, ride to the arena in a convertible through streets captured in a traveling point of view shot. It is now 8 P.M.; there are still two hours to go before the fight. Kubrick continues to compress the time in a further series of shots of Walter in his dressing room, with the last pre-fight rituals being carried out. Unlike *Killer's Kiss*, the implicit homoeroticism of boxing (as discussed by Joyce Carol Oates) is alluded to only briefly here; the commentator points out that, while the two men have never met before, "when the fight's over, they'll both know a lot about each other."[106] The predominant tone in this film is that of brotherly love and devotion. But as Walter is bandaging and flexing his hands, shot in a medium close-up while his brother watches in the background, out of focus, we are given a powerfully dramatic reminder that despite the brothers' close bond, the coming fight is something Walter must experience alone. Indeed, as the voice-over informs us, "Walter is slowly becoming another man. This is the man who cannot lose, who must not lose," adding a further sense of tension to Walter's last and most difficult period of waiting. But as the soundtrack informs us, this is a waiting that is always moving towards something; and finally it arrives — the summons to the ring.

And now the film suddenly picks up speed: the commentary disappears as the soundtrack switches to the natural sounds of the ringside. We hear the hum of the crowd, the clang of the bell, the boxing ring announcer's declaration of the upcoming fight. There is a cut back to dressing room, and we see Walter finally released from his agony of waiting. The fight itself was shot live, with Kubrick shooting the handheld material, and Singer using a tripod. An extreme high angle shot looks down on the boxing ring, as two beams of intense spotlight illuminate the canvas and ropes while the surrounding crowd is lost in blackness. Heavy shadows in the fight scene also nudge the film towards a film noir aesthetic, foreshadowing *Killer's Kiss* and *The Killing*. The only sounds are the roars and exclamations of the crowd, and the voice of the boxing commentator. A shot from between Walter's knees is a stunning reminder of Kubrick's compositional flair. The fight is mainly is shot from oblique angles, or from ground level. At times, when the two fighters were within a reasonable distance of the ropes, Kubrick shot the action by running and extending his arm out low to the canvas, pointing his camera straight up at the fighters and shooting blind to capture the shot. This kind of shooting was derived from photojournalistic practice, where the photographer often had to shoot above crowds and other obstructions that blocked the camera lens. Singer was in position to capture the culminating knockout punch, but that Kubrick was in control of the action was never in doubt: "What you saw watching *Day of the Fight* was the Stanley Kubrick everybody knows and the Stanley Kubrick who has received the recognition. He was fully formed, and that's a very rare thing."[107] With Cartier's knockout, the voice-over suddenly makes a reappearance; abruptly, the film ends with a final declamation from Douglas Edwards: "It's a hard life, but to him it's worth all the hardship and risk. He's just moved up a place in the line that leads to the championship."

Unlike Kubrick's subsequent two documentaries, *Day of the Fight* still appears fresh and undated, in spite of its portentous commentary and bombastic music. The naturalistic detailing of the activities leading up to the film's climax are captured in a classic direct cinema style that emphasizes the story's dramatic structure and predates the movement's official inauguration at the end of the 1950s, while the fight itself is shot with a degree of skill and brio that prefigures Scorsese's virtuoso camera movements in the fight scenes in *Raging Bull* (1980). Not surprisingly, Walter Cartier went on to have a successful acting career, appearing in films such as Robert Wise's biography of Rocky Graziano, *Somebody Up There Likes Me* (1956) and Elia Kazan's *A Face in the Crowd* (1957), as well as numerous television shows.

A friend of Singer's, Gerald Fried, composed the music for the film. Intent on the cinematography, Kubrick hadn't considered the soundtrack, but Fried convinced him that the film needed a score to have any chance of a commercial release. The music cost more to record and mix than Kubrick expected. Having shot the film for less than $1,000, Kubrick found himself spending more than $3,000 to record and lay the sound effects, music and commentary.[108]

Consequently, Kubrick was forced to draw on his savings to cover the final $3,900 cost of the film, a cost that was eventually recouped not by the anticipated sale to *The March of Time* series, but to one of the few distributors still handling shorts, RKO-Pathé. The latter also provided Kubrick with his next project, *Flying Padre* (1950–51), a film about New Mexican priest Father Fred Stadtmueller, whose parish was so geographically large that he commuted among his eleven congregations in a small airplane. The budget was $1,500.

Like *Day of the Fight*, the nine-minute film covers a number of carefully selected incidents in the peripatetic priest's life. His parishioners are mainly Spanish-Americans who are modest farmers and ranchers. For dramatic purposes, Kubrick has condensed the action over two days, during which we are given a glimpse of the kindly "flying padre" ministering to his scattered flock. As the film opens, we see a number of elegant aerial shots of Stadtmueller spending his first typical day flying over vast expanses of land and cattle to conduct the funeral of a ranch hand. Two men wait on the makeshift airstrip to take him to the small mission church, alongside the cemetery where the man is to be buried. Back in his plane, Stadtmueller returns to his main parish in time to conduct the evening devotions. The next day, we see a young girl arriving at the padre's door with a problem. She wants him to speak to her young friend Pedro, who has been cruel to her. The priest immediately takes the matter in hand, and peace is restored — at least momentarily, as is clear from the final shot of the boy dropping his hand from the girl's shoulder as they walk away from the house, a detail which the voice-over comments on, in case we should have missed the point. As we see shots of the priest working on his plane, another drama is introduced: a man arrives to impart the news that a young mother on an isolated ranch fifty miles away needs help. Her husband is away, and her baby is sick and getting sicker. They must get to the nearest hospital; a solution only possible with the help of the padre. As the film crosscuts between the anxious mother and shots of the priest's hand on the throttle of the plane as he urgently makes his way to the ranch, we understand how essential he and his trusty small plane are to the wellbeing of his parishioners.

The film owes even more to the conventional expository style of documentary than *Day of the Fight*: again we have a declamatory voice-over (here spoken by Bob Hite) and the aggravatingly jaunty music endemic to the genre in that period. The voice-over is more typical of the expository documentary where the tone of the film is more fully carried by the soundtrack than by the images, rather than the poetic flights of fancy of the Cartier film. The voice-over is also more or less constant throughout the film: describing the images, and at one point linking two disparate locales. This style owes much to the Griersonian school of documentary as it developed in the late 1930s (after an initial exploratory phase in the non-naturalistic use of sound), where speech is yoked to rhetorical assertion, which in America was adopted by New Deal documentarists such as Pare Lorentz and rigidified in the *March of Time* and other newsreel formats. Kubrick himself was not averse to the use of voice-over, despite the strictures against it in screenwriting manuals — whether the subjective interior monologue of *Killer's Kiss*, *Lolita* or *A Clockwork Orange*, or the more objective, third person commentary of *Paths of Glory* or *Barry Lyndon*. The film is rescued from most of the sins of this genre by the cinematography, as might be expected: as well the exhilarating aerial shots mentioned, high and low angle shots punctuate the mise-en-scène, and a close-up of an old peasant woman adds aesthetic interest. A beautiful image of the priest's canaries, shot through the bars of their cage, is a typical Kubrickian touch, as is the final shot of the priest. As the narrator is bidding farewell to the flying padre, Kubrick operates his camera while secured in a vehicle that swiftly pulls straight back from Stadtmueller — looking proud and heroic — getting smaller and smaller.[109]

The film opened in March 1951. In April, *Day of the Fight* went out as part of the supporting program to *My Forbidden Past*, starring Robert Mitchum and Ava Gardner. Emboldened by this recognition of his filmic talents, Kubrick decided to leave *Look* and become a full-time filmmaker. With no immediate projects, his film-going activities became even more intensive: as well as every change of program at The Museum of Modern Art, he saw at least two first-release films every weekend. He scoured the pages of *PM* magazine, which listed every film playing in the five boroughs, and would travel as far as Staten Island for an obscure revival. He absorbed film styles as varied as Italian neo-realism and Jean Cocteau's poetic surrealism.[110] Determined to direct his first feature film, he worked with Howard Sackler, another former high school friend then installed in Greenwich Village as a poet, on a screenplay inspired by the war which had just then erupted in Korea. In the film itself however, Kubrick never identifies the location or the war in which his protagonists are fighting, giving the story an eerie elemental power, despite the moments of portentous dramatics and risible acting. Filming took place in the San Gabriel mountains near Los Angeles, as the severe New York winter precluded any exterior shooting on the East Coast. As with *Day of the Fight*, post-synchronization problems drastically increased the cost of post-production; while trying to raise money to finish it, Kubrick went looking for work as a cameraman and director of sponsored documentaries. Only two short films from this period have been identified: one, a U.S. State Department–sponsored documentary made in 1952 about the World Assembly of Youth, a precursor of the Peace Corps, no longer extant,[111] and a thirty-minute documentary, in color, *The Seafarers*.

The Seafarers was commissioned by the Atlantic and Gulf Coast District of the Seafarers' International Union in the hope of encouraging membership by showing the facilities and advantages membership conferred. The thirty-minute film was again photographed and directed by Kubrick — his first in color — while the staff of the *Seafarer's Log*, the union's house newspaper, supervised the production (an arrangement obviously imposed by the union that is hard to imagine in practice, given Kubrick's notoriously self-contained way of working). The film has all the hallmarks of a typical promotional or industrial film of period, including the ever-present booming narration and jaunty music.

Despite the constraints of the film's material, however, from the beginning Kubrick manages to invest it with a large degree of his personal imprint. Kubrickian touches abound, from the arresting close shot of a knot on a rope that begins the film, with the sea just visible in the background, to the dissolves which merge one scene into another and the oblique upwards camera angles. The tone of the color film, warm and rich, strikes the eye immediately, an indication that Kubrick has used a more expressive lighting schema than the even, flat lighting more common in the industrial film genre. A montage of machines near the beginning of the film has a constructivist framing reminiscent of Kubrick's photographic work. Whether consciously or not, they also serve to link the film's extolling of the benefits of collective bargaining to the ideological underpinnings of this Soviet and Bauhas aesthetic, repeated in the film's closing shots, which are a muted version of the heroic worker stereotypes of early Soviet filmmaking.

Having established the milieu of the film, Kubrick cuts to an on-screen narrator, Don Hollenbeck, reading from a script into the camera as he delivers a homily on the function of the seafarers and their union. We are then shown a number of scenes, punctuated with dissolves, of sailors coming off their various ships and finding refuge, a home away from home, as the voice-over informs us, in the Seafarers' International Union headquarters. Here, in contrast to the punitive function of time in *Day of the Fight*, the commentary emphasizes that time is not to be killed, but to be enjoyed. We see scenes of the men looking for a new berth at the hiring hall, industriously reading or writing letters in the library, relaying their grievances to a union official. The hiring hall is the dramatic centre of the activities, and a long sequence is devoted to the "fair and democratic" system under which the men can find a place on a new ship, its close-ups of anxious-looking men waiting for confirmation of berths emphasizing the fact that despite the diversions, brutal economic realities are an inescapable part of their lives. This sequence also illustrates Kubrick's growing talent in visual storytelling and the creation of dramatic interest.

While many of the succeeding scenes are fairly pedestrian depictions of the further benefits of unionization, such as disability and maternity payments, in others, Kubrick's visual flair renders the subject matter more interesting. Depicting one of the homely comforts available to the men, the cafeteria, Kubrick employs a continuous fifty-second dolly shot tracking across the room and the food displayed. A sudden cut to a pan up a naked pinup is a shock in the domestic atmosphere that has been evoked by the scenes we've witnessed, as well as shots of one of the men at home with his family; a sudden reminder that the film is aimed at the hard-living sailors who will be its main viewers. The domestic air is further dissipated by a series of overhead shots of men and machines which shift the action from the intimate world we've been observing to the wider sphere of the seamen's activity, and also link us back with the film's opening shots. The film ends with another homily from Don Hellenbeck, read straight to the camera, situating it firmly back in the promotional documentary genre.

While *Killer's Kiss* has its roots in *Day of the Fight*, neither of the other two documentaries made at this early stage of his career suggest a maturity of cinematic style. What they do indicate is that Kubrick, from the beginning of his professional entry into filmmaking, was able to take less than promising material and endow it with his own dramatic and aesthetic sensibility. *Day of the Fight* fits more easily into his later work, with its finely calibrated depiction of the tension and boredom concealed behind the public façade of this quintessential American sport. *Flying Padre* and *The Seafarers*, on the other hand, remain notable as examples of the way in which Kubrick synthesized his photographic apprenticeship and knowledge of film culture in ways that enable the films to transcend the limitations of their genre. His two first features in turn betray the influence of his photographic and documentary beginnings. *Fear and Desire's* opening sequence of panning shots of hills and valleys accompanied by a third-person narration is an attempt to fuse sound and imagery that recalls the New Deal documentaries of Pare Lorentz, while the opening shots of *Killer's Kiss* mirror almost exactly those of *Day of the Fight*. Whatever his later disavowal of this early work, it was an important stepping stone in the career of one of the most enigmatic and interesting directors in the history of cinema. As Kubrick himself acknowledged in an interview in 1980,

> The best education in film is to make one. I would advise any neophyte director to try to make a film by himself. A three-minute short will teach him a lot. I know that all the things I did at the beginning were, in microcosm, the things I'm doing now as a director and producer.[112]

3 The Art of War (Films):
Fear and Desire and *Paths of Glory*

Charles Bane

> War is neither magnificent nor squalid; it is simply life, and an expression of life can always evade us. We can never tell life, one to another, although sometimes we think we can.
>
> — Stephen Crane, "War Memories"

Though trends in cinema come and go and often come again, the war film is a genre that consistently remains popular among filmmakers, critics, and audiences. Every generation, it seems, has its war, and every war has its film or films. Though filmmakers vary the formula of the genre, sometimes focusing on military life during war —*M*A*S*H* (1970), sometimes on combat during war —*Platoon* (1986), and sometimes on a particular battle in a particular war — *The Longest Day* (1962), the intent tends to be the same: to capture realistically the life of the soldier. Stephen Crane admitted the difficulty of attempting "to get to the real thing" in his "War Memories" and ultimately regarded it as an impossible task.[113] According to Michael W. Schaefer, the most famous statement regarding this problem is Whitman's claim that "the real war will never get in the books."[114]

In *Acts of War*, Richard Holmes argues that the problem with representing war artistically is that "the battlefield [is] given color and texture by the rich palette of artists, writers, and filmmakers," when in reality the battlefield is "empty and drab to many of those who live upon it. It is sometimes so unspectacular that it may not even be identifiable as a battlefield."[115] Based on Holmes's assertion, the Technicolor carnage of *Pearl Harbor* (2001) is probably a less accurate description of war than the empty sand dunes of *Jarhead* (2005). Interestingly enough, while *Pearl Harbor* is based on a real battle in a real war, the narrative that frames the battle is a fictional account of a love triangle between two childhood friends and the woman that comes between them. By contrast, *Jarhead* is a first person account of the first Gulf War based on the memoirs of Anthony Swofford, a Marine scout-sniper who served in the war. Perhaps the fact that the basis for the movie was penned by a "real soldier" lends to the accuracy of the film's battlefield.

Whatever the difficulties in accurately portraying the soldier's life, the war film remains a popular genre. So popular that many filmmakers return to the war film again and again throughout their careers. Stanley Kubrick is one such filmmaker. Kubrick began his feature film career with a war film, *Fear and Desire* (1953), and returned to the genre three more times with *Paths of Glory* (1957), *Dr. Strangelove or: How I Learned to Stop Worrying and Love the Bomb* (1964), and *Full Metal Jacket* (1987).[116] This essay will explore why war was such an intriguing topic for Kubrick and will examine his first two war films, *Fear and Desire* and *Paths of Glory*. The latter will be considered alongside the film's source text, Humphrey Cobb's 1935 novel by the same name.

In a 1958 interview, Kubrick explained his interest in soldiers and their lives:

> The soldier is absorbing because all the circumstances surrounding him have a kind of charged hysteria. For all its horror, war is pure drama, probably because it is one of the few remaining situations where men stand up for and speak up for what they believe to be their principles.... The soldier at least [has] the virtue of being against something or for something in a world where many people have learned to accept a kind of grey nothingness, to strike an unreal series of poses in order to be considered normal.[117]

Fear and Desire, Kubrick's first attempt to capture the "charged hysteria" and "pure drama" of war, was written for the screen by Kubrick and Howard Sackler, who went on to win the 1969 Pulitzer for his play *The Great White Hope*. Though in the public domain, the film is difficult to find due mainly to the fact that Kubrick himself dismissed the film as "a very inept and pretentious effort."[118] Believing the film to be an amateurish "student film," Kubrick personally oversaw the destruction of the original negative and several prints and spent much of his life tracking down other prints of the film so that he could purchase and destroy them as well.[119] According to his wife, Christiane, Kubrick "disowned [*Fear and Desire*] and would have happily gathered together every print and neg and consigned them all to an incinerator had it been possible."[120]

The contemporary reviewers of the film were much kinder and more forgiving than Kubrick. While admitting that the film was obviously made on a "shoestring budget,"[121] *Variety* noted that *Fear and Desire*'s "blend of violence and philosophy, some of it half-baked, and some of it powerfully moving" was in the end a "literate, unhackneyed war drama, outstanding for its fresh camera treatment and poetic dialog." *The New York Times* likewise called the film "uneven," "experimental," and "more intellectual than explosive" but ultimately declared the film a "thoughtful, often expressive and engrossing view of men who have 'traveled far from their private boundaries.'" Many reviewers praised the film for its technical achievements on such a low budget, citing particularly the film's cinematography and often comparing Kubrick's eye for chiaroscuro to Akira Kurosawa's, particularly his 1950 film *Rashômon*.[122]

Fortunately, Kubrick was not successful in eradicating the film from existence. A few prints still exist and are occasionally shown in film forums. One such print is in the archives at the George Eastman House in New York; the Eastman House exhibited the film shortly after Kubrick's death. The film has also recently become available on DVD. Unfortunately, the DVD is a transfer from a VHS recording of a television broadcast that appears to have been through several generations of copies. This is unfortunate for two reasons: one, the quality of the DVD does not accurately represent the film; two, because the film is surfacing 50 years after its release, viewers are watching it through the lens of Kubrick's later canon and are expecting to see a masterpiece by Stanley Kubrick, not the first film by the young filmmaker who would become Stanley Kubrick. Reviews of the DVD bear this expectation out. According to Phil Hall, "this is perhaps the single worst debut feature helmed by an internationally acclaimed filmmaker.... *Fear and Desire* is a clumsy and unintentionally funny work which bears none of the trademarks of the Kubrick style. Had it not been a Kubrick production, no one would give a damn about it today." Hall goes on to criticize Kubrick's camera work, referring to it as "shabby shenanigans" that litter the film with an unnecessary surplus of "intense" and "surreal" images. Hall ultimately concludes that the "film is silly ... [and] so earnest in trying to be intellectual that you inevitably feel sorry for Kubrick and his colleagues for mucking up." Although Hall states that he would like to see a fully restored version of the film, he is concerned that having *Fear and Desire* "easily available would clearly tear away at the reputation" of Kubrick as a filmmaker. Shane Burridge is not much kinder with his declaration that the "*only* reason this low-budget indie film is still being hunted down" is because Kubrick directed it (emphasis mine). He goes on to call the film a "slightly odd" yet "technically efficient" B film. Burridge's conclusion is that *Fear and Desire* is "less a film than a diversion [that] never rises above its limitations.... No wonder [Kubrick] didn't want us to see it." Other reviews call the film "laughably bad," or "not quite 'Ed Wood' bad, but close" and refer to it as "weak and tedious" and, at 68 minutes, seemingly longer than *Barry Lyndon*.[123]

The truth of the film is that it is not nearly as bad as recent reviewers claim. It is not a great film and it does, at times, border on tedious, but it is still a fair representation of Kubrick, the genius, in his early stages. It is, as most contemporary reviews pointed out, beautifully shot. For Kubrick, a young photographer with little film experience working with no budget and shooting on location, to have his first feature compared to Kurosawa was a monumental compliment. Kubrick's eye as a photographer turned cinematographer added new depth and dimensions to a film industry that was still tied to the "big Hollywood production" that used contract stars and shot virtually everything on a controlled soundstage. Nineteen fifty-three was the year of *The Robe, From Here to Eternity, Shane, Moulin Rouge, Julius Caesar*, and *Roman Holiday*. Movie audiences were bombarded with images of Burt Lancaster, Montgomery Clift, Deborah Kerr, Donna Reed, Frank Sinatra, Marlon Brando, Greer Garson, Gregory Peck, and Audrey Hepburn. The same year also saw the introduction of new film technology. Anamorphic lenses developed by the French astronomer Henri Chrétien led to the invention of CinemaScope, a new process that allowed films to be projected at a 2.66:1 aspect ratio, twice the size of the conventional format. The process became popular in Hollywood as film companies began to compete with television as well as other innovations within the film industry.[124]

In contrast to Hollywood's big productions, Kubrick's *Fear and Desire* was a small, quiet film that didn't rely on gimmicks and innovations to reach its audience. Although that audience was small, the film still resonated enough for Kubrick to be given a second chance with another film and a bigger budget. The reason for this resonance could be attributed to the aforementioned talent that Kubrick showed in framing shots in interesting ways. It could also be attributed to the motifs that occur in the film, motifs that Kubrick would return to throughout his career: the inability to communicate as the two sides only exchange two words which are either not understood or ignored; the dehumanization of man as the "innocent" Sidney rapes and kills a young village girl[125]; and the duality of man as represented by the double casting of Kenneth Harp and Steve Coit as both Lt. Corby and Pvt. Fletcher and as the enemy soldiers they kill.

For his next war film, Kubrick opted not to work from an original screenplay but chose to adapt a novel written by a "real soldier." Humphrey Cobb served as an infantryman in the Canadian Army during World War I, where he was gassed and wounded.[126] In an attempt to "get to the real thing," Cobb brought exacting detail to his narrative. Perhaps it is this exacting detail that so appealed to Kubrick when he chose to film this novel that first came to his attention at the age of 14.[127]

In the note at the end of *Paths of Glory*, Humphrey Cobb states that if "the reader asks, 'Did such things really happen?' the author answers 'Yes.'"[128] Cobb then goes on to refer the reader to several sources including a dispatch published in the July 2, 1934, edition of *The New York Times* titled, "French Acquit 5 Shot for Mutiny in 1915; Widows of Two Win Awards of 7 Cents Each."[129] The novel was critically acclaimed and regarded as an antiwar masterpiece. However, it was not a great popular success even though it was a Book of the Month Club selection.[130] Perhaps the novel did not find an audience because of Cobb's brutally realistic portrayal of life in the trenches, what one reviewer referred to as "the slaughter and stink of the 'field of honor'"[131]:

> "Flesh, bodies, nerves, legs, testicles, brains, arms, intestines, eyes..." [Dax] could feel the mass of it, the weight of it, pushing forward, piling up on his defenseless shoulders, overwhelming him with an hallucination of fantastic butchery. A point of something formed in his stomach, then began to spread and rise slowly ... he recognized it for what it was: the nausea induced by intense fear.[132]

The novel not only illustrated the cruel violence of war and Cobb's hatred of it, but also the incompetence of the officers who conducted the war and the suffering of the soldiers who dutifully obeyed these officers. The book vividly depicts "the rotten, ruthless system of militarism that robs men of their most primitive rights" by allowing the reader to connect with brave soldiers who are tried for cowardice and condemned to death by officers who are more concerned with personal advancement than the lives of the soldiers they command.[133]

Structurally, Cobb's novel is divided into three parts. It opens with two soldiers, Langlois and Duval, meeting each other on their search to find their regiment, the 181st French Regiment serving under Colonel Dax. Langlois is a seasoned soldier who is returning from leave, while Duval is an idealistic younger soldier who admires Langlois' medals and hopes to win his own. Langlois points out that he won his in a lottery, but this revelation does not deter Duval, who later in the novel becomes "intoxicated almost to the point of hysteria by the vibration of the gunfire, oblivious of all danger."[134] The two men finally catch up to their regiment, which is long overdue for rest after several days in the trenches. But rather than being allowed any recreation, the regiment is ordered to attack and capture a well-fortified position in no-man's-land known as "the Pimple." General Assolant delivers the news to Colonel Dax who argues that his regiment has recently suffered heavy losses and that his new recruits are untrained and unprepared for such an attack. Assolant is unconcerned and relentless:

> It was quite clear to [Dax], depressingly so, that the hour or more he had spent at his headquarters pointing out the difficulties of the attack and the exhaustion of his troops to the general had been wasted. The discussion, moreover, had ended on a note ... which had only served to wound Assolant's vanity and to solidify his stubborn refusal to consider the attack in any way a questionable one...." Please confine yourself to obeying the orders of your superiors, Colonel Dax, not to criticizing them."[135]

For Assolant, a man who rarely goes into the trenches to mingle with his men, "it was all a question of percentages. Men had to be killed, of course, sometimes lots of them. They absorbed bullets and shrapnel and by so doing made it possible for others to get through."[136] Troops are expendable as long as the mission is accomplished. Dax reluctantly accepts his orders.

Part II of the novel focuses on the attack itself, which is an abysmal failure. Dax was correct in his assessment that his men were unprepared and that the Pimple was too heavily fortified. His men advance as far as they can, only to be driven back. Furious, Assolant orders the artillery to fire on the infantry, orders that are refused. When the battle is over, Assolant demands justice for the cowardice of his men. Initially, he wants a section from each of the regiment's four companies, about 200 men, tried for cowardice. Eventually, General de Guerville convinces him to compromise and settle for one man from each company. Dax offers to take full responsibility and be the "example" that the generals so dearly want, but his offer is refused. Dax then sends out a memo to each company leader requesting that they arrest one man each and send him to the guardroom at the château "to appear before a court martial on charges of cowardice in the face of the enemy."[137] Everyone involved knows that the men who are chosen will stand no chance of acquittal and will be condemned to death. Since the soldiers did not act cowardly, each company commander is ordered to select a representative scapegoat.

Part III focuses on the court-martial and execution of the men. One company leader,

Captain Renouart, refuses to follow orders and writes a lengthy reply to Colonel Dax. He then writes two shorter drafts before writing a final simple memo stating that he is "unable to comply with your instructions because there is no member of my company against whom charges of cowardice in the face of the enemy can either be made or found tenable."[138] Believing that Renouart is related to a high-ranking politician, the generals accept his memo and try only one man from each of the three other companies: Férol, Didier, and Langlois. Férol is selected for being "incorrigible." Didier is the only witness to the murder of Lejeune by his commanding officer, Roget, on a reconnaissance mission. Langlois is chosen, ironically, by lot. The men are allowed a representative during the court-martial, Captain Etienne of the 7th Company, but he will not be allowed to call any witnesses nor refer to any of the men's former valor in action. He eloquently defends the men, but the decision had been made before the court even convened. The men are given their last meal and are allowed to see a priest. Langlois writes one final letter to his wife asking her to hire a lawyer to investigate the case. Didier is injured trying to escape and suffers major head trauma that will keep him unconscious for the remainder of the novel. He is carried to his execution on a stretcher. The following morning, a firing squad of thirty-five soldiers— including Duval — is selected. The accused men are led to and tied to posts where they are shot dead. The book closes with a sergeant major, Boulanger, shooting each man in the head to deliver a *coup de grâce*. Cobb ends his terrifying vision of war where he began, with Langlois, the soldier who won both honor and death by the luck of the draw:

> It must be said of Boulanger that he had some instinct for the decency of things, for, when he came to Langlois, his first thought and act was to free him from the shocking and abject pose he was in before putting an end to any life that might still be clinging to him. His first shot was, therefore, one that deftly cut the rope and let the body fall away from the post to the ground. The next shot went into a brain which was already dead.[139]

As Thomas Allen Nelson has pointed out, Cobb's *Paths of Glory* was "an ideal source for the filmmaker of *Fear and Desire, Killer's Kiss,* and *The Killing.* Its style and narration develop an ironic contrast between public and private worlds, the fictions of officialese and the fluctuations of an indeterminate truth."[140] Nelson goes on to say that the novel's passages of "hallucinatory intensity" that depict both the "actual and imagined horrors of war" and the "empty and formal masking of that truth" would have an "obvious appeal to Kubrick's demonstrated interests."[141] In the "Afterword" to the 1987 edition of the novel, Stephen E. Tabachnick states that Cobb's "eminently cinematic" style made the novel "relatively easy" to transform into a film.[142] Earlier, Tabachnick discusses the failed attempt by playwright Sidney Howard to bring the novel to the stage. Howard's play closed after only twenty-three performances because of "technical difficulties."[143] In Eleanor Flexner's assessment, *Paths of Glory*'s attempt to create the "audible and visual illusion of ... a heavily-shelled ... front-line trench during a major attack" simply "asked too much of the theater."[144] But film was a medium that could create the illusion of war, and Kubrick does so with horrifying precision. In an essay on films about World War I, Tom Wicker argues that *Paths of Glory* is the best film ever made about World War I in that Kubrick captures "another true story of individual lives ruthlessly sacrificed to a commander's or a nation's vanity and indifference to justice and humanity."[145]

But how exactly does Kubrick approach the text? At one point in Cobb's novel, Dax says that the soldier rarely "see[s] with naked eyes. He is nearly always looking through lenses."[146] Through what lens does Kubrick look at Cobb's novel? Although *Paths of Glory* has had "the least attention in terms of comparing the film to the source novel,"[147] three major critical studies of Kubrick's films— Norman Kagan's *The Cinema of Stanley Kubrick* (1972), Mario Falsetto's *Stanley Kubrick: A Narrative and Stylistic Analysis* (1994), and Thomas Allen Nelson's *Kubrick: Inside a Film Artist's Maze* (2000 revised edition)— do make reference to Kubrick's treatment of Cobb's novel.

Kagan points out that the major difference between the novel and the film is that the focus of the novel is on the soldiers who are to be executed by introducing the "three doomed soldiers" at the beginning of the narrative and ending the novel with "the bullets of the firing squad."[148] The film, however, moves the soldiers to the background and gives them a "passive" role so that the audience will identify with the character of Colonel Dax (played by Kirk Douglas) and his battle with the "treacherous and scheming staff officers" Mireau and Broulard (Assolant and de Guerville in the novel).[149] To further place the focus on Dax, Kubrick allows him, rather than Etienne, to defend the men at the court-martial. These changes center the story on "Dax's struggle to save the three and learn with whom he is fighting and why."[150] Falsetto echoes Kagan's analysis by pointing out that Kubrick's "one crucial decision in translating the novel" was to amplify "the role of Colonel Dax ... from the marginal character depicted in the book to the central character" of the film.[151]

Nelson gives the fullest consideration of the transformation from novel to film by stating that though the film follows "the novel's three-part organization (before the attack; the attack and after; the court-martial and execution), Kubrick did not choose to work out its ironic patterns of fate."[152] Like Kagan, Nelson notes that the novel begins and ends with the doomed soldiers but goes on further to point out that the novel's beginning and ending focus specifically on the two soldiers Langlois and Duval. Langlois, the veteran who won his medals in a lottery, is now condemned to die as "the result of another lottery."[153] Duval, a young recruit "who dreams of glory and especially admires Langlois," is chosen as a member of the firing squad.[154] Langlois becomes Corporal Paris in the film, a conflation of Langlois and Didier, while Duval's character is dropped completely. Nelson's strongest assertion is that ultimately the film "duplicates neither the nightmare landscapes of the novel nor those found in [Kubrick's] earlier films."[155] Whereas Cobb's novel is manipulative and expressionistic, Kubrick's film is objective and realistic.[156] For Nelson, this claim is not a negative criticism but an "impressive" example of Kubrick coming into his own as a director.

Though all three of these critics are correct in their assessments of the changes Kubrick made when adapting the novel to film, none of them seems to consider why those changes were made. What was Kubrick *doing* with the novel? Both Kagan and Falsetto claim that Dax is a "marginal" character in the novel, but this is not a true claim. Dax does appear in the novel less than the doomed soldiers, but at the same time, he is the novel's most well-developed character. All of Cobb's other characters are stereotypes designed to strike a chord with the reader. Langlois is the soldier with a wife back home to whom he is constantly writing letters. Ferol is the soldier with a lurid past who is using the military as a means of escaping that past. Didier is the good soldier who witnesses an atrocity and keeps his silence but is still betrayed. Duval is the young, idealistic soldier who is ready for the glory of war. The generals are the political chess masters who manipulate their pawns for their own personal advancement. Dax, on the other hand, is a contemplative and brooding figure whose main concern is the well-being of his men. He is the prototype for George C. Scott's Patton. He is Faulkner's "human heart in conflict with itself."[157]

Throughout the novel, Cobb gives the reader insight into Dax's mind through long passages of thought. When the reader is first introduced to Dax, he is considering why his subordinate, Major Vignon, cannot understand that though Dax wants his company as they walk, he is not in the mood for conversation:

> It's too bad ... that you can't ask a man to walk with you without his jumping to the conclusion that you want him to talk to you too. Why can't I say to a man, "Look here, I'm getting into a blue funk, as I always do at this point, and I really need your companionship. But it must be your silent companionship" ... [Vignon] just hasn't the faculty for knowing what I'm going through now. If he suspected the crisis I'm getting near, he'd consider it his duty, probably, to pull his pistol and put a bullet through my head.[158]

Elsewhere in the novel, the reader witnesses events through Dax's present perspective as when he leads Assolant through the trenches or through flashbacks in Dax's mind as when he recalls the argument with Assolant over whether or not the troops were prepared to take the Pimple. Therefore, Kubrick is not really making a marginal character the focal point so much as he is highlighting the character of Dax as the focal point.

But what about the doomed soldiers that are so central to Cobb's narrative? They are still central. If Cobb's novel is an indictment of the horrors of war and the treatment of the soldiers who give their lives—sometimes to enemy bullets and sometimes to "friendly fire"—in war, how can Kubrick present the same indictment if he makes the doomed characters passive and places them in the background? It is a question of form. In a novel, if a novelist wants the reader to sympathize with certain characters, then those characters must be foregrounded. The characters must stand out from the crowd. They cannot be faceless entities. Cobb achieves this sympathy through the use of compelling, if stereotyped, characters. If the reader is to care that these men are wrongfully executed, the reader must care about the men as individuals. However in a war film, the audience is predisposed to care about the soldiers. The audience does not have to visualize the atrocities of war; the atrocities are visualized for them. The audience feels sympathy when a soldier, any soldier, is cut down. In fact, too much attention to one soldier can actually cause an audience to question what is so special about this particular soldier, unless of course, the story is being told through the soldier in question's perspective, i.e. Oliver Stone's *Platoon* (1986) or Sam Mendes's *Jarhead* (2005) and, to some extent, Kubrick's own *Full Metal Jacket* (1987), which all contain first-person narration.[159] During a major battle scene in almost any war film, whenever an anonymous soldier is cut down by enemy fire, struck by shrapnel, or decapitated by an explosion, an audience will wince and audibly gasp at the horror of the carnage they are witnessing. A novelist must give the reader a reason to care about a particular soldier. Consider the following passage from Cobb:

> Charpentier climbed onto the smoking parapet, shouting and waving his men to follow. He stood there ... an heroic-looking figure, fit for any recruiting poster.... [He] turned to lead the way. The next instant his decapitated body fell into his own trench.... Four other bodies followed right after his, knocking over some of the men who were trying to get out.[160]

The impact of this passage is not the same as a ten-second celluloid clip that depicts the same incident. Even though Cobb gives this faceless soldier a name, the character is only introduced a few pages before his death. The reader has not been given a chance to develop an attachment to the character. The reader has not been following Charpentier from the beginning of the novel, so his death may not resonate for the reader the way that it would if Duval were killed at this moment. To compel his reader to further sympathize with this "heroic-looking figure," Cobb conjures up images of recruiting posters in the hope that the reader will develop the necessary attachment to the character to actually care that he has died a terrible, unnecessary death.

Knowing that his audience would already "care" about the soldiers, Kubrick is able to dispense with any unnecessary character development. Rather, he focuses immediately on the generals and their politically-charged reasons for taking the Ant Hill (Kubrick gives the target a more interesting and believable name than Cobb's "Pimple"). Mireau greets Broulard at the chateau where the court-martial will take place later in the film. Throughout the film, Mireau and Broulard will spend most of their time at this location, dining and hosting balls, far from the trenches where their men are dying. Shooting on location in Munich, Kubrick used an existing eighteenth-century chateau and had the interior redecorated to match the description in Cobb's novel. When the generals are the only ones present, Kubrick uses level medium shots to frame them, representing the fact that they are "at home" in the chateau. However, when the condemned men are brought out of the real world of the soldier's battlefield into the artificial world of the chateau, Kubrick switches to long shots—often shot from slightly high angles—

to dwarf the men in their surroundings. Dax, interestingly enough, is almost always shot in either slightly low angled medium shots or close-ups, showing that he is not out of place no matter what his surroundings. The slightly low angle also gives his character a sense of command even when he is answering to the orders of others.

By beginning with the generals and their politics, Kubrick is able to move quickly to the real conflict in Cobb's novel, the distance between officers and their soldiers. Kubrick brings the social structure of Cobb's characters to the forefront in the film. As Gavin Lambert has noted, the world of *Paths of Glory* is "cruelly divided into the leaders and the led. The officers conduct their foxy intrigues in the elegant rooms of a great chateau.... The men go to the trenches and into battle."[161] The class structure of this society is cruel and dehumanizing — a common Kubrickian theme. The lives of the citizens, or soldiers, are short and expendable as they are used solely for production, or advancement of the cause. Advancement in class or stature is achieved only through aggression and dominance, as portrayed by General Mireau. Hard work results only in the receiving of meaningless accolades, i.e., the winning of medals in a lottery. In this society, there is no justice, only treachery and vain ambition. Of course, the powers that be must maintain good public relations by occasionally visiting the trenches and prosecuting and punishing the guilty. Above all, in this uncivilized world, they must remain civilized, as evidenced by life in the chateau. Kubrick reinforces the fact that no one can escape his place in this society, that all decisions have already been made by the powers that be, through the brilliant use of tracking shots. As Dax moves through the trenches, his path is already laid out. He has no choice but to play the role that has been given him by Mireau.

Nelson's claim that by opening with the generals rather than the soldiers, Kubrick is choosing not "to work out [the novel's] ironic patterns of fate" is simply not true.[162] The film is full of ironies, as evidenced by Kubrick's juxtaposition of scenes. Throughout the film, Kubrick cuts from the beautiful chateau to the blood-filled trenches. The doomed soldiers die at the hands of their comrades because, according to Mireau, "if those sweethearts won't face German bullets, they'll take French ones!" After the court-martial judge announces that "the hearing is closed," Kubrick cuts to the firing squad receiving its orders. While the generals host a ball following the decision, Dax broods alone in his quarters. Immediately after watching the execution, the audience is treated to Mireau and Broulard eating an elegant meal. Both Mireau and Dax walk the trenches: Mireau, "pompously and hypocritically," Dax, "quietly and sincerely."[163] To further reinforce the ironies of the film, Mireau stops three times and addresses three different soldiers who just happen to be the three men he will later condemn as cowards. Finally, rather than being executed, the one true cowardly soldier in the film, Roget, is put in charge of the firing squad. All of these ironies help to capture what George Bluestone and André Bazin refer to as the "spirit" of Cobb's book.[164]

Kubrick further captures the book's spirit through the film's soundtrack and final scene, a scene that does not appear in Cobb's book. Early in the novel, the young idealistic Duval, upset that he has not yet seen combat, "console[s] himself with the sound of distant gunfire. At last, he reflected, he had heard the noise of war — The Orchestration of the Western Front."[165] The reader is told that Duval had seen the phrase, "The Orchestration of the Western Front" in a newspaper headline. It is repeated throughout the novel, usually by Duval, and represents the seeming wall of sound that is the noise of war. The closer to the battlelines the men get, the more the noise increases until the noise becomes "a din, the din an uproar, a crescendo of sound so deafening that you had to shout in a man's ear to make yourself heard. 'The Orchestration of the Western Front.' The phrase again came into Duval's head. 'And I've got a front-row seat.'"[166] Kubrick captures this orchestration through the film's score, which, according to composer Gerald Fried, "was the first all-percussion score" ever used in a film.[167] Fried, an acquaintance of Kubrick's from the Bronx, had previously worked with him on the documentary *Day of the Fight* as well as his first three feature films. The two collaborated well together; however, by the time production commenced on *Paths of Glory*, Kubrick was, in Fried's words, "already 'Stanley Kubrick,' and then it was a struggle — I had to rationalize every note."[168] The percussive soundtrack, occasionally interrupted by machine-gun fire and distant explosions, drives the film forward. Kubrick emphasized the film's soundtrack in the promotional materials, including the posters and tagline, which stated: "BOMBSHELL! the roll of the drums ... the click of the rifle-bolts ... the last cigarette ... and then ... the shattering impact of this story ... perhaps the most explosive motion picture in 25 years!" Since the film was not a huge box office draw, there was never a demand for the soundtrack to be released. However, in 1999, Gerald Fried oversaw production of a compilation of music from Kubrick's films and included one track, "The Patrol," which captures the intensity of the film's score.[169]

Throughout production, the filmmakers wrestled with how to end the film, a problem that caused several delays and arguments. United Artists, the film's distributor, wanted an upbeat ending in which the soldiers are given a last-minute reprieve. According to various sources, several different endings were written including one in which Dax and Mireau sit down to have a drink together after the men are sentenced to thirty days in the guardhouse. Some sources mistakenly claim that the various endings were actually shot, but according to the film's producer, James B. Harris, and others who worked on the film, Kirk Douglas refused to shoot any ending that betrayed the message of the novel.[170] However, there seemed to be disagreement on what exactly the final message was. Though the novel ends with the execution of the men, there is the implication that even in the direst of circumstances, human decency survives, as illustrated by Boulanger firing a shot "to free [Langlois] from the shocking and abject pose" in which the bullets from the firing squad had left him.[171] This implication of human decency would be all but impossible to capture on film. An audience watching this scene visualized would simply see three men who had just been executed by the firing squad receive a killing blow to the head. The novelist has the power to convey the thoughts of a character to the reader. The filmmaker can achieve the same result through voice-over, but the voice-over of a minor character would have been out of place in a film in which voice-over had not been previously used, save for the opening narration by the unseen Peter Capell. Furthermore, it would have seemed contrived.

While filming in Munich, Kubrick settled the dilemma by opting to script and shoot a scene that did not appear in the book.[172] It involved the regiment relaxing in a tavern and becoming increasingly belligerent until the tavern owner offers them entertainment in the form of a young German girl who has been captured by the French. The girl, portrayed by Kubrick's future wife Christiane, is forced to sing a folk song, "Der Treue Husar" (The Faithful Soldier). Harris argued that the scene did not belong in the film and was only an excuse for Kubrick to cast his new girlfriend in the film, but Kubrick, becoming more and more sure of himself as a director, insisted and the scene, fortunately, was shot.[173] While the young girl is dragged onto the stage, the soldiers jeer her with humiliating catcalls, driving the girl to tears. When she first begins to sing, the men are so loud that her song cannot even be heard. However, as the girl continues singing, the men are moved to silence, then to tears, and finally begin humming with her. Unknown to the men, Dax is outside the tavern listening. Having just left Broulard and Mireau, Dax is disillusioned with humanity. He hears the commotion in the tavern and goes to investigate. As evidenced by his grimace, he is at first disgusted that the men in his squadron are as heartless as the generals. However, as the men begin to quiet down and eventually sing with the young girl, the grimace becomes a slight smile. When informed that it is time for the regiment to return to the front lines, Dax pauses before uttering the last line in the film, "Give the men a few minutes more, sergeant." The film ends with Dax's faith in humanity restored.

The scene is important on multiple levels. One, without seeming sentimental or contrived, it conveys the idea that human decency can survive in the worst of times. Secondly, though completely original, the scene seems neither out of place nor betrays the book's message. Finally, it allows Kubrick to place his own stamp on the film and work out issues that he raised in *Fear and Desire*. The emotional raping of this young girl is comparable to the literal raping of the young girl in *Fear and Desire*. The difference is that in the first film, Kubrick allowed the inhumanity in his characters to take over, resulting in the death of the girl. However, in *Paths of Glory*, the girl is not only spared, she wins over her aggressors and connects with them on a level that breaks through the barriers of their nationalities. She is not the enemy. The men are their own enemies. In Private Joker's words, the film is "trying to suggest something about the duality of man.... The Jungian thing."

Though Kubrick showed promise with his first feature, it is with *Paths of Glory* that he becomes the genius we associate with his later films. With this single feature, he proved himself to be not only a great adapter of literature but an auteur in his own right. *Paths of Glory* is not only a great adaptation. It is not only a great war film. It is also a great film.

4 The Dream Landscape of *Killer's Kiss*

Tony Williams

According to one main concept of post–1968 film criticism concerning Hollywood narrative, the beginning of a film often anticipates its conclusion.[174] Although it is dangerous to follow this particular theory in a dogmatic manner, it is often true that certain films contain recognizable formal styles which often re-occur with necessary variations so that each manifestation does not become merely mechanical. Associated with the work of Roland Barthes and other theorists, this concept often appears in various theories concerning the role of authorship in cinema.[175] While critics may discover explicit traces of personal expression in more accessible directors, it is more challenging in terms of other talents whose very idiosyncratic use of style and meaning is by no means easy to comprehend.

The work of Stanley Kubrick resembles a palimpsest, a constantly inscribed text containing features that the artist attempts to erase but which often remain stubbornly present and discernable in more creatively realized achievements. Despite their respective positions at the beginning and end of Kubrick's career, *Killer's Kiss* and *Eyes Wide Shut* contain certain similarities. Both use a recognizable narrative structure. But different stylistic overtones dominate a content which may not appear to be exactly what it narrates. Although the story may appear logical, elements of doubt concerning the reality of what has actually happened inflect the nature of each text.

Kubrick's attempts to suppress access to his first independent production, *Fear and Desire* (1953), are well known. Had the rights of *Killer's Kiss* (1955) not passed beyond the control of its director, it would also have remained in limbo. Although critics such as Thomas Allen Nelson and Mario Falsetto see several flaws in this early work, *Killer's Kiss* does contain features that occur in refined and sophisticated ways in more accomplished films such as *Eyes Wide Shut*.[176] Dana Polan also notes that Kubrick's second film appears to have a direct continuity with these later achievements despite its low-budget technical deficiencies:

> Indeed, one might argue that it is because of its meagerness that the film fits so well. In its reduction of narrative spaces to a few claustrophobic sites, in its reduction of narrative to a bare outline of conflictual interaction, in its confining of character within a few social types, *Killer's Kiss* sets out as a visual matrix many of the stereotypes, images, and social fixities that Kubrick's cinema will return to again and again.[177]

Polan's essay is one of the very few detailed explorations of this early film. However, *Killer's*

Kiss is not merely an archaeological work exhibiting an early apprenticeship which will be over-shadowed by its more accomplished successors. It is a film set in the urban jungle of New York and foreshadows the director's last film in many ways. While *Killer's Kiss* is a late example of classical film noir, *Eyes Wide Shut* represents a refined director's vision of the visual style of neo-noir which he incorporates into his own unique signature.[178] Despite intervening decades and different production circumstances, both films feature characters trapped by different forms of fear and desire undergoing their own types of personal odyssey within the New York land-scape. One couple exists on the margins of society while the other enjoys a more affluent lifestyle. Both films involve traumatic events leading to a psychological odyssey on the part of its male characters initiated by the action of a female whose very nature remains unknowable to the very end. While Davy Gordon undergoes his dark purgatory within the impoverished urban landscape common to classical film noir, his more economically privileged counterpart begins a journey within a privileged landscape he is familiar with depicted in the more nuanced visual tones of neo-noir cinematography more indebted to the sophisticated usages in British films such as *Stormy Monday* (1988), *Croupier* (1998) and *I'll Sleep When I'm Dead* (2003) than its more stylistically empty American counterpart. *Eyes Wide Shut*'s foreboding neo-noir cine-matography depicts an affluent landscape that is equally as threatening as that contained within the different world of *Killer's Kiss*. Each film involves a climactic ritual contest involving older and younger generations. In *Killer's Kiss*, the son fights the father for Oedipal supremacy while *Eyes Wide Shut* involves the implicit threat of violence by older, more affluent, establishment figures against a young intruder in their midst. Davey of *Killer's Kiss* kills the father and redeems his lady in an ending resembling a fairytale romance. By contrast, an anonymous female redeems Bill Harford. But an extended epilogue involving tracing the path he took on his night journey suggests that things will never be the same for him again and that even his "lady fair" may be contaminated by her obscure involvement in his night fantasy. *Killer's Kiss* concludes with its own version of a Hollywood "happy ending." So does *Eyes Wide Shut*. But can we really trust these characters and can they trust each other? *Killer's Kiss* and *Eyes Wide Shut* contain charac-ters trapped by dark features within their personalities that they can not consciously compre-hend. It is coincidental and ironic that Kubrick shot his second and final features within the same deadly environment of New York.

Like the early works of George A. Romero and the 1950s films of Samuel Fuller, *Killer's Kiss* is the ultimate auteur film. Co-produced, edited, photographed and directed from Kubrick's own story over a twelve- to fourteen-week period on an initial budget of $40,000, this sixty-seven minute feature certainly exhibits features of a sparsely financed independent film, includ-ing post-synchronization of dialogue.[179] It opens with Davy Gordon (Jamie Smith) standing by his suitcase in Penn Station. His voice-over begins the narrative which moves from the docu-mentary landscape familiar from earlier 1948 noirs such as *Naked City* and *Call Northside 777* to Davy's apartment as he examines his face in a mirror for scars before his big fight. Previ-ously, Kubrick shot poster images announcing Davy's imminent fight with Rodriguez in a man-ner familiar from his first short film, *Day of the Fight* (1951). However, even in these relatively brief scenes, Kubrick suggestively reveals the result. One poster of Davy is in the gutter while the other hangs loosely from a wall. These images suggest the operation of deterministic fea-tures common to the literary world of naturalism which influenced not just the American tra-dition of Dreiser and others but also film noir, and possibly Kubrick himself.[180]

As Davy examines his face in the first of many mirror shots which appear in *Killer's Kiss*, photographs of a farm, aunt, cows, uncle, and dog are reflected there. The contrast between the Edenic country landscape and the dark world of the city has long existed in both natural-ist-influenced fiction dealing with boxing such as Jack London's *The Game* (1905) and *The Abysmal Brute* (1913), as well as cinematic variations such as *Kid Galahad* (1937). But while escape from the city may have been possible in the early decades of the twentieth century, little likelihood exists in its mid-point as the doomed hero of John Huston's *Asphalt Jungle* (1950) learns.[181] The camera pans right as Davy moves away from the mirror to frame Gloria (Irene Kane) standing before her window frame in the tenement apartment block opposite to Davy's. Davy's window frames her in a trapped position. It thus operates as a double framing device. This is the first of many dualities that occur in *Killer's Kiss,* a device Kubrick develops further in his later films. As viewers, we voyeuristically look at Davy and the attractive woman framed in the background. The camera then pans right as Davy goes to his goldfish bowl before cutting to an extreme close-up of him seen through the goldfish bowl, showing his face in a grotesque manner as fish swim around it. As Davy answers the phone, the frames of his bed surround him. Sequentially, Gloria moves to her window and the following mid-shot contains a *noir* image of her looking at Davy framed by the bars of her window with the right side of her face in shadow. These economically shot images suggest the deadly operation of the forces involving psychological and environmental urban entrapment seen in the fiction of Zola and his American successors such as Theodore Dreiser and Frank Norris. Davy and Gloria are dual images within a visual landscape. Their first encounter will result from Kubrick's fascination with those accidental forces of contingency governing human personality and historical events that Nelson sees as a major feature of the director's work. The mirror imagery governing their first scenes in *Killer's Kiss* suggests the presence of deterministic psychological features buried deep inside them that they do not understand. Both characters are self-absorbed within their individual dilemmas. They anticipate the characters of Bill and Alice Harford in *Eyes Wide Shut,* who live in a blissful state of ignorance until a nighttime incident provokes disturbing consequences.

As Vinnie Rapallo (Frank Silvera) waits for Gloria in his car, an overhead shot shows her and Davy walking in parallel formation to the street before parting. This accidental circumstance immediately evokes jealous feelings from the older man. As he tells Gloria, "You're doing all right for yourself," the next shot shows Davy descending the steps to the subway. Rapallo perversely continues to undermine the younger man. "He used to be a pretty good fighter. We can watch him on television." Kubrick then makes significant comparisons between hero and heroine as they prepare for their respective occupations. On his subway journey, Davy reads Uncle George's folksy Norman Rockwell–type letter from Washington State. The tones represent an older man existing in a state of denial as he expresses the virtues of the rural landscape. As Davy prepares for his fight in scenes reminiscent of *Day of the Fight,* accompanying shots show Gloria preparing for her nightly ritual as a dance hostess.

Before these scenes, Kubrick inserts several shots of Broadway. The most significant is an image of a clockwork toy swimmer moving rapidly in a circular position in a bucket of water. It is followed by a shot of a record on a phonograph. Kubrick then cuts to Rapallo's dancing establishment. As the camera moves left to right, the dancers rotate in circular patterns. Bouncers, ready to use violence against any customer who does not follow the rules of the game, observe the male customers. Kubrick not only introduces us to "a world of aimless repetition, culminating in the image of Gloria stuck in her boring dead-end job as a dance hostess" (in Polan's words) but also injects into his montage surrealistic elements from footage depicting unusual aspects of everyday life.[182] A furry animal incongruously dressed in a Santa Claus outfit, food such as apples, hot dogs and sundaes, photos of individuals and families, and a mechanical baby doll appear. Kubrick obliquely refers to certain elements from literary naturalism such as animal imagery and food. These basic elements condition human desire no matter how much civilization attempts to deny them. In *Killer's Kiss,* certain discontents exist in New York's supposedly civilized landscape in a manner paralleling Freud's well-known text *Civilization and its Discontents.* As a voracious reader, Kubrick must have been familiar with Freud as well as many works representing literary naturalism.

The ritually controlled world of the dance hall also contains images of violence paralleling the boxing arena. Davy has to fight in a ritually proscribed manner. Rapallo's dance hall customers have to follow certain rules of behavior. Rapallo's office contains posters displaying a violent confrontation between two men, the romantic silent film *The Winning of Barbara Worth* (1926), and two clowns who mock human efforts at control. Kubrick's ironic use of *mise-en-scène* depicts Rapallo's world as containing irreconcilable contradictions. After listening to a television commentary describing the twenty-nine-year-old Davy's career involving "one long promise never fulfilled," Rapallo goes to the dance floor. He interrupts Gloria's dance with a soldier, who objects before bouncers eject him from the building. Rapallo feels excitement over the humiliation of a younger man he does not know and whose motives he has misinterpreted. He forces Gloria to watch Davy's defeat on television. In many ways, this sequence evokes the first part of Freud's essay "Totem and Taboo," with the father figure still in control of the female. Kubrick's neo-realist boxing sequence concludes with Davy's defeat and the embrace and kiss between Rapallo and Gloria. The screen then fades to black suggesting the older man's sexual victory according to the contemporary censorship mechanisms mandated by the Hays Code. The older man has won? Or has he? Did Gloria submit? Perhaps her later rejection of Rapallo depicted within her later flashback may be due to denial mechanisms deeply entrenched within her own psyche? We cannot be sure.

The second set of tenement apartment sequences reinforces voyeuristic patterns seen within the first sequence. But this time, it is Davy who looks at Gloria like a Peeping Tom. He is now framed before the bars of his window as he watches her undress. But a phone call from Uncle George interrupts his gaze. Although the camera moves right to show him answering the phone, the audience can still see Gloria's apartment window from the mirror of Davy's dressing table. Uncle George consoles him, suggesting Davy return to the comforting rural landscape of Washington State. Davy remains non-committal. He tells his uncle that he is feeling "a little dopey, tired." These lines suggest his vulnerability to forces over which he has no control. By the time he returns to his voyeuristic activities, Gloria is already discreetly clad in a dressing gown. Davy smiles, sets his alarm clock, and goes to sleep. He is about to begin a journey in which boundaries between fantasy and reality may collapse.

Kubrick uses negative images of the New York landscape in a manner anticipating Bowman's more sophisticated astral journey in *2001: A Space Odyssey* to depict Davy's nightmare odyssey through the urban jungle. However, a scream awakens Davy from his dream. He sees Rapallo assaulting Gloria. The older man shields his face as he attempts in vain to close the blinds of Gloria's apartment window. It is almost as if Davy witnesses a dark reenactment of Freud's primal scene. He rushes to her apartment to save a surrogate image of the mother from a powerful father. Once there, Davy finds Gloria alone. He listens to her version of events via her flashback. Although flashbacks are generally supposed to provide clarity and knowledge in Hollywood narratives, ambiguity and contradiction often occur. Kubrick uses these elements for his own ends. Gloria mentions that the incident occurred "one hour ago." But this statement represents a contradiction between the actual time of the incident which she narrates as well as the time it took Davey to run to her apartment. This temporal discrepancy anticipates techniques Kubrick will use in *The Killing* (1956) to undermine audience acceptance of voice-over narration.[183] Earlier, Gloria succumbed to Rappallo's embraces. She now tells Davy a different version of the relationship. The older man had knocked on her door and asked forgiveness. "I'm sorry. I really am sorry. Can you forgive me?" She refuses this request. Viewers may ask what Rapallo needs to be forgiven for. As in Alice's flashback in *Eyes Wide Shut*, truth and illusion are mixed together in an incomprehensible structure. Former tough guy Rapallo now behaves like a castrated father figure in Gloria's flashback. "All my life I've always spoiled the things that meant the most to me." Rapallo acts in contrast with his other appearances in the film. He now performs a role in what appears to be a sado-masochistic fantasy on the part of the narrator. "I'll be your slave for the rest of your life." Gloria humiliates him like a powerful daughter figure who has taken on the role of a dominatrix in a bondage scenario. "To me, you're just an old man. You smell bad." Her lines also evoke Kubrick's continuing fascination with the atavistic components of the human personality as well as the ironic aspects of Jonathan Swift's excremental imagery that plays a key role in *Full Metal Jacket*.[184] The sequence may not be realistic but a nightmarish performance involving dark psychoanalytic mechanisms buried deep within the human personality. After Gloria screams, a zip pan returns us to the present.

Davy has woken up to witness the final act of this flashback. He has seen Rapallo's ineffective assault but has not witnessed preceding events. Gloria has screamed. But has she lost her nerve following an attempt to seduce an older man in a perverse example of the female Oedipus complex? Did the incident actually happen according to information contained in the flashback? Or did she create a situation to bring a younger man to her rescue in a macabre version of a Freudian family romance? Earlier apartment scenes revealed Davy and Gloria voyeuristically devouring each other's bodies, suggesting the operation of dark sexual psychological mechanisms ready to initiate a particular dramatic turn of events. *Killer's Kiss*'s flashback sequence and its entire narrative construction have many relationships to the type of particular cinematic narrative surrealism Kubrick will perfect as his career develops. Surrealism attempted to depict the activities of the unconscious mind by means of images frequently juxtaposed without apparent order or sense. Like Luis Buñuel in his later films, Kubrick utilized those formal structures of narrative cinema as a framing device.[185] But he extracted deeper levels of meaning from situations deceptively depicting mundane reality by often using excessive, contradictory images (whether involving actors or sets) to show the operation of unconscious forces dominating everyday life. *Eyes Wide Shut* represents a more sophisticated version of an unrefined structure governing *Killer's Kiss*. Both films involve characters and events that are difficult to decipher. Their boundaries between reality and fantasy are deliberately obscure, often due to the characters who are governed by psychological mechanisms over which they have no control. Davy states in his voice-over the morning after: "The thing that was apparent in my mind was not to ask her what her boss Rapallo was sorry for." Why not? If Davy does not ask, enough information appears on the screen to provide answers he may not wish to know himself.

Two photos appear at the right of Gloria's dresser. They show an older man and a ballerina who we later learn are her father and sister. The older man resembles Rapallo. Davy is too immersed in his romantic feelings for Gloria to interpret certain evidence which may provide a darker version of events. He inspects her room while she sleeps, noting a doll above her bed and underwear on a rack. He touches her nylons in a fetishistic manner. Here, Kubrick intuitively evokes two elements from the cinema of the past and an imminent future. The doll reminds viewers of the one seen in Susan Alexander Kane's "doll house" bedroom prior to her refusal of further objectification by a dominant male in *Citizen Kane* (1941). Davy's inspection of Gloria's underwear anticipates Scotty's knowledge of Madeline's intimate parts in Alfred Hitchcock's *Vertigo* (1958). Ironically, all these male characters are dominated by romantic fantasies concealing the operation of dark, destructive internal psychological mechanisms.

During breakfast, Gloria narrates her second flashback to Davy. But this time, it is more stylized, displaying significant elements from her own family history unconsciously revealing deep psychological scars. Kubrick's second wife Ruth Sobotka plays the role of Gloria's deceased older sister Iris. "I suppose it is really Iris's story." In a way, Gloria is correct, since her sister's narrative has deeply affected her. The ballet constantly recurs during Gloria's narration. It contains suggestive analogies to that clockwork swimmer seen earlier in Broadway moving in a circle without beginning or end. Both involve a particular repetition-compulsion form of movement that parallels Freud's findings concerning those unconscious motivating forces affecting human personality. Gloria tells Davy that their father was a writer with a growing reputation. But her birth led to the death of her mother on the same day. Her father then went on a two-week drinking binge "and I don't think he ever thought of another woman." Apparently, Gloria fulfils her dark version of the Oedipus complex by disposing of her mother as a rival for her father's affection on the very day of her birth. But she still has to reckon with the presence of her older sister, Iris, who, in Gloria's words, "was the image of her mother." She was also "Daddy's favorite and, maybe, I began to hate her."

There is certainly no "maybe" about this. Iris is the more talented sister, performing at the Ballet Rus at the age of thirteen. When their father became seriously ill, Iris married a rich man who insisted she give up her career in exchange for paying expensive medical bills. Following their father's death, Gloria delivered an emotional assault against Iris which led to her suicide and a note absolving Gloria of the responsibility. "She said she loved me. She was sorry she made a mess of things between us."

Masochistic guilt feelings over Iris's suicide began to control Gloria. After visiting New York for legal matters, she decided to take a job as a dance hostess in Rapallo's "Pleasureland" which she describes as a "depraved place, a human zoo." It is a "lower depths" version of her sister's former prestigious appearance at the Ballet Rus. Gloria takes pleasure in her nightly painful humiliation as a taxi dancer. She tells Davy that "I felt that at least Iris never had to dance like this, and then I felt less unhappy." But she is fooling both herself and Davy. Like Bill Harford, he takes the story at face value and does not attempt to decipher its real meaning. But while Alice narrates a story designed to unsettle her complacent husband, Gloria's version of her past history reveals disturbing elements in her own personality that Davy chooses to ignore. They then kiss before a window frame ominously suggesting double entrapment. Gloria tells Davy, "It's a mistake to confuse pity with love." He does not listen to her. The sequence ends with the bars of her bed framing them both.

By this point, irrational elements begin to dominate the narrative, making the real world resemble a fantasy landscape. Gloria decides to go to Seattle with Davy. His voice-over mentions something whose implications he ignores. "She was so scared, she'd grab at anything." Davy is entering into a problematic relationship with his "eyes wide shut." Both characters barely know each other. They have dark, secret desires existing within their unconscious minds which resemble each other. Davey has been in the fight game for far too long. A television commentator on his last fight described him as a perpetual loser whose career comprised "one long promise never fulfilled." He has fetishistic components within his personality paralleling many bizarre characters in the cinema of Luis Buñuel, to say nothing of voyeuristic tendencies anticipating Norman Bates in *Psycho* (1960). Gloria is also a loser as well as a glutton for sadomasochistic punishment at the hands of a father figure she both desires and rejects in very much the same way as her actual father. Can these two characters live happily ever after with Uncle George on a rural farm in Washington state?

The final chapter begins. Rapallo broods in his office which contains ominous mise-en-scène elements akin to those in Gloria's apartment. A poster of a barroom fight appears behind him, indicating the usual masculine primeval reaction to conflict. One photo represents an older woman. Perhaps his mother may have played a role in his particular version of a family romance that affected him psychologically? Unlike Gloria, we know nothing about his mother nor do we know anything about Davy's. Two laughing clowns jeer at Rapallo from a picture. They foreshadow those two drunken pranksters who will later accidentally prevent Davy from meeting a violent fate. Rapallo throws his glass at them, which also shatters the camera lens framing his gaze. Kubrick's fascination with the operation of accidental forces of contingency now appears. Rapallo's hoodlums kill the wrong man. Playing his own fantasy role of a knight in shining armor out to rescue his lady fair for the second time in the film, Davy sets out in pursuit. He wins a temporary victory over his adversaries before they overpower him. While recovering, he overhears Gloria's betrayal. She offers herself to Rapallo in the same way that her sister Iris offered herself to an older man many years ago. But this time, the motivations are ambiguous. She may wish to save her own life. But she may actually intend to consummate her masochistic fantasies involving a father figure in the most direct manner possible. However, Rapallo rejects Gloria's overtures in a manner perversely evoking her father's rejection of her for Iris years ago.

The final segment of the drama occurs in the surrealistic, but everyday environment of a warehouse containing nude female mannequins. It represents another Kubrick sequence where boundaries between reality and fantasy become deliberately blurred. Father and son confront each other in a dark film noir version of Freud's "Totem and Taboo." They battle for control of Gloria. But the battle appears to be a deliberately absurd ritual occurring in a nightmarish environment.[186] Although many mannequins are whole, others are dismembered body parts such as hands and severed heads. The female body as an obscure object of desire becomes fragmented in a battle between two males who fear each other, in an eternal contest involving age against youth. The final violent context in *Killer's Kiss* represents a dark, patriarchal struggle for the female as an object of desire on the part of two males who regard her as a vehicle for their objective sexual desires and not a person in her own right. Kubrick reveals the violent aspect of this

The dream landscape of *Killer's Kiss* (1955): Davy Jones (Jamie Smith) in the film's mannequin factory.

recurring dilemma within the male personality. He does not condone it but instead unveils its destructive dark mechanistic psychological operations. One mannequin is even employed as a weapon in the contest. Rapallo wields an ax while Davy uses a shutter pole against a rival he will eventually penetrate in a final violent act. As the son finally kills the father, the latter's head cuts into a mannequin's thus anticipating the final surrealistic image in Alex's murder of The Cat Lady in *A Clockwork Orange*. It underlines the surrealistic and dreamlike quality of the event whereby characters act not out of their own volition but from psychological forces beyond their control. Rapallo's scream merges with a train whistle at Penn Station. It appears indebted to that famous sound montage used by Hitchcock in *The 39 Steps* (1935) when the landlady's scream after discovering a body in Richard Hannay's apartment immediately merges with a train whistle in the next scene.

However, the scream device may not be solely due to a young director borrowing from another. It has ominous overtones blurring again boundaries between reality and fantasy. A scream earlier awoke Davy from his dream nightmare into another dangerous world. This scream appears to restore Davy to the world of normality. He waits for Gloria in the realistic landscape of Penn Station. He does not expect her to appear. She has betrayed him before Rapallo and he had left her to escape his fate. But Davy's lady fair suddenly appears to join her knight to begin their odyssey to the rural alternative represented by Washington state. It seems a happy ending in which both lovers have forgiven each other. However, any positive resolution appears dubious. The audience has seen too much if their eyes remain open and not shut. Like Bill and Alice Harford in *Eyes Wide Shut*, Davy and Gloria have survived their adventures "whether they were real or only a dream." Bill replies, "And no dream is ever just a dream." Both couples decide to deny what has happened and live blissfully in a world in which eyes remain shut and questions will remain unanswered.

Despite the aesthetic and temporal distance between *Killer's Kiss* and *Eyes Wide Shut*, dark continuities exist. Both dramas take place in the urban landscape of New York. Characters journey into a psychological heart of darkness involving romance, sexual betrayal, and violence, an arena dominated by irrational, instinctual forces existing within the human personality. *Killer's Kiss* is a film of denial like *Eyes Wide Shut*. Both use various forms of *noir* imagery, New York locations, and Kubrick's brand of surrealistic imagery to present a world in which characters are controlled by dark instinctual desires that may result in individual or universal (*Dr. Strangelove*) destruction. The most dangerous mechanism of all is denial, a device Kubrick criticizes in his many films. He makes films for audiences he hopes will question fictional narratives and move beyond those acceptable formulas he satirizes in his reworking of various cinematic genres. *Killer's Kiss* is an early example of a theme he will often rework, modify, and constantly change in his own unique artistic palimpsest. Despite its status as a primitive work, it contains elements that will frequently appear throughout his artistic career. His dream landscape contains both powerful imagery and warnings concerning the destructive nature of human personality affected by fantasy elements within which they attempt to seek refuge. But the cost of denial is more dangerous.

5 One Watches Cells:
Kubrick's Films Noirs in Context

Hugh S. Manon

In the limited scholarship on Stanley Kubrick's first feature films—*Fear and Desire* (1953), *Killer's Kiss* (1955), *The Killing* (1956), and *Paths of Glory* (1957)—critics have tended to position the director's early efforts not in their own historical and generic context, but as highly revealing precursors, diamonds in the rough that "set the pattern" for trends that will emerge full-force in the director's later career.[187] In such accounts, Kubrick's originality and innovation transcend Hollywood convention, and bold markers of his conscious vision consistently reemerge across the years. As an example, consider the brief but much-remarked sequence in *Killer's Kiss* in which we witness the surreal nightmare of protagonist Davy Gordon (Jamie Smith), a simple but effective series of high-speed tracking shots down an empty city street with tall buildings looming on either side. The sequence is identifiably Kubrickian, many say, owing to its graphical symmetry, its penetrative movement forward, and because it has been negativized (the series of four process shots renders light areas dark and dark areas light). Add into this concordance the jarring edits and enigmatic soundtrack, and it becomes no great leap to connect Davy's nocturnal vision with Kubrick's airborne shots of an alien landscape in the "cosmic trip" sequence from *2001: A Space Odyssey* (1968), some of which are also rendered as photographic negatives, albeit richly colorized.[188] In a quasi-algebraic correlation, film X, *Killer's Kiss*, is said to anticipate film Y, *2001*. Or as it is more commonly formulated by critics, film Y "recalls" film X.[189]

Given Kubrick's extremely rich but limited output, as well as his notorious perfectionism, this search for coherence in the details of his films is both expectable and useful, and should not be dismissed out of hand. However, because such auteuristic analyses are only ever undertaken retrospectively—charting a past career from the vantage of the present, with the gravity of the director's more recent films pulling his nascent productions into line—they implicitly endorse an unsatisfying tautology: Kubrick was Kubrick because, against all odds, he persisted in being Kubrick. Equally disconcerting is the tendency to explain the director's first major works in terms of a well-rehearsed catalogue of prehistoric Kubrick trivia, all of which points in the same direction. Here, Kubrick's youthful efforts as a photojournalist, or his three documentary short films, figure as archeological traces of the author's ever-cohesive self.[190] The problem with such biographical, determinist narratives is not that they are misleading, but that they too often abort a second, equally profitable discussion about external influence. That is, in accounting for Kubrick *the master*, they inevitably ignore the equally salient question of Kubrick *the moviegoer*. It is as if, in the eyes of some critics, the impulse to borrow from, modify, and expand on other films' successes is not a pure enough creative act — it is too bastardized and messy to be considered worthy of an auteur. Yet if a directorial self exists, can it not also be understood as a more-or-less idiosyncratic reservoir of preexisting cinematic techniques, motifs and themes — a culturally shared, yet inherently contradictory set of sources that are not "selected" so much as they are unconsciously coughed up in the various phases of a film's production?

In a number of articles and interviews, Kubrick has been noted for his omnivorous viewing habits. According to biographer John Baxter, by the time Kubrick made *The Killing*, he "had seen almost every major Hollywood film of the previous decade."[191] This essay takes such a claim seriously — not as historical fact, but *as a claim* — understanding Kubrick not necessarily as the one who has seen it all, but as a figure around which such lore tends to accumulate. In his book on *2001: A Space Odyssey*, film theorist Michel Chion observes that Kubrick "presents the reassuring portrait of the 'complete director.' Like others, however, he was operating in the real world, and like others he worked with collaborators, based on concrete conditions on the one hand and with his unconscious on the other."[192] The series of textual comparisons to follow heeds Chion's admonition regarding auteur theory: that although the singularity of the director as a film's driving creative force has been contested by many, the concept of the auteur nonetheless remains useful, but only insofar as the individual film is "considered in a *contradictory* relationship with its director and with the director's intention, of which it is far from being merely the obedient reflection."[193] Against the unitary and, at its core, Cartesian notion of the auteur that we have come to expect, Chion's rationale presses beyond the idea of a director's signature as a pervasive, quantifiable, and consciously constructed pattern. Instead of assembling a dossier of characteristic repetitions (visual motifs, narrative themes, camera techniques, etc.), the goal of the critic should be to locate and analyze the gaps that appear across a body of work — a relatively consistent pattern of inconsistencies, conflicts and resistances — thus admitting that the directorial unconscious most often emerges in a vexed relationship with the rationalized productions and generic conventions through which it is finally expressed.

In a profound sense, Stanley Kubrick was the sum of all that he had seen; yet, in an equally profound sense, the specific history of his viewership, and the uses he made of that viewership, can only ever be hypothesized, never proven. Even in the rare moments when Kubrick publicly proclaimed some of his favorite films — *Citizen Kane* (Orson Welles, 1941),[194] *I Vitelloni* (Federico Fellini, 1953),[195] and later *Eraserhead* (David Lynch, 1977)[196] — there is no way to verify that the director was being truthful, nor is there any reason to assume that such proclamations certify the direct influence of any of these films on his own. While it is tempting to draw the line somewhere — asserting *yes, here Kubrick is clearly borrowing from film X* — such affirmation leads down a slippery slope. Suddenly every resemblance seems to be both a conscious choice and a final answer. For instance, whereas it has been reported that the mannequin-factory climax of *Killer's Kiss* was "cribbed from the Girl Hunt ballet of Vincente Minnelli's *The Band Wagon* [1953],"[197] might we not more profitably connect the sequence to the profoundly *noir* hall-of-mirrors climax of Orson Welles' *The Lady from Shanghai* (1947)? In terms of structure, the scenes are in many respects homologous: both involve human simulacra, graphical repetition, and the visually arresting technique of camouflaging bodies among other pseudo-bodies. Moreover, both scenes manipulate their viewer through a disorienting refusal of classical continuity — a tactic of which *The Band Wagon* is certainly not guilty. However, when pressed to historically document the connection between *Killer's Kiss* and *The Lady from Shanghai*, the position appears less tenable. There is no way to prove that Welles's famous scene provided inspiration, however vague or direct, for Kubrick's later scene, although it may indeed have. Even were a document to surface, verified by experts to be Kubrick's own handwriting, proclaiming *The Lady from Shanghai* to be a direct model for the climax of *Killer's Kiss*, we would still have to doubt whether "influence" had occurred, since in a non-unitary conception of auteurism, cognition and intent are not the bottom line. One thing is sure, however: Kubrick's productions, like any auteur's, incorporated *both* a direct appropriation of structures from other films *and* a nebulous, impossible-to-articulate, and ultimately unconscious "feel for the game." While the existence of the authorial unconscious does not cancel out the possibility of consciously borrowing from textual precedents (if that is what we mean by "influence"), at the same time it guarantees that, in terms of interpretation, all bets are off — both for the director, who is denied clear access to the basis of his creativity, and for the scholar, who in the end cannot fail to encounter a partly unified, partly contradictory body of work.

In an effort to "think outside the oeuvre," this essay does not attempt to locate Kubrick's early work in relation to all of Hollywood cinema, but in the narrower context of a highly periodized genre — the rich, but internally contradictory corpus of classic American film noir. Appearing roughly between 1941 and the mid–1950s, *noir* is both a set of films and a broad cultural predisposition or attitude — a nexus of crime, deception, and dark fantasy in which Kubrick was ostensibly invested, and which two of his earliest features both assimilate and develop in complex ways. By isolating *Killer's Kiss* and *The Killing* as generic exempla, this essay seeks to answer two questions. First, how might Kubrick scholarship profit from a discussion of his films noirs in context, examining them alongside a selection of classic-era *noirs*, both famous and obscure, but without ever referring to the director's later works? Secondly, and in a reverse trajectory, how might an analysis of certain provocative moments from Kubrick's two *noirs* help to illuminate the structures, themes, and generative principle of film noir itself, an "absent cause" which, as Joan Copjec notes, has yet to be identified.[198] This latter question is particularly salient given the appearance of *Killer's Kiss* and *The Killing* very late in the *noir* cycle — in the company of such highly reflexive films as *Kiss Me Deadly* (Robert Aldrich, 1955), *The Big Combo* (Joseph H. Lewis, 1955) and *Beyond a Reasonable Doubt* (Fritz Lang, 1956) — as well as the hypothesis, advanced by a number of critics, that Kubrick's films noirs are best understood as parodies or burlesque caricatures, ironically resuscitating a clichéd set of generic conventions.[199]

The Woman (and the Man) in the Window: Airshaft Voyeurism in *Killer's Kiss*

In his essay "Materiality and Sociality in *Killer's Kiss*," Dana Polan compares Kubrick's second feature film to other low-budget films noirs like *Detour* (Edgar G. Ulmer, 1945): "*Killer's Kiss* has a *huis clos* ambiance to it, a 'no exit' claustrophobia in which a few ill-fated losers endlessly confront one another in miserable little bouts of aggression."[200] Though Kubrick's film is not entirely consistent in this attitude, it is nonetheless possible to pinpoint the crux of the *noir*-ness Polan identifies. More than anywhere, we sense that we are watching film noir during the sequences constructed around the narrow "airshaft" that separates two city apartments — an urban architectural feature which, given our heavy reliance on air conditioning today, has lost much of its connotative value. In many low-rise tenements built in the late nineteenth and early twentieth century, the windows of the less desirable interior rooms opened onto a ventilating shaft (or in newer buildings, a wider, but still fairly small "courtyard"). According to New York tenement inspector Lewis E. Palmer, such an arrangement was utilitarian by design, but social in practice:

> The air shaft is one of the greatest elements in destroying privacy in the tenement house. Through it one hears the sounds that occur in the rooms of every other family in the building, and often in these narrow shafts the windows of one apartment look directly into the windows of another apartment not more than five feet away. Privacy under such conditions is not only difficult, but impossible.[201]

Residents whose windows opened onto an airshaft would have been privy to scenes of undressing, romantic embraces, etc., and during warm summer months, the sounds of music and pets, domestic squabbles and sexual activity. However, such encounters would have been relatively unremarkable — more a matter of course — and one can even read Palmer's practical concerns with privacy as presaging a memorable line of dialogue from Alfred Hitchcock's *Rear Window* (1954): "We've become a race of Peeping Toms."

In his analysis of *Killer's Kiss*, Alexander Walker understands the airshaft more metaphorically, as a push-pull of tantalizing nearness and abrupt separation: "One life can look through the New York darkness into another life, yet the two lighted squares of glass only emphasize the couple's apartness. They are unaware of each other to the point of invisibility, each self-isolated, virtually imprisoned in lives that are soon revealed as humiliating and hopeless."[202]

Though this assessment of the protagonists' cell-bound existence is broadly correct, like many analyses of Kubrick's *noirs* it stresses the existential metaphor of incarceration,[203] while overlooking a deeper structural connection with the morphology of the cell — enclosed on all sides not by walls, but by other cells. Configured as a perfect one-to-one symmetry, the airshaft view in *Killer's Kiss* is at least as concerned with being sealed out as being locked in, and in generic terms can be understood as an updated, compartmentalized version of the ominously locked upstairs room at the center of Gothic melodramas such as *Rebecca* (Alfred Hitchcock, 1940), *Gaslight* (George Cukor, 1944) and *The Two Mrs. Carrolls* (Peter Godfrey, 1947). However, in contrast to the Gothic window, in which the protagonist glimpses a strange silhouette that quickly disappears in a rustle of curtains, the airshaft window in *Killer's Kiss* does not frame an isolated clue. Instead of contributing a small piece to a developing mystery, the window across the way reveals *the whole solution* and thus hermetically "locks in" the lone eyewitness, who is unable to prove what she has seen. Film noir distinguishes itself from other crime genres by playing up the thresholds of criminal perfection — the everso-tenuous membranes that both separate and serve as an interface between the observer and the observed, the public and the private, the oblivious and the unsuspected. And although such perfect façades are always susceptible to failure, the cellular ruptures and breaches enacted on screen only help to affirm the *noir* ideal of a hermetically flawless, "airtight" seal on knowledge.

Within a honeycomb of seductive partial access, *Killer's Kiss* presents a quickly developing affair between two low-rent urbanites, each of whom earns a living largely on the merits of their physical body. In the first of three airshaft sequences, veteran boxer Davy Gordon mentally prepares himself for that night's bout. He remains mostly oblivious to the presence of Gloria Price (Irene Kane) in the opposing window as she readies herself for her job as a "hostess" at Pleasureland, a seedy Times Square dance hall. Contrasting the boxer's self-absorption, a cut to Gloria's apartment reveals her sipping a cup of coffee as she intently contemplates the figure of Davy in the window across the way. The change in perspective marks the beginning of a series of parallel edits which compare Gloria's experience at the dance hall with Davy's routine at the boxing arena.[204] That the first true point-of-view sequence in the film belongs to a female character is a bit of a coup — with the camera lingering on Davy's tight-fitting clothes and athletic physique — and only after the boxing match does he return the look, objectifying Gloria and reclaiming the gaze as masculine.[205] In these initial reciprocations, however, Davy and Gloria are not positioned as surreptitious or perverse, but as jaded — strangely matter-of-fact in their willingness to see and be seen, and conspicuously devoid of the thrill we see in the eyes of "Jeff" Jeffries (James Stewart) in Hitchcock's *Rear Window* (1954).

In the story-world of *Killer's Kiss*, voyeurism and exhibitionism are far from remarkable; they comprise part of a normal, routinized pattern of behavior. Davy's initial peek at Gloria, and the lingering look she returns, metonymically stands for a whole series of other, similar moments we have not witnessed—a kind of benign voyeuristic habit on both of their parts, which on this particular day will be interrupted when the cell wall they share is breached by a real communication. Like downtown pedestrians who indifferently pass by an endless series of shop-window mannequins (a motif that will return in the film's famous climax), Davy and Gloria watch each other as dispassionately as one might watch television.[206] In several shots, the well lit, doubly-framed airshaft view evokes the scopic fishbowl-effect evoked in any number of paintings by Edward Hopper.[207] This sense of hermetic division is shattered, however, when Davy awakens from his nightmare (discussed above) to accidentally glimpse Gloria grappling with her boss and would-be lover Vincent Rapallo (Frank Silvera).[208] Only once in the film do we witness a two-way interaction across the airshaft—when Davy shouts "Hey! What's goin' on in there?" At this instant of cell-to-cell connectivity, Rapallo looks back, locking eyes with Davy, and tries in vain to cover his face by pulling down the blind.[209] When Davy runs over to assist Gloria, Rapallo is gone. However, the real problem is not that Rapallo has escaped, but that Davy has been *seen seeing* across the airshaft, and this accidental rupture of a mutually shared cell wall motivates the remainder of the film's action.

In a calculated reversal of the first two airshaft scenes, the third airshaft sequence places Davy alone in Gloria's apartment, just as the newfound lovers are about to leave town together. As soon as he enters, Davy knows something is wrong. He drops his suitcases to the floor and we hear muffled pounding and deep male voices: "Hey, you—open that door!" But the hail is not coming from outside Gloria's apartment door; it is drifting in from across the airshaft. Davy lifts the

An airshaft affair: Davy Gordon (Jamie Smith) and Gloria Price (Irene Kane) in *Killer's Kiss* (1955).

edge of the roller blind and sees his own apartment come to life. The effect is uncanny: Davy looks back to see his own familiar domain and refuge, metaphorically represented in an earlier scene as his fishbowl, now swimming with police officers. Confirming the goal of their pursuit, one cop says, "They found his manager's body about an hour ago with his head bashed in." As the words are spoken, we see a close-up of Davy's eye, widening as it peers through the crack. On one level, this antipodal cell-to-cell view is a simple plot-advancer: Davy learns that he has been framed for murder, and in a classic *noir* "wrong man" scenario, he must take action to set the record straight.[210] At the same time, however, the scene portends a semantic irony, a play on the double meaning of the word "frame." Though Rapallo's initial goal was to kill Davy, the inadvertent killing of his manager makes the scenario even better. Rapallo has evened the score by placing Davy in the precisely the same frame Rapallo himself previously occupied: the horrifying position of looking out the window, only to see another window looking back. Davy has learned vicariously from Rapallo's mistake, however, and is careful to not to reveal himself to the eyes of the police. Even the wanted man himself can understand the desire to track down a fleeing murderer named "Davy Gordon," the vacated cell of his apartment having confirmed his guilt in the eyes of the other.

By problematizing Davy's entrance to Gloria's apartment — the vantage point of the other — Kubrick adds a kind of auto-critical appendix to the book of *noir*, not only adopting and revising, but also working to theorize the structure of film noir in cellular terms. Such a connection comes into focus, however, only when we consider the concrete details of other precedent films noirs, especially those which employ the conceit of a window-to-window view. Indeed, it would not be wrong to suggest that the matrix of separation of contiguity we see in *Killer's Kiss* constitutes an overarching *noir* trope, a cellular epistemology that dates back at least as far as the proto-*noir* writings of Cornell Woolrich, and which is engaged by Kubrick in a particularly reflexive way at the close of the *noir* cycle. The following section, then, both theorizes and provides some generic context for a conception of the *noir* cell, and in doing so bridges the gap between the directorial experimentation of *Killer's Kiss* and Kubrick's 1956 film *The Killing* — a cellular crime fantasy par excellence.

"If You Ripped the Fronts Off Houses": The Cellular Epistemology of *Film Noir*

In Alfred Hitchcock's 1943 film *Shadow of a Doubt*, Uncle Charlie (Joseph Cotten) expresses his cynical views to his adoring niece (Teresa Wright) in a short monologue. "Do you know the world is a foul sty?" the murderous uncle asks his naïve younger counterpart. "Do you know that if you ripped the fronts off of houses you'd find swine?" In such statements, Uncle Charlie acts as a kind of a spokesperson for film noir, laying bare its thematic concern with an imaginary/impossible stripping away of cell walls to expose the internal truth. Later, while jawing with brother-in-law Joe (Henry Travers) at the bank where he works, Uncle Charlie says, "Who knows what goes on when the doors are closed?" As both quotations imply, such a clear view can only ever be hypothetical — not "I know" or "You should see," but instead "*Who knows?*" In contrast to other genres' representations of criminal procedure — machinations which occur either well before the fact (classical detection) or in full view of a stunned public (gangster film) — *noir* deceptions occur both secretly and right under our noses. Film noir often creates this sense of unsuspicion by transporting viewers beyond the surface of crime, immersing us in the details of a conspiratorial cover-up. Indeed, it would not be wrong to suggest that Walter Neff's unsuspiciousness within the story world of *Double Indemnity* (Billy Wilder, 1944), like that of all the great *noir* deceivers, succeeds to the precise extent that he is able to enunciate and render visible his secret plans for the cinematic audience. With regard to its greatest conceit, an impossible "behind the scenes" view of crime and conspiracy, *noir* is nothing if not paradoxical: as viewers, we look in only so as to recognize the impossibility of looking in.

Although it may seem as if the primary fantasy of film noir concerns visual penetration, investigation and solution (via the figure of the private eye, various camera techniques, etc.), the opposite is in fact true. By switching perspectives back and forth across a fastidiously maintained boundary, granting the audience access to both the keepers of the façade and their dupes, *noir* reinforces a sense of impermeability in everyday reality. Consequently, it is not the luridly fascinating inside view itself, but instead the real impossibility of such epistemological peeling, and a reaffirmation of the cell-intact — sealed up on all sides, a site of pure speculation — that dictates a wide range of *noir* structures. By defining the *noir* cell as a hermetically sealed envelope, rendered both stylistically and in narrative, we can begin to understand some of the ways in which film noir in general, and Kubrick's *noirs* specifically "rip the fronts off" a mundane, ordinary world in order to thrill audiences with their own potential side-by-side relation to crime. A primary concern, then, lies in the "buzz" evoked by *noir* — a cultural resonance or aura, as well as a well-defined set of conventions that keep audiences in theater seats. In this context, the proximity and separation of two airshaft apartments in *Killer's Kiss* sets the stage for a late-cycle, almost cartoonishly literal enactment of a dynamic that is, in the first instance, a popular *fantasy* of cellular transgression.

To suggest that *noir* is "cellular" is to indicate the proximity of behind-the-scenes crime and conspiracy, but only insofar as it is hermetically foreclosed, an impossible to verify hypothesis. Correspondingly, in invoking the word "cell," table any specific reference to prison architecture (or cellular telephones) in order to address its more elemental, quasi-biological features. Distilled to its basic structure, a cell is not usually understood as simply a box or sphere. Instead, a cell must be surrounded by other cells. At the very least, a cell is presumed to have at least one other cell attached to it — otherwise we must clarify the exception (i.e. "this is a single-celled organism"). Transposing this sense of mutually exclusive attachment into the realm of the social, among film noir's highest priorities is to focus the viewer's attention on the absoluteness of the interstitial, on the existence of absolute locks on knowledge that permit the contiguity of private conspiracy and public routine, the ominous and the ordinary. Most succinctly, the cell of *noir* can be defined as a fantasy of side-by-side obliviousness — an impossible, purely hypothetical supposition that "if you ripped the fronts off houses...." The airshafts, courtyards and balconies frequently seen in film noir can be understood as a particularly apt reification of this cellular structure — materializing, and thus calling into question, a morphology of hermetic apposition that in other genres remains entirely unremarkable. To be clear, however, the cellular structure of *noir* does not imply any inordinate emphasis on rooms or material partitions as a subject matter. Though in certain instances a *noir* cell may be coextensive with a room, house or physical wall, this need not be the case. Instead, the *noir* cell constitutes an invisible, epistemological architecture in which the obstruction of knowledge is fetishized, taking the form of a vacuum-like seal, a kind of blindness-in-seeing. Accordingly, the *noir* cell does not anticipate detection in the classical sense, but rather the impossibility of detection, particularly vis-à-vis an unsuspecting public.[211] In terms of genre, the *noir* cell dialectically revises the Holmesian crime scene, which the sleuth presumes to be full of detectible clues, and instead presents a variable locus of deception that ideally goes unnoticed as such — an unseen scene that does not so much forbid investigation as it deflects recognition. Given this hermetic structure, the innocuous surface of the cell becomes our best (and only) indicator of its inner duplicity. Viewing the world from a *noir* perspective, everything is suspicious because nothing is suspicious.

The connection of *Killer's Kiss* to the structure of the cell becomes acutely clear when we locate Kubrick's film among a selection of other films noirs that represent the proximity and fragmentation of modern life, and the possibility of accidental witnessing, in an airshaft-like arrangement. Based as it is around a central courtyard, it is perhaps unsurprising that the Monogram B-picture *I Wouldn't Be in Your Shoes* (William Nigh, 1948) was adapted from a story by Cornell Woolrich — the author of the 1942 short story on which Hitchcock's *Rear Window* is based, and an enormous literary influence on *noir*. At the film's beginning, it is late at night and the apartment windows of Tom Quinn (Don Castle) are open in the stifling heat. Tom cannot sleep, and turns on the phonograph in order to take his mind off the absence of his wife and the nature of her work (she is a dance instructor who, like taxi-dancer Gloria in *Killer's Kiss*, grapples with many male patrons on any given night). In response to the music, a voice is heard from downstairs: "I'm a milkman. I have to get up at 5 A.M. Want me to come up there and kill ya?"

What are we supposed to glean from this rather mundane bit of exposition? For one, we know that if the protagonist was quiet enough, he could get away with murder, but if he was too loud, he would be aurally witnessed by his neighbor (via a scream, thud, or other sound). Here, we find a basic template for *noir*'s appropriation of the airshaft as a metonym for metonymy itself, standing for the partialized contiguity of urban life. In this case, however, the inadvertent "tuning in" of a neighboring scene bears the structure of radio, of hearing without seeing. Unlike *Killer's Kiss*, in which Davy is a kind of televisual voyeur, Tom (and the viewer) can only imagine what the downstairs milkman looks like, just as the milkman might never know if or when a murder was taking place upstairs. Owing to their physical separation, such close quarters not only produce various fragmentary bits of information, fodder for fantasies about the "who knows what" which, in the old cliché, "goes on behind closed doors," but also opportunities for a kind of perfect misunderstanding. When Tom throws his custom made pair of tap dancing shoes out his window at a yowling cat, the next morning the shoes mysteriously turn up outside his apartment door. Later in the film, it is revealed that an old miser was killed by a man wearing the discarded shoes, framing Tom, whom we know to be innocent, as the murderer in "an unbeatable, airtight case." In this context, Tom's earlier comment that "every window in New York is open tonight" takes on a new meaning: despite the faceless anonymity of the city, someone may be listening and looking in, waiting for a happy coincidence (the thrown shoes, with their distinct tap and footprint) to provide the impetus for a perfect hermetic frame-up.

Closer visually to *Killer's Kiss* is the 1946 film *Shock* (Alfred L. Werker). At the beginning of the film, a young woman named Janet Stewart (Anabel Shaw) takes a room at the Belmont Arms hotel in San Francisco. She awaits the return of her husband, a former prisoner of war whom she thought dead for two years. Awakening from a bizarre nightmare (just as Davy Gordon does), she walks out on the balcony only to overhear a conversation emanating from an open window across the way. In an extreme long shot, revealing only a sliver of the remote action, a woman (whose face we never see) accuses her husband Richard (Vincent Price) of having an affair. When Richard calmly asks for a divorce, the woman becomes hysterical, threatening to make public his indiscretion. Her white-gloved hand reaches for the telephone. "Leave that phone alone!" Richard commands, picking up an ornate candlestick. "I hate you!" he says, and hits her over the head with great force. Janet, mouth agape in a silent scream, watches the woman fall to the floor. Failing to notice that he has been spotted, Richard pulls the curtains shut and the scene fades to black. In this sequence, as in the brief moment at which Davy spots Gloria struggling with Rapallo, it is above all the coincidental nature of the discovery — the sense that the cellular interior can only be glimpsed under special circumstances, or by accident — that conveys a *noir* aura. As in *Killer's Kiss*, the main plot of *Shock* is initiated by a localized (i.e. "over here") reception of the space of the other (i.e., "over there"), a cellular arrangement that supplants the voyeuristic "keyhole peeping" of the past with a screen-like reception akin to the contemporary phenomenon of television. But whereas early television touted its ability to place the viewer "in two places at one time,"[212] *noir* understands such views as remarkable, insisting upon a rigid boundary between seeing and knowing.

In a characteristic *noir* plot twist, subsequent scenes in *Shock* reveal the murderer to be Dr. Richard Cross, the very psychiatrist called in to treat Janet, who has lapsed into a state of "amnesia shock." With the only eyewitness now mute and confined to bed, the narrative shifts focus from Janet's plight to Richard's cover-up, subtly transforming the murderer into the film's protagonist. Having examined Janet, Richard glances out the window, assuming precisely her position from the previous night, and begins to realize that he killed his wife in full view of Janet's open window, and that the traumatic scene triggered her shock. As with Davy's view of the police search, the significance of the shot lies not so much in the contents of the window (Richard's curtains are drawn) as in the recognition of the perspective itself — a point of view which, if Janet ever remembers it, could get Richard twenty years in prison for manslaughter. Of the innocent characters in the film, only Janet sees things as they are, and for most of the film she cannot speak — a seal on knowledge that Richard works diligently to maintain. The scenario certainly feels like *noir*, owing not to any hard-boiled dialogue or chiaroscuro lighting effects, but instead to the epistemologically hermetic structure the narrative strains to establish. Unlike the scores of other peacefully sleeping neighbors who failed to witness what was right under their noses, Janet is exceptional in having horrifyingly seen too much, yet her position *as exceptional* reaffirms unsuspicion as the normal state of things. If not for a remarkable coincidence (Janet's nightmare, the position of her room, the warm night, etc.) the criminal interior would have remained hermetically sealed in its cell, "right next door," but unsuspected. However — and this is a crucial narrative tactic in establishing *noir*'s cellular arrangement — even with the existence of an eyewitness, the truth of the murder remains sealed tight.

The airshaft eyewitness again appears, in a somewhat novel form, in the 1949 film *The Window* (Ted Tetzlaff), also based on a story by Cornell Woolrich. Here again it is a hot night, and when ten-year-old Tommy Woodry (Bobby Driscoll) climbs up his apartment's fire escape to catch a cool breeze, he glances through a nearby casement only to see his upstairs neighbors kill a man with a pair of scissors. A variation on the fable of "The Boy Who Cried Wolf," the conflict escalates when no one, including Tommy's parents, will believe his story and he reports the crime to the police. The suspense-thriller predates *Killer's Kiss* by a number of years, and was popular enough to be invoked in a 1954 *New York Times* editorial about *Rear Window*, to which the earlier film was judged superior.[213] Above all, it is the striking closeness with which Tommy witnesses the crime (along with a number of rooftop traversals) that links *Killer's Kiss* to *The Window*. However, at no point does Tommy enter the neighbor's apartment to investigate; that task is left to a sympathetic police detective. Consequently, we never see Tommy inhabiting the malevolent other's return perspective on Tommy — no jarring coincidence of the gaze. Nevertheless, the film clearly describes the relation between the cell of the observer and that of the observed in hermetic terms. When Tommy's mother (Barbara Hale) tells her son that "the Kellersons are nice people — they never bother anybody," Tommy replies: "They just act that way, Mom, so you won't know anything about them." In other words, they act normal so you'll be oblivious. Later, when a police officer asks Tommy what the murderers are like, Tommy bluntly states *noir*'s hermetic paradox: "Well, they don't look like murderers." Given this investment in a perfect simulacrum, the duplicitous interior of which is glimpsed through a pane of glass, *The Window* can be understood as an evolutionary step in the cellular structuration of film noir, a trend which culminates not only in Hitchcock's much-praised, big-budget experiment *Rear Window*, but also, I would argue, in Kubrick's oft-maligned, low-budget experiment *Killer's Kiss*.

Thematically similar to *The Window*, but closer to *Killer's Kiss* both in release date[214] and in structure, is *Witness to Murder* (Roy Rowland, 1954), in which a well-to-do Los Angeles apartment dweller named Cheryl Draper (Barbara Stanwyck) views a late-night murder in the window across the street. When the police find no evidence and refuse to believe her story, she decides to investigate, gaining entrance to the murderer's apartment by masquerading as a prospective tenant. Despite her (pointedly televisual) claim to police that "I saw it when it happened!" for each new piece of evidence Cheryl produces, the killer, Albert Richter (George Sanders), is able to supply equally convincing evidence that she is insane. Following Cheryl's release from a mental institution, the body of the murdered woman is found and Cheryl decides to confront Richter directly. In a resoundingly *noir* moment, the killer, whom we have known all along to be guilty, freely admits his guilt, but only to Cheryl, who can do nothing about it: "Of course I admit it. I have nothing to fear from you. You're insane. It's recorded in the police files and in hospital reports. Anything that you might foolishly say concerning my admission would merely corroborate their findings. You have an *idée fixe* about me — possibly dangerous." For all her sleuthing across the way, Cheryl finds herself nonetheless locked out. The more she attempts to penetrate the hermetic cell of *noir*, the more territory it subsumes. Like Davy Gordon, who is made to pay for having accidentally seen too much, Cheryl's look implicates her in what she has seen. Yet unlike *Killer's Kiss*, only the killer is permitted a look back; at no point does the camera depict Cheryl as looking back into her own window the way Davy does.

Collected together, films such as *I Wouldn't Be in Your Shoes*, *Shock*, *The Window* and *Witness to Murder* comprise a glut of courtyard *noirs*—certainly a thematic trend, if not a full-fledged subgenre. While it would be nearly impossible to declare any of these films a direct influence on Kubrick, taken as a set they certainly appear to loom in the unconscious periphery surrounding *Killer's Kiss*. This is to say that *Shock*—and/or other films noirs like *Shock*—clearly have some bearing on the articulation of space, desire, and deception in Kubrick's film. But while all of the films discussed incorporate the voyeuristic thrill of seeing without being seen, and while most invoke some sense of a redoubled gaze — a look which sees the act of seeing itself — only in *Killer's Kiss* does the camera travel with the protagonist to the opposing cell in order to look back the other way. Twice in *Killer's Kiss* we follow Davy up the stairs, across the rooftop, and down into Gloria's wing of the building, entering the space of the other with unsettling impunity. The expectation that the camera will remain both attached to the protagonist and fixed on the near side of the airshaft — a convention most clearly upheld in *Shock*— is flaunted, destabilizing the subject-object binary by calling into question our sense of a reassuring "here" versus an alien "there." The result is an unsettling sense that, even when unoccupied by any onlooker, a multiplicity of other points-of-view exist. Despite other lamentable failings in *Killer's Kiss* (the flat acting, tinny post-synchronized dialogue, uninvolving plotlines, etc.), this complex articulation of the gaze — represented by Kubrick not as a monolithic, fixed point-of-view, but as a field of vision in which the subject sees only at the risk of being *seen seeing*— is surely the film's strong suit, legitimating comparisons to a revisionist film noir like *Rear Window*, while helping to mitigate the film's other flaws. As a testament to Kubrick's originality in *Killer's Kiss*, we need only consider the numerous more recent films that have successfully revamped the once-exceptional ploy of transposing the protagonist into the dangerous cell of the other "across the way." At the same time, it is important to note that by 1955 film noir itself has all but expired, with its penchant for cellular metaphors reemerging only occasionally in the late 1950s and 1960s, and usually in the form of reflexive parody and nostalgia.[215] In this context, *Killer's Kiss* can be understood as an underappreciated generic capstone, both crystallizing the hermetic structure of the cell, and suggesting, with a bluntness verging on self-reflexivity, that at any given moment, and in any given place, despite the fact that we inhabit one cell, we are always/already scrutinized by an obscure other across the way.

Backwards and Forwards:
The Killing and the Film Noir Caper

In *The Strange Love of Martha Ivers* (Lewis Milestone, 1946), Sam Masterson (Van Heflin) and Toni Marachek (Lizabeth Scott) enter the lobby of a city hotel and approach the front desk. The hotel cashier/clerk (Frank Orth) literally pops up from behind the desk, and when told they want two rooms, he launches into his well-rehearsed patter: "There's half as many baths as there is rooms. Half the rooms has baths and half hasn't — that's one way of looking at it. Another is: for each two rooms, one has a bath in the middle and the other hasn't. Or, you might say, there's a half a bath to each of two rooms." What the clerk is trying to articulate is a paradox, one of *noir*'s many paradoxes where space is concerned, though the paradox becomes clearer when we replace the word "bath" with the word "wall," the only other noun that could make sense here: "There's half as many *walls* as there is rooms. Half the rooms has *walls* and half hasn't — that's one way of looking at it. Another is: for each two rooms, one has a *wall* in the middle and the other hasn't. Or, you might say, there's a half a *wall* to each of two rooms."

In such convoluted statements, *noir* effectively theorizes itself. To overstipulate what it means to be a wall is to obsess over the interstices at the expense of what is central — to fixate on the envelope instead of the letter, the husk instead of the kernel. As with Uncle Charlie's sinister hypothesis about "ripping the fronts off houses," to conceptualize the "half a wall" is to figure the point of interface between the subject and the world as vexed or barred — a juncture at which the viewer is ignorant of his or her own ignorance. To the extent that a hotel guest thinks of himself as "renting a room" he misrecognizes the less comforting state of affairs in which he is in fact renting halves of walls — cellular barriers that simultaneously unite and divide individual subjects with/against one another. This is precisely the sort of psycho-topology Kubrick delivers vis-à-vis the interstitial airshaft in *Killer's Kiss*, and the structure of the "half a wall" becomes even more highly formalized in his next work, a meticulously plotted crime film in which a series of hermetic cells — each engineered to obviate the possibility of any outward, public suspicion — together add up to a nearly perfect caper. Drawing comparisons with a range of other films noirs, this section explores two distinct manifestations of the *noir* cell in *The Killing*: first, what might be called the "dollhouse" tracking shot, a shot which dynamically represents a cross-sectional view of the private domain of crime; and secondly, the film's several instances of cellular coincidence, moments at which two of the film's isolated narrative threads collide, revealing to the viewer an already familiar event from a new and jarringly orthogonal perspective.

In a review appearing in the June 4, 1956, issue of *Time*, Stanley Kubrick's new film *The Killing* is described an audacious reworking of "the familiar story of a stick up" in which "the camera watches ... the whole shoddy show with the keen eye of a terrier stalking a pack of rats."[216] This metaphor of stalking is not a broad generalization; it refers to a specific set of shots in the film, a trend Michel Ciment identifies as a "somewhat systematic use of lateral tracking shots" in *The Killing* and Kubrick's other early works.[217] At numerous moments in the film, the camera tracks members of the heist mob as they proceed through various environments, both public and private, and in doing so helps to define the film's mise-en-scène as cellular in precisely the sense outlined above. The two most striking tracking shots appear in the film's exposition, in a railroad apartment[218] belonging to Marvin Ungar (Jay C. Flippen). The first follows mastermind Johnny Clay (Sterling Hayden) through a series of three rooms as he explains the caper to girlfriend Fay (Coleen Gray). The second shot tracks mobsters George Peatty (Elisha Cook, Jr.), Mike O'Reilly (George Sawyer) and Marvin Unger through the same set of rooms after Johnny discovers George's wife Sherry (Marie Windsor) eavesdropping on their planning session. In each of these shots, Kubrick stages the action in the form of a cross-sectional cutaway, not only tracking past the interior of rooms, but also traversing the wall boundaries in between.[219] For instance, when Johnny walks through a doorway, the camera tracks past a black border representing the edge of the wall in which that doorway is housed. Because there are three rooms, the divisions appear twice in each tracking shot, underscoring the effect through staccato repetition.[220]

Not entirely unique in film noir, these cutaway sets recall the stylish opening sequence from a little known B-picture entitled *Open Secret* (John Reinhardt, 1948). Here, the camera is positioned at a high angle, impossibly revealing the "tops" of walls, as it tracks a shadowy figure from a city sidewalk into a bar called the "19th Hole," past a portly bartender and his card-playing customers, and finally into the darkly-lit back room, in which a secret society of anti–Semites is about to pass judgment on a local businessman. In turn, this cell-to-cell tracking shot in *Open Secret* may owe its technique to a famous long-take from Maurice Tourneur's seminal gangster film *Alias Jimmy Valentine* (1915), wherein the bird's eye view of the camera figuratively "rip[s] the roof off" a bank to reveal wall boundaries and the maze-like cluster of rooms in which the gang members commit their caper. Kubrick's architectural cross-section resembles these shots, but categorically avoids anything like a bird's eye view. *The Killing*'s two apartment sets (Ungar's and the Peattys's) are constructed less like a top-down, ichnographic blueprint than like the backless arrangement of a traditional dollhouse,[221] revealing interstitial boundaries on a horizontal plane. As a result, Kubrick's shots are more subjective and voyeuristic, less objective and surgical than their precedents, positioning the viewer "in amongst it" in the realm of the fiction. At the same time, the missing wall approximates the so-called "fourth wall" of the cinematic screen, reflexively implying that while this epistemological peeling is the province of cinema, such transparency is unavailable in real life.[222]

The two "dollhouse" tracking shots in Marvin's apartment (both of which dolly from left to right) are not merely a style-driven anomaly, but instead represent a private, behind-closed-doors analogue for a series of other orthogonal, left-to-right tracking shots in the public environment of the racetrack betting area. Although no wall-boundaries are visible in these shots, Kubrick nonetheless creates a palpably cellular mise-en-scène by bringing the cinematic foreground into play. In each of the four shots, the camera tracks a character through the crowd in front of the betting windows and toward the bar. We follow Marvin twice, once at the film's very beginning, and again when he is drunk on the day of the heist; as well as Maurice the Wrestler (Kola Kwariani) as he lumbers into position, ready to create his diversion; and finally Johnny, as he surveys the various other participants, and takes his place next to the door to the locker room and cash office. Crucial to these shots' effect is the periodic obstruction of our view by various randomly-placed bystanders— dimly lit extras who are too near the lens to be crisply in focus, but who are deliberately stationed between the camera and its nominal object. The result of this is not so much that Kubrick breaks the fourth wall, as that he reaffirms it *as a wall*. The scenes support Michel Chion's assertion that whereas "for other directors, such as Hitchcock or Bresson, the image is centrifugal: it constantly points to what it does not contain and what is external to it. The image in Kubrick, in contrast, is very clearly centripetal, attracting attention to what is at its centre."[223] By "centripetal," Chion indicates not a visual implosion or collapse, but what might be termed a *wallification* of the image — a deliberate staging of action that implicates the space (and walls) surrounding our central focus, but not what lies beyond that space. Accordingly, the central walking characters at the racetrack are bounded by objects on all four sides, not just three, as is conventional in Hollywood cinema, and consequently the events taking place in front of the camera are reified as cellular, suggesting not just private conspiracy but the oblivious other at its margins. The shots do not merely "single out" the various characters; they call into question the very structure of singled-out-ness.

Kubrick's technique in *The Killing* usefully compares to a series of exterior tracking shots in the 1951 Tay Garnett film *Cause for Alarm!* In this film, protagonist Ellen Jones (Loretta Young) attempts to cover up the death of her husband George (Barry Sullivan). Ellen did not kill her husband — he died of a stress-induced heart attack — but the cover-up is nonetheless necessary since, prior to his demise, the psychopathic George sent a letter to the district attorney proclaiming that George's physician and Ellen were conspiring to kill him. The envelope is collected by the postman early on the day of George's death, and for the rest of the film we see Ellen scrambling around the neighborhood trying to retrieve it. Ellen's neighborhood, like the airshaft in *Killer's Kiss*, is represented as a matrix of simultaneous connectivity and separation (one imagines backyard gossips talking over the hedges about "Mrs. Jones's fit of hysteria the other day"), and the cellular tracking shot — keeping pace with Ellen as she passes by yard after yard, house after house — lends emphasis to the tenuous hermetic barrier that has been thrust upon her. As in *The Killing*, the tracking shot accomplishes a dialectics of space even when no direct interaction is visible between the two (or three or four) spaces present. In moving through a series of conceptual frames, such shots call attention not only to contiguity and separation, but also to notions of mutuality, liminality, and the thresholds of knowledge and perception. The key, however, lies in the tracking camera's subjectification of the spaces being passed. To track smoothly by a series of discrete places is to create a reciprocal sense of "the one who is being passed" — not a singular, confirmable and persecuting pair of eyes, but a diffuse field of vision consisting of many potential vantage points. In contrast to the camera's lateral movement, static shots would prove relatively mute about the horrifying indeterminacy of another's gaze, or at least less articulate.

A different approach to constructing the *noir* cell, and one which similarly stakes its effect on camera movement, appears in the bravura long-take heist sequence from Robert Siodmak's 1946 film *The Killers*. The single long crane shot tracks a disguised heist gang into the Prentiss Hat factory during a shift change, then up to the paymaster's office where they steal the semi-monthly payroll, and back out of the factory grounds to their getaway cars. On the basis of this specific scene, Robert Porfirio makes the following generalization: "As it had with deep focus, the film noir assimilated the moving camera and the long take into its own closed form, controlling diegetic space in an architectonic manner (like any of the planned and edited sequences of Hitchcock) that ideally provides the viewer with a metonymic "lock" on its hermetic world."[224] While Porfirio uses the word "hermetic" to indicate the interconnectedness of all the action on screen, it is clear that his sense of hermeticism derives from the events having transpired in real-time — the fact that the diegesis unfolds not as an artificially continuous montage, stitched together from a collection of separate shots, but instead that it is "really" continuous, with the time of the performance precisely matching what we see on screen. What Porfirio seems to overlook, however, is the content of the shot itself, the fact that our window-framed view of the bandits in the paymaster's office *both is and is not* a separate shot, since for a significant portion of the sequence the camera ceases to move, remaining static while we peer in. Though the overall effectiveness of the scene clearly depends on its fluid camera work, I would argue that the result of this extreme continuity is not a monolithic "hermetic world," but instead a set of adjacent "hermetic *worlds*," plural. As in *The Killing*, it is precisely the unflinching persistence of the shot, traveling apace through a number of architecturally differentiated spaces, which sets the sequestered robbery in high relief against a blinded public view — here, the unsuspecting workers in the yard.

If the kitsch icon for the concept of hermeticism is the snow globe, with its tiny aqueous interior perfectly sealed in a sphere of glass, the object's resonance derives not simply from its smallness and shimmering movement, but also from the snow globe's encapsulation of an inside world within an outside world. The swirling flakes of plastic snow lend definition to the effect that we are seeing two worlds apart.[225] The Prentiss Hat robbery in *The Killers* is precisely like a snow globe in its depiction of two hermetic spheres: the inside world of the paymaster's office, and the outside world of oblivious passersby. The long-take, then, does not simply form a "lock" on the film's diegesis (as Porfirio would have it), but also works to establish a decidedly *noir*-ish sense of oblivious adjacency. The paradox becomes clear at the moment we recognize that the workers in the yard are both locked out of the cell of criminal conspiracy, and at the same time locked into their own hermetic sphere of day-to-day activity; the distinction that party "A" is "outside" and party "B" is "inside" is purely semantic. The point of *noir*'s hermeticism is not simple continuousness, but connectivity and mutual exclusion, and the boundary-defying tracking shot, of which the Prentiss Hat sequence is one remarkable example, highlights this cellular equanimity.

As with any tracking shot, the shots analyzed above have the effect of making the tracked figure "pop," or stand out, in the context of the numerous other static objects and events that the camera passes by. Correspondingly, regardless of their position in the depth of the frame, any objects that remain static in a tracking shot are coded as "background," even when — as in the racetrack sequences described above — they are in the extreme foreground. Given this binary, it is important to recognize that Kubrick's tracking shots in *The Killing* form part of a broader narrative strategy, creating an effect that becomes clear only later, when the moving camera has "settled in," so to speak. Having distinguished the tracked characters as visual primaries — special in comparison to the anonymous extras that surround them — each character is then permitted to reintegrate, taking his place in a conceptual background that, in earlier tracking shots, was passed by and thus rendered unimportant. In other words, Kubrick makes his characters *stand out* in the tracking shots, so as to convey a special status on them when later, in the moments prior to the heist, they *recede*.[226] As viewers, even while we definitively know who is involved in the caper and who is not, we cannot help but entertain the possibility of a second, naïve and unsuspecting view of things: a hermetically sealed-out perspective in which George is just another fastidious clerk, Marvin is a stereotypical racetrack drunk, Mike is a characteristically oversolicitous bartender working for tips, Maurice is a stoic high-roller waiting to meet a friend, and Johnny is a slightly disheveled salesman who, while spending an afternoon at the track, just happened to prop himself next to a door marked "NO ADMITTANCE," briefcase in hand. In the film's diegesis, this naïve viewpoint belongs to the many undifferentiated passersby, the very people who, in the words of bag man Randy Kennen (Ted de Corsia), "won't get any funny ideas about it." By individually escorting his crew of "seemingly normal" mobsters through the highly routinized and eminently public environment they are about to turn on its head, Kubrick creates a profound sense of visible invisibility, of seeing the unseen — a paradoxical state of affairs which accords precisely with *noir*'s insistence on the hermetic epistemology of modern crime.

In his several "dollhouse" tracking shots, Kubrick creates a sense of cellular unsuspicion not only in space but also in time, setting up the viewer for a series of quick 180-degree reversals of meaning. In terms of genre, the "heist" or "caper" narrative — of which *The Killing* is a stellar example — provides a particularly fertile ground for such temporal play, especially given its conventional insistence on synchronization. Along with *The Killing*, films such as *Armored Car Robbery* (Richard Fleischer, 1950), *Roadblock* (Harold Daniels, 1951) and *Kansas City Confidential* (Phil Karlson, 1952) comprise part of what James Naremore calls "a whole sub-genre of 'caper' movies" spawned by the success of *The Asphalt Jungle* (John Huston, 1950).[227]

These films also exploited a topical interest, appearing in the wake of the January 1950 robbery of the Brinks Armored truck office in Boston—at the time, the largest heist in American history.[228] Indeed, the hobo/clown mask Johnny Clay dons in *The Killing* directly echoes the use of children's Halloween masks by the Brinks mob. Moreover, two popular releases prior to *Asphalt*, both directed by Robert Siodmak, featured heist-related subplots: *The Killers* (1946, discussed above) and *Criss Cross* (1949). In all of these films, the complex planning of a heist plays out as a series of carefully timed events, any one of which, taken by itself, would be dismissed by bystanders as something other than what it is. Of all the caper films, however, only in *The Killing* do we get a series of literal "double takes"—identical replays in which a shot we have already seen returns later in the film to be viewed in a new context. Initially appearing under the credits, a series of shots of racehorses approaching the gate reappears at three separate points in the film. More strikingly, at two different points in the narrative we see a pair of racetrack security guards run past a calm-looking Johnny Clay in order to subdue Maurice.[229] However, the most memorable filmic epistrophe occurs at the racetrack bar, replaying the line of dialogue Maurice speaks to initiate his diversion. The wrestler's scripted words are distinct, his heavily-accented phrasing unmistakable, when he turns to bartender Mike and says: "Hey, how about some service you stupid looking Irish pig!" While the first invocation of these words is followed by a long fight sequence between a shirtless Maurice and a swarm of guards, the subsequent replay of the phrase, appearing as part of Johnny's plotline, is followed by an immediate fade-out, acknowledging that we already know the rest of Maurice's story. Moreover, the first time we see Maurice accost Mike, Johnny has already taken his place by the door; yet only in the second series of shots do we see him enter the room and take up this spot. Anchoring this sense of temporal concurrence, Maurice's words create an effect the opposite of déjà vu— we have the feeling not that we've seen something before, but that we *missed* something the first time, only later to have the missing details filled in. Yet when the details are finally supplied, they overflow, orienting us in time, but also creating a surplus of repetition.

While Stephen Mamber is correct that the narrative overlaps in *The Killing* clarify the story's complex temporality while offering "glimpses of a grand design,"[230] the repetitions also index the film's generic difference, its particularly *noir* brand of "grand design." Here again, we find Kubrick assimilating established conventions, but at the same time "bring[ing] something new to it."[231] Expanding on a device used by Lionel White in *Clean Break*, the film's source novel, Kubrick's narrative overlaps and plotline collisions push the caper film's conventional obsession with time to its breaking point, risking moments of overt parody in an otherwise involving narrative. In earlier films noirs, such overlaps are rarely executed as an actual repetition of footage. Instead, we get a more linear "rewind effect," in which something we have just seen is revealed, by way of a change in character and/or an explanatory speech, to have been a hermetically-sealed deception. That is to say, whereas classic *noir* tends to figuratively rewind, inviting the viewer's retrospective consideration of an unsuspicious scene, in *The Killing*, Kubrick *literally replays* his narrative, placing that which we have already witnessed side-by-side, as it were, with our memory of it.

Perhaps the most useful parallel to Kubrick's temporal repetitions in *The Killing* is afforded by André De Toth's 1954 film *Crime Wave*—a film noir to be sure, and one which builds to an elaborate bank heist in the third act. Despite thematic similarities, most viewers will connect the two films based on two shared casting choices. In *Crime Wave*, Sterling Hayden plays Detective Lieutenant Sims, a hard-nosed but brilliantly deceptive cop whose scrupulous planning of a sting operation prefigures Johnny Clay's *modus operandi* two years later in *The Killing*. At the same time, cast in the role of psychopathic heist gang member Johnny Haslett, we find character actor Timothy Carey, whose histrionic teeth-clenched performance carries over into *The Killing* as Nikki Arane, the racist, beatnik, puppy-loving sniper who Johnny pays to gun down a racehorse and not "squawk." Interestingly, Johnny Haslett is identified as the mob's hired

A scene twice seen: Johnny Clay (Sterling Hayden, with briefcase) mans his post in *The Killing* (1954).

"hooligan," precisely the role Sterling Hayden played in *The Asphalt Jungle*, suggesting that a kind of tripartite intertextuality is at play in Kubrick's film. In contrast to the relative toughness and cynicism of *Crime Wave*'s characterizations, *The Killing* appears as both a nostalgic caper film — recalling a day in which there was some degree of honor among thieves, as in *The Asphalt Jungle*— and at the same time a postmodern caper film, insofar as the equine assassination at the center of the heist, like Nikki Arane himself, is supposed to strike the audience as unthinkably bizarre, a cartoon.

As are all the *noir* caper films, *Crime Wave* is premised upon long-held popular notions about the impossibility of the "perfect crime." Like all the heist masterminds, "Doc" Penny (Ted de Corsia) thinks he has everything figured out, having spent a lengthy prison term engineering a scheme to accomplish the impossible — boosting the Glendale office of the Bank of America in broad daylight.[232] In the end, however, Penny's caper is not derailed by the unforeseeable "possibilities" he tries to anticipate, but by an even more perfect simulacrum than his own. In the moments just prior to the heist, a mobster named Zenner (Jim Hayward), disguised as a meter reader, takes his place in the power terminal down the street, ready to cut off the bank's electricity supply at precisely 12:05. A thug named Hastings (Charles Bronson, in an early role), having arrived at the bank well in advance, blends with the customers inside. Steve Lacey (Gene Nelson), the getaway driver, waits outside to transport the mob to the airplane that will carry them out of Los Angeles. As Penny says to Lacey, "We'll be ten jumps ahead of those dumb cops and their roadblocks. No roadblocks in the air. This one's perfect." Despite Penny's seven years of planning, however, when the power is cut to the bank and the heist begins, the bank lobby inexplicably erupts into chaos. In a series of rapid cuts we see Hastings firing away like a madman and Penny on the floor with blood coming out of his mouth. Even Lacey, who stands the best chance of escaping the scene, is instantly accosted by Lieutenant Sims on the street outside.

So what happened to bring this well-planned caper to a screeching halt? After a short chase sequence, Sims tersely explains his own meticulously engineered deception to Lacey: "A bank full of cops — tellers, clerks, customers, even the vice president — every last one a cop. You didn't expect that, did you?" Thinking back to the scene before the lights went out, the viewer recalls seeing an elderly doorman, several guards, a number of female customers milling about, and a slightly stoic, if otherwise unremarkable bank manager. Having conceptually rewound the fiction to a moment "just before," we come to the perverse and paradoxical object of *noir*— the fantasy that when we see a teller in a bank window, a security guard manning a door, or even a cop on the street, he may not be just a cop, but a cop "playing a cop," since the absence of all law enforcement would make certain scenes appear unnatural. Though no formal flashback or replay occurs, Sims' hyperbolic explanation compels the viewer mentally rewind, recollecting the utterly unsuspicious, airtight deception that just moments before went unquestioned as real. As is the case with Kubrick's overlaps, the climax of *Crime Wave* confronts the viewer with the hermetic seal between present and future time. However, whereas Sterling Hayden "talks us through" a temporal reconsideration in *Crime Wave*, in *The Killing* he enacts a replay, and thus brings the paradoxes of unsuspicion to life in a much more palpable way.

It is commonplace to point out that the intricate temporal structure of *The Killing* sets the film apart, providing an inspiration for contemporary directors such as Quentin Tarantino, Steven Soderbergh and Guy Ritchie. The legacy of *The Killing*'s non-linearity clearly can be seen in Tarantino's *Reservoir Dogs* (1992), *Pulp Fiction* (1994) and *Jackie Brown* (1997), Soderbergh's *Out of Sight* (1998), Ritchie's *Lock, Stock and Two Smoking Barrels* (1998), and many others. In these films, Kubrick's nonlinear plotting most strikingly emerges in moments of seemingly random cellular collision — moments at which the concurrence of the various narrative threads becomes subjectivized as coincidence. When Marsellus Wallace (Ving Rhames) unexpectedly passes in front of Butch Coolidge's (Bruce Willis) car in *Pulp Fiction*, or when a flame-engulfed man sails out the front door of Samoa Joe's past Bacon (Jason Statham) and the rest of the gang in *Two Smoking Barrels*, any devotee of classic *noir* will inevitably recall George Peatty suddenly emerging from the front door of the meeting place, obliviously bumping into the hood of Johnny's station wagon as he staggers across the street. Such jarring plot coincidences represent an intensified version of the figure-ground *gestalt* we experience in the racetrack betting area, establishing a dialectics of place in which a discrete action "adds up," or makes sense, only when considered simultaneously from two different perspectives. George's sudden appearance with a face full of buckshot would be superfluous if not for the fact that we see the action from Johnny's angle, though the windshield of his car. Not only does the viewer align with the shock of the character's inexplicable encounter, but we also understand its cause, having spent time with the intersector as well as the intersectee. At the same time, Johnny's brush with George reverses an earlier sequence, shot at night, in which the camera tracks Marvin as he exits the meeting place, lights a cigarette, and walks up the hill. Here, the camera's leftward movement is dramatically interrupted when we encounter a sedan containing Val Cannon (Vince Edwards) and his partner, whose goal is to steal the money from Johnny's mob. When George stumbles into Johnny's car, Johnny occupies the same location Val did, but the directional axis of the scene has flipped. Yet however variable its function and meaning, the place itself remains a constant, and Kubrick's depiction of the world as a series of punctiform spots — invoked in the very first scene when Marvin scribbles "504 W OLIVE, APP 4B, 8 P.M." on the back of his winning ticket — speaks directly to the hermetic structure of the cell, an outwardly banal coordinate in time and space that will become truly comprehensible only with the arrival of the next morning's newspaper.

Conclusion

In the end, if we are to take seriously Michel Ciment's assertion that "Kubrick learned his craft in the school of film noir" and that *noir* "colored his artistic vision,"[233] it is crucial to look beyond surface level similarities such as voice-over narration, lighting design, etc., and instead interrogate the deep structures on which these conventions are predicated. Clearly there exists something like a specifically *noir* fantasy, and this fantasy both inflects the films noirs of Stanley Kubrick, and further develops within them. The object of the *noir* fantasy, here characterized as cellular and hermetic in structure, correlates with the past-tense innocent object that will "add up" only in a hypothetical future revelation. In the present it is only supposable, fixed in a state of non-signifying ordinariness. In other words, the *noir* object is that object which may be significant, but about which we do not know that we do not know. Or, to put it in spatial terms, the *noir* cell is a real kernel of truth which would have been seen, if anyone had been there to see it. The structure of the cell, already well articulated in film noir, is clearly developed in *Killer's Kiss* and *The Killing*. The fact that characters like Davy Gordon accidentally glimpse this usually sealed-off cellular interior, and that characters like Johnny Clay inhabit it, is what makes their experience remarkable, their stories worth telling. At the same time, the hermetic knowledge-barrier in these cinematic worlds inevitably points outside the film to a whole host of analogous real-world views, scenes which, because they are beheld from the outside, refuse to disclose their secret, whether or not there is any secret to disclose. The *noir* fantasy depends on this suturing of fiction and reality — on ordinary, everyday scenes imagined as duplicitous, and as unwilling to surrender their meaning. In this sense, the phenomenological locus of the *noir* cell is far more commonplace than any carceral metaphor would allow. If the denizens of *The Killing* are imprisoned, they are trapped in the fantasy of the perfectly perfect crime, forced to defend their hermetic territory in a world where anyone, at any time, might "get wise." It's up to the reader to determine the extent to which this cellular epistemology, at once spatial and temporal, inflects Kubrick's later work.

By focusing on a series of genre-specific resemblances about which *one may only suppose*, this essay has sought to counter the tendency, implicit in much biography and auteurist critique, to construct a false sense of exclusivity between interior "signatures" and outside influences. When we consider Kubrick's early films chiefly in the context of his later, more fully realized productions, we run the risk of transforming the director's career from a living, evolving process into a kind of conceptual "box set" — brick-like, proprietary, and sealed together in cellophane — while dismissing a vast, and by definition heterogeneous array of external source-texts as irreconcilable with the directorial "I." In its most egregious form, this unitary approach to auteurism results in the anachronistic fallacy of reading the earlier films of a renowned auteur in light of an oeuvre which, strictly speaking, did not yet exist. By retrospectively mining a director's early work for evidence of what "has always been,"[234] such accounts play to the reader's innate desire for consistency and narrative completeness while masking over the awesome gap that appears at the end of any film production, that troublesome fact that, at any given point in a director's career, "the pattern" we equate with auteurism could have either been extended and thus reaffirmed, or undermined and thus transformed. As the comparative analyses above have hopefully demonstrated, a great deal can be gained by refusing to engage in an encyclopedic (and falsely comforting, confirmative) look at a director's career from beginning to end, instead adopting a speculative look outward, and to the side.

Part I Notes

1. Norman Kagan, *The Cinema of Stanley Kubrick* (New York: Continuum, 2000) 1.

2. Thomas Allen Nelson, *Kubrick: Inside a Film Artist's Maze* (Bloomington: Indiana University Press, 2000) 3.

3. Michel Chion, *Stanley Kubrick: l'humain, ni plus ni moins* (Paris: Cahiers du Cinéma, 2005) 12.

4. Vincent LoBrutto, *Stanley Kubrick: A Biography* (New York: Da Capo, 1997) 19–69.

5. Alexander Walker, *Stanley Kubrick Directs* (New York: Harcourt Brace Jovanovich, 1971) 7.

6. Rainer Crone and Alexandra Von Stosch, "Kubrick's Kaleidoscope: Early Photographs 1945–1950," *Kinematograph* 20 (2004) 21.

7. Rainer Crone and Petrus Graf Schaesberg, *Stanley Kubrick: Still Moving Pictures, Fotografien 1945–1950* (Munich: Schnell & Steiner, 1999) 24.

8. Chion 12.

9. Crone, "Kubrick's Kaleidoscope" 22.

10. Janet Staiger, "Authorship Approaches," *Authorship and Film*, ed. David Gerstner and Janet Staiger (New York: Routledge, 2003) 40–43.

11. Philippe Mather, "Stanley Kubrick: Photography and Film," *The Historical Journal of Film, Radio and Television* 26.2 (June 2006): 203–214.

12. George Ritzer, *Toward an Integrated Sociological Paradigm* (Boston: Allyn and Bacon, 1981) 12.

13. *Ibid.*, 25.

14. *Ibid.*, 24.

15. *Ibid.*, 223.

16. *Ibid.*, 25.

17. *Ibid.*, 27.

18. *Ibid.*, 83.

19. Gardner Cowles, *Mike Looks Back* (New York: Gardner Cowles, 1985) 147.

20. Cowles 113.

21. LoBrutto 35.

22. *Ibid.*, 20.

23. Cowles 194.

24. *Ibid.*, 194.

25. James Guimond, *American Photography and the American Dream* (Chapel Hill: University of North Carolina Press, 1991) 152–153.

26. *Ibid.*, 153.

27. Cowles 190.

28. *Ibid.*, 102.

29. Arthur Rothstein and Douglas Kirkland, "The Editor-Photographer Team," ed. R. Smith Schuneman, *Photographic Communication* (New York: Hastings House: 1972) 92–99.

30. Schuneman 91.

31. Cowles 188.

32. Michelle Renee Bolack, "Constructed Images: The Influences of News *Organizations and Socialization in Photojournalism*" (diss., University of North Texas) 2001, 27.

33. Cowles 108.

34. Beaumont Newhall, *The History of Photography* (Boston: Little, Brown and Company, 1982) 260.

35. Joseph Kastner, "Writing for the Picture Magazine," ed. R. Smith Schuneman, *Photographic Communication* (New York: Hastings House, 1972) 122–25.

36. LoBrutto 15.

37. Bolack 36.

38. Arthur Rothstein, *Photojournalism*, (New York: A.M. PHOTO, 1979) 20.

39. LoBrutto 73.

40. *Ibid.*, 37.

41. *Ibid.*, 35.

42. Daniel D. Mich and Edwin Eberman, *The Technique of the Picture Story* (New York: McGraw-Hill, 1945) 198–207.

43. Ritzer, *Toward an Integrated* 19.

44. John Baxter, *Stanley Kubrick: A Biography* (New York: Carroll & Graf, 1997) 28.

45. Arthur Goldsmith, "Photojournalism," ed. Willard D. Morgan, *The Encyclopedia of Photography*, vol. 15 (New York: Greystone, 1963) 2761–2790.

46. Rothstein, "The Editor-Photographer Team" 97.

47. Bolack 26.

48. *Ibid.*, 35.

49. LoBrutto 38.

50. *Ibid.*, 38.

51. Baxter 28.

52. Rothstein, *Photojournalism* 12–13.

53. *Ibid.*, 115.

54. Cowles 189.

55. Rothstein, *Photojournalism* 120.

56. *Ibid.*, 131.

57. *Ibid.*, 120.

58. *Ibid.*, 12.

59. LoBrutto 431.

60. Rothstein, *Photojournalism* 121.

61. *Ibid.*, 131.

62. Gene D. Phillips, "Early Work," *The Stanley Kubrick Archives*, ed. Alison Castle (Köln: Taschen, 2005) 268–276.

63. Cowles 189.

64. Rothstein, *Photojournalism* 173.

65. LoBrutto 37.

66. Chion 17.

67. Rothstein, "The Editor-Photographer Team" 98.

68. Bolack 10.

69. Mich 15.

70. *Ibid.*, 46–7.

71. *Ibid.*, 78.

72. *Ibid.*, 79.

73. *Ibid.*, 79.

74. *Ibid.*, 106.

75. Cowles 110.

76. Ritzer, *Toward an Integrated* 19.

77. *Ibid.*, 210.

78. Cowles 202.

79. LoBrutto 297.

80. Cowles 202.

81. LoBrutto 34.

82. *Ibid.*, 53.

83. Nelson 89.

84. Gene D. Phillips, ed., *Stanley Kubrick: Interviews*, (Jackson: University of Mississippi Press, 2001) 114.

85. Rothstein, *Photojournalism* 159.

86. LoBrutto 38.

87. Rainer Crone, *Stanley Kubrick: Drama and Shadows* (London: Phaidon, 2005) 16–29.

88. Elisabetta Sgarbi, ed., *Stanley Kubrick: Ladro di sguardi, fotografie di fotografie 1945–1949* (Milano: Bompiani, 1994) unpaginated.

89. Rothstein, *Photojournalism* 161.

90. *Ibid.*, 159–161.

91. Baxter 54.

92. Bolack 43.

93. Phillips, "Early Work" 268.

94. Stanley Fish, "Biography and Intention," *Contesting the Subject*, ed. William Epstein, (West Lafayette: Purdue University Press, 1991) 13.

95. George Ritzer and Douglas J. Goodman, *Modern Sociological Theory* (New York: McGraw-Hill, 2004) 406.

96. John Baxter, Stanley Kubrick (New York: Carroll & Graf, 1997) 56.

97. LoBrutto 15.

98. Michel Ciment, *Kubrick: The Definitive Edition* (New York: Faber and Faber, 2001) 34.

99. *Ibid.*, 34.

100. Quoted in Baxter 40.

101. Quoted in LoBrutto 58.

102. LoBrutto 62.

103. *Ibid.*, 60.

104. Ciment 190.

105. Crone, *Stanley Kubrick: Drama and Shadows* (London: Phaidon, 2005) 106 and 114–115.

106. Joyce Carroll Oates, *On Boxing* (New York: Dolphin/Doubleday, 1987).

107. Quoted in LoBrutto 64.

108. Baxter 38.

109. LoBrutto 73.

110. For a description of this period in Kubrick's life, see Baxter 43.

111. Baxter 51.

112. Ciment 36.

113. Stephen Crane, "War Memories," *The Works of Stephen Crane*, vol. 6, ed. Fredson Bowers (Charlottesville: University Press of Virginia, 1970) 222.

114. Michael W. Schaefer, *Just What War Is: The Civil War Writings of De Forest and Bierce* (Knoxville: University of Tennessee Press, 1997) xi.

115. Richard Holmes, *Acts of War* (New York: Free Press, 1985) 150.

116. War and war scenes also play a significant role in

117. Joanne Stang, "Film Fan to Film Maker," *The New York Times Magazine*, 12 Oct. 1958. Available online at http://partners.nytimes.com/library/film/121258kubrick-profile.html.

118. Robert Brustein, "Out of This World," *The New York Times Review of Books*, 1964. Reprinted in Mario Falsetto, ed., *Perspectives on Stanley Kubrick* (Boston: G.K. Hall, 1996) 136.

119. David Hughes, *The Complete Kubrick* (London: Virgin, 2000) 21.

120. Christiane Kubrick, *Stanley Kubrick: A Life in Pictures* (Boston: Bulfinch Press, 2002) 44.

121. Estimates vary greatly on the production cost of the film. What is known is that Kubrick borrowed an initial $10,000 from his father and a wealthy uncle, Martin Perveler. His uncle later loaned Kubrick an additional $5,000. Though this investment allowed Kubrick to shoot the film, he still had to record the sound, synchronize the sound, edit the film, and add titles. In order to raise the money, he worked on "miscellaneous television and State Department trivia" including *The Seafarers* (1953), his third documentary and first film in color. In the end, Fear and Desire was produced for approximately $50,000.

122. Norman Kagan, *The Cinema of Stanley Kubrick* (New York: Holt, Rinehart and Winston, 1972) 17.

123. These anonymous reviews can be found, along with many others, online at various websites including www.rottentomatoes.com.

124. 1953 was also the year that a 3-D film, *House of Wax*, first broke the box office top ten.

125. The rape scene bears striking similarities to Brian De Palma's *Casualties of War* (1989), a fact that might indicate the film's influence on a later generation of filmmakers despite Kubrick's attempts to bury it.

126. Gene D. Phillips and Rodney Hill, *The Encyclopedia of Stanley Kubrick: From Day of the Fight to Eyes Wide Shut* (New York: Checkmark Books, 2002) 65.

127. *Ibid.*, 282.

128. Humphrey Cobb, *Paths of Glory* (New York: Viking Press, 1935) 265.

129. The other sources mentioned by Cobb are R.G. Réau's *Les crimes des conseils de guerre*, J. Galtier-Boissière and Daniel de Ferdon's *Les fusillés pour l'exemple*, Paul Allard's *Les dessous de la guerre révélés par les comités secrets* and *Images secrètes de la guerre*, and Blanche Maupas' *Le fusillé*. Maupas was a widow of one of the executed men. She obtained exoneration of her husband's memory and was awarded damages of one franc.

130. Phillips and Hill 286.

131. W. A. Berendsohn, "War Memories in Literature," *Christian Science Monitor* 24 Jul. 1935: 10.

132. Cobb 31–32.

133. Berendsohn 10.

134. Cobb 75.

135. *Ibid.*, 102–103.

136. *Ibid.*, 99.

137. *Ibid.*, 156.

138. *Ibid.*, 166.

139. *Ibid.*, 263.

140. *Ibid.*, 39.

141. *Ibid.*, 39.

142. Stephen E. Tabachnick, "Afterword," *Paths of Glory: A Novel by Humphrey Cobb* (Athens: University of Georgia Press, 1987) 275.

143. *Ibid.*, 268.

144. *Ibid.*, 268.

Spartacus (1960) and *Barry Lyndon* (1975), both of which accurately represent the battlefields and war techniques of the time period in which they are set.

145. Tom Wicker, "World War I," *Past Imperfect: History According to the Movies* (New York: Henry Holt, 1995) 186.
146. Cobb 103.
147. Phillips and Hill 287.
148. Norman Kagan, *The Cinema of Stanley Kubrick* (New York: Holt, Rinehart and Winston, 1972) 63.
149. *Ibid.*
150. *Ibid.*
151. Mario Falsetto, *Stanley Kubrick: A Narrative and Stylistic Analysis* (Westport, Conn.: Greenwood Press, 1994) 176.
152. Thomas Allen Nelson, *Kubrick: Inside a Film Artist's Maze, New and Expanded Edition* (Bloomington: Indiana University Press, 1982) 40.
153. *Ibid.*
154. *Ibid.*
155. *Ibid.*
156. *Ibid.*
157. For more connections between Cobb and Faulkner, see Julian Smith's "A Source for Faulkner's A Fable" in *American Literature* 40 Nov. 1968: 394–397. The article considers similarities of plot, characters, and minor details between Cobb's novel and Faulkner's *A Fable* (1954). For example, "both novels take place in France during World War I and start with the same basic incident, the failure of a French regiment to attack an impregnable German position.... The remainder of each novel is concerned with the aftermath of this failure. (In Cobb's novel, three scapegoats are executed; in Faulkner's, the corporal responsible for the passive rebellion is executed between two criminals [395])." For those who question whether Faulkner had read Cobb's novel, see Joseph Blotner's *William Faulkner's Library: A Catalogue* (University of Virginia: Charlottesville, 1963) 93.
158. Cobb 31.
159. This idea of focusing on one soldier and raising him to a level of importance above his peers is a theme explored by Steven Spielberg in *Saving Private Ryan* (1998), a film whose battle scenes have been compared to Paths of Glory. Spielberg himself has acknowledged the influence of both *Paths of Glory* and *Dr. Strangelove*, particularly the recapturing of Burpleson Air Force Base, on his own film. See Spielberg's forward to *Stanley Kubrick: A Life in Pictures* (Boston: Bulfinch Press, 2002) 9.
160. Cobb 129–130.
161. Gavin Lambert, "*Paths of Glory* Reviewed." *Sight and Sound* (Winter 1957–58) 144.
162. Nelson 40.
163. Kagan 64.
164. As Brian McFarlane has noted, the "spirit" or "essence" of the work is difficult to determine. The simplest definition accepted by adaptation critics has to do with a film, regardless of changes to storyline, characters, etc., capturing the meaning of the book. See McFarlane's *Novel to Film: An Introduction to the Theory of Adaptation* (Oxford: Clarendon Press, 1996), as well as Bluestone's seminal text in adaptation studies, *Novels into Film: The Metamorphosis of Fiction into Film* (Berkeley: University of California Press 1957), and Bazin's "Adaptation, or The Cinema as Digest," *Bazin at Work: Major Essays and Reviews from the Forties and Fifties*, trans. Alain Piette and Bert Cardullo (New York: Routledge, 1997).
165. Cobb 7.
166. *Ibid.*, 75.
167. Hughes 58.
168. *Ibid.*
169. Originally released as *Dr. Strangelove: Music from the Films of Stanley Kubrick*. New York: Silva Screen Records, 1999. The compilation was reissued in 2005 with a few alternate tracks as *2001: Music from the Films of Stanley Kubrick*. New York: Silva America, 2005.
170. Hughes 54.
171. Cobb 262.
172. In September 1957, co-screenwriter Calder Willingham claimed credit for the scene and "99 percent" of the total screenplay. He took his case to the Writer's Guild of America, which decided in Willingham's favor and demanded that he receive co-credit with both Kubrick, and Jim Thompson. However, all others associated with the production of the film, including producer James Harris and Christiane Kubrick, claim that the scene was completely Kubrick's idea.
173. Hughes 55.
174. See Thierry Kuntzel, "The Film Work 2," *Camera Obscura* 5 (1980) 7–69.
175. See the various essays contained in John Caughie, *Theories of Authorship* (London: Routledge & Kegan, Paul, 1981).
176. See Thomas Allen Nelson, *Kubrick: Inside a Film Artist's Maze: New and Expanded Edition* (Bloomington, Indiana: Indiana University Press, 2000) 20–31; Mario Falsetto, *Stanley Kubrick: A Narrative and Stylistic Analysis: New and Expanded Second Edition* (Westport, Connecticut: Praeger) 85–86, 102–103. Both see the acting (except for Jaimie Silvera), voice-over, and ballet sequence as representing youthful flaws on the part of a director who would soon overcome such deficiencies. Nelson regards the ballet sequence as "gratuitous" in terms of failing to provide motivation for Gloria's character and lacking any form of visual coherence to the rest of the film. By contrast, Falsetto finds the disparity between the visuals and Gloria's voice-over the most interesting element in a sequence that he critiques as containing too much narrative information "to be especially convincing or moving" (86). Apart from the ballet sequence, he finds the voice-over commentary one of the film's "most routine components" (103). Kubrick's use of these formal elements may suffer from inexperience and low-budget problems. Such features also occur in his later narratives. For example, Joker's voice-over narration in *Full Metal Jacket* (1986) often sounds as dreary as Davy's in *Killer's Kiss*, but it is an integral component of the film. Also, the August 4, 1996, screenplay of *Eyes Wide Shut* contained voice-over which Kubrick dropped from the final film, voice-overs which share the same characteristics of deceptive banality that occur in *Killer's Kiss* and *Full Metal Jacket*.
177. Dana Polan, "Materiality and Sociality in Killer's Kiss," *Perspectives on Stanley Kubrick*, ed. Mario Falsetto (New York: G.K. Hall, 1996) 99. See also Foster Hirsch, *Film Noir: The Dark Side of the Screen* (New York: Da Capo Press, 2001) 85–86; Gene B. Phillips, "*Killer's Kiss*," *The Stanley Kubrick Archives*, ed. Allison Castle (New York: Taschen, 2004) 278–287.
178. For relevant material on neo-noir, see *Film Noir: An Encyclopedic Reference to the American Style*, ed. Alain Silver and Elizabeth Ward, 3rd ed. (Woodstock, New York: The Overlook Press, 1992) 398–443; Alain Silver, "Son of Noir: Neo-Film Noir and the Neo B. Feature," *Film Noir Reader*, eds. Alain Silver and James Ursini (New York: Limelight, 1996) 331–338; William Covey, "Girl Power: Female Centered Neo-Noir." *Film Noir Reader 2*, eds. Alain Silver and James Ursini (New York: Limelight, 1999) 311–327; and Constantine Verevis, "Through the Past Darkly: Noir Remakes of the 1980s," *Film Noir Reader 4*, eds. Alain Silver and James Ursini (New York Limelight: 2004) 307–322. Other informative essays also appear in these anthologies.

179. For relevant production information see David Hughes, *The Complete Kubrick* (London: Thames Publishing, 2000) 23–34.

180. For the relationship between the literary naturalism of Emile Zola and American film noir see Foster Hirsch, *Film Noir: The Dark Side of the Screen* New York: Da Capo Press, 2001) 46–50. See also Dudley Andrew, *Concepts in Film Theory* (New York: Oxford University Press, 1984) 105–106, for examples of naturalism's influence on cinema. For the relationship between the boxing movie, especially noir examples such as *The Set-Up* (1946), *Body and Soul* (1947), and *Champion* (1949), whose visual style certainly influenced Kubrick, and American literary naturalism, see Tony Williams, "'I Could've Been a Contender': The Boxing Movie's Generic Instability." *Quarterly Review of Film and Video* 18.3 (2001) 305–319. Kubrick began his career as a still photographer and his photographs certainly bear several traces of the naturalist influence of Emile Zola. For Zola's own later career as a photographer see Francois Emile-Zola, *Zola-Photographer* (New York: Seaver Books, 1988).

181. Although Andrew Spicer refers to idyllic images of the countryside that occur in classical film noirs such as *Out of the Past* (1947) and *The Asphalt Jungle*, he defines the country noir features of postmodern film noir as anti-pastoral, with the countryside no longer being an "innocent wholesome idyllic retreat from the depraved city" but now claustrophobic and corrupt. However, even the Edenic countryside in *Out of the Past* contains negative features involving the suspicion of its inhabitants against Jeff Bailey and the jealousy of a former lover against him. See Andrew Spicer, *Film Noir* (Harlow, Essex: Pearson Education Ltd, 2002) 157–158.

182. Polan 90. For Kubrick's employment of an aesthetic type of surrealism associated with the cinema of Luis Bunuel, see Nelson 30, 54, 164, and 196. Nelson sees *Killer's Kiss* as the first example of this style that he would develop in his later films. His associations among food, violence, and childhood in the Broadway montage sequences in *Killer's Kiss* receive particular emphasis in the concluding scene of *A Clockwork Orange*, as Nelson succinctly notes. "Of all the ritualized eating scenes in Kubrick — the post-execution breakfast on *Paths*, the buffet in the War Room in *Dr. Strangelove*, Moon-Watcher's first carnivorous meal, and Bowman's last meal — this scene from *Clockwork Orange* best captures a Bunuelian conjunction of civilization and its primitive discontents" (164).

183. See Maureen Turim, *Flashbacks in Film* (New York: Routledge, 1989). For the operation of deliberate errors in *The Killing's* voice-over narration see Falsetto 4–5, 96–97, and 181.

184. For Kubrick's fascination with Jonathan Swift see Ciment 70; Nelson 138–139; and Tony Williams, "Floating 'in a World of Shit': *Full Metal Jacket*'s Excremental Vision," *Film and Philosophy* 1 (1994) 121–135. For the oscillating nature of sado-masochistic feelings within the human personality see Sigmund Freud's 1915 essay "Instincts and Their Vicissitudes," *On Metapsychology: The Theory of Psychoanalysis*. The Pelican Freud Library, ed. Angela Richards (London: Penguin Books, 1984) 105–138.

185. See Nelson 30.

186. For parallels between the mannequins in the warehouse and the hostesses in *Pleasureland* see Nelson 29; Luis M. Garcia Mainar, *Narrative and Stylistic Patterns in the Films of Stanley Kubrick* (Rochester: New York: Camden House, 1999) 7, 17, and 50; and Geoffrey Cocks, *The Wolf at the Door: Stanley Kubrick, History and the Holocaust* (New York: Peter Lang, 2004) 82. The last book contains a convincing analysis of the film in terms of film noir and

Freudian associations, but the holocaust interpretation is forced.

187. According to Robert Kolker, *The Killing's* protagonist, Johnny Clay, "is a loser diminished by the gaze of authority; and the collapse of his plans, so carefully calculated that all they can possibly do is fall apart, *sets the pattern* for the characters in every Kubrick film" [italics mine]. Kolker, *A Cinema of Loneliness* (Oxford: Oxford University Press, 2000) 101.

188. For examples of this frequently made connection, see John Baxter, *Stanley Kubrick: A Biography* (New York: Carroll and Graf Publishers, 1997) 65; Geoffrey Cocks, *The Wolf at the Door: Stanley Kubrick, History and the Holocaust* (New York: Peter Lang Publishing, 2004) 81; and Alexander Walker, *Stanley Kubrick, Director: A Visual Analysis* (New York: Norton, 1999) 48, 53, and 190.

189. According to Alexander Walker (89), the single example of hand-held camera in *2001: A Space Odyssey* — capturing Dave as he floats through HAL's memory bank — "recalls" Kubrick's hand-held point-of-view shot just following the shootout in *The Killing*.

190. Baxter connects *Killer's Kiss* directly to Kubrick's 1951 documentary short about a day in the life of boxer Walter Cartier. Kubrick "unashamedly recycled *Day of the Fight* for the first reel of *Killer's Kiss*." Baxter 65. Dana Polan's assessment is more circumspect: "Kubrick began filmmaking in the area of documentary, and even in his most interventional moments in his later films, there is frequently the impression of a dispassionate, even antiseptic study of a found world." Polan, "Materiality and Sociality in *Killer's Kiss*," Mario Falsetto, ed., *Perspectives on Stanley Kubrick* (New York: G.K. Hall & Co., 1996) 97.

191. Baxter 79. Thomas Allen Nelson goes so far as to list the various screening venues the young Kubrick frequented in New York. Nelson, *Kubrick: Inside a Film Artist's Maze* (Bloomington: Indiana University Press, 2000) 2.

192. Michel Chion, *Kubrick's Cinema Odyssey*, translated from the French by Claudia Gorbman (London: British Film Institute, 2001) 41.

193. *Ibid.*

194. Ciment 310–11.

195. *Ibid*, 34.

196. David Lynch, *Lynch on Lynch*, ed. Chris Rodley (New York: Faber and Faber, Inc., 2005) 77.

197. Baxter, 65. The likeness derives from a short sequence in a mannequin storeroom in which a gangster swings an axe at Tony Hunter (Fred Astaire); he in turn deflects the blow with a mannequin torso.

198. Joan Copjec, ed., *Shades of Noir* (New York: Verso, 1993) xii.

199. Foster Hirsch calls *Killer's Kiss* "almost a parody of noir motifs.... Clearly derived from other movies rather than from life, *Killer's Kiss* has a ready-made, hand-me-down quality." Likewise, in *The Killing*, Marie Windsor's "dialogue sounds like a parody of the hardboiled school; and the exaggeration is a tip-off that noir conventions are being burlesqued." Hirsch, *The Dark Side of the Screen: Film Noir* (New York: Da Capo Press, 2001) 136, 202.

200. Polan 90. Robert Kolker makes a similar point regarding *The Killing*. Kolker 100.

201. Lewis E. Palmer, "The Day's Work of a 'New Law' Tenement Inspector," *Charities and the Commons* 17 (1906-1907) 80–90, referenced in William L. Crozier, "On the Lower East Side: Observations of Life in Lower Manhattan at the Turn of the Century," <http://www.tenant.net/Community/LES/palmer.html> (7 May 2006). Owing to various tenement reform laws, the narrow airshafts were

increasingly replaced by wider courtyards. However, the term "airshaft" continued to designate both arrangements.

202. Walker 45.

203. For an interpretation of *The Killing* based on a "prison cage" metaphor, see Nelson 36–9.

204. The parallelism of the film's exposition strongly resembles Robert Wise's *noir*-ish 1949 boxing film *The Set-Up*. Wise's parallel edits appear throughout the entire film, cutting back and forth between protagonist Bill "Stoker" Thompson (Robert Ryan) and his despondent wife Julie (Audrey Totter), and ceasing only when the couple is reunited at film's end. Kubrick's alternation is less extreme, occupying only part of the film's exposition, but in the end it is more cleverly reflexive, recombining the split narrative lines in the form of a television broadcast: Gloria and her boss engage in foreplay in his office while they watch Davy's ill-fated bout unfold on the screen.

205. Gloria's unilateral courtyard perspective resembles that of another Gloria, actress Gloria Grahame, in her role as Laurel Gray in Nicholas Ray's 1950 film *In a Lonely Place*. Laurel says to her new neighbor, murder suspect Dixon Steele (Humphrey Bogart), "I have no idea what you did after you closed your Venetian blinds." Dixon returns, "Perhaps I shouldn't have closed my blinds. You know, Miss Gray, you've got one up on me. You can see into my apartment, but I can't see into yours."

206. Compare this jaded ambivalence and lack of involvement to the more light-hearted airshaft scenes in *Gold Diggers of 1933* (Mervyn LeRoy, 1933). In one scene, Trixie Lorraine (Aline MacMahon) uses fireplace tongs to reach across the airshaft and gently pilfer a quart of milk from a neighbor's fire escape. Later, Brad Roberts (Dick Powell) serenades Polly Parker (Ruby Keeler) from that same apartment. Compared to *Killer's Kiss*; the airshaft in *Gold Diggers* is a catalyst for interaction, including both romance and communal *esprit de corps*.

207. In particular, see Hopper's *Apartment Houses* (1923), *Night Windows* (1928), *Room in New York* (1932), *Office in a Small City* (1953), *City Sunlight* (1954), and *New York Office* (1962).

208. As Dana Polan points out, it remains entirely unclear what Rapallo did to offend Gloria in the apartment. "Did he force himself on her? Was he inadequate?" Kubrick leaves the cause of the problem deliberately ambiguous. Polan, "Materiality," 93.

209. Kubrick later represents Rapallo's jealous, persecuted frame of mind in the form of a cartoon drawing of two smirking men in hats looking directly at the viewer *through a window*. The image, shot in extreme close-up, reiterates the theme of window-views that occurs throughout the film, and the sight (or thought) of it compels Rapallo to throw a drinking glass at the mirror, itself positioned as a "window" between Rapallo and the viewer. For a provocative reading of this cartoon image in terms of race, see Cocks 83.

210. A perfect explication of the predicament of the "wrong man" comes near the end of *They Won't Believe Me* (Irving Pichel, 1947), when Larry Ballentine (Robert Young) speaks from his jail cell to Janice Bell (Jane Greer). Though the viewer knows he's innocent of murder, Larry says, "I listened to my story. I brought in my own verdict." As in *Killer's Kiss*, lacking any way to prove his innocence, even the accused man himself would be compelled to bring down a guilty verdict.

211. In this context of public unsuspicion, the so-called noir "private eye" is a special character — not a detached, rational solver of puzzles (*à la* Sherlock Holmes), but a cellular boundary-crosser. The P.I. knows as little about the crime as the average man or woman on the street, but brings with him one distinct advantage: *he knows that he does not know,* and plays his cards accordingly. In contrast, as noir envisions them, members of the public are categorically unsuspicious of what is going on right under their noses; they *do not know that they do not know.* For an extended discussion of an unsuspicious public encounter in a touchstone *film noir*, see Hugh S. Manon, "Some Like It Cold: Fetishism in Billy Wilder's *Double Indemnity*," *Cinema Journal* 44.4 (Summer 2005) 21–3.

212. Richard W. Hubbell, *4000 Years of Television: The Story of Seeing at a Distance* (New York: G. P. Putnam's Sons) 4, 217.

213. Bosley Crowther, "A Point of View: Hitchcock's 'Rear Window' Provokes Contrast of This and Other Films," *The New York Times*, 15 August 1954: X1.

214. *Witness to Murder* was released on April 15, 1954; *Rear Window* on August 1, 1954; and *Killer's Kiss* on September 28, 1955. Before asserting *Rear Window*'s precedence, however, it is important to remember that the twelve-week production phase of *Killer's Kiss* began in October of 1953. See A.H. Weiler, "Of Pictures and People: New Drama 'Kiss Me, Kill Me' Filmed Here in Its Entirety," *The New York Times*, 23 May 1954: X5. At the same time, Woolrich's story, "It Had to Be Murder" (a.k.a. "Rear Window"), first appeared in the February 1942 issue of *Dime Detective*, predating all the films discussed here.

215. The morphology of the motel, which closely resembles a filmstrip comprised of individual "cels," features prominently in three remarkable post-*noir* texts: *Touch of Evil* (Orson Welles, 1958), *Psycho* (Alfred Hitchcock, 1960) and more recently an episode of the television series *Homicide: Life on the Streets* (NBC, U.S., 5 April 1996), in which two detectives investigate a killing at the New Moon motel. The episode is the series's homage to film noir, and concerns a bullet which passes through several contiguous rooms of the seedy motel, killing one of its permanent residents.

216. "The New Pictures," *Time* 4 June 1956: 106.

217. Ciment 75. A number of lateral tracking shots also appear in *Killer's Kiss*, but they are employed less systematically than in *The Killing*.

218. The term refers to a linear apartment without a hallway, in which one must walk through one room to get to the next, as on a passenger train.

219. For associate producer Alexander Singer's account of the production of these shots, see LoBrutto, *Stanley Kubrick* 118–120.

220. Similar, though less rhythmically punctuated, tracking shots depict the Peattys' apartment and the locker room at the racetrack.

221. Hal Jeffries, the protagonist of Cornell Woolrich's short story "It Had to be Murder" describes his view into a particular apartment building in precisely these terms: "I could see into it ... as freely as into a doll house with its rear wall sliced away." *The Cornell Woolrich Omnibus* (New York: Penguin, 1998) 6.

222. For a discussion of the two equivalently "impossible" shots of Davy's fishbowl and Rapallo's shattering mirror in *Killer's Kiss*, see Stephen Heath, "Narrative Space," Philip Rosen, ed., *Narrative, Apparatus, Ideology* (New York: Columbia University Press, 1986) 401–2.

223. Chion 78.

224. "The Killers: Expressiveness of Sound and Image in Film Noir," Alain Silver and James Ursini, eds., Film Noir *Reader* (New York: Limelight Editions, 1996) 178.

225. The airport runway climax of *The Killing*, with its swirling dollar bills, directly invokes the appearance of a snow globe. The metaphoric significance of this resemblance is in no way diminished by the scene's liberal

borrowing from the similarly-staged airstrip climax of *Armored Car Robbery* (Richard Fleischer, 1950), which in turn resembles the fate of the gold dust at the end of *The Treasure of the Sierra Madre* (John Huston, 1948).

226. At this point in the narrative, the track announcement that "the horses are at the gate" clearly takes on a secondary meaning, captioning the various gang members who wait, unsuspicious, in the wings for their parts to begin.

227. James Naremore, *More Than Night:* Film Noir *In Its Contexts* (Berkeley: University of California Press, 1998) 128.

228. The publicity materials for *Kansas City Confidential* advertise the film as "particularly fascinating to all those who have their own pet theories on how the Brinks Armored car robbery of a few years back was pulled." Pressbook for *Kansas City Confidential* (New York: Exploitation Dept., United Artists Corp., 1952) 13.

229. A close comparison reveals that these shots are actually different takes, yet their content is so close that a first-pass viewer would scarcely notice the difference.

230. Stephen Mamber, "Simultaneity and Overlap in Stanley Kubrick's *The Killing*," *Postmodern Culture* 8.2 (January 1998), par. 4. Though Mamber does not employ such terminology, his graphical analysis clearly intuits the logic of the *noir* cell: "Even though no more than a door or a window may separate two spaces, they are as likely to be shown to us in separated temporal segments." Mamber, par. 8.

231. Chion 44–45.

232. It is a rigid convention for every caper film to explicitly position its plan as *the impossible caper*. In *Criss Cross*, an armored car service employee named Johnny (Garry Owen) spells out the stakes of the film's heist for his co-workers: "I'll tell you something. Nobody ever got away with a heist on an armored truck in twenty-eight years. As a matter of fact, they don't even try anymore."

233. Ciment 114.

234. Ciment 78, 264.

6 Patterns of Space, Sound, and Movement in *Paths of Glory*

Eric Eaton

Themes and Structure

In all his works Stanley Kubrick was so much more than a storyteller. Yet, while this fact has been appreciated in *2001* (1968) and to some extent in *Barry Lyndon* (1975), criticism of his other works has concentrated mainly upon his characters, narratives, and social commentary. For example, the much admired *Paths of Glory* (1957) has been praised over the decades mostly for the extraordinary economy with which Kubrick has told this story that so bitterly attacks the military. This carefully constructed film of Kubrick's youth has, however, more in common with *2001* than any other of Kubrick's works, in that it relies heavily upon complex aesthetic patterns that support and yet to some extent transcend the narrative.

In *Paths* the story itself — one that concerns the struggle between the generals and the men they command — possessed a natural polarity and symmetry that Kubrick exploited in many ways and on many levels. Within it were numerous fundamental oppositions, among them (1) the enemy and the French; (2) the chateau and trench worlds; (3) the officer class and the enlisted men; (4) the generals and colonel Dax; (5) cynical opportunism and altruistic concern; and (6) lies and truth.

Out of such polarities and conflicts, Kubrick has constructed an overall, multi-leveled structure founded upon a series of confrontations that are reinforced and joined together by "permutations" of patterns formed from camera techniques, images of symmetrical structures, and specific, recurrent images of movement. Moreover, these patterns rest in a matrix provided by a unique system of highly abstract, polarized space.

One limited but useful way of visually conceptualizing this system of abstract space is as a long axis with the French state at one end and the opposing German State at the other (*see* Figure 1). Although these entities that demark the ends of this axis are alluded to many times and figure so importantly in the action, they are never represented concretely. In fact, the closest contact the audience has with these entities is in the several glimpses of the remote enemy Anthill, seen through rangefinders, and in the presence of the emissary of the French general staff, General Broulard. Neither the audience nor the characters, then, have any direct contact with these entities that exist in and define the film's abstract space. They remain remote, mysterious, and frightening.

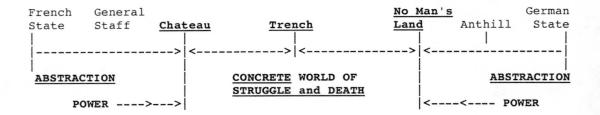

Figure 1: Aesthetic Space and Movement of *Paths of Glory*.

Yet however remote and inaccessible they seem, it is from them that emanate the powerful social forces that determine all lives. For instance, the initial disturbing force that begins the story comes from the French public and state toward the members of the general staff, who with deference to the aroused public decide upon the desperate plan to attack the Anthill. The first concrete actions depicted in the film occur in the chateau, in the middle area of the spatial axis (*see* Figure 1), when in the first of a long series of confrontations, General Broulard arrives from a meeting of the general staff to persuade General Mireau, a division commander, to order the attack. After this meeting General Mireau then travels to the trench to observe the Anthill and to bully Colonel Dax into leading the attack. The actual attack is, of course, a continuation of the force directed from the French state across the axis toward the Anthill and the German state beyond. But the thrust of the attack never moves beyond the halfway point in no-man's-land, where it bogs down and disintegrates into a rout as the French regiment is raked by machine gun and artillery fire from the unseen enemy. The film's action then moves back across the spatial axis to the chateau where occur the trial, the executions, and the final encounters between the generals and Dax.

In short, the spatial axis (*see* Figure 1) represents the conceptualization of at least two fundamental, polarized properties: (1) abstraction-concretion; and (2) the opposition of the powerful cultural forces emanating from the two states toward the concrete world of struggle and death. The actual story is, then, a sequence of confrontations that occur in the middle or concrete range of the overall system of polarized space. But the film as a whole is not simply a series of such confrontations, but rather a larger whole formed from patterns within patterns of conflict that are all brought together within and through this system of strongly conceived, polarized space.

Two Worlds

The conflict and contrast between the worlds of the chateau and the trench were an aspect of the film recognized early by the critics.[1] Each of these worlds functions as both a definite place and also as a symbol — the chateau as a symbol of the cold, impersonal system and world of the generals, and the trench as a symbol of the enlisted men and the death they face. The various rooms and "spaces" associated with the chateau and the generals contrast starkly with those associated with the enlisted men and Colonel Dax. The rooms of the chateau are not only very large and luxuriously furnished, but they are also brilliantly illuminated by numerous large windows and doors. Often in filming the generals Kubrick has these windows and doors in the far background, as if to emphasize the abundance of light as well as space. In sharp contrast, the spaces and rooms occupied by the enlisted men and Dax — the trench itself, the dugouts, the regimental command post, Dax's room, the guardhouse — appear bare, dark, and confining. For instance, when Kubrick films the dark, low-ceiling room of the guard-house (which is actually a small stable), he has the light entering from one small window in the near background in order to stress the confinement and to give the room the appearance of the inside of a rathole.

Another difference between these two worlds is that the form of the chateau, which is associated with the power of the implacable social system the generals serve, contains many hard, symmetrical and orderly lines. For example, the chateau is surrounded by a large, symmetrical formal garden and park (in which the men will be executed). The forms of the trench world, on the other hand, are composed of chaotic and non-symmetrical lines. That is, the trench itself is surrounded by the strange landscape of shell craters, ruins, and dead bodies—a harsh contrast to the formal garden of the chateau.

Kubrick has also furthered this contrast between these two worlds through use of different lenses. That is, since he photographs the generals mostly with a short lens and the enlisted men and Dax with near normal and even longer lenses, he ends up associating the spatial characteristics of the short lens with the chateau world and those of the normal and longer lenses with Dax, the enlisted men, and the trench world.

The short lens, of course, accentuates the already large spaces of the chateau while its deeper depth of field keeps all the luxurious furnishings in sharp focus. This directs some of the audience's attention away from the characters to the chateau itself, resulting in the depiction of the generals and their aides as products and aspects of a strongly delineated social environment. On the other hand, when filming the trench world Kubrick has relied mainly on the normal or near normal lens (except for the action in no-man's-land) and shallow focus; and thus he has accentuated somewhat the spatial confinement while at the same time concentrating on the enlisted men and Dax as individuals.

But Kubrick's use of camera techniques goes far beyond this chateau-trench world polarity, becoming a vital part of this film's structure that deserves consideration in itself. For example, Kubrick has used the shorter lenses not only because they exaggerate the perception of the space and the strong line patterns of the chateau, but also because they can be unflattering to the subject and can have a disorienting effect on the viewer. This is especially true when the short lens is combined with low camera angles at psychologically strategic points in the story (e.g., during Mireau's inspection of the trench, the "toast to success" at Mireau's observation post, and at the execution). When such a combination is used, the effect is disorienting and the generals appear grotesque and even monstrous. In contrast, Dax is seldom photographed from a low angle. And when this is done, Kubrick uses a normal or moderately long lens, a combination of lens and angle that ennobles his appearance as he pleads during the trial for the lives of his men.

Another interesting aspect of this particular substructure of camera technique is that Kubrick seldom allows an officer to appear alone within the frame. The exceptions are few, such as when the peeved General Mireau plays with his gloves during the trial or when the drunken, cowardly Lieutenant Roget explains the night patrol assignment to Corporal Paris—but even here Kubrick frames Roget's face with two wine bottles. In short, whereas the officers are often filmed in groups and almost never as individuals, the enlisted men and Dax are depicted numerous times as individuals in medium shots and even in close-ups. This difference seems designed to suggest that the officers overcome the obvious insecurity that drives their ambitions by grouping together as they play their roles within the social system. By contrast, the condemned men and Dax seem unprotected and frustrated, but they stand always as individuals. Consequently, Kubrick has used his camera to contradict the observation that Major Saint-Aubain (General Mireau's aide) makes about the enlisted men's strong "herd-instinct" and their tendency to group together in fear.

Images and Patterns

The specific, recurrent images that permeate *Paths* and reinforce Kubrick's use of the camera are few in number. One such image is that of recurring spiraling movement through space that builds up to climactic points that are usually shot in close-up. This image occurs in at least three key scenes, in which it is associated with a conflict of wills. The first of these scenes is in the chateau, when General Broulard convinces General Mireau to order the attack against the Anthill. At the opening of this scene, Broulard compliments Mireau on the chateau's furnishings and especially his taste in carpets. When he mentions the attack, Mireau's initial response is to comment on its impossibility. Then, as the conversation continues, the two generals begin a circling movement. They come together, walk arm in arm, turning, moving apart, then joining again. The camera tracks the two generals, adding to the overall impression of space and movement in their "little waltz" among the pieces of elegant furniture.[2] During this spiraling little dance, Broulard "charms" Mireau into ordering the attack through appeals to his vanity and ambition. And thus the whole of the "dance" moves toward the climactic point (shot from a distance) when Mireau states dramatically that "my men can do anything when they set their minds to it."

The same image and several other attributes of the "generals' waltz" appear in the following scene, in which Mireau enters Colonel Dax's command post at the trench. Just as General Broulard, did Mireau has come to convince a subordinate officer to order an impossible attack — the vital difference is, of course, that Dax must actually lead the attack. Ridiculously Mireau tries the same tactic that Broulard used on him. He begins by complimenting Dax on his accommodations. "A nice little place you have here," he says as he looks around the extremely cramped, dark, dirty little hole in the ground. When Dax responds with a friendly laugh at what he thinks is a joke, Mireau tries to appeal to his vanity, his ambition, and eventually to his sense of patriotism. When none of these tactics works, Mireau finally coerces Dax into leading the attack by threatening to remove him from command of the regiment for which he is so concerned. That is, whereas Broulard convinces Mireau to accept his plan through an appeal to vanity and ambition, Mireau triumphs over Dax through threats and an appeal to his concern for his men. And during the whole of this scene the action is supported by a variation of the same rhythm and spiraling movement that builds up to a climactic point, as did the earlier confrontation between the generals. Only this time the spiraling movement is much less obvious while the climactic point is of far greater intensity, i.e., a slow, abbreviated spiraling (accomplished through reframing and editing) that moves to a close shot of a frustrated yet determined Dax, who says, "All right. We'll take the Anthill."

The same image of spiraling movement that builds up to a climax is also part of the confrontation between Lieutenant Roget and Corporal Paris (a subplot that parallels the main plot in many aspects) after their night reconnaissance. During this argument Paris threatens to reveal Roget's drunkenness, cowardice, and his killing of one of his own men. The whole of this scene is held within the most subtle variation of the spiraling image and pattern. Instead of an outright spiraling, the two men simply exchange positions several times within the frame in a most unobtrusive manner, forming in effect the spiraling pattern that builds up to a climactic point and close-up of Paris's face — who incidentally is the character most closely associated with Dax. Within this scene one is reminded of the quiet beauty of the confrontation in *Citizen Kane* (1941) between Geddes, Susan, Emily, and Kane. Kubrick's scene has the same quality of "visual music" formed from permutations of images and patterns created through editing and reframing.

But even more important than the spiraling movement is the image formed out of longer, usually horizontal movements across the film's several polarized spaces which seem miniature replicas of the overall system of space. In all, this complex image of long directed movement holds together, indeed provides the very basis for, at least six key scenes. The shortest and least complex of these is the officers' ball that immediately precedes the execution. The large ballroom very much resembles the large room in which the three enlisted men were tried and condemned a couple of hours earlier. Only now the flag is absent, and refreshments and musicians have been brought in so that the officers can dance with their ladies while the three condemned men wait in the guardhouse to face the morning firing squad. The action begins when Colonel Dax arrives uninvited for a last attempt at convincing General Broulard to stop the executions. As the space in this scene is conceptualized, Dax arrives at the right of the frame and must send a message to Broulard, who is at the extreme left of the room and frame. A fat little colonel, who seems more a maitre d'hotel than a soldier, carries Dax's message. The camera tracks the whole of his long walk across the room, as he carefully makes his way, smiling and bowing to the spiraling, waltzing couples. After he gives the message to General Broulard, Broulard walks back through the dancing couples as the camera tracks him across the long room to Dax. In addition to the obvious presence of the major themes and irony, this scene combines feelings of hope and suspense with both the image of horizontal movement through polarized space and the image of spiraling movement. Lastly, in examining this short scene, one also realizes that it is formed from essentially the same location and movement of subject and the same camera angle, position, and movement as are certain tracking shots of Dax in the more complex trial scene which precedes the officers' ball.

The two inspection scenes at the trench, one by General Mireau and one by Colonel Dax, are also founded on the image of long, straight movement associated with force, conflict, and the film's abstract, polarized space. The first of these two scenes, General Mireau's inspection of Dax's regiment at the trench, is filled with irony that comes mostly from the conflict between pretense and reality. The general, who regards himself as a brave soldier of France, strides along the trench and at regular intervals stops to greet a soldier with the same question: "Hello, soldier. Are you ready to kill some Germans today?" Obviously the men see through his little game, but Major Saint-Auban, the general's aide and the man who will serve as the prosecutor in the trial, tells the general that his visits to the trench encourage and stimulate the troops.

This entire inspection scene is accompanied by the sound of a martial theme played on a snare drum, and the scene is filmed with a short lens from a low angle. The total effect is slightly disorienting and heavily ironic. Adding to this effect is the fact that the camera photographs the action distantly from in front of the walking general as it tracks and shoots from the low angle. This angle combined with the short lens and camera movement creates, of course, an intense feeling of space and motion in the audience.[3] The overall movement of the scene is depicted on the screen as left to right but includes one abrupt camera shift. This occurs toward the end of the scene, when Mireau encounters a soldier who suffers from shell-shock. In anger Mireau slaps the man, and then walks past the momentarily stationary camera, which then cuts to tracking him from behind after he passes. The effect is to portray Mireau as if he is fleeing down the trench after he has struck the soldier.

In many ways Colonel Dax's inspection of his men in the trench immediately before the attack is a reverse mirror image of General Mireau's. While the men might fear their colonel as they do the general, they clearly have much respect for him. And whereas the general's inspection was a public relations gimmick, Colonel Dax inspects the regiment in order to show himself and to give encouragement to the men with whom he will soon face death. In addition to this difference in action, Kubrick has further contrasted these two scenes with both the soundtrack and his use of the camera. For instance, in the background of this second inspection is not the off-screen sound of martial music, but the actual sound of war, the deafening roar of the artillery barrage. And whereas the dominant movement of the general's inspection is clearly from left to right, the dominant movement of this inspection is from right to left as it will be in the attack itself. Also, although the camera tracks this scene from in front of the approaching subject as in the general's inspection, Kubrick has now used an eye-level camera angle and a near-normal lens. This combination of movement, lens, and closer and higher camera angle results, of course, in an intense sense of movement and space as in the previous inspection, but it does not convey a feeling of disorientation.

Lastly, another contrasting parallel within the inspections can be seen in the comparison of the basic rhythm of the two scenes. That is, at approximately the point in Colonel Dax's inspection equivalent to the slapping incident in General Mireau's inspection, the camera shifts momentarily to several shots of a subjective camera (from Dax's point of view). The effect of this change is exactly the opposite of the change in the previous scene when the camera momentarily stops moving and cuts to the shot that follows the general's retreat away from the camera after he has slapped the soldier.

Attack Against Anthill

Obviously the attack on the Anthill is the scene that is most clearly founded upon conflict and a long movement across a polarized space. The attack has, of course, already been "introduced" since it was preceded by the night reconnaissance that entered the space of no-man's-land and which also contained the same basic structure — i.e., the night patrol also moved across this space toward opposition to a stop that is photographed from close up in front of the subjects. Yet while the attack has common structural features with the night patrol, it also differs in that it occurs in the day, a feature that seems to stress the irony and sense of disorientation in the fact that the real slaughter and hell occur not in the darkness men usually fear but in the light of day. Kubrick has prepared for the shock of the attack by keeping the camera down in the trench and by using a normal lens during Dax's inspection. In this way he allows us, his audience, to hear the roar of the explosions but not yet to see that fearful place that the frightened men will soon enter. Of course, this only increases the suspense and leads to the shock that comes when Kubrick cuts to an astounding overhead, panoramic view of the battlefield.[3]

This exciting attack was filmed with six cameras, one of which was hand-held by Kubrick as he followed actor Kirk Douglas across the field. As the space of this scene is conceptualized, this movement into no-man's-land is from right to left, "against the grain." Just as with the officers' ball, but on a grander scale, Kubrick here blends two movements together, one the long movement of the attack itself and the other the zooming of his hand-held camera. At the time of the production of *Paths*, the zoom lens was new to the cinema and one of the few unwritten rules for its use was that one should not zoom while moving because this would result in a sense of disorientation in the audience. Young Kubrick, however, saw that in breaking the rule with this new lens (which he only uses twice in the film), he could both attain an important emotional effect and at the same time conceal his method under the extreme tension of the attack. Kubrick thus created a stunning scene, filled with death and the din of battle, that is ingeniously contained within the blending of the disorienting movement of zooming back and forth and the larger, horizontal movement through polarized space.

In addition to this aspect of the scene's overall rhythm, the scene also contains the pervasive pattern of movement toward a climactic point that is attained and emphasized with a close-up of the main character (Dax) photographed from the front, a characteristic the attack shares with five other scenes. And lastly, the scene's polarity is, of course, further enhanced by the cross cutting of the din and the slaughter in no-man's-land with several shots of the calm and the safety of General Mireau's observation post.

Court-Martial

The court-martial that follows the attack is easily the most complex and imaginative scene of the work. Once again, an entire scene is based upon a conflict played out in a strongly conceived system of polarized space, here delineated by a symmetrical arrangement of characters. And yet however symmetrical and definite these patterns, so subtly are they conceived that the audience is not consciously aware of how Kubrick has manipulated their perception to his purpose. To begin, the action takes place in a large, brilliantly illuminated room of the chateau that seems far removed from the world of the trench and the attack, the place and event with which the trial is concerned. Moreover, Kubrick enhances the sense of space, emptiness, and cold impersonality by allowing the speeches in the room to echo faintly. The hard, symmetrical lines and the chessboard pattern of the immense floor reinforce the feeling that the chateau is the place of the system and the generals, a place where the system controls and lives are determined without compassion.

The symmetrical arrangement of the characters is closely associated with the symmetrical lines and the patterns of the room itself and with the conflict that involves images of movement through polarized space. For example, the room contains three tables. At the largest of these sit the officers of the Court-Martial Board, the president in the middle with two officers on each side (*see* Figure 2). In front and on either side of these officers are two smaller tables; i.e., to their left is the defense, Colonel Dax, and to their right is the prosecutor, Major Saint-Auban. Behind and to the right of Saint-Auban sits General Mireau on a divan, and along the wall on his side of the room sit the other officers of his command grouped together. The three prisoners sit in chairs across from the president, facing the action. Behind them stand three armed soldiers at parade rest. On the wall is a very large painting of a pastoral scene that ironically contrasts with the action below. (Kubrick used the same device of ironic juxtaposition of pastoral paintings and absurd cruelty in the scene when the officers bicker over how many men should be executed.)

Within the space of this symmetrically defined arena, Kubrick uses many technical devices to involve the audience subliminally in aesthetic patterns that are founded upon conflict. For instance, Kubrick photographed the actions of Saint-Auban from a position behind and level with the heads of the board members, and this viewpoint results in Saint-Auban's actions being perceived between the heads of these officers who are in soft focus and partially framed. As Phillips has noted, this composition connects Saint-Auban to the officers, and it is obvious that he speaks only to them and is thinking more of his career than of justice.[4] In opposition to this, Dax is photographed from behind the prisoners, resulting in the prisoners and parts of the bodies of their guards and their guards' weapons being seen in soft focus as Dax speaks in front of the Board. This obviously connects Dax to the three men over whose fate he anguishes.

Within this scene Kubrick has also extended fundamental patterns and the sense of space and conflict by carefully "choreographing" the movement of the two main actors to correspond with their speeches. That is, Saint-Auban moves (screen right to left) from his side of the room against Dax. And when he is closest to Dax and states that the actions of the enlisted men are "a stain on the flag of France," he seems almost to spit out the last phrase as if to challenge Dax. Dax's speech is exactly the opposite. Whereas Saint-Auban spoke with his hat on, as dictated by military custom, Dax (a renowned civilian lawyer) attempts to relax and to be more natural by taking his hat off as he begins to speak. And whereas the major was photographed from behind the heads of the board members, Dax is photographed, of course, from behind the prisoners as he makes the long, horizontal movement in the opposite direction (screen left to right), across the large room toward and "against" General Mireau and his officers (*see* Figure 2). He makes two such "trips" back and forth across the space in front

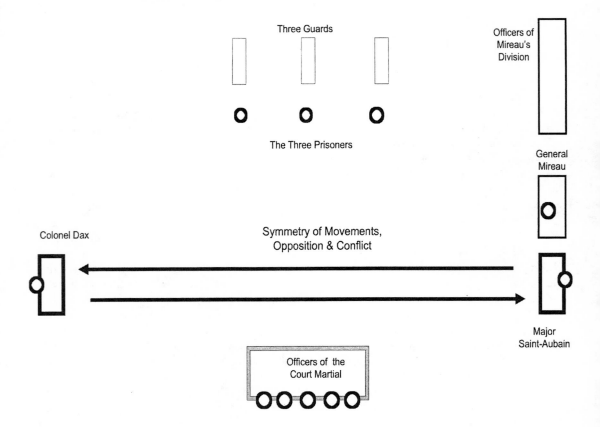

Figure 2: Aesthetic Space and Movement of the Court-Martial Scene.

of the board and prisoners. And at one point near Saint-Auban, he seems almost to spit back the major's phrase, saying that "the actions of these men were not a stain upon the flag of France. But this trial is."

Further examination of this same sequence of shots gives the impression that Kubrick's powerful style is endlessly complex, in that he communicates such an abundance of information on so many different levels. For he has not only used the setting, the placement of cameras and characters, the properties of different lenses, the composition of the frames, the movement and dialogue, but he goes even further to use the motion and the lack of motion of the camera. That is, Kubrick knew that not only does any movement of the camera involve the viewer in a strong sense of movement and space, but that different movements — e.g., panning, tracking, tilting — involve the viewer in different ways and in different degrees of intensity. He takes advantage of these differences in photographing the speeches of Saint-Auban and of Dax. Specifically, he pans the camera as he photographs Saint-Auban's speeches and for the most part tracks (a more complex movement) Dax as he defends his men. In fact, the last speech of Dax is even more complicated; for Kubrick tracks Dax as he first walks to Saint-Auban's desk, pans as he walks back to his own and then returns to Saint-Auban's desk, and then ends this sequence by tracking Dax's final movement back to his own desk. Kubrick has thus created a symmetrical pattern of opposition within such a pattern, and then concealed this structure within the narrative action which it reinforces — a superb cinematic example of the blending of form and content.

Executions

Following the trial, the relentless plot of *Paths* leads quickly and inexorably to the executions. But this scene is linked to the trial and to other scenes not simply by narrative, but also through its heavy irony and patterns of polarity and conflict. During much of the ceremony the chateau stands like a silent, ominous witness as it looms in the distant background. Looking down from its point of view at the three distant stakes, one would see the hard symmetrical lines of the formal garden and that the many characters are arranged into opposing sides (*see* Figure 3). On the left are the representatives of the state and the chateau world: i.e., a large number of officers, newspaper reporters and photographers, the two generals, and invited dignitaries. On the right stand the division band and Colonel Dax in front of his regiment, and closer to the stakes waits a wagon with three empty coffins. Starting from a point near the chateau, the three prisoners, accompanied by their guards and the priest, must walk down the corridor between the two opposing groups to the stakes where they will be bound and then shot. In short, the whole of the execution scene is oriented around the pervasive image of one long, harrowing movement through a polarized space toward a dreaded climactic point.

As in his later films, Kubrick has in the execution and other key scenes of *Paths* used the soundtrack — and especially music or the sounds of musical instruments— to create a high level of suspense and irony. In particular, he has used the drum in three scenes. In the Mireau inspection scene he uses an off-scene drum to play a martial theme in an ironic, downbeat manner which mocks Mireau and emphasizes his pretentiousness and hypocrisy. In the night reconnaissance the use of an off-screen drum again matches and reinforces the events and mood of the scene, in that it instills fear and suspense in the viewer. And in much the same way the driving rhythm of the rolling drums at the execution is used by Kubrick to intensify the feeling of fear and doom and the inevitability of these deaths in the garden of the chateau.

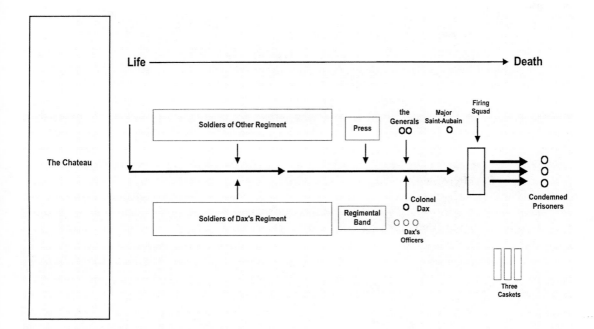

Figure 3: Aesthetic Space and Movement of the Execution Scene.

In addition to this use of the soundtrack, Kubrick has in the execution scene also increased the volume of certain almost extraneous sounds to make them figure importantly in the action and mood. Apparently he has done this in order to represent and to emphasize the psychological state of the condemned men whose perceptions are sharpened by their intense fear in these last moments of life. That is, while such sounds as reading the death warrant seem almost inaudible and insignificant, other sounds seem strangely and surprisingly magnified out of proportion. For example, after the reading of the death warrant Kubrick cuts to a shot in which the camera is situated at near ground level about twenty-five feet in front of the three prisoners who are now tied to the stakes. Suddenly, into the extreme foreground of the frame, enter the marching feet and legs, the arms and rifles of the firing squad. This particular viewpoint makes believable both the surprisingly loud sound of the marching feet that appear close to the camera and also the almost piercing sound made by the soldiers as they load their weapons. In addition to Kubrick's use of sound, what is also impressive in this complex shot is both the shock on the faces of the prisoners and the non-human appearance of the firing squad. Filming from this low angle and with a short lens, Kubrick thus achieves a sharp contrast between the three helpless "little men" tied to the stakes and the large, frightening bodies and aimed weapons that in another moment will destroy them.

Kubrick's sense of suspense, irony, and rhythm can also be demonstrated by another aspect of the sound in this scene. Up to the point of the blast from the rifles, the soundtrack has been very loud. Then suddenly, just before the loudest and most frightening of all sounds, there is unexpected silence. And buried within his stunning silence is the almost inaudible bird song and then rifle fire with which Kubrick ends the scene. Kubrick then dissolves to the sounds and image of the breakfasting generals who discuss the execution as they drink coffee and munch their croissants.

As in other scenes Kubrick has also increased the emotional impact of the execution through the use of different lenses and camera techniques that are by this point in the film a strong part of the fundamental structure of the work. He accomplishes this first of all by having the camera again track the subjects from in front as they move down the long corridor toward the stakes and coffins. As in Dax's inspection, Kubrick switches momentarily to a subjective camera (from Corporal Paris's point of view) for shots of Dax, the generals, photographers, and the three stakes. During the execution Kubrick also continues to contrast the generals with Colonel Dax by filming them with different lenses and from different angles. But in this particular scene he goes beyond this simple polarity that he has thus far constructed with these techniques; i.e., he forms out of the polarized structure of camera technique a climatic pattern that reinforces the events of the scene. He accomplishes this by moving steadily away from the normal lens and camera angle in two opposing directions at the same time, until he ends with the conflict of two extremely different images, each of which is associated with certain characters, events, themes, motifs, and patterns.

This whole system is formed primarily out of six shots, three of the generals and three of Dax, which are interspersed within the last minutes of the execution scene. This structure begins with the subjective camera shot (from the point of view of Corporal Paris) of the two generals, a near-normal lens, and an eye-level camera angle. The second shot of this pattern is that of Dax who is also photographed with the subjective camera, the same lens and camera angle; i.e., we see Dax as the prisoners do, standing in front of his men who are in focus. As the prisoners pass, Dax turns his head to follow them. The next shot of this structure begins the departure from the norm, for in it the two generals are shot with a stationary camera, a short lens, and a very low camera angle. Standing in their long, great coats, this combination of lens and angle makes them appear somewhat grotesque and communicates a slightly disorienting feeling to the audience. Next, as the prisoners are being tied to the stakes, we see Dax, who is now photographed with an ennobling, moderately telephoto lens which concentrates more on his individual face as it throws his partially visible men into soft focus. This shot ends as Dax glances over to the generals; and the camera then cuts to the last shot of the generals, who are photographed again through the unflattering short lens and from a ground-level angle. After a couple of shots of the activity at the stakes, we see Dax for the last time in this scene. And he is now photographed in an extreme close-up with a very long lens that separates him from the background that is completely out of focus and that concentrates on his anguish as he stands helplessly, watching his men die.

Conclusion

A careful study of *Paths of Glory* illustrates the extraordinary understanding and control of every aspect of filmmaking that Stanley Kubrick possessed as a twenty-seven-year-old director working on his first major film. In *Paths* he created an ingenious array of "aesthetic parameters" out of both the narrative and the technical properties of film. And from these parameters he created a complex yet subtle structure of polarity and conflict that reinforces the story while heightening both the emotional and the cognitive response of his audience.

He carried this structure and technique to the very end of his film. For whereas the film begins with a shot of the chateau and a nationalistic song, the "Marseillaise," played off-key by a band, it ends in a dingy cafe with a simple German song about love and family, sung by a captive German girl for the saddened troops of Dax's regiment. With a long lens selected for the kind of close-up photography that with few exceptions has been so carefully avoided, the camera moves slowly over the tearful faces, presenting us with over thirty close-ups. Surprisingly, the faces are either very young or old, an illustration of the pathetic state of the French army at this stage of the war. The implication is, of course, that in the other direction, in the Anthill and beyond, the enlisted men of the German army suffer the same existence. Outside the cafe stands the old sergeant who thoughtfully waits until the end of the song before giving the order for these disheartened men to return to the trench where they will again face their German enemy. And thus, whereas the climax of the narrative occurs in the last encounter between General Broulard and Dax, the resolution of the film as a whole is in this last scene — a strange and brilliantly conceived inversion process through which the conflicting patterns of the entire film close upon one another to form a final, "unresolved harmony."

7 *Spartacus*: The Specter of Politics and the Politics of Spectacle[5]

Reynold Humphries

Kubrick disowned *Spartacus*. There is little to be gained here by going into the reasons, ethical or narcissistic, why a director, working within the commercial framework of Hollywood, acts thus over a film he has helmed. However, since the primary aim of this essay is to offer an analysis of the film from the standpoint of its concerns with money, power, politics, freedom and sex, a few remarks are in order.

In his autobiography *The Ragman's Son*, actor-producer Kirk Douglas writes about how Kubrick proposed to solve the problem of credits by taking credit for the script. This problem arose, of course, because scriptwriter Dalton Trumbo was still blacklisted as one of the Hollywood Ten; officially, therefore, his name could not appear on the screen.[6] Douglas decided to brave the blacklist by giving Trumbo screen credit.[7] Certain other facts should not be forgotten. Douglas had already removed Anthony Mann shortly after shooting began and placed Kubrick in the director's chair.[8] Such power is just one of the privileges of a producer and was hardly likely to go down well with an independently minded artist like Kubrick. However, his desire to have his name on the screen as author of the screenplay suggests a commitment to his own (self-) image as auteur, although it was only later in his career that he was in a position to impose it. We shall see in due course that the director had every right to be proud of his work on the film, by far the most impressive of his credits prior to *Dr. Strangelove* (where, it might be added, he was not the sole author) and one of his most enduring achievements. However, most of the credit for the qualities of *Spartacus* must lie with Trumbo's script, a quite remarkable piece of work when one considers that he was addressing a mass audience supposedly more interested in spectacle and entertainment than with reflections on power politics. Such reflections are precisely what the audience got.

The theme of money is a major leitmotif and is introduced in ways that insist on its privileged place within a network of political power and physical domination. Money, as we shall discover, is not just a question of coin of the realm; it also has a metaphorical dimension that Trumbo exploits to introduce his analysis of politics. The seeming banality with which the concept of money is introduced serves to highlight its ubiquity in contexts that make it seem the most natural thing in the world. Thus the commentary with which the film opens informs us in the space of a sentence how a slave woman added to her master's wealth by giving birth to a son. This not only sketches in the background of Spartacus (whom we see working as an adult slave as the words are pronounced by the off-screen narrator), but brings to the fore the inter-related questions of money, power and the place of women. Although no information is forth-coming, it is possible that she became pregnant as a result of being forced to sleep with another slave or, like the women at the gladiatorial school whom we see shortly after, with gladiators.

At this juncture, however, it is the theme of exploitation, along lines of both class and sex, which is paramount, taking on a most interesting twist by the introduction of the character of Batiatus (Peter Ustinov), owner of the above-mentioned gladiatorial school. Complaining of the heat (from which he is protected by a servant with a parasol), he refers bitterly to this man and the other members of his escort: they cost him money. Rather than see this merely as a sign of avarice, we should interpret it as a subtle comment on the question of surplus value pro-duced by the worker for his or her employer. Such surplus value is massively increased in the case of the slave who works without a wage, even though he or she must be fed, clothed and housed. The escort, however, is not composed of slaves, so Batiatus is forced to spend some of his ill-gotten gains in an attempt to earn even more money by procuring slaves to be trained as gladiators. The economic and political situation at the time enabled men like Batiatus to treat people both as chattels and a source of extra revenue: a slave woman bears a child who is later sold into slavery at the age of 13. The human body produces other bodies that are at once exchanged for cash without the "producer" having any say in the matter. The parallel with the worker who has no control over the use of the product of his labor could hardly be more plain. Thus, in a couple of scenes, Trumbo introduces neatly and succinctly the concept of the exploita-tion of the proletariat by the capitalist, setting the scene for his Marxist investigation into money, class and politics.

Kubrick exploits the considerable comic talents of Ustinov in the delightful scene where Batiatus receives the unexpected visit of Crassus (Laurence Olivier) and his companions. A mock-titanic struggle lasting five seconds troubles the serenity of Batiatus: his first reaction is to offer his second-best wine, then he thinks better of it and orders his best wine to be served — but in small goblets! Both director and writer have clearly understood the need to vary the moods in so long a film (over three hours) as shall be seen on other occasions in Kubrick's use of actors, close-ups, shot-reverse-shots and group shots. The insistence on the importance of money to the character of Batiatus is necessary to set up an opposition between him and Cras-sus when it comes to money, just as Trumbo is anxious at a later stage for the audience to grasp the nature of the values that separate Crassus and Gracchus (Charles Laughton).[9] Deeply dis-turbed by the request of his guests, who have come to watch gladiatorial combats to the death, because of the bad feeling this will create within his school, Batiatus also has recourse to the little matter of the financial cost, which he assumes will convince Crassus to change his mind. In other words, Batiatus is naive and Trumbo uses his astonishment when Crassus agrees to the huge sum for which he asks to introduce a theme that will occur periodically in other, more political, contexts: that of believing that one's own ideological view of the world and human relations is natural to the point of assuming it is shared by everyone. Unfortunately for Batia-tus, money is no object — and certainly no obstacle — for Crassus and a deadly spectacle is thus mounted for the group, particularly for the two women: Helena, the wife of Crassus, and Clau-dia, the wife of Glabrus (John Dall) whom Crassus nominates at this point to the post of com-mander of the garrison in Rome as a wedding present. Class and nepotism take precedence over merit even in so vital a nomination.

Crassus and Gracchus are vastly more sophisticated than the other representatives of power in the film. If they hate each other, they also understand each other and the systems they defend: dictatorship based on the patrician order for the former, the republic with all its flaws for the latter. Crassus despises Gracchus, whom he considers to be the leader of the mob, the populace, those who are hardly better than slaves. Gracchus, however, is no more opposed to slavery than is Crassus and sees in Spartacus a danger to the hierarchy within the republic that he serves and defends in his own interest: it brings him wealth, luxury and slave women.[10] However, Gracchus is a politician to his fingertips, as we can ascertain from the way he can turn a potentially explosive situation to his advantage, a domain where Crassus, however, shows himself to be even more clever and subtle when the die is cast. Thus Gracchus draws attention in the Senate to the fact that many Romans have no bread (therefore are starving) because the city's grain supply has been cut off as a consequence of one of Rome's imperial wars. He thereby attempts to exploit the contradictions within the patrician system to which he is opposed. The slave uprising, however, cuts the ground from under his feet, since Crassus is able to displace the issue from one of potential chaos *within* Rome to one of danger *from without*. He does this by appealing to fear and to prejudice towards the other, while presenting himself as savior. Once the uprising has been crushed, it is Gracchus who becomes "the enemy within." If this works, it is because the ordinary Roman citizen has no voice and, crucially, no power. The film makes this abundantly clear in the final sequences where the imprisoned survivors of the uprising are being led along the Appian Way to be crucified. Kubrick alternates shots of Spartacus and his comrades on the one hand and of the populace on the other. There is no mistaking the looks on the faces of the latter, a mixture of fear, despair and compassion indicating that they secretly identified with the slaves. They, too, have little to lose but their lives under the undemocratic Roman system, especially now that Crassus is dictator.[11]

One discussion between Crassus and Gracchus suggests, however, that the latter is not being simply opportunistic when he evokes the question of hunger. Faced with an opponent as intelligent and dangerous as Crassus, he knows that he must be able to think quickly and to exploit any weakness that may present itself. This discussion turns on what Gracchus significantly

In Kubrick's 1960 film *Spartacus,* Kirk Douglas leads a slave army as it ambushes and burns a Roman legion encampment.

calls "the price of patriotism," thus giving to the theme of money the status of a signifier whose meaning changes with context. What is being broached here is fundamental to the film's political project and opens it out to matters in no way limited to ancient Rome. Crassus is making use of that imaginary binary opposition "us vs. them," to which even the victims of exploitation can identify in times of crisis, turning to an authoritarian father-figure and thus regressing to an infantile stage of dependence. Crassus, both as a patrician and as a soldier, fills the role perfectly, but he has his price: absolute dictatorship. The situation thus created is a history lesson on Trumbo's part. Franco used the threat of atheistic communism to overthrow the democratically elected republican government of Spain.[12] Pétain exploited the Judeo-Bolshevik conspiracy evoked by the nationalist right to hand France over to the Nazis. Kissinger decided that a democratic election in Chile could not be allowed to spread further afield, what he saw as the cancer of democratic socialism, and engineered a fascist coup. In all cases "patriotism" is a discourse claiming to save those who vote badly from themselves, a way of masking the class and economic interests of those who cannot tolerate a democratic vote. Thus the enemy of the state becomes its saviour in order to destroy it from within.

The whole point of this "group psychology" is to encourage the subject as individual to identify unconsciously with the desire of the tyrant in what is seemingly a sort of pact between two individuals.[13] Hence the crucial role of the subject's unconscious regression to the child/adult relationship, with the adult functioning as a stern superego. This fetishization of the individual is inherent to capitalist society, with its attendant ideology of success based on effort, so it comes as no surprise that everything in *Spartacus*, both in the script and in Kubrick's direction, tends to give pride of place to solidarity and collective acts: any decision involves others and is made with their consent. From the moment in the film's opening sequence where Spartacus goes to the aid of a slave who has collapsed and hamstrings a guard who tells him to go back to work, the tone is set. Spartacus is condemned to death, not only because he has attacked a guard but because of his sense of solidarity and compassion. A simple example of this is the march to Brundisi. We see an old man being helped along, indicating that this is more than just an army: it is also a manifestation of class solidarity.[14] The attitude of Spartacus must be punished as threatening the entire political system of exploitation which thus takes precedence over any question of money. Making an example of one slave as a lesson to all other slaves is far more important ideologically than the loss of a trivial sum of money. However, money does have a role to play even here, but it is limited to individual profit. Batiatus has an agreement with the soldier in charge of the group of slaves: he will take Spartacus off his hands in exchange for money. Thus private enterprise on a small scale flourishes and can coexist within what we can see as an early example of a "global system," which Gracchus later nicely refers to as taking two-thirds of the world from its rightful owners. And "ownership" of one's body and one's mind is central to Trumbo's way of discussing solidarity as a political and historical phenomenon.

Let us return, then, to the film's early sequences involving the gladiators, in particular to the way Kubrick shoots the gladiatorial contests imposed on Batiatus by Crassus and his group. The devices to which the director resorts both reinforce and render even more complex the notions put forth in the script on a wide variety of subjects. When Spartacus, Crixus (John Ireland) and the other ex-slaves arrive at the gladiatorial school, Batiatus gives them a lecture where he paints, in glowing terms and without a trace of conscious irony, the quasi-idyllic existence they can look forward to. They will be well looked after and can expect to live from five to ten years before dying gloriously in the Roman arena. Some might even obtain their freedom and become trainers, at which point Batiatus introduces Marcellus the trainer (Charles McGraw), whose sadism will be his downfall: he will die ingloriously, drowned by Spartacus in a vat of soup! Batiatus also makes the interesting remark that they will be taught to use their heads, whereas Marcellus, in a brief confrontation with Spartacus immediately afterwards, remarks that being intelligent is "dangerous" for a slave. What Marcellus really means, of course, is that the established order of which he is an integral part — much like a foreman who acts in the interest of his employer against the workers whom he oversees — is endangered once a slave starts to use his head, not in order to calculate how best to stay alive and thus to kill an opponent (Marcellus teaches the noble art of killing with gusto and delectation), but to reflect on who his real enemy is, something which Spartacus learns in a very special manner as a result of the gladiatorial contests about to follow.

At one point when the gladiators have gathered to bathe, Spartacus turns to a black man and asks his name. He receives a reply which makes its mark on him: you don't want to know my name, I don't want to know yours, here we have no friends. This is, in fact, a form of self-defense: if one treats one's fellow-gladiators with the same indifference as that shown by Marcellus, one has a chance of killing and not being killed. Things, however, are not so cut and dried and a certain solidarity is created — which Crassus sneers at when he forces Spartacus to fight the former servant of Crassus, Antoninus (Tony Curtis), who has left him to join the uprising[15] — if only due to the gladiators being constantly in one another's company: *esprit de corps* means something in this context too. This is a psychological detail which Batiatus has grasped intuitively when he uses the expression "bad feeling" to try to dissuade Crassus from going through with his request/command. For this "bad feeling," as Batiatus can see, would be directed against him, Marcellus and those responsible for forcing X to kill Y. So deeply entrenched is the patricians' belief in the inferior social and intellectual status of the gladiators, however, that they cannot see beyond the immediate gratification of a whim. The gladiators are being trained to kill other gladiators *with whom they will never have come into contact*, which is a very different state of affairs. It is precisely this intimacy — which, for reasons which will soon become clear, we can also call "promiscuity" — that provokes the temporary downfall of the established order.

Once Batiatus has been obliged to grant the wish of Crassus, the film turns its attention to those concerned: the gladiators themselves. The long sequence ending with the aftermath of the death of Draba the Negro (Woody Strode) can be divided up as follows: (1) a discussion between Spartacus and Crixus; (2) Helena and Claudia, accompanied by Batiatus, choosing the men they want to see fight; (3) the four gladiators (Crixus and Galino, Spartacus and Draba) being led out through the stockades to a sort of antechamber where they wait to be called out for combat; (4) the combat between Crixus and Galino, while Spartacus and Draba await their turn; (5) the combat between Spartacus and Draba and what happens; and (6) the aftermath. The discussion between Crixus and Spartacus, who are shown to be friends, turns on this friendship where both men are faced with a choice: kill or be killed. At this point in the action the situation is presented as an "either … or" choice, with Spartacus insisting that it is a case of survival and that, faced with this, one cannot but be forced to kill the other, even if he be a friend. Spartacus, therefore, is functioning along the ideological lines laid down by Batiatus and Marcellus: the survival of the fittest. The fact that things will soon change, however, is already indicated by the way Kubrick films the discussion: Crixus on the left of the wide screen, Spartacus on the right. Elsewhere, for reasons to be elucidated, the director has recourse to shot-reverse-shots, but the co-presence of the two friends — and, at this stage, possible opponents — on opposite sides of the screen at once makes manifest both their potential forced antagonism and an incipient solidarity, a form of understanding, inasmuch as their discussion affords them a sort of passive intimacy that is destined to be transformed into an active solidarity that only the superior might of Rome will destroy.

Leaving a discussion of the second scene to later, since it introduces elements that will lead to considerations of a different nature, we pass on to the scene where the four gladiators are escorted to the place from which they will emerge to fight before the Roman quartet. As the men pass through the stockades, Kubrick has filmed their progress as if they were about to participate in a bullfight, but as the bulls, not the matadors. This question of "bestiality" is very much the continuation of the theme of the slave or gladiator as object to be used, then cast aside. The four men are told to sit down in a sort of pen from which they are to emerge two by two into a small arena and fight to the death. Should the victor refuse to kill his opponent, he will have his throat cut by Marcellus, much as one kills and bleeds dry an animal.[16]

Kubrick only has to show us the four gladiators in the pen for us to understand the trap in which they find themselves. But is it really a case of "kill or be killed" as Spartacus and Crixus believe? It is here that Kubrick introduces a new dimension into the drama that enhances remarkably the work of Trumbo. To start with, he gives us close-ups of the two friends, but in alternating shots, not together. Each is reflecting, each is being called upon to kill his opponent, but the latter is someone else, not the friend one feared one would have to kill in order to survive. By filming the two gladiators/friends separately, Kubrick neatly draws our attention to the fact that, at this juncture, each man is reacting as an individual faced with death: his own or his opponent's. Kubrick even goes to the length of making us identify with the gaze of Spartacus. He looks out at Crixus and Galino fighting (it is Crixus who wins) through the narrow gap between two of the planks that make up the pen. We see them from his point of view, where this gap corresponds to the format of the wide screen, thus insisting on the spectacular nature of the fight and encouraging us to see it for what it is, at least in the minds of those involved: a contest where the survival of one man automatically means the death of the other. The ideology of the survival of the fittest is applied literally here, but figuratively elsewhere: physical might and economic power used to subjugate, exploit, and exterminate if necessary. The clearly *spectacular* nature of the fight is communicated to us visually so that we can better grasp its *political* significance for what is to follow.

Given that they are about to find themselves in an identical position, it is revealing that Kubrick shows Spartacus looking in the direction of Draba, who keeps his gaze fixed on the ground before him. In other words, he is avoiding eye contact as this could compromise his resolve to survive. Suddenly, Draba raises his eyes and looks upon Spartacus; we see only Draba and his gaze off-screen right. It is one of the most remarkable moments of the film. Just how remarkable, we shall discover a few minutes later. For Draba wins the contest, but instead of plunging his trident into the throat of Spartacus, he throws it at Crassus and attempts to climb up into the balcony. A soldier hurls a spear at him, so it is Spartacus who wins by default. What has happened here? The meaning of Draba's gaze now becomes clear and shifts the film into new territory, or rather it enables Spartacus — and the audience — to *see things differently* and to act accordingly by killing Marcellus and thus triggering the revolt. "Kill or be killed" has been re-cast by Draba, who refuses this binary opposition, the sign of the subject's alienation. To kill is to accept to continue a life of degradation where one is forced to act according to values imposed but never accepted. To be killed certainly puts an end to this alienation but in a purely passive fashion. Draba adopts the third way: to choose to die without killing his opponent in order to give meaning to his own life even at the moment of death, to instigate an act which is a call for action, a refusal to submit. Although he does not know it, this decision by Draba to die *as a subject* rather than live as a gladiator/slave will lead Spartacus to reflect, with all that this will entail for what follows.[17]

After Draba's death, Kubrick has recourse to a fade. A high-angle shot shows us the stockades, then the camera cranes down in such a way that the image insists on the spikes of the railings, symbols by their form of the prison that the gladiatorial school represents for the men, but also of the trident that Draba refused to use against Spartacus — whom he had never wanted to call a friend — but which he turned against their common oppressors and tormentors. Draba preferred to choose death over an imposed *performance*, thus creating a sense of solidarity in protest over a choice which had nothing free about it. The grey paint of the spikes and the uniform brown of the gladiators' tunics adds to the sombre and negative tone of this sequence where the men are forced to walk past Draba's body, strung up like a slaughtered animal, which is all he is for the Romans, but certainly not for Spartacus. Alone in his cell, he is clearly thinking and is therefore now in the throes of being transformed into that "dangerous" person feared by Marcellus.

Let us go back now to the second scene in this long and crucial sequence. Two details are of particular note as Helena and Claudia choose "their" gladiators in the presence of Batiatus: their behavior and his reactions. I find it most revealing that Trumbo should introduce the element of apparent choice in the way the two women proceed, rejecting the suggestions made by Batiatus and casting their gaze over the assembled men. Batiatus has underrated them: they are more determined to make their own choice than he expected and do not seem to treat the situation as a simple game. Something else is at stake and it soon becomes apparent, although Kubrick does not insist on it. He does, however, invite us to be vigilant and to have an eye for details. Batiatus is obviously not happy with their choices, most particularly when they designate Draba, then Spartacus, as the second couple. Kubrick shows the man clearly downcast and resigned. Is this because he dreamt of better things for the two of them, or because he reckoned he would make an unusually large sum of money by having them fight in Rome? But Batiatus also looks *sickened* by the whole business, which suggests that it is something other than money that is worrying him, especially as he will be handsomely compensated by Crassus. Kubrick and Trumbo want us to see another dimension to the character of Batiatus. It cannot be called "decency," rather it's an opposition, which he shares with his old friend Gracchus, to the selfish, arrogant and irresponsible lifestyle of the patricians.

Even more revealing, however, is the behavior of Claudia. After she has chosen Draba, Kubrick tracks left to follow the movement of the two women as they continue their search. Claudia is in the centre of the screen. Suddenly, she glances rapidly and surreptitiously off-screen right, in the direction of the now invisible Draba. The significance of this gesture, which she is anxious not to reveal, can only be that she is fascinated by the massive physique of the man. And the manner chosen by Kubrick to communicate the clearly lascivious content of her gaze indicates that this is a hint to the audience in order to introduce the theme of sexuality. Or rather, to further elaborate on it, as the question of the woman's body and sexuality has kept on returning. Here, in the case of Claudia, it returns like the repressed. Prior to the contest beginning, she requests that the contestants wear "just enough for modesty." Hypocrisy? Nymphomania? Perhaps. Certainly the script makes comments elsewhere to the effect that Crassus and his group are decadent and self-indulgent, including in the realm of sexuality. And the scene, long censored, between Crassus and Antoninus (his "body servant," a delightful formula!) suggests subtly but clearly that Crassus is as fond of young men as he is of young women. We should grant the situation far more interest than if it were yet another moralizing denunciation of upper-class debauchery, always an easy way out if one is anxious to evacuate politics.

Trumbo is surely raising here the oft-mentioned notion of the Protestant tendency to experience both fascination and disgust when contemplating the other, when we are dealing with the very particular relations between the pioneers and the Indians, for example. It is well known that one attributes to the other certain deplorable and uncivilized desires that amply justify exterminating him, but we must not lose from sight that this goes hand in hand with a displacement onto the other of desires one harbours unconsciously but that a combination of social repression and self-restraint forbid. Finding sex dirty or considering that the other has a dirty and ugly attitude to sex can thus be interpreted as a sign of conflict within the subject's unconscious: between a desire to carry out a certain act and the sentiment, imposed socially, that such an act is disgusting, uncivilized, "bestial." Thus a slave owner rapes one of his slave girls and transforms this act of violence (committed from a position of power and oppression) into a feeling of disgust at the promiscuity of the woman on the receiving end.[18]

It is in such a context that we must interpret the scene where Batiatus and Marcellus act as voyeurs once Varinia (Jean Simmons) has been introduced into the cell of Spartacus as his companion for the night. This is part of the treatment of slaves: the men receive compensation in the form of women who, of course, have no more choice in this domain than in any other. More to the point, perhaps, is the dimension of the extra twist given to alienation in the case of the men. All the slaves are alienated socially by the very nature of their working for nothing and of having no say in the use of the products of their labor. However, the men are further alienated because they interpret the situation where the women are sent to them for their pleasure as perfectly natural, whereas the women are not alienated in a like fashion as they have no choice in the matter: socially, it is "normal" for women to serve men in this fashion.[19] Moreover, the men are expected to "perform" sexually for their masters, like trained seals. Varinia, however, has a point of view of her own. When an enraged and humiliated Spartacus shouts at the two men, "I'm not an animal," she states, "Neither am I." The reference to animals is revealing: we find ourselves once again in the domain of attributing to the rejected other desires one craves to assuage, while feeling disgusted at their very existence.[20] Kubrick films this first encounter between the hero and heroine in a way that suggests Spartacus is, on the one had, a victim of the notion that the woman is an object and, on the other hand, a man whose hesitancy is due to his lack of sexual experience (he has never had the opportunity) and to an inherent sense of the *dignity* of the other. If Varinia is removed because Batiatus and Marcellus are not going to be given the sort of show they want, the contact between Spartacus and Varinia is decisive for both of them. As the film shows in subsequent sequences, neither can exist without the other.

Earlier, the intimacy existing between the gladiators was termed "promiscuity," which might seem strange. It should be clear by now, however, that this promiscuity is rather a way of life imposed upon them by intimate contact and by the "contract" by which the gladiators are allowed periodically to release sexual tension by spending the night with a woman, another instance of an exchange economy. It is the woman, therefore, whose existence is "promiscuous," and this can be compared favorably with the promiscuity of the patricians: they, after all, are free to choose. It can perhaps also be compared with the lives of the women who live under the roof of Gracchus, who makes no attempt to hide his sexual needs. These women are presented by the film as happy. Their existence is a far cry from the life of the slaves who cook, serve meals and serve as sexual objects in the gladiatorial school. Significantly, the dissolute life of Gracchus disgusts Crassus, for the simple reason that Gracchus rejects the hypocrisy of monogamous marriage to which patricians like Crassus only pay lip service for reasons of power politics. It is in this context that Gracchus refers to Rome taking most of the world from those to whom it belongs, therefore underscoring the notion of individualism: you get people to invest in a relationship that eschews any contact of a collective kind the better to impose a political and economic system based on the self. It is not difficult to see the situation outlined here as a comment by Trumbo on the conservatism of America in the 1950s and the ideology of the nuclear family underpinning it.

One critic has used the word "contrived" to describe the scenes involving Varinia on the one hand and Antoninus on the other.[21] This remark is not only for the most part inaccurate, it also betrays an ignorance of Hollywood in general and the thrust of Trumbo's script in particular. Any big-budget spectacle is going to bring in a love interest in some form or another, alternating action sequences, scenes of drama and moments of intimacy. To criticize the script of *Spartacus* in these terms and on these grounds is frivolous. The scenes between Spartacus and Varinia are not just "love interest" but a means of introducing the necessary Hollywood couple whose relationship will be over-determined by factors other than physical attraction. It is a tribute to Trumbo the writer and Kubrick the director that these scenes make sense in the overall context of ethical commitment, something shared by writer and director, and clearly present in the evolution of the relationship from the first night in the gladiator's cell to the concluding tragic moments where Varinia holds up their baby to the crucified hero whom she begs to die quickly.

Antoninus is just as essential a character, partly, too, in relation to the theme of sexuality. If he flees the home of Crassus after the latter's attempt to seduce him, then this is perhaps less because he is not attracted to the older man than because the relationship will be one of *submission* by Antoninus to the desire of Crassus. This finds an exact parallel in the way Varinia is courted by Crassus who, despite his love for her (which the film in no way questions), cannot but behave as one who has power. Let us not forget the love scene between Varinia and Spartacus where she says, "Forbid me to leave you," which is a way of asking him to show that the incipient tenderness of the sequence in his cell can now be given full rein in a context of freedom and mutual respect. There is no longer any trace of submission in the air, from whatever source or for whatever reason. Nor must we forget the final fight to the death between Spartacus and Antoninus— yet another case of an imposed "choice"— where each tries to kill the other in order to spare him the agony of a lingering death on the cross. The fact that Spartacus declares his love for Antoninus as he kills him with a thrust of his sword both refers back to the seduction scene between Crassus and Antoninus in the bath and places love between men in a context of respect and solidarity.

However, Antoninus has another, more openly political, role to play in Trumbo's scheme of things. It is through his character that the script raises the crucial class dimension of history. When Spartacus first meets Antoninus, the latter has just joined the army of gladiators and slaves. Spartacus asks him what he does and is bemused to learn that he is a scholar who taught songs to his master's children. At first amused, Spartacus is quick to learn, for he has just recognized the usefulness of another slave who has been a carpenter for eighteen years. What we are dealing with here is the question of *knowledge*. One of the great lies of capitalism is the *absence of the past* (except for supposedly patriotic purposes, such as those evoked by Crassus to justify his dictatorship). It is essential for economic and ideological reasons to repress the simple fact that people do not learn everything anew but learn from what has gone before, in particular from the knowledge — manual and intellectual — handed down from generation to generation. Without this transmission of knowledge and a recognition of its importance, we would still be living in caves. When Spartacus orders Antoninus not to abandon this gift, he is making a dramatic historical gesture, or rather a gesture that encompasses the role of history and recognizes its importance. Trumbo takes this up in a later scene between Spartacus and Varinia where he states, "I am free but I cannot read," and goes on to say he wants to know where the sun goes at night and why the moon changes shape. The answers to these questions are taken for granted by us, but only because at a precise point in time *someone* provided humanity with the answer and changed the way we now see the world and the universe. For Trumbo, knowledge is always already collective and historical.

We are now dealing with the symbolic order of language and everyday social intercourse as distinct from the imaginary order of ideology and binary oppositions rooted in a dependence on the other dating back to infancy. It is his arrogant and blind belief in his natural authority that makes Glabrus, the pawn of Crassus and the new commander of the garrison in Rome, fall into a trap of his own making: he has come to believe in the discourse of the ideological big "other." Thus, convinced that the gladiators and freed slaves are not opponents worth taking seriously, he neglects the basic duties of a professional soldier and fails to dig moats and build a stockade to protect his position and thus his troops during the night. The result: a massacre and a humiliation. By identifying with an image of the slave as the signifier of radical otherness, Glabrus has fallen victim to the *effect* of that signifier and placed ideology above knowledge. In so doing he has behaved in a way diametrically opposed to that of Spartacus in the presence of the carpenter and Antoninus. But if Glabrus cannot learn from history, Crassus can. And he can also understand that Caesar (John Gavin) has betrayed Gracchus and joined his side, less from his patrician beliefs than because it is in his political interest. Hence the uncanny prescience shown by Crassus when he lets Caesar know that he, Crassus, has nothing to fear except from him.

Thus both Spartacus and Crassus are men who can learn from history, which helps explain why Crassus can show no mercy, and yet fears Spartacus: what if another like him comes along? Trumbo is anxious to keep alive the notion of rebellion against tyranny and therefore "contrives" to have Varinia, escorted by Batiatus, ride off at the end with the son she has borne to Spartacus. This final scene gives a particular meaning to the remark Spartacus has made to Varinia prior to the final battle which ends with the annihilation of the slave army: "As long as one of us lives, we all live."[22] It also gives meaning to her own enigmatic observation in the presence of Crassus, who assumes her reticence is due to grief, "I'm not grieving, I'm remembering." This in turn refers back to the essential moment where Spartacus contemplates, after the successful revolt of the gladiators, the rope from which the body of Draba was suspended. His gaze indicates that he is remembering the man and that he, Spartacus, has finally understood the full meaning of his opponent's gesture of sacrifice. We thus return to the intimately linked questions of knowledge, history and the role of the latter in the transmission of the former: only after the event can a subject possible know the meaning of an act and its consequences. Yet a subject does decide to act, a decision to which history gives a retroactive significance. Draba acted thus. Kubrick offers us both a materialist and an imperialist vision of history through an alternating montage where Spartacus addresses his army the night before the final battle and where Crassus assumes full dictatorial powers in the name of saving Rome. Both are filmed alone in the frame, but whereas Crassus addresses a faceless mass which submits willingly to him as saviour,[23] Kubrick alternates shots of Spartacus alone and the faces of his army. Young and old, men and women are shown literally looking up to him, but as to someone who can federate disparate victims ready to take their own destiny in hand, if only to lose at this particular moment of history.[24]

If it is high time that *Spartacus* be recognized as one of Kubrick's finest achievements as a director, one aspect at least of the film is due to Trumbo alone: its status as an allegory on blacklisting, which does not go without saying. This is an aspect of filmmaking throughout the 1950s that must not be neglected. Nicholas Ray's *Johnny Guitar* (1954) is an obvious example, as are certain films of that other progressive figure of the period, Robert Aldrich: the theme of betrayal in *Vera Cruz* (1954), paranoia and surveillance in *Kiss Me Deadly* (1955), and the forgotten causes of the New Deal, with gossip columnists dredging up past indiscretions and naming names in *The Big Knife* (1955) spring to mind as instances of the climate of fear.[25] Aspects of the film can be interpreted both literally as a comment on the characters and their relation to power and figuratively as a transposition into another time and society of the fears and concerns of post-war America, of which the Hollywood witch-hunts were a very special manifestation.

Towards the end of the film the triumphant Crassus makes it abundantly clear to Gracchus, not only that the latter has lost, but that Crassus is not going to be content with his old enemy simply bowing out of public life: not only must he go but he must participate in his own humiliation. As Crassus pointedly remarks "The enemies of the state are known," and hands Gracchus a "list of the disloyal." the senator's name figures at the top of the list. It would be easy to put the name of Senator McCarthy in the place of Crassus and see the list as standing in for both his notorious (and non-existent) list of "communists in the State Department" and the list of those named as communists or sympathizers by denizens of Hollywood who gave in under pressure. However, something more complex and subtle is at work in Trumbo's script and that we should see in Crassus something extending beyond the person of the junior senator from Wisconsin.

NY 105-22020   SECRET

labelled "front" or "Communist dominated". He stated that at the end of his association with these organizations, certain political positions taken by the organizations proved to him that there was a definite alignment with Soviet and Communist policy. As a result of learning this, he terminated all his ties with these groups.

The CP, USA has been designated by the Attorney General of the United States pursuant to Executive Order 10450.
                              b2
STANLEY KUBRICK   b7D

[   ] on September 8, 1960, advised that STANLEY KUBRICK indicated to the subject's wife that he had recently arrived in New York City from California to do publicity work for the motion picture film "Spartacus", which he had directed.

On September 12, 1960, [   ] advised that KUBRICK   b2
had spent the evening and the early hours of that morning   b7D
in the [   ] apartment. On this same date, [   ]   b7C
[   ] KUBRICK [   ] old chess-playing [   ]

The files of the Los Angeles Office, territory in which KUBRICK resides, and the New York Office contain no derogatory information concerning KUBRICK.

[   ]   b7C

New York City, New York

On September 8, 1960, [   ] advised that the   b2
subject [   ] individual [   ]   b7D
[   ] him and his wife in the near future.   b7C
He [   ]

The files of the New York Office contain no information pertinent to this investigation that can be identified with [   ]

- 5 -

A (now declassified) page that mentions *Spartacus* from Stanley Kubrick's FBI file.

The point is, Crassus represents less a person than a political state of mind that has become increasingly powerful since the collapse of the Soviet Union. The script of *Spartacus* shows an uncanny grasp of the direction in which modern capitalist democracies were moving, although the signs were visible by 1946. Crassus represents the new corporate order that came into existence in the United States in the immediate aftermath of World War II, one based on a "liberal consensus" determined to eradicate all memory and trace of the New Deal, particular the notion of class solidarity, and to transform Hollywood into the privileged handmaiden of that "new order" of which Crassus significantly boasts.[26] This new order demanded that people "name names" to save their jobs, thus elevating betrayal of convictions and one's comrades into the highest form of patriotism. It is impossible not to see a reference to this sorry and sordid aspect of Hollywood's recent past in the confrontation between "Senator" Crassus and Spartacus prior to the fight to the death between him and Antoninus. "You must answer when I speak to you," he says. Yet Crassus cannot be reduced to this one symbolic function, however pertinent. Yet another line of argument is less concerned with individuals and more with the implications of their values and behavior.

Crassus and his like submit to *drives* in an endless and repetitive pursuit of pleasure. He is not after some precise object — money, a luxurious house, slaves, women — for the simple reason that he has them already. But he must convince himself that there is a *purpose* in his quest, hence his need to seduce Varinia, to bring her to submit herself physically and mentally to him. He has convinced himself that he will have succeeded if he possesses her. If we consider that "the real purpose of the drive is not some mythical goal of full satisfaction, but to return to its circular path, and the real source of enjoyment is the repetitive movement of this closed circuit,"[27] then we can perhaps better grasp what is at stake and what Crassus represents. Unconsciously, Crassus wants more than just power; his is an insatiable drive that must perforce go ever further in its search. Perhaps we could say that he is in search of "the great Whatsit," like Mike Hammer in *Kiss Me Deadly*.[28] Certainly they have one thing in common: nothing must stand in their way, no restraint can be accepted in this frenzied striving to *reach beyond*. From this standpoint Crassus is a perfect early version of that contemporary phenomenon, the "neo-liberal."

This new species lets nothing stand in its way in its attempt at global control: nothing must be allowed to stand outside its sphere of interest. Now that Crassus has obtained absolute power, what is his reaction? Fear of Caesar who might adopt the same logic and seek to replace him. In other words, Crassus will feel constrained to go further, to impose limits on more and more freedoms, to start having spies keep an eye on Caesar, and so on. *There can be no end to this cycle.* Significantly, after Crassus astonishes Caesar by stating that he, Crassus, has only him to fear, Kubrick films the two men exiting from the frame, Crassus moving off-screen *left*, Caesar off-screen *right*. It is as if a new drive for power were already under way.

Yet perhaps the simplest way to interpret *Spartacus* as a political statement is to see Gracchus and Crassus as representatives respectively of the Old Right (i.e. enlightened capitalism) and the New Right (i.e. Eric Johnston, Ronald Reagan, et al.). In which case Trumbo shows that he, for one, has no intention of forgetting the struggles of the 1930s and the alliances, however tenuous and problematic, forged during that decade. And whatever Kubrick might have said later, his mise en scène is an eloquent contribution to the spirit of resistance: that of Spartacus and that of the Hollywood Left. *Nos morituri te salutamus*?

8 Believing Is Seeing:
Surveillance and
2001: A Space Odyssey

Gary D. Rhodes

During the forty years since its release in 1968, *2001: A Space Odyssey* has simultaneously been revered and reviled. This was, after all, a film that was embraced by the Catholic Legion of Decency ("It's God! It's God!" one viewer famously shouted at a screening attended by *Rolling Stone* magazine's Bob McClay) and the drug culture ("The Ultimate Trip," the film's promotional materials proclaimed, with or without intending the oft-perceived double entendre).[29] It was also a film excoriated by reviewers like Pauline Kael and embraced by critics like Penelope Gilliatt.[30] Like Dave Bowman transforming into the Star Child, some reviewers went through their own evolution, assailing the film and then later recanting. Swayed, either by seeing the film on a second viewing or by buckling under the weight of its widespread audience support.

2001: A Space Odyssey has also been famously "understood" and "misunderstood." To help us understand, some theorists assume the role of interpreters at the United Nations, speaking in our ears the meaning of a film (and in some cases, by attaching intentionality, a filmmaker named Kubrick). They are privy to the truth of *2001*, it would seem. But the conflicts between their words suggest the problematic, even oxymoronic position of partial truth. Instead, we are left with visions in competition with one another.

Words might well be the source of the problem. As Kubrick told *Playboy* magazine in 1968:

> It's not a message that I ever intend to convey in words. *2001* is a nonverbal experience.... I tried to create a visual experience, one that bypasses verbalized pigeonholing and directly penetrates the subconscious with an emotional and philosophic content.... You're free to speculate as you wish about the philosophical and allegorical meaning of the film — and such speculation is one indication that it has succeeded in gripping the audience at a deep level — but I don't want to spell out a verbal road map that every viewer will feel obligated to pursue or else fear he's missed the point.[31]

There is, of course, a problem, or at least an irony, in using Kubrick's words to suggest the problem of logocentric interpretation. But perhaps that irony is altogether appropriate for attempting to discuss a film that is ironic, starting as it does with an onscreen title that reads "The Dawn of Man" and then concluding with an image of an infant male.

More importantly, Kubrick's quotation proposes a democratic argument that denies fixed meaning and singular truth in *2001*, embracing instead all reactions, responses, and, yes, readings of the film. Monoliths exist in the film, but not in the interpretation of it. For him, it seems, a viewer's direct contact with the film will be personal and subjective. To see *2001* is then to wield power over it, and the experience of it.

> There isn't a single aspect of ship operations that's not under his control.
> — Frank Poole on HAL in *2001: A Space Odyssey*

The reasons why critics and audiences, when speculating about their experiences with *2001*, often seized upon the HAL-9000 computer is easy enough to understand. HAL is arguably (and ironically) the most human character in the film. HAL is representative of a kind of "progress" that is both a progression forward technologically and a progression backward to the murderous impulses of the australopithecines at the "Dawn of Man." To be sure, an entire volume of essays is devoted to him.[32]

HAL is also the antagonist, the villain, really, in the section of *2001* (the film's second epoch/evolution, but its third distinct storyline) that represents the most traditional narrative structure in the entire film. A clear three-act storyline unfolds during the Jupiter Mission: introduction, conflict, and resolution. Dialogue exposition from a BBC broadcast early in the segment sets up the characters of Dave Bowman, Frank Poole and HAL; their actions and dialogue — while rich in textures and themes — are readily understandable and connected by clear causality.

Critics and audiences have also labored over the Homeric allusion in the film's subtitle, sometimes concluding that HAL — with his singular eye and violent behavior — is a technological cyclops who combats Bowman's Odysseus. Certainly no writer has explored this allegory in as much detail as Leonard F. Wheat, whose book on *2001* provides the following analysis:

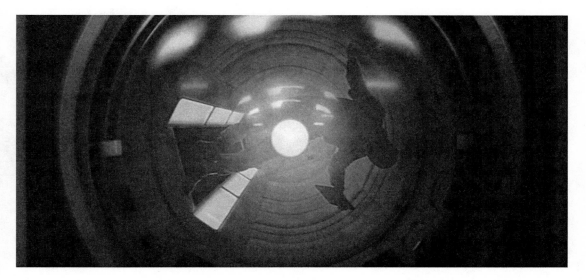

HAL's first appearance in the film underscores the emphasis on his constant visual surveillance. Within his red eye, the viewer can see a reflection of what HAL sees: he is observing Bowman's (Keir Dullea) every move.

> Bowman has a one-eyed adversary. He is HAL, the malevolent computer who reads the lips of Bowman and Poole with his sinister red eye. HAL is the cyclops. His red eye is the eye of the cyclops, and his gigantic body — the spaceship Discovery — makes him a giant, like the cyclops. Also like the cyclops, he is a killer of crewmen: he kills Frank Poole and the three hibernating astronauts. As Odysseus did, Bowman fights back. Again as Odysseus did, he attacks his adversary's forehead, although this time from the inside (inside the brain chamber behind Discovery's forehead). Once more as Odysseus did, Bowman uses as a weapon an elongated object, a key, which symbolizes the stake used by Odysseus.[33]

Wheat's desire to argue in favor of this notion (as well as two others, one being the Zarathustra and the other being the "Man-Machine Symbiosis") results in an extremely detailed allegorical study. But his zeal to make detailed one-to-one connections between the entirety of *2001* and the *Odyssey* emerges as a forced and reductive argument. His allegorical arguments also lead to several bizarre suggestions: that, for example, Bowman's green helmet and orange space uniform when he disconnects HAL might be a Kubrickian reference to the Troubles in Northern Ireland and, by extension, to Nietzsche's proclamation that "God is Dead!"[34]

To fix meaning precisely in *2001* creates a problem, as the process creates more fog than it clears. The very act of taking measurements skews the results. Exactitude breeds inexactitude. As Ciment wrote of Kubrick's work: "To describe film in words — which is to say, present to the reader in conceptual terms a series of associations of animated images — is in itself a challenge. With films which their filmmaker has always described as a 'non-verbal experience,' the task is rendered even more difficult."[35]

The task is also rendered difficult due to the presence of alternate possibilities. However detailed Wheat's study of the film and whatever value it holds, it is still one interpretation of many. A different reaction to HAL, for example, might emphasize the fact that he possesses not one eye like Homer's cyclops, but many. He has an unknown number of eyes throughout the Discovery, transforming his sight into oversight. One (or more) is in the centrifuge. One (or more) is in the pod bay. One (or more) is in the airlock. One (or more) is inside the "Logic Memory Center." One (or more) is on each of the pods, which means he can see Poole quite clearly as the pod stalks him outside the ship and causes his death. One (or more) eyes is also on the outside of the ship, which means he can see Bowman's pod clearly as he refuses him reentry. Furthermore, given his own eye on the pod, he can see "himself" (or at least a part of himself) being disallowed reentry. Perhaps HAL even has many more eyes than those catalogued here; extreme close-ups of them sometimes elude precise spatial orientation.

Thanks to an array of monitors that show the inner workings of the ship, we also learn that HAL has various kinds of "eyes," many unseen. Some are within the ship, connected to circuitry. As HAL tells the BBC: "My mission responsibilities range over the entire operations of the ship, so I am constantly occupied." As an example, he not only causes, but also sees the failing life support systems of the hibernating crew members. He has more than sight; he has vision, a plan for the future. "This mission is too important for me to allow you to jeopardize it," he tells Bowman.

It is possible then to see this world of the Jupiter Mission as nothing short of a space governed by HAL's inescapable gaze. Constant surveillance occurs aboard ship, which noticeably guides and affects the behavior of Bowman and Poole. The eye of HAL is upon all. Instead of (or in addition to) citing Homer and the *Odyssey*, in other words, a viewer could just as readily invoke Bentham, Foucault, and the Panopticon.[36]

British philosopher Jeremy Bentham finalized blueprints of his Panopticon prison-house in 1791. He believed it would become "a new mode of obtaining power of mind over mind, in a quantity hitherto without example."[37] Planned as a half-moon-shaped prison building, the Panopticon would also feature a tower building that could see into every cell. Prisoners would have the impression that their inspection by others was constant, that the jailers' gaze upon them was never averted. But the Panopticon would create just that, an impression, as the prisoners would only see the tower building, not the faces of guards who may or may not be watching them at any particular moment.

Bentham's Panopticon arose from his humane attempt to find a cost-effective solution to the 18th century penal system. For Michel Foucault, whose work investigates knowledge and power, the Panopticon is a representation for the ways in which observation and examination function in modern society. In *Discipline and Punish: The Birth of the Prison*, Foucault writes: "The panoptic schema, without disappearing as such or losing any of its properties, was destined to spread throughout the social body, its vocation was to become a generalized function."[38]

In *2001*, that social body now extends outside the earth. HAL is constantly discovering new images, as the ship's name suggests. He scrutinizes the vastness of space, ostensibly for the benefit of the Americans and U.S. astronauts who have begun to colonize space, those who are mapping the lunar surface and who wish to extend their reach into the solar system. HAL will witness that journey for them, as well as observe all that occurs within the Discovery spacecraft.

For Bowman, Poole, and the hibernating crew members, HAL's gaze is inescapable and omnipresent. HAL's first appearance in the film underscores the emphasis on his constant visual surveillance. He is first seen in the eighth shot of the Jupiter Mission segment; it is a close-up of one of his eyes. Within its red coloration, the viewer can see a reflection of what HAL sees: he is observing Bowman's every move. And HAL's eye does not blink. It does not look away, even for a moment.

In a sense, then, Bowman and Poole are prisoners aboard the Discovery, even if Bowman is officially the "mission commander." Trapped in a distance from earth gauged by space (800,000,000 miles) and time (18 months, with transmissions to Mission Control taking seven minutes), they have no ability to leave the ship. Their pods are suitable only for brief excursions into the dangers of outer space. That Bowman and Poole appear on a BBC program called *The World Tonight* while so far away from "the world" ironically serves to comment on their situation.

Realizing that they are both subject to the power of HAL's gaze, Bowman and Poole importantly see "eye to eye" on three key occasions. They look at one another in an equally quizzical manner after scanning the AE-35 unit and discovering no technical failure. They look at each other with mutual anxiety and fear after HAL reassures them that the discrepancy with the fellow 9000 computer on earth should cause no "worry." And notably, they look at each other while inside the pod when they discuss the possibility of disconnecting HAL. A single medium shot of the duo discussing that issue lasts nearly two minutes.

"There of course was no way of knowing whether you were being watched at any given moment," Orwell wrote in his 1948 novel *Nineteen Eighty-Four*. And HAL, like Big Brother, commands technological capabilities that extend well beyond anything Bentham described. Another passage from Orwell mentions that: "The telescreen received and transmitted simultaneously. Any sound that Winston made, above the level of a very low whisper, would be picked up by it; moreover so long as he remained within the field of vision which the metal plaque commanded, he could be seen as well as heard." Similarly, HAL can also see *and* hear, and connects the aural with the visual highly efficiently, as he does when he reads lips.

When HAL does read Bowman and Poole's lips, it is with an eye that is some distance from the pod into which they have retreated. A closeup POV shot shows him panning back and forth their mouths with extreme precision. Earlier, however, he has asked Bowman to bring his sketches "a bit closer" to his eye to get a better look at them. The marked discrepancy in his eyesight suggests he knowingly hasn't allowed Bowman and Poole to understand the strength of his vision. Perhaps he is intentionally deceptive on this point, as his deception certainly manifests elsewhere in the plot. For example, HAL slyly broaches a discussion with Bowman regarding "rumors about something being dug up on the moon." In reality, as Dr. Heywood Floyd's pre-recorded message later reveals, HAL officially knows the full details of the TMA-1.

As the segment unfolds, HAL's surveillance capabilities (d)evolve towards totality. Thanks to alleged problems with the AE-35 unit, HAL severs communications with earth. Curiously, he is actually speaking about Mission Control's "tight security" when he interrupts himself to announce the impending AE-35 failure. Bowman removes the AE-35 at HAL's request, which effectively removes any oversight by the "Twin Triple-Niner-Zero" computer. Any semblance of equivalence has been dismantled. This action simultaneously removes oversight by Mission Control, the source of "human error." HAL knows best, and he sees with the greatest clarity.

HAL not only sees/oversees Bowman and Poole, but he also controls what *they* see. This is true of the birthday message from Poole's parents, as well the messages from Mission Control. It is true when HAL allows Poole to view Bowman's spacewalk retrieval of the AE-35 unit, apparently "filmed" by some unseen eye of HAL's on the ship exterior and displayed on a monitor. The reverse situation allows Bowman to watch Poole's attempt at replacing the AE-35. He sees Poole emerge from a pod that is a short distance from the Discovery, and then sees another image, this time revealing the ship's satellite dish. A change of camera angles presumably caused by a change of "eyes." It is a decision that prevents Bowman from seeing the pod attack Poole.

HAL's control also extends to the images that appear regularly on the ship's monitors, which seemingly reveal only what HAL *wants* to reveal: fragmented visuals without narrative logic, not dissimilar to how McLuhan described television in the 1960s. Television is actually something that HAL understands in a way that inverts McLuhan, who believed TV is extension of our eyes. The interview footage of Bowman and Poole has taken place aboard the Discovery after the mission has begun; HAL has apparently seen *and* filmed the duo for the broadcast. His vision is an extension of television, for he has (however briefly) become the eyes of the BBC. HAL's position of power extends to the degree that he has filmed one of his *own* eyes for the broadcast, which we see playing on one of many monitors surrounding another of his eyes. It stares forward, always watching, and sometimes recording. HAL can view, and re-view.

The BBC example also highlights the fact that the power of HAL's gaze is temporal, and time is a panoptical device. Habits form as time passes, as we are watched day after day, week after week, month after month. Lewis Mumford and others have described time as a "machine," a threat to personal freedom.[39] It is, as Eric Mark Kramer has claimed, "the most powerful form of self-ordination."[40] The prisonhouse of time, inescapable even in the further reaches of the solar system. Poole still observes his "birthday," and receives messages from his parents on Wednesdays, markers of time that would have little meaning outside of earth. Only the hibernating crew members (who have "absolutely no sense of time") are immune, but their immunity renders them completely powerless.

Bowman and Poole face the repetition of HAL's ongoing stare, month after month. A series of HAL POV shots throughout the segment reinforce its ongoing power, "seeing" into the ship through an iris shot (combined with a fisheye lens) that mimics his circular eyes. This shot is seen once during the BBC broadcast, thrice as Bowman shows HAL his sketches of the hibernating crew members, twice as the AE-35 unit is checked, and twice as we see the two empty seats used by Poole and Bowman. Most famously, of course, the iris shot pans across Bowman and Poole's mouths during the lip-reading.

But the consistency of the iris shot is lost once, crucially, when the trio discusses the discrepancies over the AE-35 unit. HAL reassures both men that all is well during a scene where the iris shot is used to suggest POV. Bowman's conclusion to the conversation is, "Well, I'm sure you're right HAL. Uhh, fine. Thanks very much." As he thanks HAL, Bowman looks directly into the camera, just as he does in all of the iris shots. And yet, *2001*'s sign for HAL's POV is not present at that moment; there is no fisheye lens and no iris. The disruption of the pattern occurs at a moment when HAL's gaze has lost some of its power. Bowman and Poole are already considering HAL's problems, which could mean shutting his eyes through disconnection.

"I can see you're really upset about this," HAL tells Bowman after he reenters the ship through the emergency airlock. His glaring red eyes, the modality of surveillance, become the recipient of the gaze. Echoing the first image of HAL in the segment, Bowman's reflection appears once in HAL's eye outside the "Logic Memory Center," and again on three occasions inside that room. But the change of context suggests HAL is now the one who is looked at. The transfer of power becomes complete when HAL's reflection — in the form of his higher logic modules — is cast onto Bowman's reflective helmet. The viewer has transformed into the viewed; the jailer is now the jailed.

Of course disconnecting HAL does not remove oversight; it simply transfers the power of surveillance to another. Initially it comes in the form of the pre-recorded message from Dr. Heywood Floyd, who stares into the camera as he announces the real reason for the Jupiter Mission. His eyes lock on Bowman's to announce that another force has been monitoring earth. Keep watching the skies, Bowman, because the skies have been watching us since the very beginning.

The Dawn of Man

—*2001: A Space Odyssey* onscreen text

In the first section of the film, australopithecines live in a world where the ability to see is directly related to the ability to survive. Coexistence with other animals means that danger is always present. The one who watches is the one who wields power; a leopard attack from above illustrates this reality. Another image shows a leopard surveying the landscape with its glowing eyes while sitting on top of a victim. Careful surveillance also includes watching rival groups of the same species. One australopithecine tribe quietly approaches another that has gathered at a pool of water. The observed discover the observers, causing a fight over natural resources.

Ongoing struggles mean that the australopithecines have to be watchful even at night. They gaze around themselves because of the sounds of predatory animals, and also because of the enormity of their environment. An adult male named "Moon-Watcher" in Arthur C. Clarke's novel looks beyond the immediate landscape to the sky above. To look and to learn. He will be one of the australopithecines who come into contact with the first black monolith in the film.

Shortly after Moon-Watcher picks up a bone, he turns his head slightly, remembering the monolith, which is illustrated by an insert edit of the same low-angle shot seen when he first encountered it. After crashing the bone down repeatedly on the skeletal remains of a tapir, he imagines the possibilities, as seen in an insert edit of a live tapir falling over as if struck by force. Instead of living purely in the present, the Moon-Watcher now has a past and future. He now has vision as well as sight; he is speculative as empirical. Time, the soon-to-be of previous desire, imposes its own form of self-ordination. After all, its fruit can be seen in the first two segment titles of *2001*, "The Dawn of Man" and the particularly-specific "18 Months Later: The Jupiter Mission."

Of course the editing *sine qua non*, the jump cut from the moon-watcher australopithecine's bone toss to a spacecraft (or, as it was originally envisioned, an orbiting nuclear weapon), is preceded by two other jump cuts. The first has placed Moon-Watcher in a new position that doesn't follow continuity from the immediately prior shot when he walks out of frame with others in his tribe; he now stands alone to hurl his weapon into the sky. Then, another jump cut occurs of the bone in mid-air. Coming at the conclusion of a scene that is otherwise meticulous in maintaining continuity, these two edits seem to prepare the viewer for the third jump forward, a jump of three million years.[41] The evolution is unseen, and an equally noticeable absence is an onscreen title or title card to herald the new age. Like moon-watcher, Dr. Heywood Floyd also seemingly exists at "The Dawn of Man," even if at more advanced stage of it.

Floyd's world has conquered the moon, perhaps, but not humankind. People must be regularly surveilled and monitored. Upon his arrival at the space station, for example, Floyd meets "Mr. Miller of Station Security" and undergoes "Voiceprint Identification," which features the pre-recorded video of a woman staring directly at him. Television and computer monitors seem to be everywhere. One flashes an in-flight movie to a sleeping Floyd; another later displays martial arts for a female viewer, a hi-tech broadcast of a low-tech system of human defense. Fragmented visuals without narrative logic, surveying other places and events. Monitors are also inside the ship's cockpit, and they are on the corridor wall on the space station.

Decades of geopolitical surveillance have extended into space as well. The Russians are watching the Americans, who are watching the Russians. Heywood Floyd's encounter with the four Russians on the space station operates as a microcosm of this larger (and mutual) form of observation, refracted through the lens of TMA-1 discovery. Dr. Smyslov carefully looks over his shoulder to see if he is being watched before asking Floyd about rumors of the Clavius epidemic. Two of the three other Russians never speak, but merely stare at Floyd's reluctant answers. Intentional reluctance, of course, only to help fuel belief in the epidemic, a cover story that covers the truth and conceals it from prying foreign eyes.

Secrecy means that only those few U.S. citizens on the moon base (and presumably a few others on earth like Floyd) know about the TMA-1. The "need for absolute security" requires that no one else can see the discovery, and even those scientists who have must take "formal security oaths." The fabricated epidemic circulates after basic communications with earth are severed, an action similar to HAL's loss of communications with earth after the AE-35 is removed. Floyd's entire briefing focuses on confidentiality; proscenium framing of him at a podium serves to emphasize its centrality. Keeping a secret is as important as the secret itself.

But the prohibitions on displaying the TMA-1 site are only temporary. Like moon-watcher, Floyd envisages the future. For example, a photographer snaps four pictures at the Floyd briefing. Though he leaves just before it begins, the photographer has been permitted access to a briefing meant for few eyes among all human existence, preserving an approximate image of it for posterity. Likewise, one of the astronauts attempts to take a picture of Floyd and a few others in front of the monolith, a site that they have previously photographed, to see and *capture* an image, holding it for future observation by approved persons at an approved time.

Absolute security. Controlling what people can or cannot view. After all, Floyd believes that "cultural shock and social disorientation" will occur without "adequate preparation and conditioning" of the masses. The world will have to be trained in *how* to see the discovery. And yet the world of Heywood Floyd is not absolutely secure. He might be able to see his daughter via the space station videophone, but directly across from the booth are two uniformed men taking a break from their duties. They aren't wearing spacesuits like the other pilots we see; are they security guards taking a break? Then, as Floyd and Halvorsen travel to the TMA-1 site, two astronauts on the lunar surface see them in transit. But who are these astronauts? Are they authorized?

In other words, the surveillance is not absolute. Even the moon is not immune to random acts of observation. Floyd's world is more precise in its approach to watching, monitoring, and recording than the australopithecines, but both environments are less secure than the

Discovery spacecraft. The Jupiter Mission, whose internal system of surveillance fails and whose actions are monitored from afar.

———————————————

It seems to have been deliberately buried.
— Ralph Halvorsen on the TMA-1 in *2001: A Space Odyssey*

After (during?) Bowman's journey Beyond the Infinite, his pod appears in a home or apartment of some kind. An "anonymous hotel suite," in the words of Arthur C. Clarke's novel.[42] Through the pod window, Bowman sees an older version of himself in a space suit, looking back into the pod. As the film cuts to a long shot of the room, the pod disappears. The older Bowman then moves through the "hotel suite," examining the features of its bathroom.

Bowman scrutinizes himself in the bathroom mirror, until a sound causes him to walk into the hallway and look into a dining room. He sees himself at an even older age, sans space suit, eating at a table. The Bowman who is dining seems to sense he is being watched. He stands up and goes to the hallway, but the Bowman wearing the space suit has vanished. The Bowman who has been dining returns to his meal. After knocking a wine glass from the table, he bends down to the shards that remain. At that moment, he squints to see himself as an even older version of himself in a bed, seemingly near death. This elderly Bowman sees a monolith, and — after pointing to it in recognition — is replaced by the Star Child.

The "hotel suite" has perhaps spurred more questions than any other sequence in the film. Are these images collapsing the passage of a large amount of narrative time, or suggesting that time no longer applies? Perhaps those are both possibilities, but at least one visual cue suggests that onscreen time might parallel narrative time. When the image of the dying Bowman in bed is first seen, it doesn't merely follow an image of the other Bowman squinting. When the dying Bowman is first seen, it is an over-the-shoulder shot of the Bowman who has been dining. Two Bowmans appear simultaneously in the same frame; they seem to coexist, however briefly.

Whatever else this scene might suggest, it represents the result of panoptical reality, the product of HAL's absolute surveillance. Bowman views himself in the pod that disappears. He leaves his reflection in a mirror to pursue his image elsewhere. He sets aside his dinner to see if he is being watched. And then he views himself dying in bed. Self-ordination guides Bowman's actions in the "hotel." As Bentham had said of the Panopticon, the "watching" would be left to the "watched." Or, to quote Foucault, Bowman "inscribes in himself the power relations in which he simultaneously plays both roles; he becomes the principle of his own subjection."[43] After all, Bowman seems to be completely alone. His solitude is aurally emphasized by various echoing sounds. His chair moving, his silverware against the plate, the breaking of his glass: these noises reverberate through the hotel suite.

However, the use of vocal sounds on the music score during the Star Gate sequence and at the beginning of the hotel scene simultaneously suggest another presence. The hotel presumably has an owner. Subordination exists alongside self-ordination. Floyd's pre-recorded message has already told Bowman that his mission is the result of the TMA-1 discovery, "the first evidence of intelligent life off the earth." But the hotel's owner remains elusive even after the guest has checked in. Unlike the iconic eye(s) of HAL, Bowman would be unaware of the focal point, the "site" of the beings' sight. The hotel room surely reinforces what the TMA-1 discovery suggested: the "sentiment of invisible omniscience," to quote Bentham. All-seeing.

But does this being(s) want to watch? Arthur C. Clarke's short story "The Sentinel," from which Kubrick-Clarke drew inspiration for the *2001* screenplay, includes the following discussion of a monolith-like device: "So they left a sentinel, one of millions they scattered throughout the Universe, watching over all worlds with the promise of life. It was a beacon that down the ages patiently signaled the fact that no one had discovered it."[44] Of course in *2001*, the alarm of discovery pierces the ears of the astronauts near the TMA-1. Deliberately buried, accidentally uncovered, and undeniably activated.

The being(s) have apparently viewed the australopithecines at the Dawn of Man, as the appearance of the first monolith suggests. That the TMA-1 was buried on the moon, however, suggests that humans hardly required or needed constant surveillance. Such an action was unnecessary for a race that would have to make their way to the lunar surface in order to merit attention. The role of the alien(s)/god(s) that have placed the monoliths has been to monitor the earth from afar. They will view us only after a screening process has occurred. Only after we place ourselves before them. When the time comes. When we are worth watching.

And we will never view them. Their power is indeed beyond the infinite. Bowman's reflection will not appear in their eyes, as it did in HAL's. He will not see them as he has seen himself. No cameras will record this entity (or entities). Like deities whose followers refuse to depict them in art, this being(s) will go without witness, without depiction. They will monitor us; we will not monitor them.

Glare: To shine with or reflect a very harsh, bright, dazzling light; To stare with a fiercely or angrily piercing look; To appear conspicuous or stand out obtrusively.
— *Webster's Dictionary*

2001 presents a view of earth (and its movement into space) in which australopithecines watch each other, in which various humans watch each other, and in which a computer watches humans. Complicated layers of surveillance emerge against the backdrop of an unseen force that has seemingly always monitored us, waiting for us to be worth their attention. Until that time, they have deliberately buried a trace of themselves. The monolith is a monument to the fact that they desire to view us eventually, but it is also an artifact of the time that they visited the moon. The lunar surface is terrain that has been surveyed before, long before man's arrival. Long before Floyd has to journey to the TMA-1 to see it in person.

Seeing, after all, is believing. Perhaps that is particularly true in a film envisioned as a Cinerama epic that would envelope the audience and their peripheral vision. A film with an attention to detailed visuals and a methodical approach to pacing that would suggest the aesthetics of a scientific documentary. *2001* certainly illustrates the influence of the Canadian nonfiction film *Universe* (1960); it may well be, as Kubrick claimed, a "mythological documentary"[45]

That the events in the film have been documented is important. Everyone in the film, everything in the film, has been looked at before. Every event has been surveyed, studied, surveilled. Stanley Kubrick (and members of his production team) bore witness to all facets of the image capture. Images kept from public view until the premiere of the film; images kept even from the eyes of the MGM hierarchy until a 1968 screening shortly before the public release.[46]

The use of Cinerama and color and sophisticated special effects and slow pacing attempt to convey these images in a manner that will intensify audience reaction by total immersion in the experience. "The Ultimate Trip," as documented by Kubrick. But these are events that acknowledge their own documentation. Occasionally *2001* reminds us that it is a film. The use of inter-titles would be an example, as would the jump cut on the bone toss. The rack focus from Dr. Floyd's floating ink pen to a flight attendant. And of course there is the inclusion of various handheld camera shots, taken by Kubrick himself.[47] Handheld camera, that curious aesthetic that invokes the realism of television news and documentary cinematography while simultaneously drawing attention to the camera itself, and thus the fact someone once saw what we now see.

Perhaps the most repeated cinematic fingerprint left from those who documented *2001* is camera glare. Lights shining directly into the camera lens cause either a soft halo effect or more pronounced circular/geometric shapes to appear on the resulting film footage. Glare draws attention to the fact that everything in the film has been documented. Every frame has been viewed at some past time, and the process of image capture has been preserved in the image itself. A visual artifact from a prior survey, just like the monolith deliberately buried on the moon.

Deliberate or not, the camera glare is not at all buried in the image. It is in fact quite noticeable, so much so that an earlier style of Hollywood filmmaking would have perceived it as a repeated visual imperfection. In *2001*, the glare appears softly in the first image in the film, the alignment of the moon, earth, and sun. It appears softly as the sun peaks over the monolith discovered by the australopithecines, just as it will do when we see a similar shot of the TMA-1 on the moon. To be sure, the soft glare is a natural effect of the camera pointed into a bright source of light.

At the same time, much more pronounced camera glare occurs elsewhere in the film on a repeated basis, creating well-defined circular and geometric shapes. For example, an octagonal glare shape appears to the left of Poole's head while he is jogging in the centrifuge. Glare here would easily have been avoidable if that had been the desire; after all, there is no glare in the bulk of the centrifuge footage. It is not the necessary consequence of having to shoot into a bright light, as with some of the monolith shots.

The same could be said of the three pod missions (Bowman's, then Poole's, then Bowman's), each of which feature pronounced and repeated camera glare as the pod's lights turn in front of the camera. In fact, on Bowman's first venture, the pod rotates in the lower right of the screen with its lights creating angular red shapes on the upper left of the frame at the other side of the Discovery's satellite. The angular shapes move and evolve during the shot's progression.

Nowhere are these visual artifacts more apparent than when Dr. Floyd and his team visit the TMA-1 site, a place where the film is assaulted by a variety of camera glare. As they descend into the location, various lights on tripods feature soft glows that — as the shot cuts to

Glare draws attention to the fact that everything in the film has been documented. Every frame has been viewed at some past time, and the process of image capture has been preserved in the image itself.

a handheld image—create white vertical streaks and rectangular red shapes on the lens. By the time the group approaches the monolith, semicircular and rectangular-shaped glare appear. As an astronaut starts to take photographs, the lights on tripods create a mirror image of themselves with eight yellow rectangular glare shapes on the lower section of the frame. Similar glare appears on screen right when Floyd actually touches the monolith. The sequence ends with the monolith sounding its alarm; the roving handheld camera captures the astronauts' reaction, as well as examples of all of the diverse kinds of camera glare seen throughout the scene.

The capturing of various *2001* images has then — intentionally or not—created a record of itself. The glare draws attention to itself, and by extension to the processes of the cinema. It acts as a reminder that someone has had a vision, metaphorically and literally. Someone has scrutinized all of these images before. He/she/they decided what we could or could not see. They were watching the australopithecines, the Russians, the Americans, Heywood Floyd, Dave Bowman, Frank Poole, and HAL. This "he/she/they" is Kubrick, of course, as well as his filmmaking team, who are even able to watch whomever or whatever lurks Beyond the Infinite.

I don't suppose you have any idea what the damn thing is, huh?
— Dr. Heywood Floyd on the TMA-1 in *2001: A Space Odyssey*

It would be possible to view the Star Child in the film's final moments as an example of the returned gaze, as its turning body fixes its eyes upon us in the audience. "It looks at you," as Wheeler Winston Dixon might suggest.[48] A taboo broken, as it was so many times in earlier Hollywood filmmaking, from Charlie Chaplin to Oliver Hardy, from Buster Keaton to Bugs Bunny. The Star Child is watching us, just as Bowman's singular eye stared directly into the camera after coming through the Star Gate. Just as HAL's eye was always looking directly into the camera, gazing directly at us as he looked at everything else aboard the Discovery.

But even if it looks at us, we look at it. Kubrick avoided interpreting the film in interviews because he believed it would deny the audience "their own emotional reactions."[49] When Dr. Floyd asks Halvorsen if the scientist has any idea as to what the monolith is, Halvorsen responds, "I wish the hell we did." The lack of clear answers, the absence of fixed meaning allows, in Kubrick's words, "the audience to 'fill in' the visual experience themselves."[50]

In other words, perhaps HAL is a Panopticon *and* a cyclops. Indeed, HAL might just be whatever the spectator wishes to make of him; the same is true of the monoliths or the Star Child. The spectator can choose to stop watching; he or she can choose to turn off the DVD player or leave the theatre. The spectator watches and controls all, finally, existing outside the film, as the intermission of *2001* suggests must be so.

Despite all of the complicated layers of surveillance in *2001*, an individual audience member is the final arbiter of the gaze, a power recognized by Kubrick, even if it was not a kind of power he could control or bestow. After all, Bentham was never able to convince the British government to build the Panopticon. But his own preserved body is on permanent display at University College London for all to see.

9 Value, Violence, and Music Recognized: *A Clockwork Orange* as Musicology

Kate McQuiston

Even without the music, *A Clockwork Orange* (1971) proves more problematic, both for the scholar and moviegoer, than most of Kubrick's other films.[51] Kubrick renders Anthony Burgess's already-alienating satire in surreal extremes. The perceiver is forced to identify with Alex (Malcolm McDowell), who is both the protagonist for us and antagonist to other characters and in all cases an antihero, and to sympathize with his violent acts against others, then the violence that is done to him.[52] The film comes coated in the sound and sheen of science fiction, making the extreme events and emotions even more strange.

The complex nature of experiencing the film owes in part to its combination of mechanisms that alienate the perceiver and those that draw her closer, and owes also to graphic depictions of violence and the film's treatment of systematic dehumanization by the government. Alex is the pawn in the battle between the church and state for the soul, and the lens—or better yet, the eyes and ears—through which the perceiver must grapple with the film's larger moral dilemmas regarding free will, conformity, and public safety. One of the film's strongest messages is that people should be free to act upon free will, even if that entails violent crime, instead of being conditioned (robbed of free will) to be law-abiding, a message for which the film has been deemed by some to be dangerous.

Added to this particularly weighty topic and complex narrative situation is the film's music, carefully placed in the diegetic or nondiegetic realm, and dominated by excerpts from Beethoven's Ninth Symphony.[53] Kubrick deals with the themes of conditioning, recognition, and the malleability of meaning with music in the film, and makes the most explicit statements of his oeuvre regarding the experience of film spectatorship and the recognition of music in the scherzo sequence and the conditioning scene, discussed below. Finally, Beethoven's music is called upon in a number of scenes to point up the bumbling and ineffectual nature of the government. Irony plays a role in these scenes, though it can be located not only in the juxtapositions between the film and the music, but also within the history and text of the Ninth Symphony.[54] Unlike certain musical moments elsewhere in Kubrick's films, Beethoven's music does not, for the most part, lend itself to a moment-to-moment analysis vis-à-vis the film.[55] Rather, the problems and paradoxes of the Ninth Symphony provide considerable insight into the film's satirical elements. The choice of the Ninth is indispensable to the film as it acts not merely as a sounding board for the major themes of the story, but grapples with many of the same conflicting elements as Kubrick's narrative.[56]

Critical writing on *A Clockwork Orange* has tended to focus on ways in which the dialogue and visual elements contribute to perceivers' repulsion. Of course the music, containing Wendy Carlos's synthesized versions of classical pieces as well as orchestrally rendered ones, is mentioned, but rarely does the music factor into analyses of the film.[57] Kubrick's deployment of the soundtrack is one of the film's primary mechanisms in dragging the perceiver into the gears of *A Clockwork Orange*. The soundtrack provides much of the power to engage, by shrinking the apparent space between the perceiver and characters, so that the world of the story may invade a perceiver's most vulnerable psychological reaches. The range of Alex's power includes not just ingratiating voice-over narration, but initial eye contact with the spectator, and the ability to

The Warner Brothers soundtrack album to *A Clockwork Orange* (1971) preserves Alex's (Malcolm McDowell) unsettling eye contact with the spectator.

vocally and musically inhabit the diegetic and nondiegetic regions so as to collapse the specta-tor's sense of distance and safety from him.

The conditioning of the perceiver's responses, crucial to *A Clockwork Orange*, relies on the film's presentations and reprises of particular recognizable pieces of music. Both subtly and overtly, the soundtrack violates conventional boundaries between diegetic and nondiegetic sound to force the perceiver's emotional investment in the events and characters, and to create Kubrick's peculiar brand of violence. Where the film or a character takes an antagonistic stance with regard to the perceiver, the soundtrack, particularly through its alternate realms of diegetic and nondiegetic sound, articulates and determines the dynamics of that relationship.[58] When the permeability of the typically discrete diegetic and nondiegetic sound spaces has been estab-lished, the subject loses her ability to be a passive spectator to the narrative.

This essay closely analyzes selected scenes with music in *A Clockwork Orange* to reveal Kubrick's sensitivity to the mutability of musical value, and the recognition of music as alter-nately a cultivated pleasure and a liability. Recognition and familiarity are running threads in the discussion, particularly as they pertain to conditioning and to the nature of spectatorship. A second task is to bring the film into dialogue with specific formal and textual problems in musicology concerning the Ninth Symphony. This approach guides this analysis of the film, bringing to light new insights on the film, and pointing to a particular reading of the Ninth Symphony: namely, *A Clockwork Orange* as musicology.[59]

Promissory Notes from Rossini

Like *2001: A Space Odyssey*, *A Clockwork Orange* includes a significant amount of classical music, but the music in *2001* is almost exclusively nondiegetic. The scherzo and finale of Beethoven's Ninth Symphony are featured prominently in *A Clockwork Orange*, in both electronic versions realized by Wendy Carlos and produced by Rachel Elkind, and an orches-tral version from a Deutsche Grammophon recording.[60] Beethoven's music always appears within the diegesis. On the other hand, Kubrick uses parts of Rossini's overtures to *La gazza ladra* and *William Tell*, Elgar's Pomp and Circumstance Marches 1 and 4, and Rimsky-Korsakov's *Scheherazade* over the course of the film exclusively nondiegetically. Besides the Beethoven, the only other clearly diegetic pieces are some popular songs, like "I Want to Marry a Light-house Keeper," whose popularity was brief and only in association with the film, and "Singin' in the Rain" which is sung by Alex. Gene Kelly's recording of the song plays over the closing credits.

In relegating Rossini to the nondiegetic soundtrack — in other words, *our* realm — Kubrick increases the sense that Beethoven, on the other hand, belongs with and to Alex. We hear it through Alex's ears when he hears it, but we are not afforded any Beethoven by ourselves. This is in keeping with Kubrick's design which clearly demarcates Alex, and builds spectator asso-ciations between Alex's experiences (and our reflections upon Alex's experiences) and the music. It also conditions the audience to associate Beethoven with Alex, both during and long after watching the film. Herein lies one of the film's most effective, distinguishing, and memorable devices, whether one wishes to remember it or not. The perceiver will undoubtedly encounter Beethoven's music again, and remember the scenes in which it was used in *A Clockwork Orange*, as well as her emotional state at the time. None of the other violent films of this time feature music that would be as frequently encountered in the real world.[61] Further, Beethoven's music is not background; it belongs to and participates in Alex's story, and Alex is aware of it when-ever it plays. There is nothing "incidental" about it. The other classical music provides com-mentary on the diegesis from the nondiegetic soundtrack. Scenes with nondiegetic music are less viscerally engaging, and less potentially disturbing than those with diegetic music. Kubrick has clearly designed and organized the scenes this way.

Elgar's marches play in the prison scenes to stand for the supposed uprightness and nobility of the state; it is the musical embodiment of good posture. In this setting, the marches take on the odor of propaganda. Alex's outward cooperation and good cheer in the prison, while the music plays nondiegetically, creates an ironic effect. Alex is not at all cheerful about his incarceration, as we know from his voice-over narration.

Rossini's music, particularly in contrast to Beethoven's, communicates in an exaggerated, cartoonish language. Themes from Rossini's overtures are prominently featured in Warner Brothers cartoons, an association which is reinforced in the scene in *A Clockwork Orange* at the casino where the two gangs engage in a balletic brawl full of the extremely physical and destructive violence typical of Warner Brothers cartoons. The film thus associates Rossini with buffoonery, and Beethoven with (among other things) sophistication and sensitivity, reflecting the polarity of Kiesewetter's characterization of the 1830s as the "era of Beethoven and Rossini."[62] Though contemporaries, Rossini and Beethoven have been characterized as sensual and superficial, and learned and elevated, respectively.[63] As Dahlhaus puts it, "There was nothing to 'understand' about the magic that emanated from Rossini's music; the emotions that Beethoven's work engendered, however, were mingled with a challenge to decipher, in patient exertion, the meaning of what had taken place in the music."[64] In giving the audience the music of Rossini, and giving Beethoven to Alex, Kubrick reinforces the notion of Alex as a sophisticated, intelligent and powerful character.[65] This is a double-edged sword; if we are to consider ourselves sophisticated, intelligent or powerful as we watch this film, we must pay the price of identifying with Alex. Further, it makes us suspicious of other Beethoven fans.

Kubrick takes advantage of the gradual crescendi in Rossini's *La gazza ladra* overture to mirror the exponentially growing violence of Alex's gang's adventures. The music begins after they beat the vagrant, and continues through the gang fight in the casino and their terroristic driving on the roads leading into the country, all the way up to the gang's arrival at the writer's house. The music provides continuity as well as the effect of accumulation and end-directedness. While the light-hearted tone of the Rossini captures the gang's feelings about the night, the spectator's feelings (likely distress) are not acknowledged. Thus, there is no emotional negative space or pressure valve between the spectator and the diegesis. The diegesis is supersaturated with the story and inner states of Alex and his gang, pulling the viewer in.

A second important function of the opposition between the music of Beethoven and Rossini in the first third of the film is in foreshadowing Alex's fall from favor among his circle of friends that precipitates his capture by authorities. *La gazza ladra*, as a representative of Rossini's style, which supplanted Beethoven's popularity with audiences of his day, foretells the change in his friends' opinions of him. That Kubrick lets Rossini's crescendi unfold completely and arrive at explosive *fortissimo* sections, is a clear indication of culminating forces and consequences. While on the surface the triumph and bombast of the music reflects Alex's pleasure in violence, the presence of Rossini also signifies, as an opposing force to Beethoven, the subtext of changing popular opinion. This subtext is conveyed most strongly in the scene at the river when Alex assaults his friends to try to bring them under his control. The scene is shot in slow motion, but *La gazza ladra* plays in real time; the visuals and music are literally out of sync, signaling the larger discrepancy between Alex's assumed domination, and the decisive moment in spurring his gang's mutiny against him. The music continues into the next scene, shot at normal speed, in which Alex reprimands his friends for having questioned his authority. His friends' growing ferment and their reticence to forgive Alex for hurting them or to accept him as their leader is obvious. *La gazza ladra* continues to play up to the moment Dim hits Alex in the face with a bottle outside the Cat Lady's house, and flees with the other two gang members, leaving Alex to be arrested. The piece represents Alex's inevitable fall from popularity, a crucial point in the plot of *A Clockwork Orange*. Thus, *La gazza ladra* serves its purpose and is not heard again. Since we have been influenced to identify so closely with Alex, this clue to his imminent demise fosters our ambivalence; now we may feel some sympathy at odds with our repulsion.

Music as an Artifact from the Real World: Violence and Recognizable Music

Films exhibiting a high degree of verisimilitude can be easier for a spectator to relate to, find believable, and engage with emotionally. Familiar settings and items can help convince the viewer to accept the characters and their interactions in these settings as, in some way, real.[66] In the absence of familiar settings and objects in *A Clockwork Orange*, the familiarity of the music becomes much more pronounced, and draws the perceiver's attention to the sonic register, and to the music itself.

It is remarkable that some of the most memorable and striking violent scenes in recent films have featured preexisting music which if not familiar when the film was released, becomes familiar because of the film. Most notably, Barber's *Adagio for Strings* was widely known and extremely popular after accompanying war scenes in *Platoon*, and Wagner's "Ride of the Valkyries" was showcased in scenes of helicopter attacks on Vietnam in *Apocalypse Now*, leaving a long-remembered impression on popular imagination that cemented the music to the film's particular images. A piece's accumulated meanings will include these associations, as well as whatever meanings they may have had at the time of their premieres and subsequent lives in the concert hall and elsewhere. In viewing these films, we are conditioned so that we recall them when we hear the music they used, in other contexts.

The visual and verbal styles of *A Clockwork Orange* are meant to be alienating and off-putting. Beethoven's music and "Singin' in the Rain" are the only familiar pieces of music — indeed, the only completely familiar objects of any kind — in the diegesis. One may think that the familiarity of music might give the spectator something comforting to hold on to, but the music is defamiliarized in the setting of a futuristic dystopia, and though Alex hears sublimity in Beethoven's music, it is also a violent force in his view. Meanwhile, "Singin' in the Rain" is used to accompany one of the most violent and disturbing scenes in the film (at the writer's house), briefly in the second scene at the writer's house, and for the end credits. The song's presence at the end of the film reminds us of the violence we have seen, and of the unpleasant conditioning we have undergone.

Alex as a Fan of Beethoven, and the Scherzo Sequence and Spectatorship

Alex's violence is extreme, and inseparable from his rapture, and Beethoven is an inspiration to his violent imaginings. Alex's experience of Beethoven is conveyed to the spectator via his voice-over narration, and the glimpses we are afforded of images from his violent imagination while he listens to the scherzo of the Ninth, and at the very end of the film when the finale blasts from huge speakers, accompanying a sexual fantasy. It may already be difficult to bear Alex's prurient enjoyment of Beethoven, but even more distressing, his interpretation of Beethoven is unfalsifiable and not necessarily wrong.

Alex's persona is largely theatrical. He presents himself in the meticulous uniform of his gang, and emphasizes his right eye with false eyelashes. His violent acts are presented as a show. His love of Beethoven, however, is not something he makes a point to display, which renders it more sincere as well as personal. Alex's sensitivity as a listener comes across in his poetic descriptions of music, discussed below. His awareness of Beethoven as a classical composer sets him apart from other characters in the film. He may be anachronistic in his love for Beethoven, and perhaps also in his familiarity with "Singin' in the Rain," but he otherwise belongs to his contemporary world as evidenced in his speech and the décor of his bedroom. As a fan of these pieces of music from other times, he is a cultural time traveler, another subtle indicator of his power in the narrative and his superiority over other characters. In the milk bar at the end of the opening series of violent adventures, a woman at the bar sings Beethoven's "Ode to Joy" (the stanza beginning, "Freude, schöner Götterfunken") from a score (for the text of the "Ode to Joy," see appendix). Alex refers to the woman and her friends as "sophistos." The connotation of sophisticated and elevated taste that Beethoven brings is borne out in the Beethoven's Fifth doorbell chime at the home of the writer and his wife. In his voice-over narration, Alex responds to the woman singing at the bar: "And it was like, for a moment, oh my brothers, some great bird had flown into the milk bar, and I felt all the malenky little hairs on my plot standing endwise. And the shivers crawling up like slow malenky lizards and then down again. 'Cause I knew what she sang. It was a bit from the glorious Ninth by Ludwig van." While Alex's response is one of inner rapture, Dim makes a vulgar sound of protest. Alex hits Dim with his cane to silence him. Dim's response to the music may be motivated by a lack of recognition or appreciation, or perhaps Dim is still in the antagonistic mood set by the earlier activities of the night. But the fact remains that the music does not move Dim; it does move Alex.

Music provides sexual invitation and accompaniment: Alex (Malcom McDowell) propositions two women (Gillian Hills, left, and Barbara Scott) in the record shop.

When Alex gets home later the same night, he puts on a tape of the scherzo from Beethoven's Ninth Symphony while he masturbates and remarks in his voice-over narration, "Oh bliss. Bliss and heaven. Oh it was gorgeousness and gorgeosity made flesh. It was like a bird of rarest spun heaven mettle. Or like silvery wine floating in a spaceship, gravity all nonsense now. As I slushied, I knew such lovely pictures." Call this scene the scherzo sequence.

Much early criticism of the symphony relied on metaphors and imagery. Friedrich Kanne describes particular figures in the winds in the third movement as "melting in graceful ecstasy like an echo."[67] A critic in the *Theater-Zeitung* also wrote metaphorically of the third movement, saying Beethoven "leads us again into the deepest caverns of feeling, where the glittering gold of the soul glows in its purity; brightly shining gems give rise to thoughts of noble deeds in the future."[68]

Despite the fact that these extracts from earlier critics of Beethoven pertain to the third movement, and Alex's responses are to the second and fourth movements of the symphony and contain some of Burgess's concocted words, the styles of expression are remarkably similar. This casts Alex as a kindred spirit to earlier listeners of the Ninth, and as an authentic listener who doesn't just like Beethoven, but who "gets" Beethoven. His appreciation of Beethoven is expressed in nuanced and fanciful descriptions similar to Kanne's, further marking him as a sort of cultural authority. The fact that Alex seems, at least in part, to "get it right" when it comes to Beethoven, makes the shock of his violent fantasies even more repulsive. And yet, Alex's verbal descriptions are so eloquent and his emotional reaction so clearly profound that the spectator must face the unpleasant prospect that there might also be some kind of truth in his violent interpretations.

As Alex listens and fantasizes in the scherzo sequence, the camera begins to cut to the rhythm of the music in measure 57, when the timpani come in for twenty-one bars, on each downbeat. Alex is looking at the four identical figurines of Christ he has on his shelf. The cutting from one shot of them to another, at various angles and showing different parts of the figurines in close-up, all in time with the scherzo, gives the figurines the appearance of doing a sort of can-can. In this crude animation, Kubrick makes the most explicit statement regarding the nature of film spectatorship and the role of music of his entire oeuvre. He focuses our attention on the medium more than on the content of the film, as far as this distinction can be made. The sequence suggests the apparent power of the cinematic apparatus to combine music and images in ways that make them seem to belong together, but he shows the even greater power of the spectator to read meaning into these coincidences. Alex enacts the active, imaginative role of the spectator while listening and visualizing that we all assume as film spectators. Alex's masturbation is a symbol of our own manipulations of image and sound to create meaning for ourselves out of the available images and sounds, and what we know and think about them. Kubrick, who prizes subjectivity, thus displays the authority of the spectator regarding the film text. This resonates with his commentary regarding *2001: A Space Odyssey*, that clearly applies as well to *A Clockwork Orange*:

> I intended the film to be an intensely subjective experience that reaches the viewer at an inner level of consciousness, just as music does; to "explain" a Beethoven symphony would be to emasculate it by erecting an artificial barrier between conception and appreciation. You're free to speculate as you wish about the philosophical and allegorical meaning of the film — and such speculation is one indication that it has succeeded in gripping the audience at a deep level.[69]

The pleasure of constructing meaning with image and sound, a pleasure that is apparently sensual rather than intellectual, works against Alex during the Ludovico treatment.

For the Ludovico treatment, which Alex agrees to undergo in the middle portion of the film, a scientist matter-of-factly clamps Alex's eyes open and prepares him for viewing, much as Alex was at ease when he bound the writer and forced him to witness the rape of his wife.

Alex is made to watch a Nazi propaganda film, apparently featuring a synthesized version of the Turkish march passage from the finale of the Ninth Symphony.[70] He objects to the use of Beethoven's music in this context, protesting to the experimenters, "It's a sin — using Ludwig van like that! He did no harm to anyone! Beethoven just wrote music!" Nurse Feeley seems surprised that Alex would even notice "the background score," as she calls it, let alone that he recognizes the composer. It seems that she does not have his sensitivity to music, or taste for it. The head scientist says to the nurse, "It can't be helped. It's the punishment element, perhaps. The governor ought to be pleased," and, "I'm sorry, Alex. This is for your own good."

"It's not fair I should feel ill when I hear lovely, lovely Ludwig van," Alex shouts, to which the scientist replies, "You must take your chance, boy. The choice has been all yours."

Alex's reactions and protests reflect and give voice to our own, as spectators of *A Clockwork Orange*. Kubrick reminds us in this scene that we have chosen to see *A Clockwork Orange* of our own free will, and that in doing so, have taken the chance of being conditioned, and subject to extremely unpleasant feelings. It is likely that, in earlier parts of the film, the spectator has felt injustice concerning Kubrick's (via Alex's) use of music in perverse, violent scenes. Alex cries out against that injustice in this scene. Alex has been unaware that he's participated in conditioning the spectator of *A Clockwork Orange*; this absolves him somewhat, but Kubrick remains completely responsible. Kubrick shows he holds the puppet strings for us, as for his characters.

Alex is in a tortured state when he screams in protest during the Nazi propaganda film, and might say anything to try to convince the scientists to turn it off. It is possible, however, that he truly believes Beethoven "just wrote music." In his earlier voice-over narration, he observes beauty and experiences something like the sublime when he listens to Beethoven's music, and it is the inspiration for Alex's violent fantasies. Nothing indicates, however, that he believes Beethoven's music is a locus of violence or that he even *thinks* about Beethoven; rather, Beethoven is a means to an end. In his voice-over narration in the scene where Alex disciplines the members of his gang, he speaks of a difference between thought and inspiration, the latter of which he associates with music in general: "As we walked along the flatblock marina, I was calm on the outside but thinking all the time.... But suddenly I viddied that thinking is for the gloopy ones and that the oomny ones used, like, inspiration and what Bog sends. For now it was lovely music that came to my aid."[71]

In referring to Beethoven's music as "background," the nurse also seems to underestimate its potential to effect Alex's (or any viewer's) perception of the Nazi film. Kubrick has already convinced the viewers of *A Clockwork Orange* that music is extremely influential in film perception, and enjoys a moment of irony here in showing the doctors to be much less sensitive than they think they are. Alex is aesthetically sophisticated while the doctors are not. In fact, there is no other significant character in the film who shares Alex's taste in music. The only other character in the film with strong aesthetic leanings of any kind is the Cat Lady whose house is full of erotic art. Her taste and Alex's face off in their grappling in the most literal way when she arms herself with a bust of Beethoven, he with her prized sculpture of a phallus.

Conditioning, Hitler, and Beethoven

The story takes as its central theme the question of whether Alex's conditioning is an ethical solution to the violent behavior he chooses of his free will. The narrative plays out in an unlikely sequence of reciprocal events that nevertheless brings Alex full circle. The conditioning plays out on two levels in the film — on Alex, but also on the viewer; Anthony Burgess explains, "As the novel is about brainwashing, so it is also a little device of brainwashing in itself — or at least a carefully programmed series of lessons on the Russian language. You learn the words without noticing, and a glossary is unnecessary."[72] By process of assimilation, the reader of the novel, or viewer of the film, begins to understand Nadsat, the Russian-based futuristic slang of Alex and his friends, and thus experiences the effects of conditioning. The film, however, in marrying specific, striking images to pieces of music, becomes a much more powerful display and device of brainwashing than the novel could ever hope to be.

Alex's experience of conditioning during the Ludovico treatment is an exaggerated microcosm of our own experience upon viewing *A Clockwork Orange*. Richard Allen detects parallels between Alex's and the spectator's experience regarding the changes between the first and second portions of the film:

> As Alex enters prison, the pace of events radically slows down, the color becomes a uniform institutional gray-blue, the music stops, and we become aware of the fact that what we are watching is only a film. It is as if the spectator is punished for succumbing to the sensory lure of those opening scenes in a manner that parallels the way that Alex is punished for the activities those scenes depict.[73]

Though it is unlikely that the spectator of *A Clockwork Orange*, or any other film, is ever really unaware that she is watching a film, Allen is right to point to this transition as one that attracts the spectator's attention to the artifice and medium of film, and away from its content. This part of the film shows Kubrick's conception of violence to have less to do with graphically depicted physical aggression and harm than with unexpected violations of associations one has with things one holds dear. The films Alex is forced to watch include graphically violent ones, but the one which distresses Alex the most is significantly low in what could be considered graphically violent content.

Alex is made to watch a Nazi propaganda film that features the entire *alla marcia* section from the finale of the Ninth Symphony (mm. 331–594).[74] The film at first *seems* to be Leni Riefenstahl's *Triumph of the Will* (1934), however, Riefenstahl's film contains neither violence nor music by Beethoven. Though the pairing of Nazi films and the Ninth Symphony, as Alex sees it, has no basis in fact, the appearance of the march portion of the fourth movement does have historical resonance with remarks made by Alfred Rosenberg, who assumed leadership of the Nazi party in 1923 while Hitler was in prison. In the *Völkischer Beobachter*, he cast Hitler as the hero described in the march's text, "Joyful, like a hero to victory!"[75] Indeed, the line appears in the text of the *alla marcia* portion of the Ninth accompanying the film Alex watches, as heard through the phase vocoder of Wendy Carlos and Rachel Elkind:[76]

> Froh, wie seine Sonnen fliegen
> Durch des Himmels prächt'gen Plan,
> Laufet, Brüder, eure Bahn,
> Freudig, wie ein Held zum Siegen!
>
> Joyful as the suns that soar
> Across the splendor of Heaven's plain,
> Brothers, run your course,
> Joyfully, like a hero towards Victory!

That the text is about the transformation from brother to hero could make us hopeful that Alex's suffering won't be for nothing, but could result in better circumstances, enlightenment, or reward that heroes often attain. But this is not the case. As it stands, the heroism in the music is ironic in contrast to Alex's desperate begging that the film be turned off.

That commentators often erroneously identify the film Alex watches as *Triumph of the Will*, or fail to question the presence of the Ninth in the film reflects the extent to which the association of Beethoven with the Nazi party is ingrained in popular imagination and even scholarly thinking.[77] And, playing into Kubrick's treatment of the conditioned response, the unquestioned status of Beethoven in the Nazi film displays a correlate to Richard Allen's claim that photographs carry a presumption of truth; stock footage, or film meant to look like documentary footage is taken at face value.[78] It assumes the guise of the factual, and does not invite speculation that it could be fictitious. Perhaps this is why no one has analyzed nor attempted to identify the Nazi film Alex is viewing.[79]

The Nazi film Alex sees resembles a relatively innocuous newsreel, in its black-and-white, documentary style, in stark contrast with the images to which Kubrick has subjected us so far. The crimes signified by the Nazi film are unquestionably heinous, yet the crimes themselves are not depicted in these scenes. There are brief scenes of soldiers breaking doors down, and planes dropping bombs, but the bombs are not shown detonating, nor are any consequences seen, such as human injury or death.

This makes one of Kubrick's strongest statements about the relationship of graphic content and effects on spectator perception. Graphic violence is not necessarily the strongest factor in spectator distress; rather, the predisposition of the spectator, and the subjective associations she carries with her regarding recognizable components of the film will be the greatest factors. [80] Additionally, as Randy Rasmussen points out, "in the context of Ludovico conditioning, that combination [of the Nazi film with Beethoven's Ninth] is a threat to Alex's very capacity for creative association."[81] This corroborates Richard Allen's claims that the spectator knows what he sees is only a film and the act of spectatorship entails participation in creating the illusion.[82] In this moment in *A Clockwork Orange*, Alex is stripped of his capacity to actively create illusion, and forced into horrifying, dehumanizing, passive receptivity.

In this scene, it is the incongruity, in Alex's view, of pairing Beethoven's music with this film that creates a deeply disturbing disconnect, an extreme cognitive dissonance. While Kubrick shows no piece of music or visual image to have any inherent moral content or value, their juxtapositions and conditioning effects on the viewer are the true locus of violence. Kubrick points to the media (combinations of images and sounds) as the real weapons that rob the spectator of a mechanism to cope with the violence in *A Clockwork Orange*: one no longer has the ability to think, "This is only a movie; it can't hurt me." The acknowledgement of this truth *within A Clockwork Orange* sets it apart from other violent films. Where self-consciousness typically distances a spectator from a film, it does the opposite here, and there is no comfort, safety, or immunity for the viewer.

By the time Alex begins his treatment, the spectator has likely built up feelings of fear, hatred, perhaps sympathy for Alex. Yet, when Alex is strapped into the chair and forced to watch the violent films, the spectator is likely to identify strongly with him, since this is a clear analogue to the spectator's own experience watching the barrage of violence in *A Clockwork Orange* up to this point. So, unexpectedly, and perhaps unconsciously, the spectator identifies and sympathizes with Alex during these scenes.

When revenge is later taken upon Alex, such as at the writer's house, the spectator cannot completely wish him harm, even if it would mean evening the score, and even though the structures of the scenes suggest a symmetrical, antecedent-consequent relationship. According to W. James Potter's studies, the one motive that consistently leads to the strongest viewer aggression is vengeance.[83] The desire to see Alex get his just desserts, however, is directly at odds with the sympathy we have been encouraged to feel for him while he was undergoing the Ludovico treatment. Potter goes on, "When a character with whom viewers empathize is then the target of violence, viewers experience an increased feeling of fear."[84] Fear is a constant during *A Clockwork Orange*, though its form changes. The spectator shifts from having a fear *of* Alex to a fear *for* Alex. This is a much more psychologically challenging and complex alternative to a storyline that would simply punish Alex without having the center portion of the film, wherein Alex's experience so strongly reflects the spectator's own. Kubrick accomplishes the unthinkable in encouraging sympathy for Alex. The spectator is ever implicated in the action, and constantly has reason to be conflicted about the violence being done (whether to the spectator herself, Alex, or someone else), as well as her beliefs and feelings about Beethoven. Relationships between judgment and emotion are, for the spectator of *A Clockwork Orange*, extremely complex.

Binary paradigms exist that tie a positive judgment of the protagonist to an empathetic response and negative judgment of the protagonist to a sympathetic response, some going as far as to say that the audience delights when the negatively judged protagonist feels terror.[85] But, in Richard Allen's more flexible and elegant formulation, "character identification runs on a continuum from detachment to sympathy to empathy that is defined by the role that reason plays relative to the emotions," better describes the dynamic play of relationships among characters, and between Alex and the spectator in *A Clockwork Orange*.[86] That the spectator's judgment of Alex is likely to fluctuate depending on Alex's relationships with other characters affects changes in point of view and emotional response in the spectator. Thus, Kubrick's perpetual manipulation of the Alex-spectator relationship takes the spectator on an exhausting, relentless, emotional rollercoaster ride.

In the third part of the film, Alex returns to the writer's house, and both Alex and the writer suffer because of associations they have with music. First, the writer shudders and is utterly horrified when he hears Alex singing "Singin' in the Rain" again. He relives the horror of the night of the assault. Alex is then tortured with the scherzo from the Ninth Symphony.

Kubrick puts a final, fine point on conditioning, as idea and experience, when Gene Kelly's version of "Singin' in the Rain" plays over the final credits. With this, the spectator is nudged back into the real world. Beethoven's music, though it also belongs to the real world, has taken on the flavor of Alex's world, and by the film's end, the spectator accepts it as such. To hear Gene Kelly singing this song, however, is a new experience. Of course, it has not been played in the film yet, and now the song does not sound the same to the spectator as it did before watching the film. There can be no doubt in the spectator's mind that she has been conditioned, as evidenced by her re-cognition of the song. It is at the same time a foreboding sign that we are now prone, in our real lives in the real world, to having unpleasant associations based on *A Clockwork Orange* when we encounter parts of Beethoven's Ninth of "Singin' in the Rain," once a light-hearted tune about love from vaudeville shows and musicals.

Interpretations of The Ninth and What They Mean for *A Clockwork Orange*

James Webster summarizes predominant trends in scholarship on the finale of the Ninth Symphony, remarking that the various concurrent "domains" of the Ninth, including "tonality, musical material, rhythm, dynamics, instrumentation, rhetoric, 'narrative' design, and so forth" necessitate a multivalent analysis.[87] He notes that the fact that the Ninth is a work with sung text already demands this kind of approach. Webster goes on to show that, time and again, scholars have not been able to neatly or completely account for or interpret the events of the finale of the Ninth by means of any one principle of organization. Because the movement cannot be described in terms of any one form, or because it is destined to imperfect description as one of a number of possible forms (variations, concerto, symphonic, sonata-allegro, rondo), Webster holds that "'the' form of the finale of Beethoven's Ninth does not exist."[88] Webster's statement is not as bleak as it may seem, however, for he goes on to suggest that if one approaches the finale free of formal expectations, one will no longer feel compelled to sweep under the rug aspects of the movement for which a particular form does not account, something that has troubled scholarship on the piece. Nicholas Cook echoes Webster's observations on the Ninth: "Every interpretation of it is contradicted by the work itself."[89] These frustrated attempts in the literature speak of a persistent desire, nearly an anxiety, on the part of scholars to safeguard the venerated status of the Ninth Symphony in the canon by situating it in the formal tradition of its classical predecessors. Michael Tusa offers an attractive refinement on the view of the finale as a four-movement symphony in which he considers the implications of each of the formal trajectories in the movement with regard to meaning, and views the movement as both a résumé of and corrective to the first three movements.[90]

Scholars who seek a program for the Ninth Symphony are stuck with the indeterminacy of the instrumental nature of the first three movements, though commonly seize upon the notions of fraternal love, struggle to better circumstances, joy, and freedom, the subjects of Schiller's text as excerpted by Beethoven in the final movement.[91] Beethoven set to music roughly one third of Schiller's Ode to Joy of 1803, a less politically revolutionary version than the one of 1785. Along with lines exalting drinking, there are a number of other lines that Beethoven did not elect to set which would have raised ideological problems particularly relevant to *A Clockwork Orange*.

Beethoven left out "All the good and all the wicked/ Will tread her rose-strewn path," which implies equality among people in spite of differing moral dispositions, though he does allow that the "Just and unjust/ Alike taste of [Nature's] gift." Missing also is the line, "Every sinner will be forgiven,/ And hell shall cease to be!"[92] Beethoven's vision of the Ode does not make any promises of forgiveness or even of brotherhood.[93] So too are the government officials in *A Clockwork Orange* conspicuously vague on their plans to deal with matters of equality, fair treatment, and what consequences come to criminals. It is as likely that they will return to conventional methods of punishment (now that the effects of the Ludovico treatment have put them in a poor light with the public) as it is that Alex will revert to his violent habits. Alex's dystopic hell is likely to prevail.

Beethoven does not include any text that describes joy achieved through suffering or struggle. Instead he offers what Esteban Buch calls "the Utopia of a Joy where Sorrow had left no trace."[94] The absence of struggle also makes an interpretation of the Ninth as heroic a difficult task. Scott Burnham summarizes the nature of the heroic in Beethoven as "the necessity of struggle and eventual triumph as an index of man's greatness."[95] In such cases, the implication is that violence, as a symptom or result of struggle, is an acceptable means to an end, but this does not describe Alex.

In *A Clockwork Orange*, we see Alex suffer and eventually his free will is restored; however, he never *struggles* with moral issues, or with himself, and the cause of his restoration is not made clear. Has the government done something to condition him back to his original state? Has the shock of Alex's suicide attempt restored him? Unlike a typical hero, Alex has not earned or fought for his recovery. He has merely been victimized and punished, and shows no evidence of benefiting from his trials. Alex is shown to be at his most vulnerable during the conditioning scene, where his physical immobilization symbolizes his inability to shut out the sound of Beethoven's music, and the sight of violence, both things against which he is being conditioned. His imprisonment in the straitjacket and clamps also stands for the government's control over him. Ironically, Alex's weakest moment is accompanied by the *alla marcia* in which the symphony's only reference to a hero is made. On a more superficial level, there is irony in the combination of unpleasant sensations and the music of Beethoven, which Alex loves, as noted above. The sung text provides another source of irony as it juxtaposes the helpless, desperate Alex with words about a hero flying to victory. Rey Longyear detects ironic juxtapositions in this portion of the Ninth, comparing it with irony in the plays of Ludwig Tieck, which present "the ultraserious with the ironic or even with slapstick comedy, the poetic with the prosaic, and commonplace reality with flights of imagination."[96] Nicholas Cook suggests the juxtaposition of the ultraserious and slapstick is best illustrated in bar 331 of the finale (Turkish march): "where the majestic tones of 'And the seraphs stand with God' are punctuated by the 'absurd grunts' (some commentators have called them farts) of the bassoon and bass drum."[97] Cook notes another opposition represented by the march, noting its appearance as "the first time key structure begins to play an important role" in the movement.[98] The move from the initial D major of the Ode, to B-flat major in the march, reflects the move from D minor to B-flat major in the sonata-form first movement. The significance Cook notes of the key shift falls into line with Alex's moment of greatest remove from his original state, a moment which occurs at about the halfway point of the film, just as the march appears at roughly the halfway point in the finale. The keys of the parts of the finale that appear in the film can be readily mapped onto Alex's original state (the Ode to Joy in D major heard in the milkbar, the first Beethoven in the film), his departure (the march in B-flat major), and his return (the coda, in D major). The contrast of styles between the Ode melody as it first is sung by the woman in the bar, and then as the electronic march provides an additional register of contrast. The question of whether this telegraphic presence of the Ninth suggests sonata form is irrelevant; Kubrick uses these selected moments in his drama to signal states of relative rest and unrest.

It may be difficult for commentators on the Ninth to accept that the most memorable, centrally-located event of the last movement of this high-art symphony embodies irony. The tone of the march undermines the seriousness of other sections in the movement. In an eerily similar way, the doctors' indifference to Alex's helplessness and anguish in the conditioning scene (in which no physical harm is done to him), is reflected in the cheerfully oblivious music.

As Alex fantasizes at the very end of the film, we realize he has forgotten his suffering, echoing Buch's description of the joyful utopia, amnesic about its difficult times. Alex will once again use his free will to harm others. The portrayal of Beethoven as a representative of the heroic has been perverted and the interpretation of the Ninth as heroic becomes suspect as far as the film is concerned.

Ideas in the Ninth at issue explicitly or implicitly in *A Clockwork Orange* include brotherhood, joy, and freedom. Pressed into a fraternal relationship with Alex through his voice-over narration, in which he calls the spectators "brothers," the spectator is not free. In other words, brotherhood with Alex comes at the expense of freedom. Further, the spectator does not have the freedom to choose to view the story from a perspective other than Alex's. As such, Alex's intense point of view presents an extremely limiting viewing predicament for the spectator compared to most narrative films in which the spectator takes a more omniscient, distanced point of view. Kubrick's demands on the spectator resonate with Burnham's characterization of Beethoven's heroic style: "There is a visceral element immediately perceptible in this music, a disturbing, invasive, and ultimately compelling interaction with the listener."[99] Kubrick's film makes us ask some rather ugly questions in connection with the idea that "All men become brothers." He suggests this alliance may not in reality be desirable. Would we really want to be brothers with *all* men? Cook's assessment of listeners' experiences with the Ninth, "Each listener ... had to find his or her own way in. Instead of offering ready-made meanings, the Ninth Symphony demanded that the listener participate in the creation of meaning," also resonates particularly strongly with Kubrick's demands on the spectator.[100]

Esteban Buch astutely observes a paradox in the Ode to Joy between the unity and uniformity implied in the line, "All men become brothers," one of the most famous lines in the Ode, and the notion of true individual freedom.[101] Schiller's text does not allow for individuality under the banner of brotherhood. This very paradox is the essence of the greatest moral issues of *A Clockwork Orange* which, like Beethoven's Symphony with Schiller's text, does not offer any satisfying answers.[102] He notes another paradox in instances in which the Ninth has been adopted by the government, in other words used as state music. But insofar as the Ninth can be used as state music, Buch notes it is "hailed as a glorification of human freedom in which any trace of the state is, by definition, absent."[103]

Alex clearly has the capacity to experience moments of elation, violent and misanthropic though they may be, prompting reflection on the nature of joy, and its relation to freedom and fraternal love. Alex shows no evidence of having moral principles or life plans. He is unchecked by the law as he carries out his crimes in the first part of the film, up to the moment of his arrest, and he lacks any sense of guilt in connection with them. His incarceration is the result of his attempts to enforce fraternity among his friends under his leadership, a situation which clearly spells out the paradox of a leader among men who are supposedly brothers and, by extension, equals.

Some interpretations of the Ninth Symphony take on the odor of self-delusion. Consider Basil Deane's assessment of the symphony as "reaffirmation of youthful idealism which remained unshaken by thirty disillusioning years," or Maynard Solomon's evocation of a dream: "The Ode to Joy revives the naïve dream of benevolent ... kings and princes, presiding over a harmony of national and class interests during a moment of shared beliefs in progress, fraternity, and social justice."[104] Underlying these formulations is the sense that the Ninth Symphony, as much as it has been adopted as a symbol of joy, freedom and utopia, does not explain how such ideals can or will be attained, and makes no mention of suffering, and no mention of means, aside from "magic power."[105] Dreams are not concerned with the pragmatic means of attaining ideals, just with the ideals themselves. Beethoven's vision is not as explicitly ameliorative, as human or as healthy as Schiller's. Beethoven's silence on matters of attaining the ideal state described in the text of the Ninth contributes to its promiscuity.

Thus, the Ninth can be a stamp of approval on tactics in which the ends are believed to justify the means, such as those of the Nazi regime.[106] Kubrick capitalizes upon this gap in the Ninth Symphony to insert his satiric message about the blundering government that must rescind its plans for a crime free state because of Alex's love of Beethoven. Superficially then, the Ninth seems tailor-made for occasions of government cover-up such as the one at the end of *A Clockwork Orange*, but at the same time it conveys the ring of unresolved problems and empty reassurance.

Endings and Conclusions:
A Clockwork Orange as Musicology

The presence of the portion of the coda (from measure 851 in the score) during the final scene of *A Clockwork Orange* suggests a reading of the coda as ineffectual. The government blares the symphony through behemoth speakers, ironically underlining their failure to make Alex part of a law-abiding brotherhood. Just as Alex's release back into society does not satisfy problems posed by *A Clockwork Orange*, the ending of the Ninth Symphony does not help in solving *its* problems. The end of the film invites ambivalence about Alex's restoration to his original state, finely pointed by the foregrounded presence of the final bars of the Ninth Symphony; the film's most apparently triumphant music comes with our knowledge that Alex will commit violent acts. Alex tells us he is "cured" but does not ever say that he is "free." The ideals of freedom and especially the natural championed in Beethoven's Ninth are myths beyond Alex's reach, and beyond the reach of all the characters of the film.[107] The spectator is left with a grim predicament: after all that has happened, Alex is neither a reformed criminal, nor is he living in the utopia described by Schiller's text.

Just as the text of the symphony's finale represents unsolved problems, so too does its form. The endings of both the film (Alex's recovery and apparent alliance with the government) and the symphony (the part of the coda in the film, from m. 851 to the end) exhibit certain superficial traits that signal conventional endings for their respective forms, and yet these endings fall short. That Solomon characterizes patterns in the Ninth as having "the shape of quests" rather than, say, the "substance" or "content" of quests implies a certain emptiness, indeterminacy, and failure to qualify as a real quest.[108] Gestures of resolution (handshakes, promises, the celebratory glittering flashbulbs of press cameras and conciliatory gifts in the film; a climactic aggregation of the instrumental and vocal forces of the Ninth, crescendo and accelerando and a final cadence with the sonic quality of an exclamation mark in the symphony) rally forth, in spite of unanswered questions. Both endings seem perfunctory and ironic for being such grand spectacles.

The final lines of text of the finale, advising us, "Seek [your Creator] in the heavens!/ Above the stars must He dwell," does not go very far as practical advice on dealing with the unsolved (and unsolvable?) dilemma of criminals in society. Examples of the problems presented over the course of the symphony, the resolution of which we may hope for in the coda of the final movement, include the juxtaposition of styles in the finale, the music's resistance to formal description, the meaning of the sung text, and whether or not the variants of the Ode to Joy melody chart progress such as might be described by a heroic interpretation. The nature of the Ode to Joy variants perhaps causes the greatest problem, as evidenced in critical commentary.

Intertwined threads in criticism on the Ninth include the loss of effect in light of the seeming incoherence of the Ode to Joy variants, and the final movement's failure to unite musically incongruous elements.[109] The resolution of these problems is further complicated by the paradoxes and unsolved dilemmas in the sung text. These questions point to another impending dilemma: if the nature of the problems of the finale cannot be determined, how can we begin to asses the function, let alone the success, of the coda? It seems that the music is either oblivious to the practical difficulties of attaining the ideal state its text describes, or it is helpless to offer answers, or it knows answers but does not offer them for fear of being silenced on counts of subversion or revolt. The coda throws up its hands, helpless to make good on its promise of a free, unified utopia in, as Fanny Mendelssohn put it, "falling from its height into the opposite extreme — into burlesque."[110] Insofar as the end of the film concludes in a similar state, it corroborates this interpretation. However, the film acknowledges that in having freedom, Alex will be at odds with the government. All men are not brothers, though as representatives of men, Alex and the prime minister are pretending to be brothers, with their disingenuous handshake.

The film also supports an interpretation of the coda as amnesic with regard to the preceding parts of the movement. Its acceleration and crescendi do not suggest to me reveling in a free or joyous state, rather, particularly in light of the film, the frantic, chaotic state of a flagging performer who beats a hasty retreat off the stage. Doubtless, Alex and the prime minister find their moment of forced alliance a source of intense anxiety and repulsion. In light of Kubrick's film, in which Alex makes motions of undergoing a transformation to a new state, it is possible to see the transformation of the Ode melody as fruitless, visiting once more the familiar Kubrick trope of the fate that cannot be avoided.

Not only do Beethoven and the Ninth carry considerable accumulation of associations, but many responses to Beethoven's Ninth are cast in emotional, personal terms, even when in a critical or scholarly context. Further, many responses to the symphony from its premiere to the present identify a dynamic, violent force issuing from the piece, sometimes heard as Beethoven's voice or intent. The object of the violent force is variously the listener, musical conventions of the past, or Beethoven's own demons.

The earliest writings on the symphony's power describe the piece as "terrifying" and "fiery," and containing a "quality of antagonism" that captured Beethoven's own struggles.[111] A critic for London's *Harmonicon* wrote, "A fanatical spirit is raging among a certain party of German amateurs, with a violence that tramples down reason, that treats the works of Haydn and Mozart as things gone by, and allows no merit but to noise, puerility, and extravagance."[112] Whether Beethoven is a praiseworthy liberator of music from old, constricting styles, or he is a violent destroyer of those styles is in the ear of the beholder. Beethoven's symphony and Kubrick's film raise the same kinds of questions about the effects of a purportedly liberating cause. An observation on Beethoven which also readily describes Kubrick's film comes from Maynard Solomon: "Beethoven's modernist contribution, then, was to symbolize extreme states by means of a host of new musical images and image clusters that we may collectively designate as authentic characteristic styles, prototypical styles which have yet to be named, let alone fully analyzed."[113]

Beethoven Forum's focus on Beethoven's music in films confirms the need to consider Beethoven reception history in this context, and it shows that in films as elsewhere, matters of the character and meaning of Beethoven's music, as well as Beethoven's identity are far from absolute or settled.[114] The tropes running throughout the *Beethoven Forum* articles broadly include political interpretations, gendered or sexual readings of his music, the problem of styles in the Ninth Symphony and the phenomenon of its unending recontextualization. These topics can become more sharply pointed with the cues provided in the narrative, verbal and visual registers of film.

Because of the immediate impact of the film medium, and wide dissemination and consumption of film (as compared, say, to musicological writings on Beethoven), films are a uniquely powerful proponent of popular perceptions of Beethoven. In her work on Beethoven and action-film villains, Robynn Stilwell notes that the popular Beethoven has often embraced aspects considered abject by the institution. Stilwell articulates a discrepancy between scholarly and popular conceptions of Beethoven: "While the more emotional, irrational, and even violent elements have tended to be neatened away, out of sight, or at times even forcibly removed by musicologists, popular culture has retained, revitalized, and recirculated the more troublesome Beethoven."[115] Stilwell overstates this divide somewhat, as evidenced by the number of musicological sources from disparate decades which acknowledge problems of Beethoven and his music. Scott Burnham also acknowledges Beethoven's distinctive treatment by the scholarly and popular realms: "Although the Beethoven myth has been dressed down in the academy, it remains alive as ever in mainstream commercial culture." He points to many films and minor novels as evidence for this claim, and even detects "a subtradition detailing the dangerous effects of listening to Beethoven's music."[116] To the extent that popular notions gain credibility over time and feed back into subsequent scholarship, one must wonder to what degree the images and ideas associated with Beethoven in *A Clockwork Orange* created a climate for Susan McClary's work on Beethoven, to take one example, and what role the film may have had, however subliminally, in inspiring her scholarship.[117]

If Alex were a fan of, say, heavy metal instead of Beethoven, he would be much less problematic for the spectator. When we first learn of Alex's feelings about Beethoven, it seems to fly in the face of what Beethoven's Ninth stands for, but this notion is quickly displaced by the more difficult truth that Beethoven's Ninth, despite its text, and popular interpretations, does not stand for anything on its own. In loving Beethoven, Alex seems to be destroying or defacing something the spectator values, or at least recognizes as a valued cultural object. This displays the illusion of proprietary rights as a symptom of fanhood. Alex's behavior is a perversion of some of the exalted values associated with the symphony, and Alex's visceral connection with the music may dismay Beethoven's less violent fans. With emotional attachment comes vulnerability; fanhood has its hazards. This is why Alex's conditioning is so painful for him and another reason why *A Clockwork Orange* may be so painful for the spectator.

Though *A Clockwork Orange* affects reassessments of conceptions and associations held before viewing the film, its greater concern is with the mechanisms by which one forms and reforms such notions in the first place. Kubrick forces a consciousness of the processes and components of spectatorship itself and he reveals associations between a piece of music and notions of meaning or value as the wayward children of happenstance and habit. *A Clockwork Orange* does not reinterpret the Ninth Symphony; rather, it makes a statement on its hermeneutic slipperiness, and promiscuous reception history. Kubrick's recontextualization of Beethoven is, in a sense, a reproduction of Beethoven insofar as it enters into a particular relationship with the listener, just as every concert performance and recording of the Ninth Symphony is a reproduction. Like Andy Warhol's mass produced images of Beethoven of 1987, and like Alex's row of Christ figurines, Kubrick's presentation of Beethoven reminds us that reproducing something also implies losing the essence of the original.[118] Kubrick, in concert with many voices from music scholarship, views the nature of the function and reception of a work and thus its value, as dynamic but therefore also as threatening (embodied in the character of Alex) to the notions of authenticity and moral high ground that are often invoked by Beethoven's champions in expositions of his value and place in western culture.

Kubrick is not suggesting we are wrong if we value Beethoven's music, but that we must acknowledge our own creative role in the production of this value, and whatever meanings we perceive. The location of meaning, for Kubrick, is not in the work, but in the listener and he puts preexisting music in his films so that they will be recreated anew by every spectator. Though Kubrick's film may at first coerce the spectator into hearing Beethoven's music as a locus of violence, he shows us that this is an illusion of conditioning. That the spectator is likely to have had associations with Beethoven that are not antagonistic, makes the new association something she wants to resist, contributing to her anxiety, and her sensitivity to the violence in the film.

Kubrick also promulgates the idea of enjoying Beethoven as a sensual experience, free of ideology, in the character of Alex. Not once does Alex divulge what he thinks of Beethoven; rather, he expresses reactions to Beethoven's music in purely experiential, emotional terms, and with fanciful, visual analogies. Kubrick's idea has a beautiful simplicity, though it wears such an ugly disguise. A similar idea informs his approach to *2001: A Space Odyssey*, in which he attempts to create a nonverbal experience. Kubrick's films celebrate the subjectivity, impermancence and reinventability of musical meaning. Like Nicholas Cook, he believes each listener has to find his or her own way into the Ninth, and actively create his or her own meaning. And, like any worthwhile investment, one's personal investment in the Ninth is both an asset and a liability, as Alex's adventures boldly attest.

Appendix: "Ode to Joy" text and translation

O Freunde, nicht diese Töne!
Sondern lasst uns angenehmere anstimmen
Und freudenvollere!

O friends, no more these sounds!
Let us sing more cheerful songs,
more full of joy!

Freude, schöner Götterfunken,
Tochter aus Elysium,
Wir betreten feuertrunken,
Himmlische, dein Heiligtum!
Deine Zauber binden wieder,
Was die Mode streng geteilt;
Alle Manschen werder Brüder,
Wo dein sanfter Flügel weilt.

Joy, bright spark of divinity,
Daughter of Elysium,
Fire-inspired we treat
Thy sanctuary.
Thy magic power reunites
All that custom has divided,
All men become brothers
Under the sway of thy gentle wings.

Wem der grosse Wurf gelungen,
Eines Freundes Freund zu sein,
Wer ein holdes Wib errungen,
Mische seinen Jubel ein!
Ja, wer auch nur eine Seele
Sein nennt auf dem Erdenrund!
Und wer's nie gekonnt, der stehle
Weinend sich aus diesem Bund.

Freude trinken alle Wesen
An den Brüsten der Natur;
Alle Guten, alle Bösen
Folgen ihrer Rosenspur.
Kusse gab sie uns und Reben,
Einen Freund, geprüft im Tod;
Wollust ward dem Wurm gegeben,
Und der Cherub steht vor Gott!

Froh, wie seine Sonnen fliegen
Durch des Himmels prächt'gen Plan,
Laufet, Brüder, eure Bahn,
Freudig, wie ein Held zum Siegen.

Seid umschlungen, Millionen,
Diesen Kuss der ganzen Welt!
Brüder! Über'm Sternenzelt
Muss ein lieber Vater wohnen.
Ihr stürzt nieder Millionen?
Ahnest du den Schöpfer, Welt?
Such' ihn über'm Sternenzelt!
Uber Sternen muss er wohnen.

Whoever has created
An abiding friendship,
Or has won
A true and loving wife,
All who can call at least one soul theirs,
Join in our song of praise;
But any who cannot must creep tearfully
Away from our circle.

All creatures drink of joy
At nature's breast,
Just and unjust
Alike taste of her gift;
She gave us kisses and the fruit of the vine,
A tried friend to the end.
Even the worm can feel contentment,
And the cherub stands before God!

Joyful as the suns that soar
Across the splendor of Heaven's plain,
Brothers, run your course,
Joyfully, like a hero towards Victory

You millions, I embrace you.
This kiss is for all the world!
Brothers, above the starry canopy
There must dwell a loving Father.
Do you fall in worship, you millions?
World, do you know your Creator?
Seek Him in the heavens!
Above the stars must He dwell.

10 The Sadness of the Gaze: *Barry Lyndon*

Homay King

The Illusion of Visual Mastery

Many have struggled to understand the emotional tone of Stanley Kubrick's *Barry Lyndon*. On the one hand, critics have frequently called the film "chilly," reacting negatively to what they perceived as an unsympathetic portrayal of the title character, and to the apparent indifference of both narrator and camera to the events unfolding before them. Penelope Houston tells us that, upon its release, the majority of critics panned *Barry Lyndon*, finding it "too cold, too deliberately beautiful, too muted, too drained of 'life'—and too baffling."[119] Robert Kolker, for one, has suggested that Kubrick's images "replace intimacy with distance, the human with the inhuman" and express "an emotionless isolation."[120] Reviewers blamed not only the film's distant narrator, and what they saw as lackluster performances, but moreover the insistent artifice of Kubrick's camerawork and shot compositions. However, while the majority of critics were bemoaning the film's chilly lack of feeling, others were praising its eloquent expression of feeling. Most notable among them is Andrew Sarris, who in a review for *The Village Voice* called the film "the most expensive meditation on melancholy ever financed by a Hollywood studio." Indeed, Sarris goes on to state that "every frame of *Barry Lyndon* is a fresco of sadness."[121]

How are we to reconcile these two mutually exclusive responses to the film? How is it possible that one viewer sees aloofness in a style of camerawork that for another evokes an unprecedented melancholy? One possible answer lies in a closer analysis of the "painterly" or "fresco"-like quality of Kubrick's images, invoked both by the film's detractors and by Sarris. *Barry Lyndon* is a film that quotes painting at every turn, sometimes directly, and more often simply through the use of fixed framings which recall the composition of a painted landscape.[122] Indeed, production designer Ken Adam notes that Kubrick "wanted to make direct reference" to painting, and studied works by Gainsborough, Hogarth, Reynolds, Chardin, Watteau, and Stubbs. Frank Cossa in turn observes the resemblance to "the hazy lemon yellow skies and classically balanced landscapes of Richard Wilson," and the "crystal grey tonalities" in the daylight interiors, evocative of Chardin.[123]

Kubrick's painterly shots are striking in that they forego the cinema's signature formal element: they are denuded of motion. But the deliberate artifice displayed in these images is also linked to their perspective: an extreme long shot, often prefaced by a slow, stately outward zoom. Many have noted Kubrick's use of this camera trope in *Barry Lyndon*; John Engell counts nineteen zooms altogether.[124] The resulting images are fixed tableaux in long shot, bathed in natural light, with their human figures dwarfed by their surroundings and historical situations.

The cinematic close-up tends to signify not only spatial proximity, but also affective proximity and intimacy. Indeed, the close-up as prompt for identification has passed into the lexicon of standard narrative filmmaking convention to such an extent that one may typically infer the importance of a given character by counting the number of close-ups he or she receives. The long shot, by contrast, usually signifies not only spatial distance, but also psychical and emotional detachment. When combined with a lack of intra-frame movement and a deliberately synthetic, period-recreation mise-en-scène, the long shot would seem to represent absolute detachment. However, Kubrick reverses the attributes normally attributed to the long shot and close-up. *Barry Lyndon* is a film that systematically interrogates many of the features generally associated with the long shot and distant gaze. It does so by giving this vantage point an unexpected affective resonance, infusing the film's landscapes with longing and desire.

Many of the qualities associated with the cinematic long shot have been inherited from eighteenth-century landscape painting, particularly those of the "picturesque" tradition.[125] W.J.T. Mitchell suggests that, at its most ideological, the landscape may serve as a means by which socio-economic or political conditions are reified:

> Landscape ... naturalizes a cultural and social construction, representing an artificial world as if it were simply given and inevitable, and it also makes that representation operational by interpellating its beholder in some more or less determinate relation to its givenness as sight and site. Thus, landscape (whether urban or rural, artificial or natural) always greets us as space, as environment, as that within which "we" (figured as "the figures" in the landscape) find — or lose — ourselves.[126]

Here, Mitchell describes the cultural work that landscape performs as genre: the way in which imagery of nature and environmental space can have a naturalizing effect on all that appears harmoniously lodged within that space. It is the second of Mitchell's points with which I am most concerned: the notion that a landscape picture interpolates or positions its spectators in an idealized and fictive relation to the space it depicts; that it encourages spectators to perceive space according to the measure of man. Broad, sweeping views, low vanishing points, balanced compositions, and panoramic scope are typical features of both eighteenth-century landscape painting and cinematic establishing shots. At its most conventional, such features have come to be associated with a human claim of mastery over nature, claims of possession over territory, conformity of the wilderness to a formal or aesthetic order, and a triumph of the static and synchronic over change and unpredictability.

Like its still-image kin, the cinematic establishing shot often strives for an effect of naturalism in the depiction of space, while simultaneously adhering to a rigid, geometrical abstraction at the level of framing, shot composition, and angle. Film scholar Stephen Heath describes how the conventions of cinematic vision demonstrate similar properties to those described above, and traces its lineage yet further back in the history of visual representation. In *Questions of Cinema*, Heath suggests that the illusion of mastery through vision so often propagated by the cinema camera dates to the Renaissance system of perspective:

> The conception of the Quattrocento system is that of a scenographic space, space set out as spectacle for the eye of a spectator. Eye and knowledge come together; subject, object, and the distance of the steady observation that allows the one to master the other; the scene with its strength of geometry and optics. Of that projected utopia, the camera is the culminating realization.[127]

In such a system, the eye of vision and the "I" of knowledge are conflated, such that subjectivity and consciousness are thought to be wholly on the side of the spectator, while the spectacle becomes a fully masterable object. As Heath notes in the same essay, the cinematic camera turns "space" into "place" and the "seen" into a "scene"—a terrain ready for modification by human activity, appearing to be both intelligible and hospitable.

Psychoanalysis has frequently theorized visual representations in terms similar to those described above. Heath's description of the conflation of "I" and eye—and the resulting illusion of human agency and subjectivity—draws upon Jacques Lacan's theories of the ego-formation and the imaginary. In a Lacanian story of cinema spectatorship, images tend to function like mirrors for their spectators, offering up pleasing reflections that depict what the spectator would like to be in wish-fulfilling fantasy.[128] As Lacan informs us in *The Four Fundamental Concepts of Psychoanalysis*, visual representations are not only indices of imaginary identifications; they also have a "belong to me" aspect about them, which Lacan says is "reminiscent of property."[129] Not only do our visual perceptions of ourselves in the mirror strike us as uniquely ours, but, in a Cartesian move, our perceptions of things and places in general are also frequently subsumed under the heading of our own personal world view. This way of understanding vision ultimately results in a kind of perceptual prison-house, whereby no individual way of seeing is shared by anyone else. The competing claims of perceptual ownership finally render the world as such inaccessible, except through the lens of proprietary visions.

No sooner has Lacan sketched this prison, however, than he alludes to several possible means of escape. One such possibility emerges during his analysis of an encounter with a sardine can. Lacan recalls a conversation he has with a young boy upon spotting the sardine can floating in the distance at sea. The boy shrewdly remarks that Lacan can see the sardine can, but that it cannot see him; Lacan in turn reports that he was "not terribly amused" by this fact. In the following passage, Lacan comments upon the feeling of consternation this simple observation provoked for him, and theorizes about the consequences of such a lopsided relation between seer and seen:

> No doubt, in the depths of my eye, the picture is painted. The picture, certainly, is in my eye. But I am not in the picture. That which is light looks at me, and by means of that light, in the depths of my eye, something is painted.... This is something that introduces what was elided in the geometral relation — the depth of field, with all its ambiguity and variability, which is in no way mastered by me. It is rather it that grasps me, solicits me at every moment, and makes of the landscape something other than a landscape.[130]

In this passage, Lacan suggests that, under certain circumstances, we may become aware of the fictive status of our vision's dominion over the perceived. Contrary to conventional wisdom, the eye does not survey and occupy the landscape; rather it is the landscape which "is painted" in our eye, which is "in no way mastered" by us, and which emphatically occupies the position of subject in this passage. Kaja Silverman lucidly describes the effects of this reversal in *World Spectators*, where she interprets a statement that Merleau-Ponty attributes to Cézanne: "The landscape thinks itself in me." Silverman writes, "Rather than aspiring to become the initiator of perception, Cézanne gladly accepts his role as recipient ... [as] the medium through which the things of the world paint themselves."[131]

The insistent language of absence and divestiture from both Lacan and Cézanne is notable. The picture may be in my eye, but, Lacan notes with concern, I am not in the picture. Here, Lacan surprisingly suggests that the desire "to be in the picture" may supercede the desire to occupy to position of seer, and may trump the desire for all privileges that convention tells us accompany that position. In the above example, the sardine can cannot see Lacan back in a way that would grant him visual "being" or mutual recognition. He remains invisible, evicted from its landscape, to the amusement of his young companion. The landscape and the light solicit and grasp him in the visual field, not the other way around. Lacan's allegory of the sardine can finally suggests that those who fail to recognize this fact — those who insist on the rules of "scenographic space," and on a strict separation between seer as subject and seen as object—do not get to be in the picture. When we submit to the illusion that we master the landscape, we willingly absent ourselves from it.

Roland Barthes is another theorist who offers a theory of the image which helps us to imagine alternatives to the qualities typically imputed to the distant gaze. In *A Lover's Discourse*, Barthes suggests that visual images exclude the spectator from what they depict.[132] Like Lacan in the story of the sardine can, Barthes describes a certain type of spectatorship which is predicated upon the viewer's absence from the visual field, and he helps us better to understand how this visual "fading" can be a source of the most heart-wrenching affect. In a somewhat surprising move, Barthes defines the image as follows: "Here then, at last, is the definition of the image, of any image: that from which I am excluded. Contrary to those puzzle drawings in which the hunter is secretly figured in the confusion of the foliage, I am not in the scene: the image is without riddle."[133] Like the Lacanian example cited above, this unusual definition suggests a way of thinking about the image in which spectatorship involves an exclusion, rather than an imaginary projection of oneself into the scene, and upon a dispossession rather than a claim of ownership. Barthes adds the following corollary: "The images from which I am excluded are cruel, yet sometimes I am caught up in the image (reversal). Leaving the outdoor café where I must *leave behind* the other with friends, *I see myself* walking away alone, shoulders bowed, down the empty street. I convert my exclusion into an image. This image, in which my absence is reflected as in a mirror, is a *sad* image."[134] Here, Barthes goes yet a step further in undoing the association of visual imagery with presence, possession, and potency. Clearly, the image Barthes describes above participates in the melancholic affect he would later associate with the medium of photography in *Camera Lucida*.[135] In place of a cool objectivity, it situates the viewer in a highly subjective and affectively-laden place of sadness, longing, and mourning. In place of the triumph of occupying an idealized, unobserved, or panoptic vantage point, this image prompts reflections on absence, exclusion, and displacement.[136]

We must return to Lacan at this point, who provides us with a final example of how the illusion of visual mastery may be challenged, this time through the experience of the work of art. *The Four Fundamental Concepts of Psychoanalysis* contains a passage which helps us to understand how an "absence from the picture" within a film's diegesis may be duplicated for the film's spectators outside of it. Shortly after the parable of the sardine can, Lacan states that the visual artist "gives something for the eye to feed on." However, this is a different kind of feeding than that of the surveying gaze which grazes upon a landscape; instead, the spectator is dispossessed: "[The visual artist] invites the person to whom this picture is addressed to lay down his gaze there as one lays down one's weapons.... Something is given not so much to the gaze as to the eye, something that involves the abandonment, the *laying down* of the gaze."[137] Here, Lacan makes the distinction between eye and gaze explicit. The work of art is addressed not to the mastering gaze, but to the "depths of the eye"—the eye, in Cézanne's terms, in which a landscape paints itself. This passage furthermore suggests that in order to accept the artist's invitation to receive the picture, the spectator must actively cede or "lay down" the gaze. The spectator, in other words, must abandon all hope of visual potency or a panoptic surveillance.

"I am not in the picture": *Barry Lyndon* and the Longing to Appear

Barry Lyndon is a film which could be said to provide something for the mastering gaze — in Heath's terms, to the vision which is hungry for scenographic space — only to take it away moments later. On the one hand, the film's long shots cannot help but participate in that cold

Ryan O'Neal as the title character in Kubrick's *Barry Lyndon* (1975).

claim of possession with which their vantage point has historically been associated. But Kubrick's camera makes the act of absention, and the longing it provokes, inseparable aspects of the long view. Through this process, a figurative "no trespassing" tape is installed between spectator and film. Ultimately, though, Kubrick also invites us to imagine how we might once again become a part of this film's landscape, re-entering it, in Lacan's terms, as an "eye" rather than a gaze. The film extends this invitation through the very affect that our absence from its pictures evokes. The critical divergence over *Barry Lyndon* could be viewed as a result of the tension between these two ways of experiencing the film's landscapes, as gaze and eye respectively.

Kubrick's frequent outward zooms, and the landscapes they frame at their culmination, seem at first glance to replicate the functions of what Heath calls "scenographic space," and what Lacan calls the "belong to me" aspect of visual images. However, closer analysis reveals that the affect associated with these long shots is less one of triumph than of melancholy. *Barry Lyndon* tells the story of a character who longs to appear in visual scenes. Indeed, Thomas Allen Nelson suggests a similar idea when he writes that the film "paradoxically implies that Barry's attraction to this world comes from his seeing it from afar rather than up close."[138] The rake's progress that this film embarks its anti-hero upon takes the form of a series of pictures to which Barry hopes to gain admittance. Kubrick makes clear that Barry's class aspirations, desire for love and marriage, and longing for social status are not simply about wealth and power, but pertain explicitly to the visual world. He does so by quoting painterly genres and compositional conventions, presenting the various socio-economic milieux in which Barry longs to appear as so many types of pictorial images.

As mentioned earlier, *Barry Lyndon* interrogates conventional features of cinematic vision first and foremost through the use of the outward zoom. However, the film accomplishes a similar task through its representation of time, as *Barry Lyndon*'s layered historical references complicate the film's status as period recreation. In a sense, historical recreation does to time what the surveying gaze does to space: it lays history out for the spectator's perusal, and does so from a vantage point that is considered superior to what it views. *Barry Lyndon* calls attention to our absence from this historical epoch through several temporal equivalents of the outward zoom. Kubrick's film is a 1975 adaptation of the novel *The Luck of Barry Lyndon* by William Thackeray, first published in 1844, which is itself set in the eighteenth century. This series of adaptations and its layering of various pasts already suggests something other than a strictly linear view of history. The film's status as historical recreation is further compromised by the musical score, some portions of which come from its future, such as the Schubert Trio heard in Part II, which dates from 1828.[139] The film's locations are crafted from composites of historically anachronous bits of architecture: Ken Adam notes that the Irish architecture was constructed "by combining three different sites" and that the Lyndon estate was also "a kind of composite architecture using castles from Salisbury, Sussex, Wiltshire, and York."[140] Thus, while the authentic costumes, natural diegetic lighting, and historically faithful décor in *Barry Lyndon* might at first suggest that it is an exercise in absolute recreation, this drive toward authenticity is counterbalanced both by the historical inaccuracies mentioned above, and by the film's highly-studied camera work. The camera's insistent artifice suggests less an attempt to recreate the past as such than to evoke different kinds of images, signifiers that are already representations in and of that past. And the film's natural lighting and extra-diegetic music are not at odds with one another; rather, they work together to provide some of its most impressive conduits for affect. Together, they form the vehicle by which we as spectators, once we lay down the gaze and exit the picture, may begin to re-enter it from the other side.

The Outward Zoom as Trope of Exclusion

The outward zooms in *Barry Lyndon* usually begin with a fixed close-up, then withdraw to a long shot, whereupon the camera pauses. The camera stops just at the point where the framing begins to evoke the conventions of a landscape with figures: the actors stand miniaturized and posed in a tableau, and both camera and intra-frame movement are momentarily suspended. One example that occurs early in the film provides a kind of allegory for the move from a notion of scenographic space to the idea of the long shot as signifying an absence or longing. This scene depicts the Kilwanger Regiment, led by Barry's rival Captain Quin, who has begun courting Barry's beloved cousin Nora. The regiment marches forward in a militaristic display across a lush green field as a large audience looks on. As the troops march, the band plays a rousing rendition of "The British Grenadiers," complementing the patriotic pageant. The image in question begins with a medium shot, and slowly zooms out to reveal the long procession of soldiers, marching toward the camera in a single-file horizontal line. The camera stops its zoom just at the point where the landscape is framed in perfect symmetry, revealing the entire line of troops, a carefully positioned group of observers in the foreground, and a quilt-like set of partitioned pastures laid out across a wide valley.

Initially, this image seems perfectly to represent the long shot as an assertion of mastery over territory. Indeed, the marching troops seem to claim more and more ground in this pastoral, domesticated landscape as they advance, and the image may thus recall Ireland's colonization by Britain. However, the voice-over narration which accompanies this image suggests an additional meaning. With unusual insight, the narrator remarks that the soldiers' "scarlet coats and swaggering airs filled Barry with envy." One might expect that the act of observing the Bradyville regiment on display would allow Barry to participate vicariously in their military conquest: the theory of the image as mirror or locus for identification would suggest as much. Instead, we are told that Barry registers his exclusion from this picture. Like Lacan's seascape or Barthes' riddle-less foliage, Barry here encounters a landscape that — at least at this point in the narrative — has no room for his own projected image. Barry's exclusion is further underscored by his love rival's presence in the scene. The handsomely attired Captain Quin, suitor to Barry's beloved cousin Nora, is as visible in this pageant as Barry is absent from it.

This scene is immediately followed by another outward zoom which continues the theme of exclusion and bereftment. The shot begins with a close-up of some logs being split by an axe. The zoom reveals the chopper to be Barry, flanked by chickens in a lush Irish countryside and apparently venting his aggressions on the wood at his feet. As the camera moves away, the narrator informs us that, following the military march and learning of Nora's courtship by Quin, Barry has resolved never to see her again. The narrator continues: "But such resolutions, though they may be steadfastly held for a whole week, are abandoned in a few moments of great despair." Once again, the voice-over and outward zoom function as enunciatory elements that makes explicit both the act of leave-taking, and the affects of bereavement and despondency which accompany it. The clouds overhead cast a shadow on the ground which seems to reiterate the melancholy affect.

Yet a third outward zoom immediately follows the image of Barry at the chopping block. Appropriately, this image firmly reinscribes the lines of the triangle comprised by Barry, Nora, and Quin, and once again places Barry at its outermost point. The shot commences with a tight close-up on two pairs of lovers' hands clasped together at chest level. The camera's slow zoom reveals these figures to be Nora and Captain Quin. The long shot at the end of the zoom results in another painterly landscape: the low vanishing point, careful placement of a tree at frame left, thin sliver of shimmering lake in the distance, and perpendicular side lighting from a source at frame right all work together to create a highly stylized tableau. Nora and Quin are positioned slightly toward frame left and in the foreground; another couple are positioned at frame right and a bit further up screen. Nora's white dress contrasts with the bright red of Quin's military uniform. Barry is excluded from this scene, denied even the reverse point of view shot which would connect him to it as observer. Nevertheless, the image clearly represents Barry's psychical point of view, insofar as it presents the picture he would like to be in, but from which he is ostracized.

Quin now confesses to Nora that his heart has "felt the soft flame" with four women besides herself, to which Nora replies, "Ah, you men. Your passion is not equal to ours. We are like some plant I read of: we bear but one flower, and then we die." Soon, Barry himself arrives, whereupon he angrily returns Nora's love-gift of a piece of ribbon. He exposes her falsehood in the process, for it seems she has bestowed the same gift upon Quin. The return of the ribbon occurs in a closer shot, which reveals longer, starker shadows upon the ground and a dim chiaroscuro vapor across the landscape, the type of lighting one might find at sunset. As Quin runs off and Nora chases after him, the camera cuts back to the same long shot which ends the outward zoom, with its original lighting scheme. In these images, the lighting disobeys the rules of chronological continuity in favor of expressing an affective resonance. Just as the film's musical score does not wholly coincide with the temporal context of the narrative, so the light follows the cues of affect rather than those of temporal verisimilitude. Here, we come to understand that Kubrick's use of natural lighting sources rather than studio lamps in no way signifies a preference for absolute realism or historical authenticity. Rather, environmental light is put in the service of artifice, and the natural is always intertwined with affect and desire.

Nora does not appear for the remainder of the film, but she is determinative for Barry: she will become the driving impetus for his quest to become part of a series of pictures from which he has been previously denied admittance. Henceforth, Barry's desire will be modeled on the template of a primal scene. This primal scene, however, is traumatic not because of the sadism imputed to it, but because of Barry's lack of inclusion in the image it forms.[141] In this sense, the images which are most influential for Barry's desire are those which are pulled straight from the throes of the Oedipus complex: they are triangulated images, where Barry is inevitably lodged in the position of the child or excluded term. The number three features prominently in *Barry Lyndon*. Indeed, one might even go so far as to say that the film is organized around a series of love triangles: Barry, Nora, and Captain Quin; Barry, the German peasant Lischen, and her husband; Barry, Lady Lyndon, and Lord Lyndon; Lady Lyndon, Barry, and the maid. Barry will find himself playing the third wheel not only to various couples, but more broadly, he will long for (and ultimately gain) access to scenes of military glory, the world of high-society gambling, the titled gentry, and raucous drunken revelries—the rival in his triangulated desire this time played by the motley collection of figures who are in the place where Barry wants to be.

Kubrick counterbalances this system of triangles through a series of duels. Duels between Barry's father and a creditor, between Barry and Captain Quin, between Barry and a gambling debtor, and between Barry and Lord Bullingdon provide narratively significant moments. The list of twos and threes could go on: like many of Kubrick's other films, *Barry Lyndon* has two parts; Lady Lyndon's theme music is a Trio by Schubert; and so on. The duels, it seems, function not merely as a way for Barry to eliminate rivals, but as a means of resignifying the triangle—of attempting to reinstate a clear division between subject and object, where perception is something that shoots outward, and where the subject with the sharpest vision reigns triumphant. The triangle, however, remains the film's dominant metaphor for Barry's insatiable desire, and each time, Kubrick figures it in terms of a visual schema where the seer occupies the absent third position.

Like Grogan, another character to whom Barry is deeply attached and who represents his Irish past, Nora disappears from both screen and story.[142] In *Barry Lyndon*, as in other Kubrick films, being visible is the sole way to have one's story told: characters who disappear from view, whether permanently or temporarily, do not get to participate in the narrative. This helps to explain Barry's driving need to be seen. Unlike in much of classical Hollywood cinema, to be resolutely embodied in a Kubrick film is actually an advantage rather than a drawback, however much his characters may suffer for it. During Lord Bullingdon's absence from the Lyndon estate, for example, we do not have access to his activities. Toward the conclusion of the film, when Barry departs for Ireland and then for America, the narrator informs us that "His life there, we have not the means of following accurately, but he appears to have resumed his former profession of a gambler without his former success." *A Clockwork Orange*—a film that directly precedes *Barry Lyndon* in Kubrick's oeuvre—contains a scene in which Alex returns home after completing his treatment at the Ludovico center, only to find that a lodger named Joe has taken his place. As he storms out of the apartment, he proclaims to his parents Em and Pee, "You'll not be viddying [seeing] me again." Here, as in *Barry Lyndon*, farewells are figured first and foremost in visual terms, as disappearances. As Barry is exiled after his duel with Quin, he appears on horseback; the image's low vanishing point, rolling hills, partly cloudy skies, and placement of horse and rider toward the bottom left of the frame are reminiscent of Stubbs. Barryville has become a landscape, a picture he can no longer enter. Kubrick's outward zoom emphasizes the connection between this transformation of space and Barry's departure from it.

The device of the outward zoom in *Barry Lyndon* is perhaps better understood in contrast to the inward zoom, which Kubrick deploys to different purposes. In most cases, the zoom-in is deployed to represent a moment of discovery or information-gathering. One early example occurs during Barry's enlistment with the British army, when he spots two bathing men in the lake, one of whom is an officer. Barry contrives a plan to escape with the officer's horse and uniform. Kubrick's use of the zoom is in this instance fairly conventional: it represents Barry's point of view, is voyeuristic, and marks his act of discovery. As John Engell notes, three of the last four inward zooms in the film provide close-ups of bills.[143] These zooms likewise draw attention to some object in the mise-en-scène to which the spectator is now being made privy.

The function of the inward zoom is in every case to *inform*. The reverse zoom, by contrast, *evokes*: rather than revealing to us a bit of information, it tends to emphasize the impossibility of an epistemologically thorough vision, and to inflect the gaze with melancholy.[144]

Another point of contrast is provided by the several outward zooms which occur in *A Clockwork Orange*, where they are used to slightly different effect. In the earlier film, the reverse zoom tends to reveal recessed spaces and the illusion of depth of field, rather than the flat, painterly spaces of *Barry Lyndon*. *A Clockwork Orange* begins with an extreme close-up of Alex in droog attire looking directly into the camera. The camera slowly zooms outward to reveal the long, narrow interior of the Korova Milkbar with its white statues lining the walls. In *A Clockwork Orange*, Kubrick explores the z-axis rather than the y-axis. Whereas the voice-over narration in *Barry Lyndon* pretends to omniscience and objectivity, that of *A Clockwork Orange* is spoken as a first-person, confession-like monologue by Alex. The film undoes similar assumptions about truth and its relation to vision, but through the notion of interior space. We may believe we are getting access to Alex's innermost thoughts, a genuine explanation for his criminal behavior, but Kubrick's camerawork puts us at a remove and undoes the possibility of such knowledge. Likewise, *Barry Lyndon*'s narrator may at times seduce us into thinking that we occupy a theological position in relation to the characters and places they traverse. However, the outward zooms emphasize our eviction from that vantage point.

Two more outward zooms that occur back to back in Part II of *Barry Lyndon* return us to the notion of exclusion from a picture as described by Lacan and Barthes, and help us to understand how this condition relates not simply to the distance from which something is viewed, but also to that picture's formal attributes. At this point in the film, Barry has wed Lady Lyndon and assumed the Lyndon title, and has also begun his descent upon the narrative arc foretold by the narrator, with a binge of overspending and profligacy. The first outward zoom in the series begins with a close-up of Barry flanked by two maids, whom he embraces. The camera's reverse movement reveals a Hogarthian tableau: Barry in the midst of a group of dissolute soldiers, drinking and fondling women, upon which the camera holds briefly. A chorus of "The British Grenadiers" recalls the earlier scene of the military pageant, in which Barry's envy of the soldiers is first made known. Now, Barry has not only become a part of that military group; he has also entered the aristocracy, albeit through the back door. The new image thus shows him included in two "pictures" from which he was previously excluded. The dim interior lighting and highly stylized positioning of the figures in the frame further emphasize the pictorial status of this image over and against its cinematic qualities.

Barry has gained admittance to this picture, it seems, but the following images make it unclear whether it is still advantageous for him to occupy it. As the camera zooms out, the narrator dryly comments that "her ladyship and Barry lived, after a while, pretty separate lives." We immediately cut to a second zoom image, this time starting with a close-up of Lady Lyndon. She is flanked by her two sons, with Bryan's crib on the left and Bullingdon on the right, mirroring the position of Barry and the two maids in the previous image. Where the previous long shot invokes a Hogarthian etching, the image of Lady Lyndon and sons invokes British portraiture. The figures' stylized poses and vacant, hollow eyes recall Gainsborough's portraits of children. The separation between husband and wife is thus rendered visible not only by the camera's reverse movement, but also by their representation in terms of two distinct styles of picture.

Barry and Lady Lyndon are each excluded from the image to which the other belongs. The Hogarthian scene represented by Barry's picture participates in a kind of didactic universalism: its warning is predicated upon the spectator's fear that anyone, lacking proper piety, might unwittingly become part of such a picture. Its mode of address resembles that of a fable or allegory. The portrait, by contrast, aims to emphasize the uniqueness of its subject. It does not invite a universal spectator to imagine herself in the situation it depicts, nor does it address her with a warning. Where the former genre aspires to narrativity, the latter aspires to timelessness. The two kinds of pictures are thus incompatible, not only in terms of their subject matter and style, but in terms of how they solicit the viewer. The affective content of these scenes has been sublimated into a highly-articulated aesthetic system. We might even say that the two shots participate in another duel of sorts, a face-off that concerns not only husband and wife, but also two distinct styles of image.

Not only are Barry and Lady Lyndon each excluded from the picture in which the other appears; they also fail to see each other in these pictures, as Lady Lyndon's blank stare emphasizes. Like Lacan's sardine can, they thus fail to confer upon each other the mutual recognition that each desires from the other. Kubrick's films are full of references to the limitations of vision, and to monocular vision in particular. The chevalier with whom Barry teams up to swindle the aristocracy wears an eye patch; Hal the computer in *2001* sees through a single convex mechanical eye; Alex in *A Clockwork Orange* wears a single false eyelash, and is later housed in a Benthamite prison, which is a kind of monocular yet panoptic structure. The very title of *Eyes Wide Shut* suggests a kind of half-vision, or a sightedness that occurs through or despite blindness. These films in turn frequently highlight the perils of seeing in only two dimensions, or failing to foresee the possible outcomes of an action. Interestingly, though, each of these characters uses his eye in some way that could be considered beyond the range of normal vision: the chevalier counts cards at candle-lit gambling tables, HAL lip-reads a conversation, and Alex envisions himself participating in sadistic erotic fantasies, of which the Ludovico treatment will attempt to cure him once again through visual means. Thus, we might initially suspect that Kubrick is merely pointing out the limits of the human eye, and simply revealing over and over again how it falls short of the fiction of the mastering gaze. But it soon becomes clear that he is also alluding to its hidden capacities.

The Mobile Camera and the Freeze Frame

Barry Lyndon challenges the notion of the mastering gaze not only through the use of the outward zoom, but also through images which unsettle the boundaries between the static and the moving. In cinema, we have come to accept the stationary shot as the signifier for an uninvolved or non-intrusive looking position. By contrast, hand-held or mobile camerawork in medium-shot or close-up has come to signify not only proximity, but also the involvement and mutual imprecation of a film's camera and what it depicts. By a sleight of hand, however, the stationary shot has come to be associated not only with lack of involvement, but also with an affectless anonymity. Kubrick uses both the static shot and the handheld camera in ways that undo these associations. He felicitously strips the distant, static-looking position of its claim to unbiased objectivity. At the same time, he reveals that a proximate, mobile camera does not automatically produce an individuated point of view, nor does it guarantee intimacy between spectator and screen. In *Barry Lyndon*, Kubrick ultimately asks us to reconsider our conventional understanding of the subjective camera or look.

There are but few scenes in *Barry Lyndon* shot with a handheld or highly mobile camera, and their infrequency makes them all the more striking.[145] The first of these occurs in a scene which takes place during the early stages of Barry's enlistment with the British army. The troops have laid camp for the night, and Barry becomes involved in an exchange of insults with a fellow soldier. The altercation escalates, and it is soon decided that the two men should settle their disagreement through a boxing match. The ensuing fight is filmed entirely with handheld camera. Here, we might expect the camera to provide point-of-view shots, aligned with Barry's looking position. However, Kubrick's camera refuses to take sides either spatially or subjectively: it simply hovers around the action at a low angle, betraying no particular bias or consciousness concerning the fight. Its movements are sloppy and disorderly, to such a degree that focus and lighting are slightly compromised, a choice that seems noteworthy given the extreme technical perfection displayed throughout the rest of the film. The human figures who form the borders of the arena serve as a container for the camera's haphazard movements. Thus, the camera, usually an agent of heavy-handed enunciation in this film, is now itself contained within a square frame composed of the very figures whose movements it formerly attempted to confine to its viewfinder. It is as if camera and characters had switched functions.

Another scene involving a significant use of the hand-held camera — also a fight scene — occurs in Part II of the film, during a harpsichord performance given by Lady Lyndon at the estate. A slow, stately pan of 360 degrees emphasizes the high level of control and decorum both in the room and on the part of the filmic enunciation, creating a foil for the chaotic movements to come. The concert is disrupted when Lord Bullingdon enters drawing room with his younger half-brother in tow. Bryan stamps noisily on the parquet floor, wearing shoes several sizes too large for him, while Bully walks in stockinged feet. Bully acerbically intones, "Don't you think he fits my shoes well, your ladyship?" The deposed elder son then publicly proclaims his disdain for his stepfather, denouncing Barry's licentiousness, profligacy, and "ungentleman-like behavior" in front of the guests. Lady Lyndon grabs Bryan by the hand and runs tearfully from the room. Barry now throws a punch at Bully, which catches him squarely on the back and brings him to the floor. With this blow, the camera commences its hand-held movement, jerking erratically around the tussle and remaining low to the ground. As in the sequence described above, the camera never settles into a genuine point-of-view shot, instead bouncing among various perpendicular views of the prone figures. But nor does it act as if it were a bystander or human observer. When the concert guests leap up from their chairs, the camera hangs back and does not intercede. If this camera is mobile, it is nevertheless unmoved by the scene it witnesses. It remains affectless and uninvolved by the ferocity of its participants.

The camera's low angle allows the walls of the drawing room, which are covered in paintings, to remain visible throughout the fight. As in the boxing scene, frames within the image serve as an order-bestowing device in contrast to the camera's sudden unruliness. Here, we see walls hung salon-style with framed oil paintings of the kind mimicked by the film's own long shots. In an interview with Michel Ciment, Kubrick remarks that Barry, like characters in several of his other films, has "clawed his way into a gilded cage."[146] Kubrick's characters are often not aware of their confinement, because their cages have been aestheticized. In *A Clockwork Orange*, Alex's bedroom seems paradoxically less cramped when his window shade is drawn, for it bears a portrait of his beloved Ludwig van Beethoven; his prison cell at Staja 84F is likewise decorated with religious artifacts that distract from its carceral function. The Overlook Hotel in *The Shining* and Bill and Alice's apartment in *Eyes Wide Shut* are also decorated, trap-like spaces, the former a temporal loop from which there is no escape, the latter a kind of erotic tomb bathed in blueish light. Like his Kubrickian kin, Barry mistakes the paintings which adorn his iron-clad walls for windows onto so many vistas of freedom.

Barry's progressive confinement culminates at the end of the film in the amputation of his leg following the duel with Lord Bullingdon, a condition that puts a permanent stop to his class mobility. Barry is not the only Kubrickian protagonist to meet the fate of paralysis at film's end: *A Clockwork Orange* ends with its anti-hero in traction in a hospital bed; *The Shining* concludes with an image of Jack Torrance frozen in the snow. In *Barry Lyndon*, Kubrick also sublimates this condition into an aesthetic trope. The film's final image of Barry, as he enters the carriage which will take him to the new world, ends in a freeze-frame, reiterating the former wanderer's now-hindered mobility.[147] It is as if we no longer need the outward zoom to render visible this final act of leave-taking. Barry is finally "in the picture," but not in the form he had originally intended. He has lodged himself into the supreme, paradigmatic confined space of the static, two-dimensional image.

Landscapes Regained

One more outward zoom from the second part of *Barry Lyndon* is an image that returns us to the question of how we as spectators re-enter the picture after our systematic absention from it. This shot occurs during a scene depicting a birthday party for the young Bryan. A magic show has been arranged for the party, and a crowd of guests has assembled to watch it. The shot commences with a close-up on Lord Bullingdon's face. At this point, we have not yet seen the surrounding context of the birthday party, nor do we realize that Bully is seated among the magician's audience. His face in close-up registers a pale, sour expression, and as the camera slowly draws back, we see that Bully is in fact seated at his mother's feet and clutching her hand, surrounded by a cadre of beaming faces. Unlike this displaced older brother — who has essentially been made to disappear like one of the magician's rabbits— Bryan's other birthday guests appear to be enjoying the spectacle. A cut reveals the stage upon which these eyes are trained, and little Bryan assisting the magician as part of the show.

Once again, we seem to have an outward zoom as signifier of exclusion: Lord Bullingdon is clearly absent not only from the show which engages this adoring audience, but also from the new, happy family triangle composed by his mother, Barry, and young Bryan. But this image can be read in an additional way as well. Unlike those described previously, the long shot in which this zoom ends does not seem to reproduce any particular painter's style or painterly genre, at least not in an immediately recognizable manner. Rather than culminate with the object of representation clearly delineated from the act of spectatorship, this image reflects the looking position back to us, showing us audience members like ourselves. It thus complicates any attempt to say who is in the picture and who is not.

Every looking position, this image seems to say, is susceptible of itself becoming part of another picture. That is, while every picture may entail an exclusion, a leave-taking, or a step backward, there is no looking position so far removed that it cannot itself be observed by someone in another position. This aspect of the field of vision has several consequences. On the one hand, it means that there is no such thing as a position of absolute panopticism, which can see without itself ever being observed. On the other hand, it means that one cannot be excluded for long from one picture without soon becoming visible as part of another. The melancholic affect of the long shot is highly situated and occurs in relation to a particular landscape. It is not a condition which need be inhabited permanently.

The few pivotal scenes in *Barry Lyndon* which dramatize a loss or a leave-taking, but without the use of the outward zoom, seem to verify this idea. The scene in which Barry says goodbye to Lischen, the German peasant woman with whom he has lodged, for example, contains no zoom, nor does the scene depicting Bryan's death. These two scenes represent some of the "warmest" in the film in terms of their affective coloring, rendered through elements such as extra-diegetic music and the luminous, candle-lit photography which won *Barry Lyndon* its few laurels. In these scenes, it is as if Kubrick were indicating that if we are indeed to enter the pictures that are Thackeray's story, we must do so through channels other than recreation or restoration. If these landscapes seem too coldly artificial to inhabit, perhaps it is because Kubrick does not mean for us to lay claim to them in the first place. If the characters seem inaccessible or unsympathetic, perhaps it is because we are not meant to merge fully with their subject positions. And if the seventeenth century of the film's events seems distant and unfamiliar, perhaps it is because that temporal landscape is itself but an aggregate of other century's' ways of seeing it, rather than something capable of being recreated with absolute authenticity. The condescending omniscience dramatized by the film's narrator, and the assertion of possession dramatized by the surveying look, Kubrick seems to say, will not get us into the scene as promised. We must instead enter the picture through affective channels. Rather than shine the powerful lamps of the twentieth century on this world, we must access it through what dim flickers of indigenous light lie waiting within it, ready to graft themselves onto the filmstrip. Perhaps, after all, we are not being excluded from this picture: we are simply being enfolded into it in a different way.

11 Reconsidering Fidelity and Considering Genre in (and with) *The Shining*

Jarrell D. Wright

Initial critical reactions to Stanley Kubrick's 1980 film adaptation of *The Shining*, the best-selling 1977 novel by Stephen King, were almost uniformly hostile.[148] A striking pattern emerges from a survey of these reviews, in which critics repeatedly cited two major problems with *The Shining*. First, reviewers often complained that Kubrick's adaptation departed too radically from the novel. According to one critic, "The truly amazing question is why a director of Kubrick's stature would spend his time and effort on a novel he changes so much it's barely recognizable, taking away whatever originality it possessed while emphasizing its banality."[149] Second, there was a consensus that the film failed to satisfy the expectations attending its status as Kubrick's entry into the horror film genre — it was not scary. One reviewer asked, "Did Stanley Kubrick really say that [it] would be the scariest horror movie of all time? He shouldn't have."[150]

Although this assessment of *The Shining* is quite different — indeed, it argues that Kubrick's substantial alterations to the structure and details of King's narrative are essential to the unorthodox, yet no less frightening, horror film he created — the purpose of this essay is not to take issue with these early reviews. Rather, this essay will offer an analysis of *The Shining* that explores in the context of adaptation theory more generally the concerns that animated those reviews: fidelity and genre.

Fidelity

The question of fidelity has vexed film theory for so long that to some scholars it has become "tiresome."[151] Yet for many observers it remains "at the center of the adaptive problem,"[152] and — as the response to Kubrick's *The Shining* (and uncounted other film adaptations since then) attests — many film critics and lay audiences continue to believe André Bazin's maxim that a "good adaptation should result in a restoration of the letter and spirit" of the original work.[153] As a consequence, no general theory of adaptation — to the extent that one is even possible[154] — can be considered complete unless it accounts for the stubbornly persistent notion that an adaptation's fidelity to its source text is, at a minimum, relevant to criticism of the filmic text.

Using *The Shining* as a test case, this essay suggests that an analysis of the differences between a film and its source might offer a useful starting point for a critique of the film by illuminating the question of what the filmmaker sought to accomplish by adapting a particular work, a necessary first step in ascertaining whether or not the adaptation is successful.

However, to frame the issue in these terms is to make two assumptions that go against the grain of current scholarship in film studies. First, it constitutes an appeal to "evaluation as a critical project," a concern that "except in the area of adaptation study" has come to be perceived as quaintly old-fashioned.[155] This essay will illustrate how the fidelity analysis I propose can also contribute to the supposedly more sophisticated task of "asking how [a film] works," and that considerations of fidelity do not necessarily amount to "an appeal to anteriority" or to "a valorization of literature as such in the face of the insurgent challenge of cinema studies."[156] Second, this essay also assumes the validity, if not the primacy, of auteur theory as a way of understanding adaptations or other filmic texts. Although a defense of auteur theory is beyond the scope of this essay, its assumption that this approach to film studies is valuable not only needs to be made explicit but also requires at least an explanatory aside.

Whatever shortcomings auteur theory may have as a general enterprise, it is certainly a useful tool for understanding the films of Stanley Kubrick in particular.[157] Perhaps more than any other contemporary director, Kubrick possessed and exercised plenary authority over his projects:

> He prefers to prepare a project, collect material for it over a period of months, even years, pore over books and magazines with the systematic curiosity of an autodidact, monitor the seating

The title card to Kubrick's *The Shining* (1980).

capacity and average takings of cinemas in each foreign capital or the design and deployment of posters or even the distance between seats and screen at press shows, not to mention the size of newspaper ads and the rates of currency exchange. He also has the subtitles of every foreign version of his films completely re-translated into English to make certain that nothing crucial has been omitted, supervises all dubbed versions, and checked out the quality of the seven hundred prints of *The Shining* which were released the same day in the United States.[158]

Needless to say, Kubrick also enjoyed the coveted right to final cut, a right he was able to exercise in the case of *The Shining* without even having to screen the film to studio executives more than ten days before its release.[159] And Kubrick himself — who wrote or co-wrote all of his feature films except for *Fear and Desire* (1953) and *Spartacus* (1960)[160] — saw his task as a director to be nothing "more or less than a continuation of the writing. I think that is precisely what directing should be."[161]

Kubrick, however, is an unusual case. One of the weaknesses of auteur theory is that it not only "privileges the contributions of directors over the contributions of other creative artists in the production of a film, but it also privileges some directors over others" — specifically directors like Kubrick who are considered to be auteurs.[162] But at least one scholar and film producer has suggested that some form of auteur theory can legitimately play a broader role in film studies: "The experience of production relations within a film makes clear how one can award an authorial primacy to the director without adopting any of the idealist presuppositions about origin or homogeneity which seem to arise unbidden in one's path."[163] The auteurist bias embodied in this essay, therefore, need not be seen as an impediment to the validity or wider applicability of the fidelity analysis. Instead, this choice of an auteur's film will elucidate that analysis is a methodological tool, simplifying the presentation of a technique that, in principle, can be employed in critical work on films that do not lend themselves as readily to approaches based on auteur theory.

Genre

In contrast to the issue of fidelity, considerations of genre rarely arise in adaptation studies.[164] At most, genre becomes a concern only in analyses of particular films that are themselves deemed to be genre pieces.[165] What makes this common omission remarkable is the fact that adaptation theory and genre theory share so many points of congruence. Most notably, genres can be analyzed as literary forms that are assembled from the gradual accretion of a diachronic series of adaptations.[166] Likewise, both genre theory and adaptation theory interrogate the Romantic notion of authorship as an individualistic endeavor and the status of texts as hermetically independent entities.[167] And a resource for adaptation theory that has yet to be explored adequately arises from the metaphorical relationship between "adaptation" in the filmic or literary sense and "adaptation" as a concept of the natural sciences, a relationship that parallels the connection between the ideas of genre and genera.[168]

Because of these commonalities, and the emerging consensus that adaptation criticism is too heavily invested in the primacy of the source text,[169] this essay proposes, with *The Shining* as an example, that adaptation theory can benefit from considering a film in relation to the history of generic conventions within which both the film and its source text are situated.[170] In other words, a film participates in — and should therefore be conceptualized as part of — a *sequence* of adaptations of which the "original" text, in turn, constitutes a segment.[171]

This interpretation of Kubrick's *The Shining* both frames and unites these two general strands of argument. In the first section of this essay, the fidelity analysis when applied to *The Shining* casts doubt upon the most common interpretation of the film: that Kubrick's adaptation is an indictment of violence on an historical scale, with particular reference to European colonial practices in America. Instead, the film's most significant departures from the novel suggest that Kubrick's primary concern is the source of evil, which Kubrick locates within the ambit of human reality rather than in the domain of the supernatural. The second section examines Kubrick's shift toward realism and away from the marvelous elements of the Stephen King novel through the lens of genre theory.[172] Treating the King and Kubrick iterations of *The Shining* as instances of the gothic, the essay explains Kubrick's modulation of the narrative in terms of the tensions within that genre between rationalistic and nonrationalistic discourses. Both aspects of the argument in this regard are offered as models that other scholars might adopt, or adapt, in taking adaptation criticism in a different, and hopefully productive, direction.

Reconsidering Fidelity in *The Shining*

Critical perspectives on the proper role of fidelity in adaptation theory have varied from the extreme of enshrining the source text as the ideal that a film must emulate at its peril to the opposite polarity of according it no importance at all. Although the first view, epitomized by Bazin's argument that an adaptation should reproduce "the letter and spirit" of the original,[173] has largely given way to the second, represented by Thomas Leitch's claim that fidelity "is a hopelessly fallacious measure of a given adaptation's value,"[174] a range of intermediate positions has exhibited a general trend in favor of fidelity's salience. For example, George Bluestone — who posits the linguistic medium of source text as so fundamentally different from the visual medium of film as to render the two virtually incommensurable[175] — argues that some degree of infidelity is "*inevitable* the moment one abandons the linguistic for the visual medium," and therefore that fidelity analysis is, if not irrelevant, then at least uninteresting.[176] Yet just as contemporary critics like Leitch and Robert Stam had less extreme analogues in 1957, more moderate versions of Bazin are now advancing the view that considerations of fidelity are germane to adaptation criticism. James Griffith, for one, suggests that "fidelity to effects rather than details" can be an appropriate element in criticism of an adaptation.[177]

What renders all of these perspectives inadequate is the assumption that to a greater or lesser extent undergirds each of them — the idea that trans*ferr*ing a narrative from one medium to another necessitates trans*form*ing the narrative in a manner coded as infidelity. Bluestone, of course, makes this assumption explicit in his analysis of adaptation,[178] but it implicitly informs Leitch's claim that fidelity "is unattainable ... and theoretically possible only in a trivial sense. Like translations to a new language, adaptations will always reveal their sources' superiority because whatever their faults, the source texts will always be better at being themselves."[179] Similarly, Griffith's dismissal of an adaptation's fidelity to the details of its source narrative relies upon a model of mimesis inspired by Samuel Taylor Coleridge's distinction between imitations and copies: "deductively abstract critics who emphasize the medium agree with Coleridge that the written work need not taste like an apple, but they insist that the film adaptation taste like ink."[180] Even Bazin, by mentioning the possibility that a film can remain faithful to the spirit of the original work, tacitly admits that fidelity to its letter is problematic.[181]

But the notion that adapting a written work for the cinema requires change is true only in the most reductive sense and false in every other. The closest a film could come to being a perfectly faithful adaptation of a novel would be for it to display the novel's scrolling text on the screen in the manner of closing credits — or perhaps to frame the opened novel from a reader's-eye view with a hand occasionally appearing to turn the pages — but even then the film would not, in Griffith's words, taste like ink. Although on one level this suggestion is absurd, it serves on another to highlight the fact that what we would deem as a practical matter to be the "perfectly faithful," or even slavish, adaptation is far from a chimera. Such films are produced routinely; critics usually hate them. When Stephen King produced a six-hour television miniseries version of *The Shining* based on the screenplay that Kubrick had rejected twenty years earlier,[182] "the result [was] what you might call a literal interpretation of *The Shining*, as dramatically attenuated and thin on emotional substance as most of King's books."[183]

One consequence of the inaccurate view that narrative transformation is an inevitable product of adapting a written work to the screen has been film criticism that all too readily explains away such changes as the necessary result of the adaptation process. Greg Jenkins, for example, states that his main objective in studying Kubrick's adaptations is to examine how and why Kubrick alters characters, narrative structures, and other elements of his sources.[184] Yet Jenkins' analysis of *The Shining* most often attributes major departures from King's novel to the requirements of the medium of cinema, particularly the financial pressures to limit running time and the resulting phenomenon of narrative compression.[185]

For instance, the interview scene in the film shows Jack Torrance (Jack Nicholson) and the Overlook's manager, Stuart Ullman (Barry Nelson), agreeably if awkwardly participating in an unremarkable ritual of the business world. King's novel, on the other hand, depicts an overtly antagonistic relationship between the characters: "I don't believe you care much for me, Mr. Torrance," says Ullman. "I don't care. Certainly your feelings toward me play no part in my own belief that you are not right for the job."[186] According to Jenkins, this change reflects Kubrick's need to streamline the story by de-emphasizing Jack's history of alcoholism — the reason Ullman is reluctant to hire him and, ironically, the reason Jack gets the job anyway (an old drinking buddy sits on the Overlook's board of directors); "Ullman's affability need not be explained — but his hostility would be."[187] A similar technical concern figures into Jenkins' analysis of the scene between Dick Hallorann (Scatman Crothers) and Danny Torrance (Danny Lloyd), in which the concept of "shining" is first introduced. In the film, Danny is reticent about the powers he shares with Hallorann; most of his closeups in the scene show him silently staring at Hallorann, and he only speaks a few lines of dialogue. In the novel, however, Danny is immediately responsive to Hallorann's inquiries and talkative throughout the scene, which consumes eleven pages consisting mostly of close dialogue (80–90). Jenkins's primary explanation for this difference is the limited ability of a child actor to memorize lines, although he adds that this "minimalist give-and-take" also builds suspense.[188]

Jenkins is by no means alone in offering a fairly narrow range of explanations for the changes Kubrick made to King's novel. Charlene Bunnell has noted that, although Kubrick's film "does not quite do the novel justice in terms of character development and suspense, it does capture the theme and atmosphere of the original and provide some effective cinematic touches."[189] And Michael J. Collins explains that Kubrick "distills the events and characters of King's novel and augments them with skill — Kubrick transforms the characters, events, and settings of the novel into elements better suited to film."[190] Perhaps more importantly, none of these critics is wrong to invoke cinematic exigencies as explanations for Kubrick's alteration of King's narrative. It is beyond cavil that a story originally presented in a textual medium must accommodate itself to the demands of cinema in the process of adaptation, and that filmmakers sometimes make changes for precisely the reasons that Jenkins, Bunnell, and Collins identify. Rather, the problem with these accounts is that they have so little explanatory power — the fact that narrative compression is necessary does not illuminate the question of why a filmmaker chooses to compress one aspect of the story rather than another.[191]

Although it would therefore be naïve to imagine that every novelistic vision can be transferred feasibly to the screen, and therefore to eschew entirely the divergent strengths of text and cinema as a potential reason for changes evident in a film adaptation, there are at least two reasons why we ought to be wary of relying upon that explanation. First, film is a much more potent and flexible medium than this rationale tends to imply.[192] Second, this theory of change fails to account for the most common differences between film and source text: small-scale omissions and interpolations that are not mandated by the cinematic context.

The first point can be illustrated by critical responses to one of the most visually striking features of Kubrick's *The Shining*— the Overlook's hedge maze. Conventional wisdom holds that Kubrick must have opted for the labyrinth because the menagerie of topiary animals featured in King's novel would have been "an insoluble special-effects problem."[193] Yet the maze itself has been called "one of the most intriguing creations in the history of motion pictures" and "one of the most pernicious sets ever to work on"; constructed of pine boughs stapled to plywood forms, the maze had to be assembled twice (once for exterior shots in the United States and again for studio work in England), but was so large and intricate that crew members frequently became lost inside.[194] Given these logistical difficulties, Kubrick probably could have created King's hedge animals without appreciably greater effort or expense. This is particularly true in light of the fact that, with the exception of one scene, fidelity to the novel did not even require the menagerie to be animated. The animals only needed to appear in different positions and locations in a series of subjective point-of-view shots, gradually becoming more lifelike, assuming more predatory poses, and moving inexorably closer to the lens. Because one can easily imagine how such an effect might look when rendered in Kubrick's distinctive mise-en-scene — I am thinking specifically of Kubrick's tachistiscopic jump-cuts to a stark tableau of the slaughtered Grady girls in *The Shining*, and to David Bowman's silent screams as he crosses through the stargate in *2001: A Space Odyssey* (1968) — one must ask why Kubrick elected the hedge maze instead.

In this connection, we should also reconsider the purpose of the hedge maze in Kubrick's film. The maze and King's animals are usually equated in scholarly commentary on *The Shining*, but from the standpoint of narrative function they have nothing in common but the fact that they are both made of hedges — in other words, nothing at all. In the novel, the animals figure in three episodes (among the most frightening King has ever penned) that have no equivalents in Kubrick's film: they menace Jack, closing in on him, by seeming to move while his back is turned (205–12); they chase Danny to the Overlook's front porch, only evidencing their progress when Danny looks over his shoulder to find them closer, yet motionless (286–94); and, their movements finally perceptible, they intercept Hallorann upon his arrival at the Overlook (408–09, 415–19). As far as narrative function is concerned, Kubrick's maze plays the same role as the Overlook's boiler in King's novel — the former is responsible for Jack's death by hypothermia; the latter kills Jack, and destroys the Overlook, when it explodes in the novel's finale (436–37). Accordingly, we must not only ask why the topiary scenes are omitted, but also why Kubrick kills Jack with ice rather than fire and why he allows the Overlook to survive at all — questions that are not easily answered by reference to the mandates of the cinematic medium alone.

The second point — that relatively small narrative changes are not explainable by the transposition of a story from one medium to another — can be illustrated by a set of minor interpolations Kubrick made in his version of *The Shining*. During the closing-day tour of the Overlook, Ullman explains to Jack and Wendy (Shelley Duvall) that the hotel "is supposed to be located on an Indian burial ground, and I believe they actually had to repel a few Indian attacks as they were building it." The film also incorporates a wealth of Native American imagery: set decorations, costumes, and even aspects of the plot evoke the motif — Danny's escape from his father by retracing his footsteps in the snow has been described as "an old Indian trick."[195] These details are absent from King's novel, which only references Native Americans in passing; Danny thinks about the subtle, barely perceptible changes he has noticed in his parents since they arrived at the Overlook, and is reminded of a puzzle-picture in which images of Indians have been

Jack Torrance (Jack Nicholson) chasing Danny in the hedge maze at the conclusion of *The Shining* (1980).

hidden: "if you strained and squinted, you could see some of them" (196). Nothing about the medium of cinema compelled Kubrick to add these minor nuances, but they were obviously significant to him. His co-screenwriter, Diane Johnson, has explained that the Indian burial ground idea was Kubrick's and that he did a great deal of research on Native American history and customs while working on the screenplay.[196] Without some other or more complete theory of narrative change in adaptation, however, these interpolations appear to be gratuitous.

In light of these examples and the problems they illustrate, the differences between a film adaptation and its source text should be understood whenever credible as the filmmaker's conscious and purposive choices rather than as matters of necessity foisted upon the filmmaker by the cinematic medium. To clarify: this not to say that there are two discrete categories of change and that the critic must assign each instance of infidelity to one group or the other. Rather, it is to acknowledge that — while the transposition of a narrative from a textual medium to the cinema might be able to explain the fact that the narrative has changed — the characteristics of cinema as a medium cannot explain why *particular* changes are made instead of others. Even if we assume, for example, the impossibility of capturing King's topiary animals or the Overlook inferno on film, that fact would not explain why Kubrick replaced these aspects of King's novel with a hedge maze rather than with one of the numberless other possible substitutes that were available to him. Similarly, the fact that Kubrick had to concretize the Overlook in order to put *The Shining* on screen does not explain why his hotel sets featured Native American designs. A filmmaker who is confronted by a cinematic imperative that makes adhering to the source text problematic must choose an alternative based upon an overall vision for the film, and the critic's task is to develop a reading of the film that provides a coherent explanation for as many of those choices as possible.

Blakemore calls details like the Indian burial ground reference in *The Shining* "confirmers" and, for him, the sum total of Kubrick's changes to the novel confirms that the film "is explicitly about the genocide of the American Indians. Every frame, word, and sound of it."[197] McFarlane examines the parts of a novel that a filmmaker discards in making an adaptation, as well as what elements the filmmaker adds that were not present in the novel, in order to analyze how the adaptation "enunciates" the narrative functions originally performed by the novel.[198] In a similar vein, fidelity should be considered as an index of the filmmaker's vision for the adaptation, a set of cues that supplies a guide for how to read the film. Of course, this approach to fidelity does not amount to a valorization of the source text. Instead, it reflects Bluestone's insight that "the film-maker merely treats the novel as raw material and ultimately creates his own unique structure.... What he adapts is a kind of paraphrase of the novel."[199]

When this model of criticism is applied to *The Shining*, it becomes apparent that the most common reading of the film is, at best, incomplete. The overwhelming majority of critics who have discussed *The Shining* tend to concur with Blakemore — the film is a meditation on historical evils, particularly racism, and how they echo down to the present.[200] Many of Kubrick's departures from King's novel tend to confirm this hypothesis, most notably the final shot showing Jack Torrance in a photograph from an Independence Day celebration at the Overlook in the 1920s. But this reading is inconsistent with the fact that Kubrick jettisoned a plethora of material from the novel that would have resonated with this theme:[201] "If Kubrick is to be remonstrated for his rendition of *The Shining*, it must be for his unwillingness to recreate any texture of the historical evil that informs King's novel, and to which the latter devotes enough attention so that the individual pasts of his protagonists merge into the collective pasts of the Overlook."[202]

Two examples should suffice to establish this point. A major narrative strand in the novel involves a scrapbook that Jack finds in the hotel basement. Reading newspaper clippings about the sensational and often disturbing events that have regularly occurred at the Overlook, Jack is fascinated, even seduced, by the hotel's story, and the scrapbook is essential to his transformation into a thrall of the hotel: "It seemed that before today he had never really understood the breadth of his responsibility to the Overlook. It was almost like having a responsibility to history" (161). Although Kubrick gives us a teasing glimpse of the scrapbook next to Jack's typewriter in one brief shot in a single scene, he never takes advantage of it to reinforce his supposed theme of historical evil.

Another major episode in the novel is Jack's discovery of a wasp's nest, which becomes an occasion for Jack to recall encounters with evil in his own personal history: a drunken fit of temper in which he breaks Danny's arm, his dismissal from a teaching post when he loses his temper and nearly beats a student to death, and his brushes with an abusive father. Jack even calls the nest "a workable symbol for what he had been through" (109). Kubrick, however, deemphasizes Jack's past and eliminates the wasp's nest from the narrative entirely, despite the fact that it evokes the idea of an evil that refuses to remain buried in history — after being poisoned with a bug bomb, the wasps mysteriously regenerate and sting Danny.

As Stephen King explains in his account of the genesis of *The Shining*: "The past *is* a ghost which haunts our present lives constantly," and the Overlook as a variation on the haunted house theme is a "symbol of unexpiated sin."[203] If Kubrick's vision of *The Shining* was informed by the notion of historical evil, then why did he omit significant elements of the novel that were palpably relevant to that vision? The fidelity analysis in this section suggests that Kubrick was doing something different. It therefore becomes necessary to offer a more complete reading of the film, one that resolves the discrepancies between Kubrick's adaptive choices and prior interpretations of his film, and one that explains the major departures from King's source text.

The fact that the various political interpretations of the film do not mesh with Kubrick's philosophy offers one hypothesis: "When Rousseau transferred the concept of original sin from man to society, he was responsible for a lot of misguided social thinking which followed. I don't think that man is what he is because of an imperfectly structured society, but rather that society is imperfectly structured because of the nature of man."[204] The argument developed in the next section is that Kubrick's concern in *The Shining* is to shift the source of evil out of the supernatural realm — where it is primarily sited in King's novel — and into the human heart.[205]

This reading of the film subsumes the historical interpretation without superseding it. Kubrick was always fascinated by man's inhumanity to man — *Dr. Strangelove or: How I Learned to Stop Worrying and Love the Bomb* (1964), *A Clockwork Orange* (1971) and *Full Metal Jacket* (1987) are particularly emphatic articulations of the theme — and the idea of genocide is too strongly evident in the subtext of *The Shining* to be ignored. Yet this is merely an aspect of the film's larger message. Moreover, this reading takes into account the fact that Kubrick's entire career was marked by an intense interest in genre, including attempts to redefine genres and experiments with generic conventions.[206] Kubrick's treatment of evil in *The Shining* is inextricably intertwined with history after all — the history of a genre, the Gothic.

Considering Genre in *The Shining*

The principal argument thus far has been that a complete and accurate interpretation of *The Shining* — or, for that matter, of any film adaptation — must account for the film's most significant deviations from its source text. Although this essay has examined a number of differences between Kubrick's film and King's novel, some more important than others, the purpose of this section is threefold. First, to identify the major points of incongruity between the two versions of the narrative. Then to argue based upon those differences that Kubrick's primary objective in *The Shining* is to use the conventions of the horror film, and the Gothic tradition of which those conventions form a part, in order to posit evil as a product of human action rather than a supernatural phenomenon. Finally, to situate this reading of *The Shining* within the evolving matrix of a genre known as the Gothic in order to establish that King's novel, no less than Kubrick's film, is an adaptation of themes and concepts inherited from other works.

The most frequently noted difference between Kubrick's adaptation and King's source text is the manner in which Jack is portrayed.[207] In the novel, Jack is a fundamentally good person — a loving husband and father, an effective teacher, a gifted writer — who nonetheless is tormented by weaknesses like his temper and his alcoholism, weaknesses that the supernatural forces of the Overlook exploit. King goes to great lengths to foster sympathy for Jack. Even after Jack has nearly succeeded in strangling Wendy to death, King has her explain to Danny: "Listen to me.... It wasn't your daddy trying to hurt me.... The hotel has gotten into him, Danny. *The Overlook has gotten into your daddy.* Do you understand me? ... It's not your daddy talking, remember. It's the hotel" (375, 380 [emphasis in original]). And at the height of Jack's homicidal rampage, Danny is able to break through to what still remains of his father: "You're not my daddy," he says, as Jack is poised to strike him with a roque mallet. "You're a mask.... Just a false face. The only reason the hotel needs to use you is that you aren't as dead as the others" (429–30). "Doc," Jack responds, "Run away. Quick. And remember how much I love you" (431).

In the film, however, Kubrick offers a characterization of Jack that is much less complex: "There appears to be no serious attempt at tracing the psychological regression involved in Torrance's breakdown and in its later stages it seems to possess little psychological subtlety."[208]

Certainly by the end of the film, in which Jack Nicholson adopts a hunchbacked posture and an Ygor-like gait that telegraph his character's utter wickedness, there is no hint that Jack is a sympathetic figure or that a kernel of goodness still resides within him — if one ever had. Indeed, many critics have complained that Jack Nicholson's portrayal of the character makes him appear psychotic from the moment he first appears on screen.[209] But this impression has little to do with Nicholson's performance or with Kubrick's script or direction. Rather, Kubrick conveys this sense in a non-narrative fashion simply by casting Jack Nicholson in the role. Particularly in light of the fact that the character and the well-known actor share the same first name, it is difficult for an audience to avoid superimposing its perception of Nicholson and his previous film roles upon his performance as Jack Torrance.[210] Yet the result is that the film version of Jack conveys a markedly different impression than does the Stephen King original.

Less commonly remarked upon, but no less significant, is the fact that the Overlook never physically harms any of the characters in the film. This departure from King's novel is most apparent in the way Kubrick renders the scenes involving Danny and Room 237.[211] King's novel is unambiguous. Halloran warns Danny to stay out of the room; Danny's "dreadful kind of curiosity" (172) prompts him to steal the hotel's passkey, but he resists the temptation to use it. On a second attempt, however, Danny gains the courage to enter the room, where he finds a "woman in the tub [who] had been dead for a long time.... The years-damp, bloated, fish-smelling hands closed softly around his throat and he was turned implacably around to stare into that dead and purple face" (219–20). Kubrick, on the other hand, never reveals what happens to Danny after he goes into the room — a ball rolls into the frame as he plays with toy cars, he follows its path expecting to find his mother, and he walks through the already opened door from which the room key still dangles. In fact, Kubrick strongly hints that Jack was the attacker,[212] and even when Jack goes into the room to investigate "we ourselves have difficulty in determining which vision is actuality and which is fantasy."[213]

Finally, whereas King takes pains to offer the reader evidence that the supernatural is a bona fide presence at the Overlook,[214] Kubrick leaves open the possibility of a rational explanation until virtually the end of the film. King's novel includes an episode — after Jack has fallen under the influence of the Overlook, and Wendy and Danny have begun to suspect that they are in danger — in which the hotel's elevator begins operating on its own. Although Jack insists that it merely has a short circuit, Wendy hears voices in her mind talking about a party, "*Goodnight ... goodnight ... yes, it was lovely ... no, I really can't stay for the unmasking*" (301). Jack stops the elevator between floors, pries the door open, and assures her that it is empty. But Wendy pulls him away, and looks inside:

> "What about this, Jack? Is this a short circuit?" She threw something and suddenly the hall was full of drifting confetti, red and white and blue and yellow. "Is *this*?" A green party streamer, faded to a pale pastel color with age.
> "And *this*?"
> She tossed it out and it came to rest on the blue-black jungle carpet, a black silk cat's-eye mask, dusted with sequins at the temples.
> "*Does that look like a short circuit to you, Jack?*" she screamed at him [303 (emphasis in original)].

One could hardly ask for more confirmation that the supernatural realm has penetrated into normal reality.[215] By contrast, "the film does a lot to discount its more conventional horrors."[216] Every scene in which Jack witnesses a "ghost" features a prominently placed mirror — in the case of Lloyd's manifestation, directly in front of Jack — which suggests that "Jack is conversing with himself."[217] Kubrick only establishes that Jack's visions have a genuine, physical existence when he absolutely must, after Jack promises that he will "correct" his wife and son and we hear the bolt slide open outside the pantry where Wendy has imprisoned him.

What all three of these major differences between Kubrick's film and King's novel have in common is a radical shift in the narrative's locus of efficacy, a shift away from the supernatural as a potent force.[218] In the novel, the spirit of the Overlook must work tenaciously and manifest itself physically in order to turn Jack against his family. In the film, as Kubrick has said, "Jack comes to the hotel psychologically prepared to do its murderous bidding. He doesn't have very much further to go for his anger and frustration to become completely uncontrollable."[219] Significantly, Kubrick identifies anger and frustration as affirmative causes of Jack's violence, not as character flaws that give the external influence of the Overlook a way to manipulate him. Jack is predisposed to lash out against his family; isolation, claustrophobia, and stress do the work of pushing him toward homicide.[220] Supernatural forces in the film become less palpably real than in the novel, serving merely to decorate or metaphorically to amplify the primary horrors that Kubrick wants to depict, horrors with fundamentally human causes.[221] The ghost of Delbert Grady can unlock a door, but only a person of flesh and blood can break through one with an axe.[222]

This aspect of the film — Kubrick's use of horror movie conventions to tell a story of human evil — accounts for the common critical view that "*The Shining* is less a horror film than a meticulous, enthralling academic imitation of one."[223] Kubrick consistently miscues the audience, priming viewers to expect the kind of story that he never delivers.[224] Danny's croaking, vaguely sinister voice for his imaginary friend Tony imply a plot focused on demonic possession.[225] References to the Donner party, and to "a little boy who lives in [Danny's] mouth" and hides in his stomach, presage a cannibalistic end for the Torrance family.[226] Because "The Disturbed Indian Burial Ground is such a Usual Suspect in horror narratives that it is almost a generic archetype itself,"[227] Kubrick's apparently superfluous interpolation prompts another distinct type of expectation. And when Kubrick arrives at frightening points in the narrative that might be handled with greater suspense, "the building of tension is often deliberately short-circuited."[228] We see Jack spying on Wendy's discovery of his manuscript well before he interrupts with the chilling question, "Do you like it?" Kubrick allows us to "see or hear nearly every vivid heft, descent, and blow of the axe" when Jack chops through the bathroom door,[229] even though the camera must execute a violently rapid pan in order for Kubrick to do so. The point is to emphasize that evil itself is not a surprise, a sudden, unexpected intrusion from an invisible domain, but a product of a very material and even, at times, mundane humanity.

By modulating King's narrative and positioning evil in the rational world, Kubrick situates his adaptation of *The Shining* within a continuing generic dialogue that has defined the Gothic tradition since it emerged in the eighteenth century.[230] The dichotomy between rational and nonrational discourses—"the tension between the desire to arouse belief and the need for verification"—is a constant feature of supernatural fiction.[231] Most famously, Tzvetan Todorov has identified these two tendencies within "the literary Gothic" as "the supernatural explained (the 'uncanny') [and] the supernatural accepted (the 'marvelous')."[232] Todorov's "fantastic," of course, "occupies the duration of [the] uncertainty" between the two extremes.[233]

Even the first Gothic novelists, perhaps uneasy with the otherworldly themes with which the form was often preoccupied, were "concerned with maintaining an external plausibility."[234] Indeed, one critic has gone so far as to call realism "the sine qua non of the ghostly tale," which "stands or falls on its power to convince the reader that the *feeling of the supernatural* corresponds to some element in reality."[235] The effort to blend or reconcile these two antithetical strains of the Gothic has been an animating force for the genre since the beginning, during its evolution through Romanticism and the Victorian era, and into the ghost story or horror story forms that it assumed in the twentieth century.[236]

The fact that the Gothic exists along a continuum defined by these polarities might explain why Kubrick was interested in *The Shining*, which has been described as an instance of the genre.[237] Kubrick was fascinated by the eighteenth century because it "saw the conjunction of reason and passion"—"the two poles of Kubrick's universe."[238] Not coincidentally, those are also the pillars of the Gothic tradition, an eighteenth-century phenomenon. And it is probably not coincidental either that Diane Johnson, whom Kubrick selected to co-write the screenplay, is a professor of literature whose specialty is the Gothic novel.[239] As a consequence, it is possible to understand *The Shining* as an adaptation not — or not merely — of Stephen King's novel, but as an adaptation of themes that King was also developing in the source text.

Although King's version of *The Shining* is located close to the marvelous end of Todorov's Gothic spectrum,[240] it involves a complex interaction between reality and the supernatural. The tradition of realism, or the uncanny, is present in the characters' attempts to explain Danny's shining and the tumultuous events at the Overlook: Jack explains that "if precognitive trances are possible, they're probably functions of the subconscious mind" (266), and the wasp attack is attributed to a defective bug bomb —"Had to have been. How else can you explain this?" (136). Fantastic elements are also evident, most obviously in the episodes with the topiary animals: Jack is *almost* convinced that his encounter was a "hallucination" or "some kind of breakdown" (224), and he consoles Danny by pointing out that there are no hedge-animal footprints in the snow leading up to the front porch (296).[241] These uncanny and fantastic elements of the novel, along with the predominating marvelous components, dynamically reflect and reinforce each other. The paranormal evils of the Overlook act as a catalyst upon the dormant tensions that the Torrance family brings to it,[242] yet those troubled familial relationships and Danny's psychic talents also fuel the hotel's malevolent power. The Overlook's refusal to allow its evil legacy to remain buried in the past is a metaphor for Jack's inability to suppress the violent potential that lurks within and haunts him, yet Jack's personal demons also represent the psychic pressures building within the hotel and rendered concrete in its "often patched" boiler —"You'll want to keep your press up to no more than fifty, maybe sixty.... She creeps" (18–20).

Kubrick, on the other hand, disentangles the two strands that are so tightly woven together in King's novel while moving decisively toward the uncanny side of the Gothic continuum, ending somewhere close to its fantastic center.[243] Throughout most of the film, Kubrick maintains a fine balance between rational and supernatural without forcing the audience into a choice between them. This might explain why Kubrick disposed of the overtly fantastic hedge animal episodes— the brute physicality of the animals would have more urgently pressed viewers to choose sides in the rational/nonrational dialectic than would Danny's intangible visions or the ambiguously rendered events in Room 237. The reverberating sound of the bolt being pulled back when Jack is released from the pantry punctuates this segment of the film, shifting it into the marvelous mode before the eerie epilogue — rife with ambiguities— returns it to a fantastic balance-point.[244]

The demands of the fantastic mode upon a filmmaker would have presented an almost irresistible temptation to Kubrick, offering another possible reason why he might have decided to adapt *The Shining*. The fantastic "constitutes the shock between what is real and what is imaginary," and it "can only originate from a background of strongly defined 'realism.' For there to exist an opposition between the real and the imaginary, and conceivably a frisson between the two, the framework of reality must be scrupulously respected."[245] Kubrick's unique mise-en-scene, what one critic has termed his "realist/surrealist style,"[246] lends itself perfectly to this effect. The cold lighting, the geometric sets and camera movements, the deliberate pacing, and the remote starkness of atmosphere — recognizably marks of a Kubrick film — in *The Shining* accentuate the reality and materiality of the story, almost wounding us with a sense of hardness and solidity and making the irruptions of violence all the more terrifying. Richard T. Jameson's assertion that "*The Shining* is a horror movie only in the sense that all of Kubrick's mature work has been horror movies," is therefore absolutely correct.[247]

Finally, Kubrick's manipulation of these themes can be seen as part of what has been called the "process of secularization of literature."[248] The Gothic novel was transformed in the nineteenth century, when fiction "increasingly began to suggest that the chaos and disruption previously located mainly in such external forces as vampire or monster ... was actually produced within the mind of the human subject."[249] A similar phenomenon was part of the evolution of the horror film genre in the late twentieth century, when Alfred Hitchcock's *Psycho* (1960) "put the horror in the here and now."[250] As a result, Kubrick has not merely adapted a novel; he has contributed to the adaptation of a genre.

Conclusion

A standard assumption in film studies and adaptation theory is that adaptations cannot cross genres, but this analysis implies that Kubrick's *The Shining* does exactly that — remaining in the field of the Gothic, of course, but modulating King's narrative so aggressively that it trespasses upon recognized boundaries within that genre. So is *The Shining* an adaptation, or something else? As asserted at the beginning of this essay, a genre can be considered as the diachronic accumulation of traces left by a series of adaptations. In this view, adaptations *cannot* cross generic boundaries because the process of adaptation is one in which those boundaries are deformed, expanded, and even defined. To the extent this view has merit, then despite the fact that Kubrick, at a minimum, violated generic norms in *The Shining*, and despite conventional wisdom to the contrary, *The Shining* is an adaptation precisely because it squarely confronted, and remade, generic imperatives.

Part II Notes

1. Gavin Lambert first called attention to the contrast between the two worlds in a 1957 article in *Sight and Sound*. But the best discussion is in Alexander Walker's *Stanley Kubrick Directs* (New York: Harcourt Brace Jovanovich, 1971) 82–155.

2. Alexander Walker, *Stanley Kubrick Directs* (New York: Harcourt Brace Jovanovich, 1971) 90.

3. Walker 106.

4. Gene Phillips, *Stanley Kubrick: A Film Odyssey* (New York: Popular Library, 1975) 52.

5. I have used the restored and uncut version of the film shown on French television, respecting the widescreen format.

6. I shall return to the question of blacklisting later in this essay.

7. See Peter Hanson, *Dalton Trumbo, Hollywood Rebel* (Jefferson, N.C.: McFarland & Co., 2001) 148.

8. A question to which I do not have the answer: is there any footage shot by Anthony Mann remaining in the film?

9. We can also note the skill with which Trumbo looks ahead to the confrontation between Gracchus and Crassus: Batiatus has a bust of his friend Gracchus whom he prudently covers up in the hope that Crassus will not see it.

10. The place and function of women in *Spartacus*, whether patricians, wives or slaves, will be discussed below.

11. Spartacus remarks at one point that the free man loses the pleasures of life when he dies, whereas the slave loses only his misery.

12. We shall have cause to evoke Communism in another context.

13. See Sigmund Freud, *Group Psychology and the Analysis of the Ego*. The Standard Edition of the Complete Psychological Works of Sigmund Freud (London: The Hogarth Press and the Institute of Psycho-Analysis, 1955) 69–143. Freud devotes a chapter to what he calls "Two Artificial Groups: the Church and the Army."

14. And also of solidarity between the sexes and the generations: elderly men and women, as well as boys and girls, are part of the mass movement led by Spartacus.

15. This contempt is, in fact, another form of self-defense, for Crassus fears that this sort of solidarity will prove contagious; it has already given the former slaves something to believe in and, as we have pointed out, might well have extended to the starving masses of Rome. Obviously the expression "bread and circuses" functions as an ideological weapon in the hands of the ruling class only when bread is available. The French aristocracy learned this to their cost in 1789.

16. The gladiators, like the slaves, are figuratively "bled dry," a suitably vampiric image much used by Karl Marx to describe the capitalist.

17. I would suggest that we see Draba looking off-screen as a displaced form of address to the audience of *Spartacus* on how to interpret what happens. The audience within the film — Crassus and his group — are also off-screen at this point, so Kubrick's mise en scène invites us to interpret Draba's gaze as a sign of the dawning of a sense of solidarity between him and Spartacus faced with the power of Crassus.

18. Thus Claudia's fascination with Draba is the conscious manifestation, through inversion, of the unconscious disgust the ideological big Other has instilled into her when it is a question of blacks. This is clearly a reference to American society in the 1950s.

19. I used the word "serve" deliberately: the women are, as it were, servants or slaves to male desires. Let us not forget the formula "body *servant*" to define the explicitly hierarchical relationship between Antoninus and Crassus.

20. Batiatus has referred earlier to the gladiators as "stallions" which have connotations of sexual potency. It would be easy to see Batiatus as impotent, but that would not sum up the character.

21. Hanson 136.

22. In a fascinating article on *Spartacus*, Douglas and Kubrick, the late Raymond Durgnat pointed out the anti–Christian meaning of all the former slaves claiming to be Spartacus: "If Christ was the individual who suffered for all, here, all suffer for one." The *individual* dying for our "sins" becomes a *collective* death having the same political meaning as Draba's early sacrifice. See *Motion* 6 (Autumn 1963) 52.

23. The cries of "Hail Crassus!" are obviously intended to remind us of "Sieg Heil!"

24. As we have already pointed out, it is of note that the army comprises gladiators and freed slaves, old men and women, boys and girls. An extraordinary shot of the corpse-strewn battlefield after the final confrontation is over gives the impression of everyone *asleep*. It is as if they died as they lived, united in a mass collective movement.

25. For a detailed and persuasive analysis of Aldrich's radicalism and his links with the Hollywood Left, see Tony Williams, *Body and Soul. The Cinematic Vision of Robert Aldrich* (Lanham, Md.: Scarecrow Press 2004).

26. On this and related issues, see Jonathan Munby, *Public Enemies, Public Heroes. Screening the Gangster from Little Caesar to Touch of Evil* (Chicago and London: University of Chicago Press, 1999). The chapter entitled "Screening Crime the Liberal Consensus Way" (pp. 144–

85) is of particular interest in this context. For more background material, I refer the reader to my articles "The politics of crime and the crime of politics: Post-war noir, the liberal consensus and the Hollywood Left." In *Film Noir Reader 4*. Ed. by Alain Silver and James Ursini. And "'Documenting' Communist Subversion: The Case of *I Was a Communist for the F.B.I.* (1951)." In *Docufictions. Essays on the Intersection of Documentary and Fictional Filmmaking*, ed. by Gary D. Rhodes and John Parris Springer (Jefferson, NC: McFarland, 2006) 102–123.

27. Dylan Evans, *An Introductory Dictionary of Lacanian Psychoanalysis* (London and New York: Routledge, 1996) 46–47.

28. Interestingly, it is Hammer's secretary Velda who levels this accusation at her boss.

29. Martin Scorsese, ed., *The Making of 2001* (New York: Modern Library, 2000) 162–163.

30. Scorsese 144–146. Also, Piers Bizony, *2001: Filming the Future* (London: Aurum, 2000) 64–65.

31. Gene D, Phillips, ed., *Stanley Kubrick Interviews* (Jackson, Miss.: University Press of Mississippi, 2001) 48.

32. David G. Stork, *Hal's Legacy: 2001's Computer as Dream and Reality* (Cambridge, Mass.: Massachusetts Institute of Technology, 1997).

33. Leonard F. Wheat, *2001: A Triple Allegory* (Lanham, Md.: Scarecrow, 2000) 53.

34. *Ibid.*, 111.

35. Michel Ciment, *Kubrick* (New York: Holt, Rhinehart, and Winston, 1983) 7.

36. In the late 1990s, I began to lecture on the idea of HAL-as-Panopticon at the University of Oklahoma in a course titled "Film History Post-1945." Later, I offered similar ideas in two other courses, one devoted to Kubrick and another specifically exploring *2001: A Space Odyssey*. As a result, I was particularly happy when Michel Chion examined panopticism briefly in *Kubrick's Cinema Odyssey*, trans. Claudia Gorbman (London: BFI, 2001) 83–84.

37. Jeremy Bentham, *The Panopticon Writings*, ed. Miran Bzovic (London: Verso, 1995) 29.

38. Michel Foucault, *Discipline and Punish: The Birth of the Prison*, trans. Alan Sheridan (New York: Pantheon, 1977) 207.

39. Lewis Mumford, *Technics and Civilization* (New York: Harcourt Brace, 2004).

40. Eric Mark Kramer, "Guest Editor's Introduction: Narrative and Time," *Tamara: Journal of Critical Postmodern Organization Science* (2004) 1.

41. In terms of editing continuity during this scene, consider for example the use of an over-the-shoulder image of Moon Watcher between two frontal views, with which features an exact placement of all gestures and other australopithecines. Also, consider the use of four match-on-action shots during the murder of the rival australopithecine. Four different attacks on his body (the second of which misses him, and the fourth of which breaks a bone on his back) are cut with precision on action.

42. Arthur C. Clarke, *2001: A Space Odyssey* (New York: New American Library, 1968) 209.

43. Foucault 202–203.

44. Scorsese 25.

45. *Ibid.*, 238.

46. "Beaucoup Secrecy (Not Just Publicity) on Kubrick's *2001*, Even From Metro." *Variety* 3 Apr. 1968.

47. Phillips 131. Here Kubrick discusses the fact that he always shoots the handheld camera shots for his films himself. "I find it virtually impossible to explain what you want to even the most talented and sensitive camera operator," he says.

48. Wheeler Winston Dixon, *It Looks at You* (Albany: SUNY Press, 1995).

49. Scorsese 248.

50. Phillips 91.

51. Many terms employed in film-music discourse fall short of capturing the full range of the subject's behavior and experience. Anahid Kassabian engages with this problem explicitly and elegantly in *Hearing Film* where she points out that "spectator" implies passive involvement with a film, while "viewer" excludes sound and music. The terms used here, including Kassabian's "perceiver," describe an active subject — an admittedly idealized subject — whose experience of the film is likely to reflect elements of this analysis and interpretation. See Anahid Kassabian, *Hearing Film: Tracking Identifications in Contemporary Hollywood Film Music* (New York: Routledge, 2001) 2.

52. As an ultimately uncurbed criminal main character without appropriate motivation for his crimes, Alex is so problematic that Nicole Rafter must put him in a category by himself: the nonhero, "a no-good bad guy." Nicole Rafter, *Shots in The Mirror: Crime Films and Society* (New York: Oxford University Press, 2000) 160. Janet Staiger points out two major complaints about the film: that Alex was made "too nice," and that "Alex's victims were set up to be destroyed." Janet Staiger, *Perverse Spectators: The Practice of Film Reception* (New York: New York University Press, 2000) 103.

53. The categories "diegetic" and "nondiegetic" were first proposed by Etienne Souriau and became mainstays of film-music discourse following Claudia Gorbman's seminal *Unheard Melodies*, in which the terms provide a running thread and theoretical touchstone. Diegetic music is understood to be coming from within the world of the film, and audible to the characters, while nondiegetic music functions as underscore and is only heard by the moviegoer. See Claudia Gorbman, *Unheard Melodies: Narrative Film Music* (Bloomington: Indiana University Press) 1987. Kubrick's film does not follow Burgess's novel closely in terms of pairing music with scenes. James Wierzbicki catalogues the differences between Beethoven's Ninth in the film and in the novel in "Banality Triumphant: Iconographic Use of Beethoven's Ninth Symphony in Recent Films," *Beethoven Forum*, vol. 10, no. 2 (113–138) 124.

54. *Dr. Strangelove or: How I Learned to Stop Worrying and Love the Bomb*, Kubrick's other and much less graphically violent satire, uses music ironically to underline the futility and ineptness of government projects and international politicians of the Cold War era. "Try a Little Tenderness" renders the midair refueling of a plane as an act of copulation, while "We'll Meet Again" is a doubtful message, couched in Vera Lynn's smooth voice accompanying scenes of the destruction of the earth by bombs.

55. One of the main musical techniques of Kubrick's oeuvre is the establishment of a specifically coded and rich moment-to-moment correspondence between music and narrative. The dramatic and emotional content of certain scenes in *Lolita* and *Eyes Wide Shut* plays out in the music of Nelson Riddle and Gyorgi Ligeti, respectively. The music, meanwhile, accumulates pointed dramatic and emotional implications. Katherine McQuiston, "Recognizing Music in the Films of Stanley Kubrick," diss. Columbia University, 2005: 49–63 and 141–154.

56. Wendy Carlos had been working on a version of the Ninth before hearing of Kubrick's intention to make a film of *A Clockwork Orange*, as discussed by Chris Nelson (see note 10). The first proposal of the Ninth for the film was lucky happenstance. Kubrick ultimately had to approve the decision, however, and decide where and how it would appear in the film.

57. Krin Gabbard and Shailja Sharma generalize that the music functions as ironic counterpoint in "Stanley Kubrick and the Art Cinema," *Stanley Kubrick's "A Clockwork Orange,"* ed. Stuart McDougal (Cambridge: Cambridge University Press, 2003) 85–108. Peter Rabinowitz's commentary mainly concerns musical differences between Burgess's novel and Kubrick's film. He describes the role of the music in the film as offsetting the violence and also the destructive force that is the potential flip side of high artistic achievement. Peter J. Rabinowitz, "'A Bird of Like Rarest Spun Heavenmetal': Music in *A Clockwork Orange*," *Stanley Kubrick's "A Clockwork Orange,"* 109–130.

58. This very phenomenon is at the heart of Stilwell's analysis of *Closet Land*, and Ken Garner's analysis of music in films of Quentin Tarantino. See Stilwell, "Sound and Empathy: Subjectivity, Gender and the Cinematic Soundscape," *Film Music: Critical Approaches*, ed. K.J. Donnelly (Edinburgh: Edinburgh University Press, 2001) 167–187, and Ken Garner, "'Would you like to hear some music?' Music in-and-out-of-control in the Films of Quentin Tarantino," *Film Music: Critical Approaches* 188–205.

59. Though Buch holds that "The 'Beethoven and us' formula is always thought to be new by those who utter it, but the terms employed are often drawn from an accepted repertory of admirative or rejective terms," it is still valuable to situate Kubrick's among the voices that comment upon the piece, and examine his cinematic tools for doing so. Esteban Buch, *Beethoven's Ninth: A Political History*, trans. Richard Miller (Chicago: University of Chicago Press, 1999) 232.

60. For a description of how Carlos and Elkind came to work on *A Clockwork Orange*, see Chris Nelson, liner notes to *Wendy Carlos's Clockwork Orange (complete original score)*, ESD 81362, 1972.

61. *Straw Dogs* features music of Bach coming from a small radio, but only in early, nonviolent scenes of David (Dustin Hoffman), to convey his civilized, mathematical mind. Later, the aria "Caro Nome" from Verdi's *Rigoletto* is performed while a beating takes place in the backstage area in a church. While this is somewhat similar to *A Clockwork Orange* in that it is diegetic art music in a violent scene, the violent characters show no sign that they are conscious of the music, much less that they are *using* it, as Alex does, or enjoying it. Rather, it is Amy (Susan George), in the audience who is affected by the music. The lines "Col pensiero il mio desir/ A te ognora volerà" (My thoughts, all my desires/ Will ever turn to you") resonate with Amy's horrifying yet ambiguous memories of her rape, conveyed in flash cuts from her distressed face to scenes of the rape. Verdi's aria is much less likely to be familiar to and recognized by the spectator than Beethoven's music in *A Clockwork Orange*, and the meaning of this aria, sung in Italian, is not likely to be understood by the audience in the absence of subtitles.

62. Raphael Georg Kiesewetter puts this concept forth in his *Geschichte der europäisch-abendländischen oder unserer heutigen Musik* of 1834, as discussed by Carl Dahlhaus in *Nineteenth-Century Music*, trans. J. Bradford Robinson (Berkeley: University of California Press, 1989) 8.

63. This formulation suggests that Beethoven's pieces are texts to be struggled with, while Rossini's music is simply to be heard and enjoyed. Kubrick does not subscribe to this attitude regarding Beethoven.

64. Dahlhaus 11.

65. An orchestral version of the Ode theme from the finale of the Ninth plays on the film's DVD menu, which seems extremely strange. The DVD menu is a strictly nondiegetic place. In using Beethoven (music for Alex in the diegesis), it is breaking with the codes the film so carefully sets forth. It is therefore highly unlikely that Kubrick chose this music for the menu.

66. The phenomenal success of "Tony and Tina's Wedding," a live show about a wedding and wedding reception that involves audience participation by turning members into "wedding guests" who interact with the actors in the wedding party, attests to the value of verisimilitude in the dramatic arts, to say nothing of the craze for reality television shows in America in the late 1990s and early years of the twenty-first century. Of course, "Tony and Tina's Wedding" is heavily scripted, and the situations in reality shows on television are contrived and later heavily edited before airing. Even if these shows are an illusion, viewers seem attracted by the "spontaneous reality" these shows sell. A film version of "Tony and Tina's Wedding" released in 2004 was a box office failure.

67. Nicholas Cook, *Beethoven Symphony No. 9* (Cambridge: Cambridge University Press, 1993) 33.

68. Cook 33–34.

69. Interview by Eric Nordern, *Playboy*, September 1968, reprinted in *Stanley Kubrick: Interviews*, ed. Gene Phillips, (2001) 47–48.

70. The Nazi propaganda film *apparently* features an electronic version of this music because while it is the music we hear, we may be hearing it as Alex perceives it, distorted because of the drugs in his system. If we were able to hear the music objectively, however (as, for example, the scientists in the room hear it), it might very well be an orchestral, non-electronic recording.

71. It is not clear that *La gazza ladra*, which we hear in the nondiegetic track, is the music Alex hears. This scene is in slow motion, suggesting a disconnect between the seen and the heard. Further, the music in this scene in the novel is music by Beethoven.

72. Anthony Burgess, "Juice from a Clockwork Orange," *Perspectives on Stanley Kubrick*, ed. Mario Falsetto (London: G. K Hall and Co., 1996) 188. First printed in *Rolling Stone* 8 June 1972.

73. Richard Allen, *Projecting Illusion: Film Spectatorship and the Impression of Reality* (Cambridge: Cambridge University Press, 1995) 133.

74. It appears that Carlos added extra measures at the end of the march section, after what Beethoven wrote in m. 594, perhaps to continue to the end of the scene, where the dialogue between Alex and the doctor is so loud that the music can barely be heard, let alone followed closely.

75. Alfred Rosenberg, "Beethoven," *Volkischer Beobachter*, 26 Mar. 1927, cited in Buch 185.

76. Beethoven commentators have long grappled with the style incongruity between the Turkish Janissary march section and the preceding elevated, holy sounding "O altitudo!" section. Nicholas Cook encapsulates the pitfalls of predominant approaches to the passage: "Romantic interpretations reduce the contradictory elements of the Ninth Symphony to a narrative thread or a series of pictures; absolute-music interpretations reduce them to an architectural plan." See Cook 93.

77. For a detailed account of Hitler's admiration of Beethoven, see Buch.

78. Allen 91.

79. This is not the only case of Kubrick fooling his viewers into believing what he shows is something from the real world. Ronald Reagan famously asked to see the War Room (the elegant set designed by Ken Adam figured prominently in *Dr. Strangelove or: How I Learned to Stop Worrying and Love the Bomb*) when he was elected president. Vincent LoBrutto, *Stanley Kubrick: A Biography* (New York: Penguin Books, 1997) 247.

80. For an explication of those aspects of media violence which have been agreed upon, and which are "objective,"

see W. James Potter, *On Media Violence* (London: Sage Publications, 1999).

81. Randy Rasmussen. *Stanley Kubrick: Seven Films Analyzed* (Jefferson, N.C.: McFarland & Company, Inc., 2001) 151.

82. Allen 3.

83. Potter 33.

84. *Ibid.*, 37.

85. Richard Wollheim espouses this view in "Wish-fulfillment," in *Rational Action*, ed. Ross Harrison (Cambridge: Cambridge University Press, 1995) 50.

86. Allen 129.

87. James Webster, "The Form of the Finale of Beethoven's Ninth Symphony," *Beethoven Forum* 1 (1992) 26.

88. Webster 36.

89. Cook 100.

90. Michael Tusa, "Noch einmal: Form and Content in the Finale of Beethoven's Ninth Symphony," in *Beethoven Forum*, vol. 7, no. 1 (2000) 113–137.

91. Buch detects the first interpretation of the Ode to Joy as an Ode to Freedom in an 1838 novel *Das Musikfest oder die Beethovener* by Robert Griepenkerl (a contributor to *Neue Zeitschrift für Musik*). Buch 116–7.

92. See Buch 46–8.

93. Maynard Solomon keenly points out the indeterminate tense of "All men become brothers," which casts the notion as an abstract idea, divorced from actuality. Maynard Solomon, "The Ninth Symphony: A Search for Order," in *Beethoven Essays* (Cambridge: Harvard University Press, 1988) 30.

94. Buch 99.

95. Scott Burnham, *Beethoven Hero* (Princeton: Princeton University Press, 1995) xiv.

96. Rey Longyear, "Beethoven and Romantic Irony," *The Creative World of Beethoven*, ed. Paul Henry Lang (New York: W.W. Norton, 1971) 149–50.

97. Cook 103.

98. Cook 36.

99. Burnham, *Beethoven Hero* 32.

100. Cook viii.

101. Cook points too to a stylistic shift in the music in which this text is set as an indication of Beethoven's distance from its message: "Perhaps the most explicit technique of Beethoven's irony is anachronism." As the music assumes a Mozartean style, "as the verbal expression reaches maximum intensity, the music goes into quotation marks. Nothing could more clearly express Beethoven's detachment from his own message; nothing could more clearly indicate the retrospective, and therefore ultimately futile, nature of the Enlightenment ideals that Schiller's words proclaim." See Cook 103–4.

102. Indeed, Ma Ting Heng also detected this problem in his description of the finale as holding out "the illusion that a progressive and just society can be achieved without class conflict." "Xiyang zichanjieji yinyue dui wo de duhai" (I was poisoned by the bourgeois music of the West), *Guangming Ribao* (*Enlightened Daily*) 4 Mar. 1965 as cited in Cook 95–96.

103. Buch 3. In a wider-reaching summation of the paradoxes of the piece, Susan McClary offers, "The Ninth Symphony is probably our most compelling articulation in music of the contradictory impulses that have organized patriarchal culture since the Enlightenment." Susan McClary, *Feminine Endings* (Minneapolis: University of Minnesota Press, 1991) 128–9. The notion of paradox defines Beethoven scholarship, evidenced by the final sentence in the "Beethoven" entry in the *New Grove Dictionary of Music and Musicians*: "It is indeed difficult, if not impossible, to imagine a time when Beethoven's music will not continue to exercise its paradoxically confounding and foundational force." Scott

Burnham, "Beethoven, Ludwig van," *New Grove Dictionary of Music and Musicians*, 2nd ed. 114.

104. Basil Deane, "The Symphonies and Overtures," *The Beethoven Companion*, ed. Denis Arnold and Nigel Fortune (London: Faber, 1971) 313.

105. In this, the Ninth shares an uncanny similarity with Nazi propaganda films, whose cheerful promises make no acknowledgment of the suffering that its cause will exact.

106. The "Ode to Joy" melody, as it has been arranged by Herbert von Karajan for orchestra, without sung text, buries its possible meanings even further from the surface. In this form, it serves as the official anthem of Europe.

107. *A Clockwork Orange* is dominated by industrialism. Alex's mother, who works in a factory, wears synthetic wigs in neon colors. Milk, a symbol of nature, is perverted with drugs. The spiked milk, Alex's mother's sleeping pills and the Ludovico treatment itself all suggest a scientific and engineering approach to the human being.

108. Solomon 13.

109. See, for example, Friedrich Kanne's 1824 response to the symphony, cited in Cook 38.

110. George Grove, *Beethoven and His Nine Symphonies*, 3rd ed. (New York: Dover, 1962) 392.

111. Cook 27.

112. Cook 46. Scott Burnham identifies a forerunner of Alex's gang in the "fatally boisterous Beethoven cult" that is the subject of Robert Griepenkerl's novel, *Das Musikfest oder die Beethovener*. "Beethoven, Ludwig van," 112.

113. Solomon 25.

114. *Beethoven Forum*, vol. 10, no. 2 (2003).

115. Robynn Stilwell, "Hysterical Beethoven," *Beethoven Forum*, vol. 10, no. 2 (2003) 163.

116. Burnham, "Beethoven, Ludwig van" 112.

117. McClary, see note 53.

118. Walter Benjamin meditates on the nature of reproduced art, and concepts of authenticity, ritual and materiality in his landmark essay, "The Work of Art in the Age of Mechanical Reproduction," in *Illuminations*, ed. Hannah Arendt, trans. Harry Zohn (New York: Harcourt, Brace and World, Inc., 1968) 219–253.

119. Penelope Houston, "*Barry Lyndon*," *Sight and Sound* vol. 45, no. 2 (Spring 1976): 77. John Engell suggests that the film is driven by a tension between the austerity of style and the content of the "moral lessons" it offers. John Engell, "*Barry Lyndon*, a Picture of Irony," *Eighteenth-Century Life* 19 (May 1995) 83.

120. Robert Kolker, *A Cinema of Loneliness* (Oxford: Oxford University Press, 1988): 153–161. Kolker in general characterizes the film as lacking affect, and interprets this gesture as a deliberate critique of melodramatic emotional content on Kubrick's part.

121. Andrew Sarris, "What Makes Barry Run," *The Village Voice* no. 20 (December 29, 1975) 111–112.

122. Interview with Ken Adam, *Kubrick: The Definitive Edition*, ed. Michel Ciment (New York: Faber and Faber, 2001).

123. Frank Cossa, "Images of Perfection: Life Imitates Art in Kubrick's *Barry Lyndon*," *Eighteenth-Century Life* 19 (May 1995) 79.

124. Engell 85.

125. Ann Bermingham suggests that the term "picturesque" was a vexed one when applied to English landscape painting, and one which stood at the very intersection between nature and culture. "Applied to landscape," she writes—paraphrasing E.H. Gombrich in *Norm and Form*—"the term referred to its fitness to make a picture; applied to pictures, the term referred to the fidelity with which they copied the picturesque landscape." Ann Bermingham, *Landscape and Ideology: The English Rustic Tradition, 1740–1860*

(Berkeley: University of California Press, 1986): 57. Bermingham also notes that the notion of what constituted a "picturesque" landscape changed by the end of the eighteenth century, from the manicured, orderly, qualities of the Brownian garden to "the smaller-scale, less obviously designed picturesque garden, which consisted of a variety of intimate occluded views in which nature appeared in its rough, shaggy, and even humble aspects." Ann Bermingham, "System, Order, and Abstraction: The Politics of English Landscape Drawing around 1795," in *Landscape and Power*, ed. W.J.T. Mitchell (Chicago: The University of Chicago Press, 2002): 82. The landscapes Kubrick constructs in *Barry Lyndon* would seem to predate this shift.

126. W.J.T. Mitchell, "Introduction," *Landscape and Power* (Chicago: The University of Chicago Press, 1994) 2.

127. Stephen Heath, "Narrative Space," *Questions of Cinema* (Bloomington: Indiana University Press, 1981) 30.

128. See Christian Metz, "Identification, Mirror," *The Imaginary Signifier*, trans. Celia Britton, Annwyl Williams, et. al. (Bloomington: Indiana University Press, 1977).

129. Jacques Lacan, *The Four Fundamental Concepts of Psychoanalysis*, trans. Alan Sheridan (New York: W.W. Norton, 1981) 81.

130. Lacan 96.

131. Kaja Silverman, *World Spectators* (Stanford: Stanford University Press, 2000) 143. The discussion of *The Four Fundamental Concepts of Psychoanalysis* is indebted to Silverman's indispensable readings of Lacan in both *World Spectators* and *The Threshold of the Visible World* (New York: Routledge, 1996), particularly pages 195–207.

132. For another analysis of Barthes's theory of the image and exclusion, see the author's essay "The Long Goodbye: Jeff Wall and Film Theory," discussing Barthes in relation to Wall's theories of the landscape as leave-taking. In *Jeff Wall: Photographs*, ed. Achim Höchdorfer (Köln: Verlag der Buchhandlung Walther König, 2003) 110–127.

133. Roland Barthes, *A Lover's Discourse*, trans. Richard Howard (New York: Hill and Wang, 1978) 132.

134. *Ibid.*, 133.

135. Roland Barthes, *Camera Lucida*, trans. Richard Howard (New York: Hill and Wang, 1981).

136. Alan Spiegel makes a similar observation about the affect attending Kubrick's reverse zooms when he writes that "the camera withdraws from that to which we would cleave close — and in this respect, our sorrow is collateral to Barry's: we too can never get what we want or keep what we get, and the motion of the camera is a measure of our bereavement." Alan Spiegel, "Kubrick's *Barry Lyndon*," *Salmagundi* (Summer-Fall 1977) 204.

137. Lacan 101.

138. Thomas Allen Nelson, *Kubrick: Inside a Film Artist's Maze* (Bloomington: Indiana University Press, 2000) 184.

139. Schubert's 1828 Piano Trio in E-Flat (Op. 100) serves as Lady Lyndon's theme song and was written well after the time period in which the film is set. Michel Ciment also notes that Handel's Sarabande is orchestrated in a "more dramatic style" than one would find in eighteenth-century composition. Michel Ciment, "Interview with Stanley Kubrick," *Kubrick: The Definitive Edition*, 175.

140. To be more precise: the Irish architecture was constructed from Caher Castle, Ormond House, and Huntingdon; the Lyndon estate used Wilton (Salisbury), Petworth (Sussex), Longleat (Wiltshire), and Castle Howard (York). Adam 205.

141. Freud writes of the childhood view of sexual intercourse as sadistic in *Three Essays on the Theory of Sexuality*, trans. James Strachey (New York: Basic Books, 1962) 62.

142. As John Engell writes, "The good old soldier admits to his young friend that he has gambled away half the money he promised him, then says, 'Kiss me my boy, for we shall never meet again.' Redmond kisses him and weeps. Grogan is dead, and like Nora will never appear again." Engell 84.

143. Engell 86.

144. The terms "inform" and "evoke" are borrowed from Lacan's "Field and Function of Speech and Language in Psychoanalysis," where he applies them respectively to what he calls "empty speech" and "full speech." Jacques Lacan, "Function and Field of Speech and Language in Psychoanalysis," *Écrits: A Selection*, trans. Alan Sheridan (New York: Norton, 1977).

145. Discussed here are the boxing scene and the drawing room fight scene; others include a marching scene after Barry has been forced to join the Prussian army, the scene of Lady Lyndon's suicide attempt, and a brief shot during the flashback scene which shows Bryan's accident on horseback.

146. Ciment 174.

147. Mark Crispin Miller reads the freeze-frame as "suggesting that the action stops when the hero no longer enlivens his surroundings." "*Barry Lyndon* Reconsidered," *The Georgia Review* vol. 30, no. 4 (Winter 1976) 827.

148. The negative response of film critics to *The Shining* is not entirely remarkable. None of Kubrick's twelve feature films released prior to 1995 "ever opened to widespread critical and commercial success." Frank Manchel, "What about Jack? Another Perspective on Family Relationships in Stanley Kubrick's *The Shining*," *Literature Film Quarterly* 23 (1995): 69. His thirteenth and final feature, *Eyes Wide Shut* (1999), continued this trend. Tim Kreider, review of *Eyes Wide Shut*, *Film Quarterly* 53.3 (2000) 41–48. The director himself was aware that his films were more often praised in retrospect than upon their initial release. Stanley Kubrick, "The *Rolling Stone* Interview," by Tim Cahill, *Stanley Kubrick: Interviews*, ed. Gene D. Phillips (Jackson: University Press of Mississippi, 2001) 203.

149. Jim Harwood, "*The Shining*: But Not Bright," review of *The Shining*, *Variety* 28 May 1980: 14. Similar evaluations of the film include Dennis Bingham, "The Displaced Auteur: A Reception History of *The Shining*," *Perspectives on Stanley Kubrick*, ed. Mario Falsetto (New York: Simon-G.K. Hall, 1996) 290: "The reviews which were angry and negative tended to be bothered by ... Kubrick's tendency to drop plot and character details out of the novels he adapts"; Noël Carroll, "The Future of Allusion: Hollywood in the Seventies (and Beyond)," *October* 20 (1982) 61: Kubrick "jettisoned Stephen King's carefully built rhythm of tension and replaced a number of King's smoothly timed shocks (in the center of the plot) with an abyss of languor"; P.L. Titerington, "Kubrick and *The Shining*," *Sight and Sound* 50.2 (1981) 117: "Any knowledge of King's novel creates an impression of remnants of the original surviving in what is otherwise a completely different kind of script"); C.T. Walters, "Stanley Kubrick's *The Shining*: A Study in the Terror of Abstraction," *Ball State University Forum* 26.3 (1985) 30: "Kubrick eviscerated Stephen King's book."

150. Richard T. Jameson, "Kubrick's *Shining*," Falsetto, *Perspectives* 243. Jameson concluded his review by describing *The Shining* as "a horror movie that isn't a horror movie, that the audience has to get into and finish." R. Jameson 252. Similar evaluations of the film include: John Brown, "The Impossible Object: Reflections on *The Shining*," *Cinema and Fiction: New Modes of Adapting, 1950–1990*, ed. John Orr and Colin Nicholson (Edinburgh: Edinburgh University Press, 1992) 117: "*The Shining* is a kind of critical parody of the [horror film] genre, which deliberately exposes and undercuts all the stock motifs of the genre while keeping within its general domain and maintaining a straight face"; Larry W. Caldwell and Samuel J. Umland, "'Come and play with us': The Play Metaphor in Kubrick's *Shining*," *Literature Film*

Quarterly 14.2 (1986) 110: "It might seem ... that we are in a horror film at last, but Kubrick will not allow it"; Jeff Conner, *Stephen King Goes to Hollywood* (New York: New American Library-Plume, 1987) 28: the film "consistently operates against historical film shock tactics" and its "balloon of tension is continually deflated"; Morris Dickstein, "The Aesthetics of Fright," *Planks of Reason: Essays on the Horror Film*, ed. Barry Keith Grant (Metuchen: Scarecrow, 1984) 65: Kubrick "appears to have forgotten that the main point of a horror film is to frighten us"; Titterington 117: "Judged simply as a horror film, or even a thriller, *The Shining* appears an odd exercise."

151. Dudley Andrew, *Concepts in Film Theory* (Oxford: Oxford University Press, 1984) 100.

152. Greg Jenkins, *Stanley Kubrick and the Art of Adaptation: Three Novels, Three Films* (Jefferson, N.C.: McFarland, 1997) 6.

153. André Bazin, *What Is Cinema?*, ed. and trans. Hugh Gray (Berkeley: University of California Press, 1967) 67.

154. See Thomas Leitch, "Twelve Fallacies in Contemporary Adaptation Theory," *Criticism* 45 (2003) 149–71; Brian McFarlane, *Novel to Film: An Introduction to the Theory of Adaptation* (New York: Oxford University Press, 1996) 194.

155. Leitch 162.

156. *Ibid.*

157. But see Bingham 288 ("Kubrick's films lent themselves perfectly to auteurist sensibilities and analysis, with one exception. The auteur himself was nowhere to be found in films which appeared to have been handed down from on high").

158. Michel Ciment, *Kubrick: The Definitive Edition* 41.

159. Ciment 42.

160. Kubrick's role as co-screenwriter of *Lolita* (1962) was uncredited. See Mario Falsetto, *Stanley Kubrick: A Narrative and Stylistic Analysis*, 2nd ed. (Westport: Praeger, 2001) 191.

161. Stanley Kubrick, "Words and Movies," *Hollywood Directors, 1941–1976*, ed. Richard Koszarski (New York: Oxford University Press, 1977) 308. See also Thomas Allen Nelson, *Kubrick: Inside a Film Artist's Maze*, new and expanded ed. (Bloomington: Indiana University Press, 2000) 8 (discussing Kubrick's "standard practice" of adaptation throughout his career as based on V.I. Pudovkin's 1929 text, *Film Technique*).

162. Michael Patrick Allen and Anne E. Lincoln, "Critical Discourse and the Cultural Consecration of American Films," *Social Forces* 82 (2004) 878.

163. Colin MacCabe, *The Eloquence of the Vulgar: Language, Cinema and the Politics of Culture* (Berkeley: University of California Press, 1999) 38. But see Leitch 150 (questioning whether, and to what degree, the production of a film adaptation is as collaborative as the production of a film based on an original screenplay).

164. The work of George Bluestone is a notable exception. His skepticism about the usefulness of fidelity as an evaluative criterion for adaptations is explicitly predicated upon his view that "the end products of novel and film represent different aesthetic genera, as different from each other as ballet is from architecture." George Bluestone, *Novels into Film* (Baltimore: Johns Hopkins Press, 1957) 5.

165. *The Shining* is an obvious example. Richard T. Jameson, for instance, argues that Kubrick's flawed direction of Jack Nicholson and Shelley Duvall "deprived the audience of any real opportunity for identifying with his characters ... thereby violating conventional theory on how to bring off a jolly good scareshow." R. Jameson 245. See also Bingham 285 ("Contempt for 'vulgar' tastes could be felt in the film itself, Kubrick's rendition of a base genre").

166. "The most distinguished authors, as well as their more mediocre contemporaries, freely adopt the plots they inherit from other writers." Heather Dubrow, *Genre* (London: Methuen, 1982) 9.

167. "The very question of whether one should accept the notion of generic classification or challenge its validity involves one of the broadest theoretical issues, the degree of autonomy that can be claimed for the work of art and its creator. The acceptance of generic categories tends to imply — and also tends to encourage — a view of the writer as a craftsman instructed by past artists, rather than a bard inspired by his own emotions." Dubrow 45. As Michel Ciment notes in reference to Stanley Kubrick's work, genre and historical consciousness are inescapable even for an artist who strives toward originality: "To affirm one's difference it is important to preserve a historical conscience, a sense of being linked with the past.... One means of distancing oneself from this tradition is to call its genres into question." Ciment 59–60. For a detailed discussion of adaptation in terms of intertextuality, see Robert Stam, *Literature through Film: Realism, Magic, and the Art of Adaptation* (Malden: Blackwell, 2005).

168. "The concept of genre (or species) is borrowed from the natural sciences." Tzvetan Todorov, *The Fantastic: A Structural Approach to a Literary Genre*, trans. Richard Howard (1973; Ithaca: Cornell University Press, 1975) 5. In literature, however, "evolution operates with an altogether different rhythm: *every* work modifies the sum of possible works, each new example alters the species." Todorov 6. In adaptation theory, a nascent awareness of the connections between film and biology is present in the work of George Bluestone, who remarked that "mutations are probable the moment one goes from a given set of fluid, but relatively homogenous, conventions to another." Bluestone 5. For a treatment of literature and literary theory from a biological perspective, see Joseph Carroll, *Evolution and Literary Theory* (Columbia: University of Missouri Press, 1995).

169. See, for example, McFarlane 194; Stam 3–5.

170. Perhaps this focus on genre will enable readers who are suspicious of or antagonistic toward auteur theory to forgive the auteurist perspective that otherwise frames this essay. Genre, after all, has eclipsed auteurism as the principal force motivating film audiences to visit the cinema. "Canning the Film Director," *Economist* (U.S. edition) 3 Oct. 1992: 92.

171. See Stam 66.

172. See Todorov 25.

173. Bazin 67.

174. Leitch 161. See also Stam 3–5.

175. Bluestone vi.

176. *Ibid.*, 5 [emphasis in original].

177. James Griffith, *Adaptations as Imitations: Films from Novels* (Newark: University of Delaware Press, 1997) 73.

178. Bluestone 5.

179. Leitch 161. Stam's similar view relies explicitly on the idea that fidelity is lost from the moment a narrative is transposed from text to screen: "It is questionable whether strict fidelity is even *possible*. An adaptation is *automatically* different and original due to the change of medium." Stam 3–4 [emphasis in original].

180. Griffith 41.

181. Bazin 67.

182. Tony Magistrale, *Hollywood's Stephen King* (New York: St. Martin's-Palgrave, 2003) 95. In fairness to King's script, it was written as part of his contractual obligation to the studio, and Kubrick, not wanting to be influenced by King's vision for the film, simply did not read it. Conner 32. See also Harlan Kennedy, "Kubrick Goes Gothic," *American Film* 5.8 (1980) 50. Magistrale reports that King, whose dis-

pleasure with Kubrick's adaptation has been widely publicized, gave his "pledge that he would not discuss further Kubrick's film in any public form" as a condition of obtaining the rights to produce his own adaptation of the novel. Magistrale, *Hollywood's Stephen King* 198.

183. Robin Dougherty, "Vanity, Thy Name Is Stephen King," review of Stephen King's *"The Shining," Salon*, 25 Apr. 1997, 9 Apr. 2005, http://www.salon.com/april97/shining970425.html.

184. Jenkins 1.

185. "In disposing of ... texture, Kubrick speeds his project, but whittles down the fullness of King's story." Jenkins 77.

186. Stephen King, *The Shining* (New York: Doubleday, 1977) 6. All further citations to *The Shining* will appear as parenthetical references in the text.

187. Jenkins 75–76.

188. *Ibid.*, 81. Likewise, Kubrick's streamlined action has the incidental benefit of making the narrative "elliptical [and] mysterious." Jenkins 77.

189. Charlene Bunnell, "The Gothic: A Literary Genre's Transition to Film," Grant 92.

190. Michael J. Collins, "Culture in the Hall of Mirrors: Film and Fiction and Fiction and Film," *A Dark Night's Dreaming: Contemporary American Horror Fiction*, ed. Tony Magistrale and Michael A. Morrison (Columbia: University of South Carolina Press, 1996) 119.

191. Perhaps this accounts for the fact that the specific conclusions Jenkins offers at the end of his study are mostly in the nature of uninteresting truisms; for example: "As Kubrick remakes the original narrative, he tends, with some exceptions, to simplify it." Jenkins 156.

192. Leitch 150–53. It is curious that Leitch resists "the essentialist view that novels and films are suited to fundamentally different tasks," yet concludes elsewhere that "re-creating specific textual details or the effect of the whole" is impossible. Leitch 151, 161. See also Griffith 192–93 ("material and technique make poor categories on which to base claims about an adaptation's fidelity to a novel").

193. R. Jameson 245. See also Jenkins 94 (Kubrick deemed "the unwieldy hedge animals" to be "dispensable"); Nelson 199 ("in an era before Computer Graphic Imaging," such effects would have been impossible).

194. Garrett Brown, "The Steadicam and *The Shining*," *American Cinematographer* 61 (1980) 785–90.

195. Bill Blakemore, "Kubrick's Shining Secret: Film's Hidden Horror Is the Murder of the Indian," *Washington Post* 12 July 1987, final ed.: F1.

196. Ciment 294–95.

197. Blakemore F1.

198. McFarlane 20.

199. Bluestone vii, 62. In the words of a Stephen King critic, "the best approach to Kubrick's *The Shining* is to divorce it from connections with Stephen King — not because Kubrick failed to do justice to King's narrative, but simply because it has ceased to *be* King's." Michael R. Collings, *The Films of Stephen King* (Mercer Island: Starmont, 1986) 62. Of course, separating the Kubrick and King iterations of *The Shining* is the very opposite of what this essay is suggesting, but the purpose in arguing that the two should be considered together is to identify exactly *how* the narrative has become Kubrick's rather than King's.

200. "*The Shining* is less about ghosts and demonic possession than it is about the murderous system of economic exploitation which has sustained this country since, like the Overlook Hotel, it was built upon an Indian burial ground." David A. Cook, "American Horror: *The Shining*," *Literature Film Quarterly* 12 (1984) 2. "The Jack Nicholson of *The Shining* is possessed neither by evil as such nor by the 'devil' or

some analogous occult force, but rather simply by History." Frederic Jameson, *Signatures of the Visible* (New York: Routledge, 1990) 90. "Kubrick seems to be saying that America has a right to be superstitious, that its ghosts are real." Flo Leibowitz and Lynn Jeffries, review of Kubrick's *The Shining, Film Quarterly* 34.3 (1981) 47. "While some critics thought *The Shining* 'airless' or 'claustrophobic,' ... I think it a terrifying commentary on the effects of consumer mentality and media violence." Tony Pipolo, "The Modernist and the Misanthrope: The Cinema of Stanley Kubrick," *Cinéaste* 27.2 (2002) 5. The film's subtext is "the indictment of American racist and sexist ideology." Greg Smith, "'Real Horrorshow': The Juxtaposition of Subtext, Satire, and Audience Implication in Stanley Kubrick's *The Shining*," *Literature Film Quarterly* 25 (1997) 300. "*The Shining* works primarily through elements that evoke America's past history and the present state of its society." Titterington 118. For a broad survey of other critical readings of *The Shining*, see Manchel 68–71.

201. There are other reasons for doubting the majority view. Caldwell and Umland argue that *The Shining* is a parody of a horror film and that it therefore "cannot sustain the ponderous social psychology which film scholars have imputed to it." Caldwell and Umland 110.

202. Tony Magistrale, *Landscape of Fear: Stephen King's American Gothic* (Bowling Green: Bowling Green State University Press, 1988) 70.

203. Stephen King, *Danse Macabre* (1981; New York: Berkley, 1983) 265 (emphasis in original).

204. Ciment 163. As Robin Wood has observed, the horror film genre can be either progressive or reactionary. Robin Wood, "An Introduction to the American Horror Film," Grant 192.

205. Kubrick admitted in a 1980 interview that one of the "deeper implications" of the film is that "there's something inherently wrong with the human personality.... There's an evil side to it." Jack Kroll, "Stanley Kubrick's Horror Show," review of *The Shining*, directed by Stanley Kubrick, *Newsweek* 26 May 1980: 96. See also Collings 62 ("Jack Torrance in large part replaces the Overlook as focus of evil"); Cook 2 ("In *The Shining* I think we're being told that true horror is not extraordinary but surrounds us every day").

206. Given Kubrick's prior work, it is not surprising that in *The Shining* he "would subvert the novel's and the genre's outward conventions in order to explore the possibilities of meaning and expression on many levels." Bingham 285. "Whatever kind of movie *The Shining* turns out to be — and with Kubrick it's reckless to conjecture — it's at least sure to be a film made challengingly against the grain of the genre Kubrick has chosen." Kennedy 51. See also Caldwell and Umland 106; Leibowitz and Jeffries 45 (noting "Kubrick's propensity to use genres merely as vehicles").

207. "Unlike the Jack of the novel, the film's protagonist is not a loving or kind husband. Whereas King stressed this positive aspect of Jack's personality, Kubrick eliminates it completely." Manchel 74. Manchel observes that another significant difference between the film and the novel — Wendy is portrayed as timid and homely in the former, as strong and beautiful in the latter — flows from the change in Jack's character; Wendy, as she is depicted in the novel, would never stay with Jack, as he is depicted in the film. Manchel 74. See also J. Brown 111; Collings 62–63; Falsetto, *Narrative and Stylistic Analysis* 126.

208. Titterington 117.

209. See, for example, Magistrale, *Hollywood's Stephen King* 201.

210. "Jack Nicholson plays Jack Nicholson playing Jack Torrance." R. Jameson 251. Manchel finds Nicholson "ideal for the part" precisely "because we do identify the

actor with his previous roles." Manchel 75. And, according to Stephen King, "People have said to me that Nicholson is crazy from the beginning of the film; there's never any progression. That is not right. The man is sane at the beginning. People impute that craziness to Nicholson because of the other parts he's played." Tim Underwood and Chuck Miller, eds., *Feast of Fear: Conversations with Stephen King* (New York: Carroll, 1992) 100. See also Falsetto, *Narrative and Stylistic Analysis* 166; and F. Jameson 93.

211. Other examples include Kubrick's omission of the wasp's nest — Jack observes that it was "as if it wasn't wasps that had stung his son ... but the hotel itself" (138) — and the topiary animals, which rip through Danny's pants and scratch him (294).

212. See Jenkins 88; Leibowitz and Jeffries 49.

213. William Paul, *Laughing, Screaming: Modern Hollywood Horror and Comedy* (New York: Columbia University Press, 1994) 349. See also R. Jameson 249; Randy Rasmussen, *Stanley Kubrick: Seven Films Analyzed* (Jefferson: McFarland, 2001) 265–66.

214. See Ben P. Indick, "King and the Literary Tradition of Horror and the Supernatural," *Fear Itself: The Horror Fiction of Stephen King*, ed. Tim Underwood and Chuck Miller (New York: Signet, 1985) 185.

215. As one critic says of King's fiction in general, "the marvelous element is introduced early and is never seriously doubted, even by the protagonist (much less the reader, with his advantage of generic expectations)." Margaret L. Carter, *Specter or Delusion? The Supernatural in Gothic Fiction* (Ann Arbor: UMI Research, 1987) 122.

216. Jonathan Romney, "Resident Phantoms," *Sight and Sound* 9.9 (1999) 11. Events on the "fantasy level" of the film, such as Jack's conversations with Lloyd (Joe Turkel) and Grady (Philip Stone), "tend to have purely symbolic or allegorical significance." Leibowitz and Jeffries 48.

217. Rasmussen 263. See also R. Jameson 248; Magistrale, *Hollywood's Stephen King* 89; Nelson 207.

218. Kubrick and Johnson "have changed the emphasis of Stephen King's best-selling thriller to a much more subtle and shocking balance between the natural and the supernatural." Kroll 96.

219. Ciment 194.

220. Two critics go so far as to blame Jack's breakdown on writer's block. See Dickstein 75–76; Darryl Jones, *Horror: A Thematic History in Fiction and Film* (London: Arnold, 2002) 141.

221. John Brown notes that the ghosts Wendy sees appear too late in the film to have any metaphorical significance, and that they are merely incitements to scream. J. Brown 115.

222. Because the Overlook is not the source of evil in the film, it need not be destroyed at the film's conclusion — and particularly not by fire, which has traditionally been associated with the purgation of supernatural evil.

223. Dickstein 65.

224. *The Shining* exhibits "a film aesthetic that continued to confound audience expectations at the very moment it appeared to fulfill them." Nelson 199. See also Leibowitz and Jeffries 48.

225. See F. Jameson 88–90.

226. See Brigitte Peucker, "Kubrick and Kafka: The Corporeal Uncanny," *Modernism / Modernity* 8 (2001) 669.

227. Jones 145.

228. Titterington 117. See also Leibowitz and Jeffries 45 ("one suspects that the 'failings' in *The Shining* are related

to Kubrick's interest in deliberately redirecting the audience's attention elsewhere").

229. Smith 304.

230. See Fred Botting, *Gothic* (London: Routledge, 1996) 23.

231. Glen Cavaliero, *The Supernatural and English Fiction* (Oxford: Oxford University Press, 1995) 23. See also Bunnell 8; Carter 2; S. L. Varnado, *Haunted Presence: The Numinous in Gothic Fiction* (Tuscaloosa: University of Alabama Press, 1987) 121.

232. Todorov 41–42.

233. *Ibid.*, 25.

234. Cavaliero 23. See also Robert F. Geary, *The Supernatural in Gothic Fiction: Horror, Belief, and Literary Change* (Lewiston: Mellen, 1992) i; George E. Haggerty, *Gothic Fiction / Gothic Form* (University Park: Pennsylvania State University Press, 1989) 3.

235. Varnado 5 (emphasis in original).

236. See Botting 11–12; Geary 12; David Punter and Glennis Byron, *The Gothic* (Oxford: Blackwell, 2004) 25.

237. See, for example, Punter and Byron 248. King himself implies an association with the genre by virtue of his many allusions to figures such as Edgar Allen Poe and Shirley Jackson, and Wendy's observation that living at the Overlook is like being "in the middle of a Horace Walpole novel" (169). See also Indick 175 ("King has constructed his work on a sure knowledge of the fiction of his predecessors.... In his own distinctive style are mirrored the major traditions he has inherited").

238. Ciment 66.

239. *Ibid.*, 293.

240. Carter 122.

241. Indick has argued that the topiary scenes are reminiscent of Henry James' 1897 short story "The Turn of the Screw," perhaps the paradigm case of the fantastic. Indick 187.

242. See Kennedy 52; Punter and Byron 249.

243. "The supernatural elements in *The Shining* are deliberately and subtly organized to *prevent* a single consistent interpretation of the ghosts and visions." J. Brown 115 (emphasis in original). "*The Shining* uses ... psychological misdirection to forestall the realization that the supernatural events are actually happening." Ciment 185. "The line between objective reality and the subjective, interior life of the characters becomes blurred." Mario Falsetto, "Stanley Kubrick: An Overview," Falsetto, *Perspectives* 15.

244. The epilogue "appears to reveal something, the final narrative turn of the screw, or perhaps an explanation of the story's ambiguities — but really it reveals nothing." Romney 9. Comments that Kubrick made twenty years before *The Shining* suggest that he designed the ending to avoid introducing a "false note" into the film. Stanley Kubrick, "Director's Notes: Stanley Kubrick Movie Maker," Falsetto, *Perspectives* 23.

245. Ciment 125.

246. Nelson 199. See also Romney 10 ("There's an unsettling tension about the film's austerity").

247. R. Jameson 245.

248. Geary 11.

249. Punter and Byron 25.

250. Stephen Prince, "Introduction: The Dark Genre and Its Paradoxes," *The Horror Film*, ed. Stephen Prince (New Brunswick: Rutgers University Press, 2004) 4. See also Peter Hutchings, *The Horror Film* (Harlow, England: Pearson-Longman, 2004); Punter and Byron 68.

12 The Mask That Conceals Nothing: On the Concepts of Marital Fidelity and the Lo-Fi Soundscape in *Eyes Wide Shut*

Randolph Jordan

When I first experienced *Eyes Wide Shut,* it left me empty. I wasn't drained from having been through an intense experience. I was simply empty, as though Tom Cruise's performance had been made manifest within my very being. I became Bill Harford, wandering the streets of a cardboard New York, desperately trying to connect with all that I was presented with on (and off) screen. Yet I felt as though I couldn't break through the film's surface, and that perhaps there was nothing lying beneath this surface to begin with. Like poor Bill, each time an inter-personal connection loomed I was thwarted by one distanciating interruption after another. As these interruptions progressed, I became interested in the fact that each of them revolved in some way around the diegetic presence of sound reproduction technology. It became clear that the film places its overarching concern for the issue of marital fidelity alongside fidelity issues that arise in sound theory, particularly debates that rage around the concepts of "originals" and their "copies." These debates are ultimately about whether or not access to a copy can yield the depth of its original, or if a copy is always and necessarily doomed to remaining little more than a surface beyond which there is nothing. Kubrick's film explores this question by translating issues of fidelity in sound reproduction into an exploration of the concept of marital fidelity. It is in this convergence of the concepts of fidelity that the film seems richest to me. However, it is a richness that exposes the inherently surface nature of the cinema, a nature that Kubrick dared not attempt to transgress.

Inside Out?

Eyes Wide Shut deals with the question of whether *thinking* about cheating on one's part-ner has the same effect on a relationship as *doing* it. The film problematizes the idea of mental infidelity in interesting ways. In an early scene, Alice Harford (Nicole Kidman) admits to her husband, Dr. Bill Harford (Tom Cruise) that she was once so tempted by another man that she was ready to give up her marriage and family for one night of passion. This suggests that Bill's reaction to her cheating would have been to break up with her immediately. So the fact that they don't break up over Alice's temptation of years past suggests that there *is* a difference between the desires that lurk in her mind and the actions she takes in the world outside. But wait ... if this is so, then why does Bill respond to her inaction by going out on the town in search of sexual adventure?

The story ends with an interchange between the Harfords in which it is decided that the events of a single night, or even a lifetime, can never be understood as the whole reality of their relationship. And, similarly, that a dream is never just a dream. There is a deliberate conflation here between thinking and acting, between dream and reality, which revolves around the basic question of where one draws the line of marital fidelity that cannot be crossed. If the line between the binaries of dream and reality is unclear, there emerges the potential for other possibilities outside of this binary construct. With this in mind, where is the line of fidelity to one's partner drawn for Bill and Alice in this film? Does the blurring of this line result in them breaking free of their established notions of monogamy? How is the blurring of boundaries represented in the film's formal and aesthetic strategies?

In his study of *Eyes Wide Shut* for the BFI Modern Classics series, Michel Chion is careful to note that the film establishes clear codes for representations of mental activity which draw a "strict line" between the real and the imagined.[1] He refers specifically to the sound of remembered phrases presented with the convention of added reverberation, and the black and white shots of Alice and the sailor which could be Bill's visualizations of his wife's potential infidelity. For Chion, there is no confusion here about what is thought and what is actually done; there is no blurred line between these boundaries. Chion uses this observation to

Nicole Kidman and Tom Cruise in *Eyes Wide Shut* (1999).

support his assertion that the film does not mingle subjective representations with more objective approaches to reality, and thus the film hovers ever on the surface of its subject matter like a mask that reveals nothing of that which lurks underneath.[2] Chion takes this as a call not to question that which might lie beneath the surface, but rather to understand that the mask hides nothing: "We must get on with what we are told and what is done. This is perhaps the message of *Eyes Wide Shut*."[3] For Chion, the film does not allow free access to the internal workings of its characters, and thus these internal workings are not important to the film as a whole. Therefore our attention is best directed at what we *do* have access to.

As Chion says, the film maintains a very precise division between inside and outside with respect to the characters as well as its aesthetic treatment of the world in general. It is for this reason that the film's one exception to the rule stands out all the more: the blurred distinction between diegetic and non-diegetic music. Though the categories of "diegetic" and "non-diegetic" sound are increasingly considered to be relics of antiquated jargon, there is no way around the fact that the film uses our conventional understanding of these categories as a crucial part of its precise unfolding. Kubrick deliberately sets up ruses whereby non-diegetic sound is revealed to be diegetic, only to turn this tactic inside out when we arrive at the Somerton mansion. So the question is this: what does the line between the inside and the outside of the diegesis have to do with the line between the inside and the outside of our featured characters in the film? In turn, how do these lines reflect the basic difference between thinking and doing that the film explores in relation to the concept of marital fidelity? The role of sound reproduction technology within the narrative provides the answer to these questions. Though he never mentions it within in his own study of the film, Chion's concept of "on-the-air" sound, as theorized in *Audio-Vision: Sound on Screen*, will provide the tools necessary to make sense of the way Kubrick represents sound technology here.[4]

Putting Things in Context

Each time Bill gets further separated from Alice through potential sexual interaction with someone else there is sound technology close at hand. In a conventional monogamous relationship, lack of fidelity to that relationship is most often defined by the degree to which a person engages in sexual activity with someone other than his/her partner. The idea that an individual could be close to one person while remaining close to another is regularly dismissed. Thus, the closer people get to someone else, the further they are from their partners. In this model, separation is at the heart of infidelity. Similarly, the concept of fidelity with respect to sound concerns the degree to which a sound is separated from its source. Separation from source is at its highest in cases of the electronic recording and transmission of sound, a fact that home stereo enthusiasts take as the basis for assessing the value of their equipment. For the audiophile, the strength of a high-fidelity music system lies in the faithfulness with which it can reproduce that which is recorded on the disc. In turn, the fidelity of a recording is allied with the degree to which it can reproduce the original sound event. The ideal in both the marital and audiophile versions of fidelity is the notion that there is a single entity to which one must remain as close as possible at all times. In *Eyes Wide Shut*, the increasing physical distance between Bill and Alice throughout his night on the town is regularly presented in the simultaneous contexts of both sexual impropriety and technologies of sound reproduction.

The relationship between the idea of separation and the technological reproduction of sound has a long history, but has been perhaps most clearly synthesized through the coining of the term "schizophonia" by R. Murray Schafer, founder of the World Soundscape Project and father of Acoustic Ecology. Schafer describes schizophonia as "the split between an original sound and its electroacoustical transmission or reproduction."[5] In *The Tuning of the World*, Schafer discusses the role of reproduction technologies in creating a disjunction between original sounds and their propagation through space, and the effect this disjunction has on humans within their sonic environments. One of Schafer's main concerns is that, with the creation of sonic environments through technologies of sound reproduction, any environment can stand in for any other, thus removing the natural context for the sound's original existence.

Awareness of environmental context is of the utmost importance to Schafer. Throughout *The Tuning of the World* he demonstrates his desire to return to pre-industrial conditions where schizophonia is impossible. He makes a distinction between the "hi-fi" soundscapes associated with the countryside — the closest relative to pre-industrial life in the modern world — and the "lo-fi" soundscapes belonging to urban space: "The quiet ambiance of the hi-fi soundscape allows the listener to hear farther into the distance just as the countryside exercises long-range viewing. The city abbreviates this facility for distant hearing (and seeing) [because] individual acoustic signals are obscured in an overdense population of sounds.... Perspective is lost."[6] His divide between the countryside and the city is based on the idea that sounds are clearly attached to their sources in the former, while being more dissociated in the latter. In short, cities are bad because we can't always contextualize the sounds we hear within our environments. This is a situation that becomes increasingly exaggerated by the amount of sound being transmitted through electroacoustical means in contemporary urban space. Ultimately Schafer describes the electroacoustical separation of sound from source as being characteristic of late twentieth century attempts to "transcend the present tense" whereby the spatial characteristics of a recording made in the past can replace the natural characteristics of a space existing within the present.[7] So both spatial and temporal transgressions are at the heart of schizophonic experience.

In making his binary distinction between hi-fi and lo-fi soundscapes, Schafer exhibits an essentialist ideal about what these two things are and neglects the blurred boundaries that exist between them in all but the most remote areas of the world. His book contains constant references to a pre-industrial past that informs his distinction along the lines of the rural and the urban. In his appeal for a high fidelity soundscape, he suggests the idea of faithfulness to an original that cannot be traced. He thus falls into the trap from which so many copy culture theorists have tried to escape since the dawn of the age of mechanical reproduction: that when one sets out in search of an original to which everything else must measure up, we find that originals are related more to the idea of Platonic "forms" than to anything tangible within the world. As James Lastra has explored in great detail in his book *Sound Technology and the American Cinema*, this is a fact particularly true when trying to discover the original at the core of any kind of sound event. Thus Lastra concludes that, when speaking about technologies of sound recording and transmission, we should move away from the idea of "reproduction" and focus primarily on the idea of "representation."[8] In this way the expectations for fidelity between "original" and "copy" can be changed according to an understanding that all copies are little more than representations to begin with. This is a reality compounded by the fact that even the events being copied cannot be pinned down to stable and original wholes. So the distinction between original and copy becomes somewhat artificial.

Nevertheless, anguish over loss of context in contemporary urban environments persists well beyond the writings of R. Murray Schafer. In *The Cultural Logic of Late Capitalism*, Fredric Jameson's classic description of the negative connotations of schizophrenic symptoms is a fine example of the continuance of such anxiety. Jameson argues that the fragmentation, isolation, and surface re-assemblage of experience characteristic of postmodernism amounts to a loss of historical context.[9] This idea of surface re-assemblage without historical context, or surface without depth, is exactly what Schafer decries. For Schafer, the negative connotations of the prefix "schizo" are used intentionally to describe a world which he feels has been drastically altered by the invention of technologies capable of pushing a sound well beyond the limits of its original source. This is an unstable world in which what one hears is not often a reflection of what one sees, a world in which sounds are not contextualized in terms of their sources.

This line of thinking from Schafer and Jameson is firmly grounded in what we might call a worship of context. Yet this worship reflects a very particular worldview that has not always been in effect. In "Accidental Voices: The Return of the Countertenor," Sherry Simon discusses the idea that a mismatch between body and voice, as was apparent with the operatic figure of the male countertenor, allowed for a "break with naturalism" which "frees the listener to hear the voice as separate from the body."[10] In the periods before and after romanticism we find positive connotations to the idea of "pure" voice, times when "voice was marvelous for its own sake, when its role was to unfold in a display of pure surface."[11] This ideal of pure surface means that a voice at a distance from its source is a voice to be praised for its potential to become completely abstracted from its grounding in the body. An infidelity of sound/image expectation thus opens up the potential for the sound of a mismatched voice to break free and become faithful to an ideal for music based on abstraction from worldly context.

This love of abstraction was turned inside out by romanticism, and to this day we still suffer from anxieties surrounding voices that are separated from their sources within the body. Such anxieties have been elevated since technologies of sound recording and transmission arrived on the scene, stemming from the early days of spiritualist beliefs in the supernatural powers underlying such technologies,[12] and evidenced more recently by the public's negative reaction to Ashlee Simpson having her lip-synch exposed on *Saturday Night Live*. Not surprisingly, the role of technology in achieving the mismatch between body and voice is another of Sherry Simon's concerns when thinking about the issue of the countertenor. Speaking of the film *Farinelli* (1995), in which a castrato voice was emulated by the post-production blending of a soprano with a countertenor, Simon reminds us that this technological morphing is very appropriate in the recreation of a voice that was itself a product of technological alterations of the body in its day.[13] She suggests that there is a basic thrill in achieving such a technological mismatch between voice and body, a thrill evidenced by the common practice of changing the revolution speed on our turntables to alter the gender of the singers with whom we are so familiar.

Farinelli is an excellent example for present purposes because it finds kinship with Schafer in its attempt to sonically recover a long lost past, yet it glorifies a sonic ideal based on notions about surface that, as Simon suggests, privilege decontextualization and abstraction in their own right. The technological manipulation of a castrato's body in order to produce a voice that seems abstracted from that body could be thought of as a precursor to the technologies that Schafer holds responsible for the emergence of schizophonic experience in twentieth century life. Similarly, the emergence of the symptoms of schizo*phrenia* described by Jameson is also the result of exposure to celebrations of pure surface where an ignorance of context is the ideal state of reception.

Something on the Air Tonight

Indeed, the thinking of Schafer and Jameson has interesting implications when considering sound/image relationships in film. The question of context when it comes to attaching a sound to its source is of great importance within an art founded upon the constant separation and attachment of sound and image. The audiovisual contract inherent in the cinema is an agreement we make to understand the relationships between sound and image based on the rules of convention to which they abide.[14] When our expectations for these rules are played with, our faith in the contract breaks down and our experience shifts to one governed by the principles of schizophonia.

Michel Chion's category of "on-the-air" sound is a fertile area for exploring the relationship between convention and subversion of sound/image relationships in the cinema. Chion describes on-the-air sounds as those "in a scene that are supposedly transmitted electronically ... by radio, telephone, amplification, and so on — sounds that consequently are not subject to 'natural' mechanical laws of sound propagation."[15] It has become quite conventional to use on-the-air sound in ways that transcend the ordinary boundaries of space and time to which diegetic sounds are usually beholden. For example, it is now a common convention to begin a film with non-diegetic music playing over the opening credits, only to reveal that a radio or record-player positioned within the diegesis has apparently been making the sound all along. Let us compare this convention with what we find in the opening moments of *Eyes Wide Shut*.

The film begins with what seems to be a standard non-diegetic use of a Shostakovich waltz. We first hear the music as the brief opening titles bookend a shot of Alice removing her clothing. In these opening moments there is no sound to be heard other than the music. Following the title credit there is a cut to the exterior of the couple's apartment block with accompanying street noises. The music continues unabated, but we are immediately thrust into a world of diegetic sound which was absent just prior. We then cut to the inside of their dwelling and find the Harfords preparing for a night out. As the dialogue begins, the music starts to get pushed down on the soundtrack in a very subtle use of the "cocktail party effect,"[16] a common strategy for ensuring dialog intelligibility that is used in cases of both diegetic and non-diegetic music alike. If there is any indication that the sound of the music has a diegetic source it is subtle enough that it is something of a surprise when Bill shuts down their home stereo unit and the music stops. This is a trick that should alert us to the importance of the line that separates the inside and outside of the diegesis, and how easily this line is crossed when dealing with on-the-air sound. In this first case there is little if any treatment to the sound of the music which suggests to us that it is coming from a small portable stereo rather than the proverbial orchestra pit more often associated with the non-diegetic realm. So upon the music's termination we are immediately put in the position of assessing whether or not the quality of the sound has been faithful to the source we are shown on screen. If not, then we are given a clue as to the film's attitude towards the distinction between the inside and the outside of the diegesis.

There are various conventions for the treatment of on-the-air sound which can be used as guides when trying to assess a film's approach to the diegesis. Chion elaborates with respect to how different qualities of on-the-air sound can manipulate the listener's understanding of its temporal and spatial dimensions. As with the inside and outside of the diegesis itself, there are two poles of on-the-air sound between which any number of variations can arise: emphasis on the *source* of the sound being propagated, or the material qualities of its electronic *transmission*: "If the sound being listened to has technical qualities of directness and presence, it refers back to the circumstances of its original state. If it has aural qualities that highlight its "recordedness," and if there is emphasis on the acoustic properties of the place where it is being listened to in the diegesis, we tend to focus on the moment where the recording is being heard."[17] In this opening scene from *Eyes Wide Shut*, the emphasis is much more on qualities of directness than on any signs of the music having been recorded and transmitted through the space of their home. So direct, in fact, that had Bill not shut the music off there would be no real evidence that the sound was ever on the air at all.

The revelation that this music has a diegetic source creates something of a paradox in which the sound refers both to the time and space presented within the narrative and the lack of time and space that exists outside the diegesis. This creates an interplay between the romantic ideal of materialization (the diegetic realm) and pre-romantic ideal of abstraction (the non-diegetic realm), or between the timely and the timeless. The film plays on this interaction throughout the film by way of its clearly modern setting which seems tapped into something much older, the transcendence of the present tense which lies at the heart of schizophonic experience. The film's opening shift between these two realms is the first movement in a gradual gesture of schizophonic inversion between the inside and the outside of the diegesis that culminates in the orgy at the Somerton mansion. This gesture passes through three phases: it begins with an initially blurry boundary between diegetic and non-diegetic music in the form of the Shostakovich waltz; it then moves towards shifting boundary lines between different registers of diegetic sound; and finally it makes a clear break between all diegetic sound and its non-diegetic oppositions, only to show that this break is really a suture that joins the two together. As we'll discover, Bill traces this gesture along a line of on-the-air sound throughout the film.

The next movement in this gesture comes at the Zieglers' party as we get our first glimpse of Bill and Alice Harford engaging in behavior which could lead to extra-marital affairs. We watch them interact with their potential partners amidst a soundscape that drifts between the live sound of the band and the recorded sound of intermission music. As we move through the Zieglers' space there is evidence that the music we hear is diegetic: we see the band playing in the main dance hall, and we hear changes to the music's spatial signature as we move in and out of this room. The band's piano player, Nick Nightingale (Todd Field), turns out to be an old friend of Bill's. The band stops playing for an intermission and some canned music starts up shortly thereafter. Bill approaches Nick who is still on the stage next to his piano, and within this room there is little change in sonic quality to distinguish the newly introduced recorded music from the live sound we heard just prior. There is a piano very present in the mix, and it is no accident that we hear this as we see Nick standing next to his instrument while on his break. We become more aware of the divide between live and on-the-air sound as we see Nick and his unplayed piano while hearing a piano on the soundtrack. A more extreme version of this split will occur at the Somerton mansion, ultimately positing Nick as a figure who hovers somewhere between the various sonic poles that concern us here.

Again the line between different registers of music has been softened. This time, however, it is not the line between diegetic and non-diegetic sound, but rather that which lies between live and on-the-air sound within the diegesis. Thus the line that was initially presented as defining the frame of the diegesis through the Shostakovich waltz has now shifted to a line existing within that frame through the live and canned music at Zieglers' party. Another example of this occurs later in this scene. As Alice's new Hungarian acquaintance drinks from her glass, the canned music comes to an end. After a few short seconds of music-free ambiance the band starts back up. The shift is so subtle that it is not until part-way into the new couple's dance that we catch a glimpse of the band in the background and realize that they are playing live once again. If on-the-air sound can be so easily mistaken for live presence, then we are getting a taste of Schafer's schizophonic environment: the lo-fi soundscape in which the sounds we hear are not well contextualized within the environment around us. Of course, this observation applies to the way this environment is presented to the audience through the film. It could well be that the characters in the film have no trouble distinguishing between the live and the canned; but as Chion suggests, we are not privy to their experience and must make sense of the events of the film from the position afforded to us by the director.

The first time we hear a piece of music that has never been associated with a diegetic source (either explicitly shown or merely suggested) is during Alice's confession to Bill about the feelings she had for the sailor.[18] This is the birth of Bill's awareness of his wife's potential for marital infidelity. It is significant that it is at this point, when he is forced to connect with what his wife was saying, that we are introduced to the outside of the diegesis as a place that exists in and of itself. Similar non-diegetic music accompanies the black and white visualizations of Alice and the sailor that later appear as Bill makes his way around the city at night. We know that the events depicted in these images never happened, just as this music never "happened" within the space of the diegesis. Yet the music is there, just as the images are, and just as Alice's confession is out on the table for Bill to deal with. This external music is thus allied with images representing very internal thoughts, be they Alice's or Bill's. Indeed, such use of non-diegetic music to reflect what is happening within a scene is one of the most common conventions in sound film, and this very fact suggests that to think of the inside and outside of the diegesis as being separate is something of a mistake. So we are presented with the idea that what lies deep within could be the same as what exists far on the outside. The use of music here thus reflects the issue that Bill Harford now has to deal with: does his wife's mental infidelity have the same effect on their relationship as if she actually had an affair with this man? Is thinking the same as doing? Is the inside the same as the outside?

Reach Out and Touch Someone

Before Bill has a chance to process and react to what Alice has told him, they are interrupted by a telephone call announcing the death of one of Bill's patients. This is the call that brings Bill out into the world at night and which ultimately leads him to the Somerton mansion. It is during his journey of the night that he begins the process of making sense out of what Alice has told him. This process is thus defined by its relationship to the technology which physically separates Bill from his wife at exactly the moment that she admits her psychological separation from him.

The telephone offers one of the most commonly shared experiences of mediated sound in today's society. It is a technology based on a schizophonic principal: the separation of the human voice from its grounding in the context of the body and its location in space. Yet it maintains a level of degradation between source and transmission such that one would never mistake the sound of a voice on the telephone for that of a person standing in the same room. Thus the distance between sound and source through the telephone is always emphasized by the characteristic on-the-air qualities of the medium. Fittingly, the film's use of telephonic interruptions is always in furtherance of Bill becoming increasingly distanced from whomever he happens to be with when the phone call occurs: first during his stoned conversation with Alice, then as he is about to engage Domino (Vinessa Shaw) for her sexual services, and again during his final conversation with Nick Nightingale at the Sonata Café. Each of these calls not only breaks up Bill's interactions with these people, but also serves to remind us of his increasing physical distance from his wife.

The film's distinctions between live, on-the-air, and non-diegetic music are first allied with the telephone as purveyor of schizophonic experience in the scene between Bill and Domino. As they begin their sexual encounter, appropriately sultry jazz music is heard. Here the sound is presented slightly to the right in the mix and with a hint of recordedness which suggests, to the attentive listener, that there is a diegetic source providing the music here. However, this scene begins after a shot of Alice sitting at home next to a small tabletop television whose sound is unquestionably on-the-air. The cut to the shot of Bill kissing Domino makes the accompanying music seem very full and direct by contrast, thereby giving it a non-diegetic feel. Then Tom's cell phone rings. He gets up to take the call and the camera follows him as he moves towards Domino's bookshelf. There we find a small stereo unit similar to the one in his own bedroom. He reaches out to push a button and the music stops, repeating the gesture made at the beginning of the film. Here our surprise is somewhat lessened, due both to the more overtly diegetic quality of the music and the fact that this is now the second time this has happened. Most importantly, however, is that within this single scene we have a double recurrence: the revelation of a diegetic source for music, and an unexpected phone call interrupting an exploration of marital infidelity. In this way the film makes it clear that this play on distinctions between diegetic and non-diegetic music is to be understood in the context of the distanciating potential of sound reproduction technology within the narrative. This marks the next movement in the film's gesture of inversion concerning the inside and the outside of the diegesis. The separation between diegetic and non-diegetic music is clearer than in the film's opening example, matching Tom's greater physical separation from his wife here. As we'll discover, the film gradually clarifies the distinctions between these realms so that it might ultimately fold them onto one another and press them onto the same surface, suggesting their inevitable interdependence.

Soon after, Bill wanders into a club in which Nick Nightingale is just finishing up a set with his band. As it was at Zieglers' party, when the band stops the canned music begins. This time, however, the distinction is made clearer by the considerable difference in volume level between the two. So this scene follows on that between Bill and Domino as clarifying the distinction between two registers of music, this time live and on-the-air sound. However, there remains an important similarity between this instance of the replacement of live sound with recorded sound and that which we found at Zieglers' party: we continue to hear piano playing as we see Nick away from his instrument. This is the next phase in the gesture of inversion which finds Nick moving away from the piano towards electroacoustically transmitted sound and finally coming to rest on the outside of the diegesis.

It is important that this next phase in the gesture of inversion comes at the point when he will provide the means for Bill to access the Somerton mansion. In their conversation Nick tells Bill about the upcoming party. This conversation is also interrupted by a telephone call, only this time the call is for Nick which informs him (and ultimately Bill) of the location of the mansion. Thus directions to the schizophonic nexus of the film, the space of the mansion in which Bill's greatest distance from Alice is achieved, are suitably provided by means of schizophonic technology. Appropriately, the password that Nick gives Bill is "Fidelio," conjuring up the notion of fidelity through its obvious etymological relationship to the English version of the word and through its reference to the Beethoven opera which is premised upon an exploration of marital fidelity.

Nick is the key to the film's general split between the inside and the outside of the diegesis, and he allows Bill to cross the divide and take a glimpse into what he thinks to be a part of the outside of his world: the Somerton mansion. The Somerton mansion is the embodiment of the outside of the diegesis, a place which can't really exist. Yet it is so much a part of what happens in this film that it must exist, and not on the outside peering in, but rather on the same surface as everything else.

The Piano Player's Gone Yet the Music Lives On

As Bill enters the Somerton mansion we hear the ritual music consisting of sustained strings, male chanting, and percussion. We hear the music as though from a distance, suggesting that it is operating in the diegetic mode. This mode seems to be confirmed as Bill approaches the ceremonial space. The door is opened for him and the volume increases accordingly until he is fully within the room. It becomes apparent that the voices of the chanting that we hear are played back in reverse, and here we discover that the source of the music is synthetic: Nick can be seen on stage playing a rig of synthesizers and samplers.

Given the gothic aesthetic of the ritual, the presence of modern electronic instrumentation seems a bit superficial. Yet this superficiality is suitably mirrored by the presence of masked guests which serves to prevent any voices heard within the Somerton mansion from being grounded in corporeality. The result is a space in which these sounds are not attributable to a tangible source. We may well understand that the spoken voices come from the bodies and that the chanting voices come from the samplers, but this is a faith in the audiovisual contract not substantiated by the film itself: we are not offered the sense of material grounding that we would get from seeing people's lips move in conjunction with the sound of their voices.

Sound mediation has reached its peak at this point in the film. So we might ask ourselves: why has Kubrick placed such emphasis on mediation? Instead of keyboards and samplers he could have had, for example, a giant pipe organ and choir. Instead of full face masks he could have had half-masks that keep the mouths visible. There are a couple of possibilities about his decisions that are worth considering. First is the obvious one: full face masks ensure protection of identity, a simple function of the idea that this is nothing more than a private party for people whose identities must be kept secret. In a similar way, the keyboards and samplers call attention to the modernity of the ritual, adding a surface sheen obscuring the ancient depths that the ritual suggests. The emphasis on modernity lends credence to the idea that this is really just a bunch of super rich white men getting their ya-yas on with little interest in the historical context or implications of their actions.

In its combination of sound technology and dissociation of sounds from their sources, the scene at the mansion is an exemplary schizophonic space. It is also a scene in which surface is celebrated within the narrative, and perhaps by Kubrick himself. Perhaps, because of the ambiguity surrounding whether or not the orgy scene holds a critical or sympathetic stance in relation to that which it represents. Fittingly, this is an ambiguity that is reflected in the various different treatments of live, on-the-air, and non-diegetic music that takes place here.

There are four distinct musical sections throughout the Somerton interlude to which we must pay close attention. The introductory music for the ritual is understood to be diegetic mainly because we see Nick playing instruments that are, through moments of precise synchronization in his fingering, associated with the sounds that we hear. This is the first and only time that we will see electronic instruments being played in the film. Up until now the music performed live within a scene has always been on acoustic instruments. This is important because the spatial signatures we attach to the sounds of acoustic instruments can be attributed to the spaces in which they're played. When Nick triggers samples of percussion, stringed instruments, and voices, there exists the possibility that the spatial qualities of the sounds we hear are inherent in the recording and do not reflect the space in which they are transmitted. This is one of the key points made by Schafer when developing his concept of schizophonia: when hearing sound transmitted electroacoustically we lose clarity on whether the sound's spatial qualities are a function of the recording space of or that of the transmission. In other words, when one spatial signature can replace another we lose context for the source of the sound. So in Nick's on-screen performance here, the sounds are samples recorded in the past while being performed in the present. There is a blurred zone between the spaces and times in which this music has been, and is being, produced.

The ritual disrobing comes to an end and the women in the circle disperse around the room to select partners and escort them elsewhere. Bill Harford is one of the chosen few. At precisely the moment that he and his new companion leave the ritual room and enter the hallway just outside, the chanting ceases and we are left with a lingering string drone. This drone decreases in volume as they get further away and begin to converse. Chion refers to this "sudden disappearance of the music" as a "hole" in the soundtrack resultant from Kubrick having died before the mix was completed.[19] It could be that he is referring to an earlier version of the film; the auditory nuances of this particular moment in theatrical screenings of the film in 1999 did not standout. However, based on both the U.K. and U.S. DVD releases, this is not a "mistake" in any way. There are two key justifications for the music ending like this. Firstly, the ritual is coming to an end as the women disperse with their various chosen partners, so it would make sense that the accompanying music also comes to an end. Secondly, and more interestingly, the music might best be understood as having a limited specificity to that space. Although the music is audible before Bill enters the room at the beginning of the scene, it has now shifted to being strictly associated with that room. When he leaves, the music falls away. This is a similar treatment to what we find in the next musical interlude.

As the string drone fades away while Bill and the woman exchange words in the hallway, a new female soprano voice emerges with a distant and highly reverberated quality. The sound is distinctly diegetic since the reverberation is similar to that which is present on the speaking voices here. Yet we are offered no source for the sound on screen. Gradually a new musical motif emerges with strings and percussion of quite a different order than what was heard before. This music seems to have no reverberation within the space, and retains qualities of directness and presence as Tom begins to move throughout various different rooms. Thus it would seem to be non-diegetic. Yet given the electronic nature of the musical apparatus we have seen, is it reasonable to expect the entire space to be wired for sound transmission, and that Nick is still playing away downstairs with his music being piped in all over the house? The fact that we can't be certain is the surest sign of all that this space is fundamentally schizophonic, and that this schizophonia is a reflection of the separation that Tom is experiencing from his life with Nicole. Adding to the uncertainty is the fact that when this second musical interlude finally comes to an end it is in precise conjunction with Bill once again being escorted out of a room by another masked woman. So in at least one sense this second piece of music has been attached to a given space as diegetic music would be. Thus it operates according to principles both diegetic and non-diegetic at once.

As Bill speaks with this woman we hear ballroom music, again as though from a room down the hall. Tom is once again interrupted and asked to follow an usher. We cut to a shot of Nick, still blindfolded, being escorted through the room in which this ballroom music seems to be originating. We see couples dancing in a style that suits the music, yet it appears to be on-the-air as there is no band visible. We cut back to Bill being brought down the hall and back to the ritual room where he began his journey. We continue to hear the distant sound of the ballroom music, yet as soon as he crosses the threshold this music disappears and is promptly replaced by the first appearance of the Ligeti piano theme. Though the ballroom music seems to have been diegetic, it has not obeyed the strict laws of the space, for it should still be audible as Bill enters the room. The Ligeti music is, on the other hand, decidedly non-diegetic.

The piano player has left the scene, never to appear again. Yet it is just after Nick leaves that we hear the introduction of the piano theme that will haunt the rest of the film in a decidedly non-diegetic fashion. This is the film's climactic auditory moment, for it is here that the separation between the inside and the outside of the diegesis becomes complete. This separation is embodied by Nick's disappearance from the narrative, fulfilling his destiny as the figure that will lead Bill from the inside to the outside so that he may find his way back again, threading the two together. The slippage between modes within the mansion concentrates the slippages heard elsewhere in the film and allows Nick to cross the boundary between inside and outside once and for all. Bill has witnessed this cross and is now faced with a choice: either he believes in the separation, and that Nick has disappeared into a mysterious unseen realm, or he believes that there is no mysterious realm and that what he has witnessed is no different from that which he experiences in regular life. This choice is a metaphor for Bill Harford's need to reconcile the worlds of thought and action so he can figure out where he stands in relation to his wife.

Laying It All on the Table

The introduction of the Ligeti piece recalls the only other recurring theme to be positioned decidedly within the non-diegetic realm: Jocelyn Pook's string piece which accompanies Alice's confession and each return of the black and white imagery of her and the sailor henceforth. The music isn't the same but its relationship to the narrative is. After his wife's revelation, Dr. Harford is plunged into a world plagued by his paranoia surrounding the possibility of her infidelity. When his identity is revealed at the mansion, his paranoia suddenly shifts from the consequences of Alice's potential infidelity to the consequences of his own. In both cases the paranoia surrounding potential infidelity is marked by the fundamental infidelity that non-diegetic music always presents towards a film's diegesis. If we take the position that such music can never be contextualized within the diegesis, then we might think of cinematic spaces marked by non-diegetic music as being fundamentally lo-fi in the Schaferian sense. The Ligeti piece calls constant attention to the absence of the piano player who Tom desperately tries to track down to no avail. It might be said that after Bill leaves the mansion he goes in search of the source of the non-diegetic music and cannot find it. This is a schizophonic breakdown of the highest order. As such *Eyes Wide Shut* joins in a long history of films premised upon the narrative trajectory of joining an acousmatic sound with its source: an early example being Fritz Lang's *The Testament of Dr. Mabuse*, and continued in fine tradition in more contemporary films like David Lynch's *Lost Highway*.

Non-diegetic music is a constant reminder that it is separate from the space that the characters occupy, and yet it is strangely reflective of that space. Now what if we consider the idea that the notion of non-diegetic music is a concept designed to add credence to diegetic events? By calling attention to the idea that musical accompaniment comes from outside of the space that the characters occupy, we understand the diegetic space as being all the more tangible. In other words, the diegesis is defined by its relationship to its opposite: non-diegetic space. This is a binary construct that draws attention away from the idea of film as a surface without depth, a single plane of expression without an inside and an outside. Yet as we have heard, non-diegetic music is, more often than not, intimately connected with that which takes place within the diegesis. So can it really be separate?

The importance of the idea of surface without depth is laid out within the narrative when Victor Ziegler (Sydney Pollack) has a frank discussion with Tom toward the end of the film. He tells Bill that he's making a big deal out of nothing, that there is no depth beneath the surface about which he is inquiring. It was just a bunch of guys having a party, and nothing bad happened to Nick, or to Amanda (Julienne Davis), the woman who apparently saved his life at Somerton and turned up dead from a drug overdose the following day. Ziegler suggests that Nick was reprimanded for allowing Bill to crash a private party, and Amanda's death was a coincidence, not to be read as having anything to do with what Bill suspects took place. The scene at the mansion was a celebration of surface without depth, Schafer and Jameson's nightmare alike. We might take this to be a metaphor for Bill's struggles with Alice's confession, for that is also something that took place within the space of the mind and finds no context in real world action. Her fantasy was separated from grounding in reality, just as Ziegler suggests of Bill's own fantasy about the events of that night at the mansion.

So perhaps the moral of *Eyes Wide Shut* is not the revelation of the fluid boundary between thinking and doing, or the realization that there is more to any relationship than can be summed up by individual thoughts or actions. Perhaps, in the end, it is about the value in celebrating surface without depth, of enjoying abstraction from grounding in the material world. Or, as Chion puts it, to "get on with what we are told and what is done"[20] rather than trying to scratch the surface in order to reveal something which doesn't exist in the film to begin with. As such, the film is aligned with pre-romantic ideals of vocal performance in the opera. This celebration would include an understanding that perhaps surface and depth are one and the same, that the notion of a lo-fi experience is really only a misunderstanding of the role of context in our environments. In the cinema, the environments created are inherent to a medium that is entirely abstract and upon which we have placed expectations for realism based on problematic notions of film's indexical relationship to the pro-filmic world. To call attention to the artificial distinction between diegetic and non-diegetic music is to acknowledge film as surface: there can be no escape from the grounding in the materiality of the medium.

The film's shifts from diegetic to non-diegetic music, through the on-the-air spaces in between, are ruses suggesting the ultimate impossibility of such shifts. Nick hasn't slipped into another realm. As Ziegler says, he's back in Seattle "bangin' Mrs. Nick." The realm of non-diegetic music is no less tangible than that. Similarly, the use of Tom Cruise and Nicole Kidman as principal actors suggests the impossibility that we can forget who they are. There is no escape from their identity as Hollywood's most celebrated couple of that day. As such, the film is about stripping surface away from context just as Tom and Nicole constantly divert attention away from the context of the film world to their status as surface icons outside of that world. We might understand this as a similar process to non-diegetic music exposing itself as being outside the space of the characters, only to point us back to the diegesis by highlighting the fact that they are each a part of the same surface. To differentiate between the two is to imagine a depth that is really just a function of juxtapositions upon a single plane. Tom and Nicole do not exist without their films, and *Eyes Wide Shut* does not exist without Tom and Nicole: they are all part of the same surface.

It might be suggested that marital infidelity is a desire to have one's cake and eat it too, to have the best of two possible worlds within a single plane of existence: to enjoy the world of a secure long-term relationship with a single person while remaining open to the diversity of potential relationships that exist beyond the confines of a monogamous marriage. *Eyes Wide Shut* examines this possibility. However, instead of employing a narrative directly concerning multiple partner relationships, Kubrick uses the film's concern for the effects of mental infidelity on a monogamous relationship as its guiding principal. In turn, this principal underlies a formal and aesthetic exploration of surface worship and the problems this worship raises for common distinctions made between diegetic and non-diegetic music. For those that question the continued relevance of the term "diegetic," particularly in a world of cinema which seems to confound the concept on a regular basis, a film like *Eyes Wide Shut* cannot exist without an acknowledgement of the poles that lie on either side of the diegesis. The film is about revealing that which is already plain to behold. It is the revelatory process itself that is most important, and this process is dependent upon the cinematic codes that have been designed to cover up the fact that no revelation is really necessary. The word "diegetic" is a code for a way of understanding film that posits an interior and an exterior, a mask that hides the fact that there really is no mask in the first place. *Eyes Wide Shut* lays the cinema bare while adhering to many of its most common conventions. For those that were dissatisfied with Kubrick's final work, perhaps the nature of the film's revelatory process is a large part of the problem. The film is one of his finest; it attains a level of reflection upon its own premises of construction without slipping into the total distanciation of the most self-reflexive films. It hovers somewhere between mesmerizing spectacle and intellectual detachment, and lays both out on the surface so that, in the end, we learn that there really isn't any difference between the two.

13 *Eyes Wide Shut*: Kubrick and the Representation of Gender

Lindiwe Dovey

The topic of this essay is Kubrick's representation of gender and, while it focuses on *Eyes Wide Shut* (1999), Kubrick's final film before his death in 1999, it also locates this film within Kubrick's oeuvre and raises questions about the engendering of gender in Kubrick's films as a complete body of work.

Studies of gender in film of course involve the examination of both male and female characters, masculine and feminine identities, but this essay focuses primarily on the representation of female characters. On a purely narrative level, Kubrick's work is striking for its absence of female characters. Three Kubrick films feature a sole woman in a world of men: *Fear and Desire* (1953); *Paths of Glory* (1957); and *Dr. Strangelove* (1964). Many Kubrick films offer only one female of any narrative importance: *Killer's Kiss* (1955); *The Killing* (1956); *Barry Lyndon* (1975); *The Shining* (1980); and *Full Metal Jacket* (1987). Indeed, *2001: A Space Odyssey* (1968) is a film in which female characters are of virtually *no* narrative importance. In Robert Kolker's words, "[Kubrick's] films are rarely concerned with women, except in a peripheral and usually unpleasant way."[21] And if Kubrick's films are concerned with men, it is not in a gesture of celebration of masculinity, but rather to see men, Kolker argues, "mechanistically, as determined by their world, sometimes by their erotic passions ... [and] always by the rituals and structures they set up for themselves."[22] Kolker's statements would imply that Kubrick levels a critique at men, whom he sees as part of a socially as well as sexually constructed—and constricted—group. Kubrick clearly locates himself within this group, approaching his subject matter from a thoroughly masculine point of view. Perhaps this exploration and critique from within partly lends itself to the pervasive sense of claustrophobia in Kubrick's films. And perhaps it is due to the fact that female characters are in abundance only in *Eyes Wide Shut* that *Daily Variety* writer Todd McCarthy finds more optimism in this film than in any other Kubrick film. McCarthy writes:

> Less ascerbic and more optimistic about the human condition than any of the director's previous films, [*Eyes Wide Shut*] remains remarkably faithful to its source, while also trading in familiar Kubrick concerns such as paranoia, deception, the literal and figurative masks that people wear and the difficulty for even intelligent human beings to transcend the base and self-destructive impulses that drive the species ... [the] film is unique in the late director's oeuvre in that it is women who far outshine the men.[23]

"Outshine" is a rather unfortunate choice of word here, considering that—as Randy Rasmussen argues—Kubrick's female characters are "not so much real women as they are abstract projections of someone else's sexual desire."[24] Do the female characters in *Eyes Wide Shut* "outshine" the men in terms of their wit and intelligence, or do they shine out as physical objects, as abstract projections of male sexual desire? Or do they "shine" in the eerie sense of the word invoked in Kubrick's horror film, *The Shining*? Before considering *Eyes Wide Shut*, however, turn briefly to the role that women play in earlier Kubrick films.

The women in Kubrick's films do indeed appear to be the projections of heterosexual male desire, and, as such, they are also often projections of heterosexual male fear of the female. Kubrick's female characters are largely schematic, ranging from the *femmes fatales* in the early, noir films, *Killer's Kiss* and *The Killing*, to the innocent, weeping German woman in *Paths of Glory*, to the young voluptuous beauties and old hags in *A Clockwork Orange* (1971), to the long-suffering Lady Lyndon in *Barry Lyndon*, to the pathetic wife and mother Wendy in *The Shining*, to the Vietnamese prostitutes and "warrior woman" in *Full Metal Jacket*. It is possible to contend, quite crudely, that we do not learn anything new about femininity from these characters or from their representation. They are situated at the conventional poles of "ideal" and "fallen" woman. Rather, they aid our understanding of masculinity.

In an article that focuses on *Full Metal Jacket*, White puts forward her theory that Kubrick's female characters reveal more about men than women:

> Woman is troped, in [*Full Metal Jacket*] and other films by Kubrick, as the "Virgin Mary," whose name is invoked in all seriousness by the drill sergeant, and simultaneously as the cloacal shit from which the fighting men are trying to emerge so that they can become "real" men. Clearly, the woman-sewer or woman-fosterer-of-regression must be destroyed, but we have seen that, to their confusion, the men find that in doing so they have also destroyed both the virgin-mother and the warrior ideal that silently pervade the film's ideological structure.[25]

Similarly, in his essay "All Roads Lead to the Abject: The Monstrous Feminine and Gender Boundaries in Stanley Kubrick's *Shining*," Robert Kilker argues that far from being troped realistically in contrast to Jack Torrance's horrific patriarchal presence, the feminine is also represented as monstrous, as something that must be expelled. Kilker argues that while "the film does make a monster out of the repressive patriarch, ... it also codes the feminine as monstrous, and equally threatening as the patriarchal forces that would try to contain it. Kubrick's film shares not only [a] fear of the female body, but also powers that are coded feminine."[26] Kilker draws on psychoanalytic theory to show how Kubrick stereotypically aligns the act of "shining"— whose origin Halloran attributes to his grand*mother*—with femininity, with the notion of a mother's "intuition." He argues that, far from fearing only Jack Torrance's violent masculinity, we as viewers are also made to fear the feminized act of shining, and the intrusion of the abject female body into the diegesis, through the horrific sights of the blood streaming out of the elevator behind the girl twins, and the rapidly aging body of Grady's murdered wife. Furthermore, Kilker argues that the feminine skill of shining is specifically located within Danny, a boy, so as to provide the safe possibility of his growing out of this dangerous feminine realm — away from the abject, horrifying body of the mother — towards the male realm of language and culture. Kilker acknowledges that his reading goes against the grain of most interpretations of gender in Kubrick's films — and he confirms the belief that Kubrick's films "have always challenged patriarchal institutions such as the army, science, government, and the family."[27] Kilker's reading, however, attempts to take us beneath the surface critique of masculinity and patriarchy in Kubrick's films to try to find deeper, unconscious fears and desires at work in Kubrick's organization of gender. This essay attempts a similar reading of *Eyes Wide Shut*, and will argue that while the film is ostensibly about a man who has to learn to accept his wife as an equal, it also associates its female characters with a horrifying power that is similar to that of shining.

Now, the film medium introduces a particular problem in the representation of gender. The manifest nature of gender (and racial) difference in the social world is transferred to the visual film medium, whereas this difference may be obscured within the non-visual, written medium of literature. Rather than complicate this immediacy of perception that is one of the effects of cinema, Kubrick seems to deliberately *mark* or *encode* gender difference in his films. Through his casting, costume design, performance direction, choreography of scenes, alteration of the narratives of adapted texts, and chosen audio-visual techniques, Kubrick makes full use of film's ability to *present* and *perform* gender difference.

The performance of gender difference in Kubrick's films often involves the encoding of the female as "other" in relation to the "self" of the male. There is an implicit assumption, a kind of inscription, of the film's normative perspective as a heterosexual, male perspective. This normative perspective becomes apparent when one considers the way in which gender, racial, and sexual difference are often represented in such a way as to send a volt of shock, surprise, or horror through the viewer. I want to consider briefly a few examples of scenes in which Kubrick constitutes gender and sexual difference as shock. At the end of Kubrick's film *Paths of Glory*, Colonel Dax's French soldiers are relaxing in a bar when a young German woman is ushered in for their entertainment — notably, the actress is Christiane Kubrick, Kubrick's third wife, whom he met during her audition for this part. An extended scene shows how the young woman transforms the men's lecherous jeers quite suddenly into tears through the song she sings. The intrusion of a woman is shown to be, in this case, the positive catalyst for a quite shocking — even sentimental — alteration in male behavior. Susan White contrasts this final sequence in *Paths of Glory* favorably with the final sequences in *Full Metal Jacket*, in which, she argues, the soldiers' contempt for and scapegoating of women is "curiously coupled with a pervasive desire for regression to the womb," evident through the singing of the infantile Mickey Mouse song.[28] In *Paths of Glory*, on the other hand, White argues that "*These* men are able to make the moment of scapegoating itself into one of community, sharing this sad song with the woman as they would a lullaby, accepting her mastery of a language they may not understand. The men in *Paths of Glory* remain 'human' because they can accept their own infantilism without violently punishing the woman who makes them aware of their helplessness. (One of the lyrics in the German song is 'Please Mother, bring a light.')"[29] Whether one passes positive or negative judgment on the representation of gender in these sequences, the fact remains that gender difference is an occasion for shock and surprise. A further example of Kubrick's exploitation of the film medium to conjoin femininity and shock is to be found in the penultimate sequence of *Full Metal Jacket*. Kubrick places considerable emphasis on the moment at which the sniper turns around, the moment at which we realize that the ruthless killer is a *woman*: he does this primarily through the use of the slow motion, which seems to encourage the viewer to gasp in shock and amazement at the sniper's unexpected gender. Similarly, at the end of *A Clockwork Orange,* a shock occurs due to the fact that we see a woman, for the first time in the film, not being violently abused, but apparently in pleasure. Alex's voice-over "I was cured all right" transitions into this shot *not* of him inflicting violence on a woman, as we would expect, but of him engaged in sex with a woman who appears to be in control of the act and visibly enjoying herself. Our eye has been trained throughout the film to see women only as sexual objects (like the statues in the Korova milk bar), not as sentient beings, and so the sudden image of visible female pleasure (even though it is Alex's *mental* vision of course) comes as a shock. The shock, as with the shot of the sniper, is magnified due to the use of slow motion. In *The Shining*, as already indicated, it is *horror* rather than shock that is allied with the female body — consider the sudden aging of Grady's murdered wife in Room 237 — and it is also associated with the male homosexual body (for example when, close to the film's end, Wendy encounters two men, one dressed in a bear suit, engaged in a homosexual act). In fact, in many of Kubrick's films — with the exception of

Full Metal Jacket, in which a discourse on homosexuality is foregrounded rather than suggestive — homosexuality is presented as deviant, shocking, and strangely alluring (or otherwise
ridiculously comic) in the same way that the female body is presented as non-normative, as
something to be both feared and desired, as something repressed which, at times, suddenly ruptures the screen with its difference.

Along with the encoding of women as men's shocking "other" in Kubrick's films, Kubrick
also crucially and consistently tropes women as works of art, *objets d'art*, from the mannequins
of women in *Killer's Kiss* (which are used in a fencing-like fight in one of the final scenes), to
the female furniture in *A Clockwork Orange*, to the paintings of nude women in *The Shining*, *A
Clockwork Orange*, and *Eyes Wide Shut*, to the statuesque, almost inanimate characterization of
Lady Lyndon and the women who participate in the orgy scene in *Eyes Wide Shut*.

It seems relevant, in light of the fact that Kubrick literally "objectifies" his female characters in this way, and also in light of the way in which he seems to accentuate sexual difference,
to consider his work in the context of the first and most famous essay on the representation of
gender and sexual difference in cinema, Laura Mulvey's "Visual Pleasure and Narrative Cinema," published in 1975. In this essay — which is a manifesto of sorts— Mulvey makes the case
that classical narrative cinema has traditionally exploited gender difference by encoding men as
the subjects of the "look" and women as the objects of the "look." In this schema, male characters signal movement and action whereas female characters represent to-be-looked-at-ness
and are visually exploited so as to "freeze" the narrative to allow for erotic contemplation. Scrutinizing the films of directors such as Hitchcock and Sternberg, Mulvey argues that female characters in such films are constructed largely for the purpose of offering visual, erotic pleasure
for male spectators— both for the male characters in the film's diegesis, and for the male spectators in the audience. She argues that if female spectators in the audience wish to participate
in the visual pleasure, they are forced to "masculinize" their perspective. Two kinds of look are
in operation in Mulvey's schema: scopophilia, that is, using another person as an erotic object
to achieve visual or sexual pleasure, which may involve voyeurism (looking in such a way as to
sadistically control the object of one's look), and fetishism, that is, overvaluing the object of
one's look. The second kind of look is identification, that is, identifying narcissistically with
another person so as to fulfill the desires of one's ideal ego. Given that classical narrative films
mirror the patriarchy prevalent in society itself, Mulvey argues, both kinds of look — scopophilia
and identification — are "owned" by men. Classical narrative films construct an implicit male
rather than female spectator. The distinction between men as active possessors of the "look"
and women as passive objects of the "look" leads to Mulvey's coining of the term the "male gaze,"
based on Lacan's concept of "the gaze," a concept to which the essay will return.

In spite of the importance of Mulvey's essay to film studies, it has been criticized by feminist and queer theorists for its heterosexual bias, and for not acknowledging the ways in which
viewers might switch — in the course of a film — between masculine and feminine positions,
between sadistic and masochistic associations. In *In the Realm of Pleasure* (1988), Gaylyn Studlar points out that spectators desire and identify with both male and female characters, and she
posits that film spectatorship is a curiously masochistic rather than sadistic activity, for both
men and women. Mulvey's essay has also been criticized for being strangely reactionary, since
Mulvey says that her intention is to "destroy" pleasure altogether by analyzing it. Kubrick is no
doubt complicit in the historical process whereby spectators are encouraged to derive visual
pleasure from the female form on the screen, but his "take" on pleasure is by no means parochial.
Unlike Mulvey's desire to banish pleasure, Kubrick seems to revel in the creation of "visual pleasures" of all kinds: there appears to be an equal weighting given to the visual pleasure of the
Stargate sequence in *2001* as to the visual pleasure of seeing Nicole Kidman slip out of her black
sheath dress in the opening shot of *Eyes Wide Shut*.

In spite of the different angles that Kubrick and Mulvey take on pleasure, Mulvey's essay does offer tools for analysis that seem highly appropriate when considering Kubrick's representations of gender. While *Eyes Wide Shut* is, on the surface, an exploration and critique of the "male gaze," it also seems to encode, perhaps unwittingly, the feminine body as shocking or horrifying. While many critics have commented on the theme of the porous boundary between dream and reality, and the theme of marital infidelity, in *Eyes Wide Shut*, few have looked at the way in which the film reveals a profound fear of death, where this death is associated with the female. The novel on which the film is based, *Traumnovelle*, published in 1926, has been translated into English as *Dream Story*, which ignores the very important pun in the German: "traum"—which means both "dream" and "trauma." One cannot focus on the interaction of dream and reality, of husband and wife, in the film without also looking at the theme of the fear of death. As Christiane Kubrick herself has said, "[*Eyes Wide Shut*] has nothing to do with sex and everything to do with fear."[30] Audiences who were expecting an erotic thriller from the film were sorely disappointed; they received, instead, a kind of horror thriller.

A number of critics—such as White and Kilker—have shown the usefulness of drawing on psychoanalytic theory in analyzing the representation of gender in Kubrick's films. Mulvey's own chief tool is psychoanalysis and Studlar also says that she "freely acknowledge[s] [her] debt to psychoanalytic film theory."[31] Psychoanalytic theory is particularly helpful when approaching *Eyes Wide Shut*, not only because the film takes as its subject human psychology, but also because it is adapted from a novel written by an author who was a colleague of Freud himself. Freud (1856–1939) and Arthur Schnitzler (1862–1931), the author of *Dream Story*, both lived in Vienna from 1902 onwards and apparently had great respect for one another. Freud in fact referred to Schnitzler, who was also Jewish and a doctor-psychologist, as his "alter ego."[32] Many thought that Schnitzler anticipated some of Freud's most important theories through his fictional writings—which included a great deal of prose, but also plays, the most famous, in retrospect, perhaps being *The Round*, which was adapted to film in 1950 as *La Ronde* by one of Kubrick's greatest filmic influences, the German-born director Max Ophüls. Notably, *La Ronde* was recently updated into a play called *The Blue Room* by David Hare, in which Nicole Kidman starred at about the same time that *Eyes Wide Shut* was released.

Schnitzler was no doubt influenced in *Dream Story* by Freud's *Interpretation of Dreams*, and by Freud's understanding of the dialectical relationship between the conscious and the unconscious, between the real and the dream worlds. The confluence of dreams and reality is deeply impressed upon the reader in the final sentence of the novel, in which Albertine (the Alice equivalent) and Fridolin (the Bill equivalent) lie in their bedroom after Fridolin's confession. Schnitzler writes: "And so they both lay there in silence, both dozing now and then, yet dreamlessly close to one another—until, as every morning at seven, there was a knock upon the bedroom door and, with the usual noises from the street, a triumphant sunbeam coming in between the curtains, and a child's gay laughter from the adjacent room, another day began."[33] By making the characters' sleep "dreamless," Schnitzler suggests that when sleep is interrupted by the quotidian, dream awakens once again. In this way, Schnitzler closes his novel on an idea that pervades the entire text—that dream, fantasy and reality are inseparable and ever-present in our lives.

While the film follows the novella's narrative quite closely, and Charles Helmetag is correct that *Eyes Wide Shut* is a relatively "faithful" adaptation in its cardinal functions, he is less so in saying that Kubrick engages the Freudian theme of the fluidity of dream and real worlds to the extent that the novel does.[34] Kubrick's film is less about the overlapping architectures of dream and reality than it is—at least, on the surface—an intriguing exploration of sexual difference and the gendered nature of looking, fantasizing and acting, and it harnesses the economy of gazes made available through the film medium to enact this thematic alteration. The film seems to be consciously or subconsciously influenced by the psychoanalytic thought not so much of Freud, but of Freud's follower and protégé, Jacques Lacan, and particularly by Lacan's concepts of the "mirror stage" and "the gaze."

The character of Bill Harford can be read with ease through the Lacanian concept of narcissism on which Mulvey's structure of identificatory looking is based. In order to understand the way in which Lacan defines narcissism, it is necessary to consider briefly his iconic essay, "The Mirror Stage."[35] In this essay, Lacan charts the entry of the child into the objective world. The child, recognizing itself in a mirror for the first time, passes from pure subjectivity into an awareness of its simultaneous objectivity in the world, and thus begins its integration into the symbolic order. The symbolic order is one of three orders into which Lacan divides experience: there is the imaginary order, that is, the pre-linguistic realm, before the child has learned to speak and is still connected to the mother's body; there is the symbolic order, which is the realm of language and culture and patriarchy; and finally there is the real order, an order which refers to the material world which it is impossible for us to access, but which we are constantly struggling to represent through the imaginary and symbolic orders. Film itself has been classified as a mixture of the imaginary and symbolic orders due to the way in which it fuses image and word, fantasy and representation.

The image the child has of itself in the mirror stage is essentially a narcissistic image — and this image is, in adulthood, projected onto others, and particularly those with whom we have intimate relationships. For, according to Lacan, love is primarily narcissistic — it is about being in love with "one's own ego made real on the imaginary level."[36] Or, as he alternatively says, "we can learn nothing from the field of love, that is to say, from the framework of narcissism, which ... is made up of the insertion of the *autoerotisch* in the organized interests of the ego."[37] In Freud's and Lacan's pessimistic view of romantic love, scopophilia and identification as narcissism intertwine — it is impossible to isolate one's erotic gaze at another from one's desire for *recognition* — for the erotic gaze to be aimed at oneself. Kubrick, however, complicates Freud, Lacan and Mulvey's theories in that both Alice *and* Bill are shown to crave erotic recognition. This bi-gendered characterization contradicts Freud's "othering" of the woman in which he refers to her as the "dark continent," as sexually unknowable, and it also contradicts Lacan's implicit understanding of the *female* desire to the gazed-at when he speaks of the "satisfaction of a woman who knows that she is being looked at, on condition that one does not show her that one knows that she knows."[38] Kubrick erodes this dichotomy through his characterization of Bill and Alice — a characterization that is achieved primarily through visual means, and through his exploitation of the star system in film.

Kubrick uses the visual prop of the mirror, in the first scene of *Eyes Wide Shut*, to characterize Bill as narcissistic, as needing to undergo a journey in which he will learn how to develop a new kind of love for his wife in which he will recognize her as an equal — a more optimistic kind of love than that imagined by Freud and Lacan. In the first scene, Bill stares at himself in the bathroom mirror and says, "Perfect," in response to his wife's question about how *she* looks, without turning to look at her. This scene suggests that Bill narcissistically sees his wife in himself, as part of his property rather than as an individual being. Bill's character is a myopic one — wrapped up in his own vision of himself, he cannot find the wallet he is seeking and he also cannot remember the name of the babysitter even though Alice has referred to "Ros" a moment prior to his query. In the second sequence of the film, the ball at the Zieglers' mansion, Bill's scopophilic and narcissistic impulses merge as he enjoys both *looking* at the two models with whom he flirts, and also being *looked at* and *desired* by them. In the ball sequence, which Kubrick adds to the film (in the novel Albertine and Fridolin merely recount their experiences to one another the day after the ball), Kubrick makes full use of the potential for the film medium to convey information through an economy of gazes. Bill does not bother to look for Alice while he is being entertained by the models, while Alice does look for and at Bill. Whereas Alice is a great deal more ambivalent about her encounter with the Hungarian man Sandor Szavost with whom she dances, gazing away from him to look with jealousy at her husband flirting with the models, and eventually breaking off the encounter, Bill, on the other hand, seems to be about to accept the models' invitation to be taken to the "rainbow's end" when he is interrupted and summoned to Victor's bathroom. Bill's willingness to be made a sexual object by the models contradicts Mulvey's claim that, in traditional film narrative, "the male figure cannot bear the burden of sexual objectification."[39] We are here presented with a character who is so focused on himself as a sex object that he is more concerned with being looked at than he is at looking at anyone else, and especially his wife. Kubrick erodes simple male/female dichotomies here since Alice's character is not devoid of this narcissistic desire to be seen as a sex object, either, as is evident in her flirtation with Szavost and also during the sequence, after the ball, in which Alice and Bill make love. Here, Alice gazes erotically at her own image in the mirror.

Bill and Alice are different on one level, but identical on another — that is, in their extra-filmic, real identities as stars, as Tom Cruise and Nicole Kidman, a married couple in real life at the time of the film's making. In his exploration specifically of narcissism, Kubrick's film seems to operate on two levels: as an exploration of the ordinary marriage of Bill and Alice, and as an exploration of the celebrity marriage of Tom and Nicole. Kubrick exploits his viewers' awareness that they are watching a real-life married star couple and thus implicates us as real voyeurs — even as viewers of pornography in the scene in which Tom and Nicole begin to make love. Through his manipulation of the star system, Kubrick seems to propel us beyond the imaginary and symbolic orders towards the real order. For we witness, in an uncanny way, the faked fidelity of Cruise and Kidman *acting* as a married couple, mimicking their real life relationship; and we also witness *real infidelity* in that in the course of making the film Cruise and Kidman, as actors, were of course required to engage in sexual acts with other actors. Apparently, Kubrick, Cruise and Kidman had long discussions on the topics of sex and obsession, and Kubrick was the only person on the set filming the sex scene between them, confirming the theory that part of the film's fascination has to do with a star rather than an ordinary marriage.

In spite of both characters being fashioned as narcissistic, Bill's narcissism is shown to be dangerous. Bill's narcissism rears itself again in the scene in which Bill and Alice fight about the events at the Zieglers' party. It becomes apparent that Bill, up until this point, has seen his wife only through an *imago* — through his *subjective* view of her. He assumes that other men see his wife and want to have sex with her because she is attractive; this does not bother him, we can infer, because (since he thinks he "owns" his wife) her being desired by other men is a compliment to him; he assumes, at the same time, that she does not feel desire for men other than himself. He claims a fundamental gender difference in which men have erotic desires, whereas women desire security. Alice derisively argues Bill into a corner in which, according to his own logic, he nearly admits that he desired the two models at the party.

Alice's attempt to claim a different identity for herself — as a desiring rather than desired being — is striking in a film in which most of the female characters are, literally or figuratively, models, and in which these characters are generally filmed or framed in a static way. Kubrick had a choice as to how to define the professions of the women in his film since women in modern-day New York are, of course, on very different terrain to the women in the novel, which is set in late nineteenth-century Vienna. Rather than making his female characters bankers or lawyers, Kubrick makes them models, housewives, prostitutes, receptionists, and barmaids. Through this choice, Kubrick would seem to acknowledge Mulvey's view that modern women are constructed by patriarchal society as *objects* to be gazed at, and also Rasmussen's point that Kubrick's female characters tend to be "abstract projections of someone else's sexual desire." The opening shot of the film — of Nicole Kidman slipping out of her black sheath dress — a remarkably static shot filmed from no particular point of view — activates our extra-textual awareness of the character as a star who frequently models various designer beauty products; it is two models who similarly seduce Bill; Mandy is a model, who is presented to us as incapacitated, vulnerable and unaware of our gaze in the first scene; the women who are present at the masked orgy scene, also models, are made even more model-like through being masked, and through the way in which they are centered, naked, in the mise-en-scène, ominously surrounded by the black-cloaked men. In this sequence, the power of the look is ascribed to men, and particularly to men of wealth and power, as indicated through the juxtaposition of the shot of Nightingale, blindfolded, and the low shot that slowly zooms in on the piercing eyes of one of the men on the balcony, who "spots" Bill, and who is clearly the orchestrator of events.

Rather eerily, if one pauses the frame on the newspaper article that reports Mandy's death, one sees that Kubrick — no doubt as a joke — constructs a backstory for Mandy in which she is said to enact stripteases for her fashion designer, who is given the name Leon Vitali — the name of Kubrick's personal assistant, who played the roles of Lord Bullingdon in *Barry Lyndon*, and of Red Cloak in the orgy scene. There is a disturbing extra-textual flavor to this story, albeit a joke. Now, one could argue that the fact that it is Christiane Kubrick's paintings of female nudes that beautify the walls of Alice and Bill's apartment might suggest that women have some degree of control over their own representation in the film. However, by making Alice a *failed* art gallery owner, Kubrick deprives even his lead female character of such agency. Largely confined to the domain of the household and to the role of mother and housewife, Alice articulates a critique of oppressive representations of women through her revelation, after the Zieglers' party, that she is not simply a "model" — an object to be desired by men — but a *desiring* woman, who has, in fact, fantasized about another man. What the protagonist in Kubrick's film cannot bear, then, is *not* his own objectification, which he quite enjoys (and which confirms Studlar's theory of masculine masochism), but rather his wife's attempt to assert herself as a sexual subject rather than object. Bill's attempt to "punish" Alice on this account leads him not on a sadistic journey, as one might expect according to Mulvey's schema, but on a journey that is at once sadistic *and* masochistic. Susan White sees the masochistic behavior of many of Kubrick's male characters as striking. She writes:

> In his analysis of *Dr. Strangelove* ("The One Woman," *Wide Angle* 6.1 [1984]: 35–41), Peter Baxter describes the "ineradicable tendency towards self-abasement, even self-destruction, that is almost universally repressed in the construction of masculinity." The joyous self-annihilation of male-dominated Western culture is made hilariously explicit in that film (viz., its subtitle, "How I Learned to Stop Worrying and Love the Bomb"). Baxter's reading of *Dr. Strangelove* concentrates on "the one woman" in the film, Miss Scott (the bikinied secretary), who, like the "single women" in *Paths of Glory* and *Full Metal Jacket*, functions to reflect and transmit various masculine concerns. Baxter notes that "the comic conceit" of *Dr. Strangelove* derives from the fact that "between men and the reality of politics and war intervenes the realm of sexual phantasy," a phantasy focused on "the nostalgic desire for a past that cannot be reached except in death."[40]

This "ineradicable tendency towards self-abasement" is clearly at work in Kubrick's characterization of Bill and what is disturbing about Bill's masochistic desire for a past that cannot be reached except in death is that it concentrates Freud's two human drives — eros, the erotic drive, and Thanatos, the death drive — onto the *female* body.

On the one hand, in imagining his wife having sex with the naval officer in images that are reminiscent of pornography, Bill relegates his wife to a genre that has been interpreted, most forcefully by Catherine McKinnon, as an oppressive and sadistic one in its representation of women. Bill thus conjures an image of his wife as pornographic "whore" so as to punish her. On the other hand, however, he replays this imagined pornographic film to himself in a masochistic way — so as to torture and abase himself — and it is these images that also propel him on a journey that is both sadistic (in his desire to be unfaithful to his wife) and masochistic (in that it leads him towards danger and possible death). Masochism and sadism thus interlock in Bill's characterization, and in the film as a whole, in a way that is perhaps best interpreted not through Mulvey but through the work of contemporary feminist film theorists, such as Studlar, who argues that there is no clear distinction between the male-active-sadistic and the female-passive-masochistic. Just as masochism is not confined to female characters in Kubrick, sadism is not confined to male characters; Alice's articulation of her fantasy to Bill is a sadistic act, intended to hurt him, just as her dreams are — albeit unconsciously — sadistic, in which she laughs at him watching her having sex with other men.

It is difficult to distinguish, then, between Bill and Alice according to the polarization of active/male/gazer and passive/female/to-be-looked-at-ness. Rather, Kubrick draws attention to their difference through magnifying Bill's narcissism and through fashioning Alice as a character seeking a more active, equal role in her marriage. Kubrick's narrative thus largely revolves around Bill's journey — which becomes a journey towards learning how to accept his wife as an equal through learning how to look, how to transform his "male gaze." Kubrick engages us in this journey particularly through exploiting the film medium's claims on the Lacanian imaginary, symbolic *and* real orders, through certain narrative choices, through camera movement, and through editing.

In the novel, the separation between fantasy and reality is much less marked than in the film. In the scene in which Albertine reveals her fantasy of the naval officer to her husband, Fridolin is not silenced, but rather responds with a fantasy of his own — Fridolin is thus immediately established as a character capable both of fantasizing and of embarking on real sexual adventures. *Eyes Wide Shut,* on the other hand, seems to go to great lengths to distinguish between Alice's fantasized sexual world and Bill's real, although interrupted, sexual adventures. To make this distinction Kubrick seems to associate a fluid, exhilarating camera movement with Alice, whereas Bill is associated with stultified movement, both in performance and through editing. In the first sequence of the film, it is Alice who provides the motion propelling the first scene in the Harfords' apartment into the second scene, at the Zieglers' party. Bill is the one who interrupts motion by switching off the diegetic music, the Shostakovich waltz. Bill suffers a journey in fits and starts, as it were, with Kubrick placing stumbling blocks in his way — at the Zieglers' ball Alice gets in his way when he is attempting to greet Ziegler's wife. In the rest of the film, Kubrick refuses to let us move by means of the kind of easeful superimposition associated with Alice in this sequence. Rather, as we follow Bill through his adventures, we become increasingly aware of his entrances and exits. While the content of his experience may seem fantastical and unreal, the interludes of entering and exiting are overly quotidian: if one jumps from chapter to chapter in the film, one notices how many scenes of entry and exit interrupt the narrative flow of the film. And before Bill visits Ziegler, his journey is represented by a shot which is only two seconds long, possibly the shortest Kubrick shot in the film, considering Kubrick's notoriously long average shot length (ASL). As Mario Falsetto notes: "[Kubrick's] films often contain moments of straight cutting from one space and time to a completely different time and space, with no establishing shot or fade-out to prepare for the transition."[41] This technique is altered in *Eyes Wide Shut* — Kubrick makes Bill's journey difficult for us as viewers to attest, it seems, to its *reality*.

Certain critics have claimed that Bill's journey is essentially a dream-like journey, and one critic claims that the dream begins, in the film, with Ziegler's summons to Bill to the room where the model Mandy is lying naked, overdosed on drugs, since this scenario resembles Freud's example of the "examination dream," where one arrives at a traumatic scene too late.[42] On the contrary, this scene is very important in establishing the reality of Bill's situation as opposed to the fantasies of his wife. Bill's fantasy of being taken to the rainbow's end by the models is interrupted because of the eruption of the bodily — of illness — in a world of ease, plenitude, and pleasure. This scene thus represents the first step in Bill's journey away from the narcissism of the imaginary towards the Lacanian order of the real. This scene is not present in the novel, but is crucial in the film in the way that it introduces us to characters whom we will later encounter during and after the orgy scene, specifically Victor and Mandy — and these are characters who represent how high the *real* stakes are in Bill's journey. At this early stage, however, Bill does not realize how crucial these characters will be to him — still immersed in his narcissism, as he tries to resuscitate Mandy, he continuously says, "Look at me, Mandy. Look at me." In the morgue scene, it is he who will be forced to take a long, hard look at Mandy's real, dead body. Mandy's death symbolically represents the limits of female objectification by men — the female object here becomes the dead object. At the same time, the character of Ziegler — not present at all in the novel — seems to have been introduced to represent the limits of narcissism — the place where Bill will arrive if he doesn't learn his lesson in looking.

Whereas in the novel, the mysterious woman at the orgy scene has not previously been introduced to us, in the film, we are introduced to Mandy precisely so as to confirm the reality of her death rather than leaving this death ambiguous. In the novel, Fridolin cannot be certain whether the woman in the morgue *is* in fact the woman from the orgy. The end of his visit to the morgue ends with the following passage:

> Adler [the morgue overseer] placed his hand reassuringly on Fridolin's arm, then asked with a certain diffidence, "Well — was it her?"
> Fridolin hesitated a moment, then nodded silently, and was scarcely conscious that this affirmation might quite possibly be untrue. For whether the woman now lying in the mortuary was the one whom twenty-four hours earlier he had held naked in his arms, to the wild accompaniment of Nachtigall's piano, or whether she was really a complete stranger, of one thing he was absolutely certain. Even if the woman he was looking for, had desired and for an hour perhaps loved were still alive, and regardless of how she continued to conduct her life, what lay behind him in that vaulted room — in the gloom of flickering gas lamps, a shadow among shades, as dark, meaningless and devoid of mystery as they — could now mean nothing to him but the pale corpse of the previous night, destined irrevocably for decay.[43]

In this way, Schnitzler, as well as Fridolin, makes a metaphor of the woman's body — she is both a pale corpse in her own right, and the previous night's corpse. Kubrick, however, does not allow us to query the reality of Mandy's death. And while it remains a mystery as to whether Mandy was killed through foul play, or through an overdose, no mystery remains as to the economies of gender power at work behind the scenes, and which manifest themselves in Ziegler's discourse. In the film, misogyny — Ziegler's misogyny — is shown to have led, symbolically, to a woman being sacrificed for the satisfaction of the men in the story. Ziegler not once mentions the name "Mandy" in the scene in which Bill confronts him — to Ziegler, Mandy is not a woman, but a "hooker," a "junkie," "the woman with the great tits who ODed in my bathroom." A tension is thus set up between the powerful men who were at the orgy, whom Ziegler *refuses* to name because it would give Bill sleepless nights, and the young woman whom Ziegler does not name because he cannot see her as anything other than a "hooker." This scene cuts directly into the shot of the mask lying on Bill's pillow — a visual warning of the hollow, narcissistic man Bill might become if he does not learn his lesson.

It is no small irony that Ziegler is played by the famous film director, Sydney Pollack, a close friend of Kubrick. In fact, one could argue that *Eyes Wide Shut* is Kubrick's first film in which he implicates himself on multiple levels. In the first place, it is the only film in which Kubrick acts as an extra, visible in the Sonata Café where Nightingale plays the piano. Bill and Alice's apartment was also specifically modeled on Kubrick and Christiane's New York apartment and, as mentioned earlier, the paintings on the walls are mostly by Christiane. Some believe that these personal references are not coincidental, but specifically related to Kubrick's investment in the subject matter of this film. He had been introduced to Schnitzler's novella by his second wife, Ruth Sobotka, in the 1960s, and he had wanted to make an adaptation of it ever since 1968, the year in which Subotka committed suicide. Somewhat eerily, Sobotka stars as a ballet dancer who commits suicide in Kubrick's early film *Killer's Kiss*. Perhaps Kubrick physically inserted himself into the film since, as one of Kubrick's biographers, John Baxter, writes: "What struck Kubrick so much about *Traumnovelle* was that it would allow him to examine his own dark side, and one can speculate that he also saw it as a way to expiate his guilt [in relation to Sobotka's suicide].... The author was from Vienna and was introduced to him by the wife who he thought for the rest of his life was the woman most suited to him."[44] If the film represents a journey both for Kubrick and for Bill, what does this journey entail? It seems that it is a journey towards an awareness of the fragility of life and the fact of human mortality. While on the surface this would seem to be a positive journey, it is not unproblematic, in the light of Kubrick's gender constructions, since it is the feminine that comes to represent the shock or horror of death: Mandy interrupts Bill's liaison with the models through illness; Marion reveals her love for him at the bedside of her dead father; Domino, the prostitute, learns that she has AIDS; and the model Mandy ends up dead after the orgy. One might argue that this emphasis on the feminine as signaling death could be attributed to the novel — but, notably, in the script Kubrick cuts the scene in the novel where Albertine relates her dream to Fridolin in which she sees him gruesomely sacrificed. In the course of the film, then, Bill moves away from a "male gaze" in the Mulveyian sense towards being the *object* of the "gaze" in the true Lacanian sense.

The term "the gaze" is elusive in Lacan's work — it does not refer to the look of a human eye, but rather to the uncanny sense that the *object* of one's look is "gazing" back at one. In his essay, "Of the Gaze as *Objet Petit a*," Lacan situates the "Objet Petit a"—a variable — as the object of the look, as the object of desire.[45] Mulvey substitutes the female character as this *objet petit a*. The gaze, in her scheme, is that which *disrupts* the desiring (male) look at the female, that which breaks through the imaginary and the symbolic orders from the materiality of the real. Mulvey understands this threatening gaze as the disruption of the male spectator's fetishization of the woman on the screen: in the moment of the look, he is made aware that his fetishization of the woman — representing lack, due to the fact that she does not posses a phallus — is merely a symptom of his fear of castration. In the case of *Eyes Wide Shut*, however, one could argue that the gaze that stares back at Bill is motivated by more than fear of castration; it is motivated by fear of mortality, of death. And this kind of gaze — a gaze of death — is the gaze with which Lacan is most concerned. This is illustrated through Lacan's use of a particular painting to explain the gaze — this painting is Hans Holbein's 1533 *The Ambassadors* (on permanent exhibition at the National Gallery in London). One's eye is first drawn in this painting to the two male figures, surrounded by objects that signal power, wealth and achievement — fine clothes, artistic and scientific instruments, a globe — and the men seem to look confidently back at us. However, the men's instruments and steady stare is then undercut when one notices the strange shape at the bottom of the painting. The strange shape is a skull. This skull that stares back at us is Lacan's supreme example of the gaze, of that which looks back at us and "reflects our own nothingness," that reminds us that bordering on the symbolic order is the threatening order of the real in all its materiality.[46]

In *Eyes Wide Shut* the "skull" that gazes back at Bill is encoded as feminine — it hovers around Marion, Domino, and Mandy. While, on the one hand, the film seems to critique the narcissistic, powerful patriarchy represented by Ziegler, and to encourage Bill to undertake his journey in learning how to look beyond himself to the humanity of those around him, and particularly his wife, it is impossible to ignore the fact that Kubrick associates femininity with horror, with the abject, and as something to fear. In this sense, I agree with Christiane Kubrick that Kubrick's final film is not obsessed with sex, but rather with death, and it is as though

Kubrick is attempting to break through the imaginary and symbolic orders in this film into the real order of death itself—but where death is coded as feminine.

In the final analysis, one might argue that in spite of his alignment of femininity and death, Kubrick's film is feminist in that Alice becomes the heroine of the story in her ability to negotiate amongst all three of the Lacanian orders in her strange imperative to her husband at the end of the film that they should "fuck": in this final word, Alice simultaneously conjures the non-linguistic sexual desire of the imaginary, the language of the symbolic, and the real (through the fact that this act will not be witnessed onscreen—it will be achieved only after the "death" of the film itself).

At the same time, Alice's words echo the sense of repetitiveness and claustrophobia experienced by many of Kubrick's characters, both male and female, and suggest that *Eyes Wide Shut* is not a wholly optimistic film. For, after Bill's complex, dangerous and profound journey towards an appreciation of his wife as more than an object of sexual attraction for men, Alice suddenly seems to demand that he once again see her in precisely such terms. Perhaps, finally, it is naïve to think that there can ever be an escape from the constraints of society or self in Kubrick's films, even in *Eyes Wide Shut*.

14 Carnivalesque and Grotesque Bodies in *Eyes Wide Shut*

Miriam Jordan and *Julian Jason Haladyn*

The Classical and Grotesque Body: "You're not even looking"

The opening scenes of Stanley Kubrick's *Eyes Wide Shut* present two contrasting visions of the human body: the classical eroticized nude and the drama of the grotesque body. In a short scene that interrupts the flow of the opening titles—cut in between the actors' names and the title of the film itself—Alice Harford is pictured in a shallow space framed by classical columns that demarcate the entrance to this dressing area. Filmed as a stationary shot on a slight angle, the scene embodies the image of the classical nude, with Alice dropping her black dress to the floor revealing her completely nude body underneath as she steps out of this fallen garment in her black high heels. Alice is represented as a classical nude with a body that is complete and idealized, "cleansed, as it were, of all the scoriae of birth and development."[47] This momentary scene of eroticism is unique in the film, with the sexual possibilities of this first glimpse into this world never reaching fruition. An abrupt cut to black ends the scene.

Following the black-and-white title of the film that subsequently appears, another cut brings us to a street level scene with cars driving by and buildings in the background, sounds of sirens punctuate the activities of New York City where the film takes place.[48] After this contextualizing prelude, we join Bill Harford, who is standing in the same dressing room that his wife had occupied in the initial scene. There are a number of significant differences that mark the transition of this space from an embodiment of Alice's eroticized classical body to the disembodied qualities of her grotesque bodily functions as she urinates in front of her husband. A quick examination of the room reveals elements visible in both scenes; the window on the back wall is dressed with voluptuous red curtains that have been drawn back revealing ordinary Venetian blinds partially closed, a row of shoes underneath the window trails towards the mirrored closet doors on the left wall. The bookshelves that line the right wall of this space are present in the shot of Bill, but are blocked by the angled perspective of Alice captured from outside of the room looking in through the classical pillars, which are not visible at the beginning of the scene with Bill—the camera having entered the space of the dressing area. These differences achieved through the framing of the scene are accentuated by the addition and subtraction of various objects within the room. Primary among these is the elimination of a floor lamp situated in the corner between the mirrored closet and the window, which provides dramatic lighting for Alice's exposed nude body. Tucked behind this lamp in the initial sequence is a pair of uncovered rackets, one of which appears again in a case and leaning against Bill's dresser within the main space of the bedroom. In the subsequent scene a golf bag replaces both the floor lamp and the rackets, which, in addition to the resulting lack of illumination surrounding Bill's scene, implies a solitary masculine game in place of a shared activity. This subtle differentiation between Alice's scene in the space and the subsequent scene with Bill highlights many of the larger problems that circulate through the narrative of the film, all of which originate from Bill's obliviousness to his own surroundings—as symbolically represented through the lack of illumination when his character first appears in the beginning scenes. In this poorly lit space, Bill fleetingly looks through the Venetian blinds into the world, "oblivious to the anonymous crisis signaled by the passing siren."[49]

The final material difference between the two scenes is the appearance of a small red patterned area rug centered in the room when we join Bill, which is not present in the scene with Alice. There is, however, a spatial correlation between the site of Alice's discarded dress and the location of the rug; Alice erotically unveils her body through the removal of her black dress that she drops on the floor in the same location where the rug is situated in the subsequent scene with Bill. The mysteriousness of the black dress—a theme that the color black is associated with throughout the film — is replaced by the ornate red carpet, which is symbolic of the sexual frustration felt not only by the characters, but also by the viewers of the film who anticipate a transparent narrative and sexual display. As Tim Kreider states in his review of *Eyes Wide Shut*, Kubrick "mocks any prurient expectations in the very first shot of this movie: without prelude, Nicole Kidman steps into the frame, her back to the camera, shrugs off her dress and kicks it away, standing matter-of-factly bare-assed before us for a moment before the screen goes black and the main title appears. It's as if to say, 'You came to see a big-time movie star get naked? Here ya go. Show's over. Now let's get serious.'"[50]

The transition from the "matter-of-factly bare-assed" show of Alice's idealized naked body to the seriousness of Kubrick's depiction of the ordinary grotesqueries of the Harford's daily life — the bodily activities that have become so routine that Bill does not even notice them — is reflected in the staging of the room, in which the moment of eroticism appears to be lost before the movie even begins, having been replaced with a rug that Bill simply walks across while getting ready for the Zieglers' Christmas party. The prelude of Alice's idealized sexual display is literally segregated from the remainder of the narrative by the title of the film, after which the idealism of Alice's body is replaced by the casual reality of her bodily functions. In Bill's eyes the presence of her body has become one of the many beautiful objects that adorn their apartment.

Another significant difference between the depictions of this space is the texture of the filming itself. Whereas the original scene of Alice is shot from a fixed point of view that is slightly off centered, Bill's presence in the same room is presented head on with a handheld camera in a constant state of visual movement. This contrasting filmic approach to the same site again punctuates the distinction between the classical and grotesque body, specifically in terms of the relationship that this private room has to the larger world outside of the Harford's window. Alice's classical nude body is represented within the closed space of the dressing room, which appears self-contained due to the framing device of the pillars; this vision exists within a brief moment that is literally contained within the black screens of the opening and is visually separated from the main narrative. A similar act of containment occurs throughout the film in Bill's black and white visions of Alice's adulterous fantasies, which are cut into the scenes of Bill's wanderings. Kubrick's use of black-and-white film functions to conceptually distinguish these scenes of fantasy from the real events of the film serves to highlight "the artificiality and inaccuracy of the story being presented to the audience."[51] The filming of both the initial scene of Alice and Bill's imagined visions of her sexual activities are fixed, with the camera placed in a single location for the duration of these scenes, formulating visually self-contained images on the screen. The second version of this room is not fixed, but is part of a larger narrative that propels us into the film; instead of remaining contained within this site, the camera follows Bill as he walks through the entire space of the bedroom, responding to his bodily movements with everything from a grand arc across the room to a slight shiver as he uncovers his misplaced wallet on the bedside table. Finally venturing into the bathroom, the camera moves into a position behind Bill, following him to the doorway and stopping. For the remainder of the scene the camera follows Alice, until they both leave the bedroom; this entire sequence, beginning in the dressing area and ending at the door leading from their bedroom to the hallway, is one take that explores the interconnected sites of their most intimate space.

The filming of this scene beginning with Bill reflects the qualities that Mikhail Bakhtin attributes to the grotesque body. As he states, the grotesque body "is not separated from the rest of the world. It is not a closed, completed unit; it is unfinished, outgrows itself, transgresses its own limits."[52] In the first sequence in the changing room, Alice's act of undressing is treated as a separate and complete unit that is not related to the rest of the bedroom: we cut in and out of the scene without any association to a larger world. Bill's scene is filmed as a continuously growing context that begins in this dressing room, but quickly ventures out and becomes part of a larger world; the classical pillars do not limit or close off this space, but are transgressed as Bill prepares to engage in a social obligation. Similarly, Alice's grotesque bodily activities and functions are realities to be ignored in order for him to be able to view his wife as "perfect." But it is ironically the grotesque body that will transgress the "perfect" boundaries of Bill's world and threaten the stability of his life.

The grotesque body becomes the centre of attention as Bill ventures into the blue and white bathroom where Alice sits on the toilet urinating, a sound that can be clearly heard over the music. She is discovered with her dress hiked up around her waist and draped down her right leg, with her left leg exposed to the camera displaying her panties pulled halfway down her thighs. This is our first true exposure to the grotesque body, that is the body in the process of excreting fluids, an act in which the boundaries "between the body and the world are overcome."[53] But Bill does not look at Alice sitting on the toilet; instead he walks straight to the mirror to look at himself as she asks him, "How do I look?" He continues looking at himself in the mirror and does not bother to inspect Alice before he responds, "Perfect," while she stands up and wipes herself. Alice disposes of the toilet paper in the toilet as she asks Bill, "Is my hair okay?" He responds, "It's great," again without looking at her as she pulls up her underwear. Alice finishes adjusting her dress and underwear as she points out, "You're not even looking at it." In response, Bill turns and looks directly at Alice for the first time as she flushes the toilet and says to her, "It's beautiful." He then leans forward to kiss her on the neck while saying, "You always look beautiful." Bill walks out of the bathroom, but the camera stays with Alice as she finishes her ministrations and then follows her out into the bedroom. The fact that Bill's oblivious comment that Alice is "perfect" occurs at the same time that she is in the process of wiping herself after she has urinated points to his inability to view her body in its grotesque reality, instead he pictures her without looking as an ideal classical beauty. Only after the evidence of her bodily function has been *flushed* away and Alice's body is again closed off from the world does Bill physically look at his wife.

As they finally prepare to leave the bedroom, Bill turns off the radio, revealing that the music that we have been listening to is diegetic, or part of their world. This one action abruptly signals the constant shifting from reality and imagination or dream that is characteristic of the film and functions to transform "the Shostakovich piece from non-diegetic to diegetic music."[54]

But even though this romantic waltz fails to cover up the grotesque reality of Alice's bodily functions, which transgresses itself and intrudes into their existence, Bill's familiarity with Alice's body is one that he in his habitual obliviousness chooses not to notice. He is so accustomed to Alice and her body that he does not even open his eyes to it when she asks repeatedly how she looks. In fact his response "appears to be the product of long habit rather than true feeling. Not a lie, exactly, but more a pro forma than a profound token of love. And Alice, *mildly* chastising her husband for it, knows that she is being taken for granted."[55] Only when she points out that he is not even looking at her does he finally look at her and, scrutinizing her appearance — which betrays the imperfections of her body, tell her that she is always beautiful. This reliance on an absolute conception of Alice as "always" beautiful points to a prevailing problem that Bill confronts throughout the film, right up until the final scene when he uses the term "forever" to describe their love, a term that Alice tells him frightens her. These absolute conceptions are again part of the ideal and classical world to which Bill continually returns when escaping his own fears of the grotesque realities of his life. Even as Bill looks at Alice and tells her she is beautiful, he is not responding to her body and its imperfect reality, but rather to the idealized classical image that he has of her, as represented by the image of Alice in all her fixed perfection in the opening shot.

The scene in the bathroom signals the shift that has occurred between the classical, eroticized nude body of Alice that we see momentarily before the film's title and the drama of Alice's grotesque body that becomes the catalyst for the entire series of events in *Eyes Wide Shut*. In the initial vision of Alice, Kubrick frames her "nakedness and our voyeurism within a painterly composition of white pillars and red curtains, bathed in a golden light that made her resemble one of those Renaissance bronzes later mentioned by Szavost."[56] By associating Alice with Renaissance statues, Kubrick is establishing a cultural ideal of classical beauty that Alice can never live up to. As Peter Stallybrass and Allon White note in *The Politics and Poetics of Transgression*:

> The classical statue has no openings or orifices whereas grotesque costume and masks emphasize the gaping mouth, the protuberant belly and buttocks, the feet and the genitals. In this way the grotesque body stands in opposition to the bourgeois individualist conception of the body, which finds *its* image and legitimation in the classical. The grotesque body is emphasized as a mobile, split, multiple self, a subject of pleasure in processes of exchange; and it is never closed off from either its social or ecosystemic context. The classical body on the other hand keeps its distance. In a sense it is disembodied, for it appears indifferent to a body which is "beautiful," but which is taken for granted.[57]

Although many of these elements of the grotesque body occur repeatedly throughout the film — most notably the grotesque costumes and masks of the climactic carnivalesque orgy scene at Somerton — it is the classical body and its grotesque double that are the focus of these beginning sequences. Bill takes this classical body for granted, refusing to see the grotesque reality that lies beneath his projected "beautiful" fantasy of Alice, which is shattered by Alice's sexual confession that sends him on a futile search for a classical fantasy — one that may never have even existed. It is Bill's inability to reconcile the classical body of his wife, the ideal vision of Alice that exists in his mind, with the grotesque reality of her bodily existence that drives the plot of *Eyes Wide Shut* forward.

The Lower Stratum of the Grotesque Body: "He glanced at me"

Although Bill is able to remain oblivious to Alice's bodily functions and needs when he avoids looking at her while she is on the toilet urinating, instead recalling his "perfect" classical image of her beauty without looking, the grotesque body becomes the site of disagreement the following evening during their argument. Before discussing this conflict, it is important to establish the parameters that lead up to this dispute, which fall into two categories associated with the grotesque body, specifically intoxication and the lower stratum of the body.

The role that intoxication plays in *Eyes Wide Shut* is confined, almost exclusively, to the beginning of the film. At the Zieglers' Christmas party both Alice and Bill appear to be drunk, likely due to the boredom of not knowing anyone at the event — their presence at this party is the result of Bill's professional obligation as a doctor, since Ziegler is a wealthy patient whose patronage presumably permits the Harfords to maintain their lifestyle. Their mutual intoxication allows Alice and Bill to engage in mild flirtatious behavior that would not be acceptable in an everyday situation. Alice dances with Sandor Szavost, who banters with her about the reason that women used to get married, "to be free to do what they wanted with other men," and attempts to seduce her by luring her upstairs under the pretext of viewing Ziegler's collection of Renaissance bronzes. At the same time Bill strolls through the party with two seductive young models on his arm, who flirtatiously ask him, "Don't you want to go where the rainbow ends?" Similar to Bakhtin's notion of the carnival as a second life, Alice and Bill's intoxicated actions are sanctioned by the "temporary suspension of all hierarchic distinctions and barriers among men and of certain norms and prohibitions of usual life" within the space of this party.[58] The prohibitions of the Harfords' married life are therefore not broken or violated, neither Bill nor Alice engage in a physical sexual tryst, but instead their drunkenness allows them to temporarily bend the rules of their relationship. This initial suspension of their everyday lives is the focus of these flirtatious activities, which are blatantly directed at the lower stratum of the grotesque body: that is at the sexual organs. As is repeatedly made clear throughout the narrative of the film, "the rainbow ends" at the site of sexual activity — the most blatant example being the sexual possibilities that are facilitated by the costume shop, ironically titled Rainbow Fashions, which provides Bill with the mask he needs to access the Somerton orgy and which is the scene of Milich's pandering of his daughter. This is obviously an ironic joke on Kubrick's part, given that a rainbow has no end.

In fact, *Eyes Wide Shut* can easily be viewed as an ironic parody of sexual fantasies, in which case these scenes of drunken flirtation function as a warning to the viewer that, as with traditional satires and parodies, the story to follow is not to be taken entirely seriously.[59] As Nelson points out, this film resembles the deceptive narrative strategies "found in *2001* and *The Shining*, in which predominantly solemn and naturalistic surface orders are at war with an internal satiric disarray caused by unacknowledged irrational forces that exist within the structures of both personality and civilization."[60] The entire purpose of Alice and Bill's drunken flirtation therefore is to fulfill, even if only at the conceptual or dream level, the fantasy of temporary sexual gratification. But the satiric disarray of their lives, which is caused by a number of unacknowledged irrational fantasies and desires, is not gratified by the mock carnival activities of the party.

These harmless acts of flirtation become the preliminary topic of conversation during the second instance of intoxication, when Alice and Bill smoke marijuana in their bedroom the night after the party. A series of montage shots document their respective activities during the course of the day. We witness Bill's professional practices as a doctor, in which he deals with the material aspects of his patients' bodies. These scenes of Bill are contrasted with Alice's domestic dealings, which are equally focused on the grotesque realities of Alice and their daughter Helena eating and grooming their bodies. As a means of relaxation at the end of the day, Alice retrieves a stash of marijuana hidden in a Band-Aid container. This scene of intoxication begins with a close-up view of Alice lying with her body facing the camera on their bed, which is covered with a patterned red bedspread and pillowcases, smoking a joint. The camera pulls back as she finishes inhaling and passes the joint to Bill, who is revealed to be sitting on the side of the bed behind Alice. Unlike the public carnivalesque qualities of Ziegler's party, this moment of intoxication is one of privacy and intimacy between husband and wife — who are both in their underwear — with the camera often framing the couple in a single shot. But, similar to the drunkenness of the party, this act of intoxication is likely functioning as a prelude to sex — real or imagined — as is evidenced by Bill's stroking of Alice's lower bodily stratum. Bill's sexual advances are ironically timed, coinciding with his deceptive explanation of where he "disappeared" to after Alice spotted him with the two models at the party. Alice draws a parallel between Bill's intoxicated advances on her and his similar advances on the models that he was "so blatantly hitting on." In doing so she associates herself with his blatantly grotesque sexual desires and articulates this by asking him if he "happened to fuck them?"

Unfortunately, Bill is unwilling to look at his beautiful wife and see her bodily desires to "fuck." Even with her use of this profane terminology, using the grotesque "fuck" instead of the socially acceptable "make love," Bill again overlooks her bodily functions and needs by naively idealizing Alice and her state of mind. The flirtations between husband and wife cease the moment that Bill obliviously remarks that it is "understandable" that Szavost wanted to "fuck" his wife, because she is "a very ... very beautiful woman." Bill's use of the classical term "beautiful" in addressing Alice's body signals his continuing idealization of her as a complete body, which again parallels his use of the term the preceding night in the bathroom when he made the blanket statement "you always look beautiful." But unlike he reaction to his prior act of inattentiveness to her physical body, Alice is not willing to simply *mildly* chastise him. Instead she questions the very foundation of his logic, asking: "Because I'm a beautiful woman the only reason any man ever wants to talk to me is because he wants to fuck me. Is that what you're saying?" This question brings about a shift in the scene's composition, with Alice leaving Bill on the bed and standing in the doorway to the bathroom, where the previous grotesque bodily encounter was avoided. In her rephrasing of Bill's would-be compliment that she is "a very ... very beautiful woman," Alice exaggerates the meaning of his statement in order to bring about a direct conflict between his vision of her as classically "beautiful" and his inability to see her bodily desires to "fuck."

The argument degenerates until Bill makes the absolute statement that "women don't.... They just don't think like men." This is the foundation for not only his lack of jealousy in regards to Alice, but also the basis for his understanding of the women with whom he works in a professional capacity. Bill is visibly offended by Alice's insinuation that his "beautiful" women patients may have sexual "fantasies about what handsome Doctor Bill's dickie might be like." This diagnosis is ironically proven correct immediately following this argument, when Marion declares her love for Bill after he has come to tend to her recently deceased father. He has obviously been unaware of Marion's sexual desire for him, proving that he has no right to claim knowledge of what women do or *don't think*. Bill's misguided statement to Alice that "women don't.... They just don't think like men" when it comes to sexual desires and fantasies sparks an argument that leads to the narrative thrust of the film: Bill's crisis in perceiving Alice as having the same grotesque thoughts and desires that he has. The fraudulent nature of their marriage centers on Bill's idealization of Alice, whom he cannot conceive as having a grotesque body and corresponding desires.

Although Bill has many opportunities to back out of this argument, Alice taunts him with her questions and exaggerated interpretations of his own words. This recourse to exaggeration, particularly in terms of sexually vulgar innuendoes, is another major element of the grotesque body. As Bakhtin points out, "Exaggeration, hyperbolism, excessiveness are generally considered fundamental attributes of the grotesque style."[61] Alice's blatant excessiveness in her argumentation — her bodily gestures of pinching her nipples when describing his examination of a female patient—serves to highlight the lengths that she is willing to go to get Bill to admit the possibility that women have the same bodily and sexual desires that men do. There is something very absurd about this argument, one that cannot be explained away by the fact of their intoxication; like many arguments between longtime life partners, there is more being discussed than simply Alice's disagreement with Bill's choice of words. As Nelson states: "Stripped down to their underwear and smoking pot, away from the masks of social civility and sexual predation, the Harfords become ensnared in a private psychosexual dispute that exposes the fraudulent nature of their 'perfect' marriage."[62] Later, Nelson addresses what he calls "Alice's satiric disbelief" that Bill has never been aroused or had sexual thoughts about one of his "beautiful" patients.[63] This again points to the possibility that the argument is staged—as is the movie itself—as an exaggerated satire or parody of married sexual relations, in which Alice is attempting through hyperbole to alter Bill's perception of her from—in relation to Kubrick's paradoxical title—*eyes wide shut* to *eyes wide open*. What Alice is asking of Bill is simply that he remove his mask of social civility and look at her as she truly is, in all of her grotesque bodily functions and desires. Even though she exaggerates the situation to the point of absurdity, Bill continues to be oblivious to the subtext of their discussion and to his obvious inability to reconcile the classical visions of his wife with the grotesque body that she is increasingly displaying to him.

Alice's reference to the sexual thoughts of Bill's female patients, beyond being simply an exaggeration meant to undermine his defense of professionalism, may be seen as parodic humor, a joke that she is playing on Bill, which in his stubbornness he never gets. This stubbornness is reflected in the filming and editing of the scene, in which, after the argument begins, Alice stands up and is mobile for much of the remaining exchange, whereas Bill sits unmoving on the bed. As Michel Chion describes: "the editing gives Alice a dominant place and it is she who is seen the most. The camera follows her various postures—standing, seated, bending over, kneeling—and stops on her face when she starts to recount the episode in Cape Cod. The reverse shots of Bill, when he has stopped talking and is sitting frozen on the bed as he takes in these revelations, are at once short and extraordinary."[64] This visual contrast between Bill's stationary position within the scene and Alice's mobility again demonstrates the distinction between the classical and grotesque body. Whereas the classical body—epitomized by the statue—is fixed, unmoving and "keeps its distance," the "grotesque body is emphasized as a mobile, split, multiple self, a subject of pleasure in processes of exchange."[65] Bill keeps his physical distance from Alice, remaining fixed on the bed, and also remains distant and fixed in his position within the argument itself: he is sure, secure and fixed in his beliefs, specifically in relation to Alice. After she comments to him, that he is "very, very sure" of himself, he replies: "No. I'm sure of you." Bill's insistence on being "sure" of Alice offends her because he is not willing to think of her as anything but a static object—that is a beautiful, faithful, and ideal wife. It is not that she wants him to be jealous of her per se, but that she needs him to acknowledge her erotic or grotesque desires and needs, rather than arrogantly pretending she is a perfect woman.

The seriousness with which Bill treats the situation illustrates that he does not *see* what is unfolding—just as he failed to see her the night before on the toilet—and this triggers Alice's "fucking laughing fit," as Bill angrily terms it. This is a significant moment in the film for two reasons. First, it signals a transition in the Harfords' relationship, because after this outburst and the story of Alice's desires that follow, Bill is no longer able to view his wife in the same way. Secondly, it is arguably the only scene of true laughter, with the possible exception of her laughter in the dream she has the next evening. All others involve laughter as social niceties or social masks. Alice's laughter in this scene is an example of what Bakhtin describes as carnival or festive laughter, which "is not an individual reaction to some 'comic' event. Carnival laughter is the laughter of all the people ... it is directed at all and everyone, including the carnival's participants. The entire world is seen in its droll aspect, in its gay relativity ... this laughter is ambivalent: it is gay, triumphant, and at the same time mocking, deriding. It asserts and denies, it buries and revives. Such is the laughter of the carnival."[66] Alice's laughter mocks Bill, denying his certainty that *women don't think like men*—a thought that appears to scare and eventually haunt him through the recurring black and white visions that he has about her adulterous thoughts. On a more general level, Alice's laughter also serves to mock the entire situation, possibly her entire "perfect" life and her willingness to throw it away for one night of "fucking." With this laughter, she throws all of Bill's seriousness in his face as a means of eliciting an *honest* answer from him. But, whereas Bakhtin's notion of carnival laughter always fulfills a regenerative role that embodies positive change, Alice's laughter is ironic and underpins the disembodied character of her situation. At no point does she appear to take pride in the irrational bodily desires that she felt for this nameless naval officer. Instead her fantasy epitomizes the struggle that she goes through in negotiating the problematic relationship between her grotesque sexual fantasies and the "perfect" world of her life. Alice's laughter is aimed at Bill—specifically his obliviousness in regards to the struggle that she goes through in balancing her reality and her fantasies— at herself and, ultimately, at us, the viewers of the film who want to see "perfection." The carnival laugh that Alice expresses underpins the "absence of narrative meaning" in *Eyes Wide Shut*, the story that the characters are engaged in being "meaningless *in and of itself.*"[67]

Alice's desire frightens her because it represents the possibility of her sexual fantasies coming into contact with the reality of her world. According to the story that she tells Bill, she is ready to throw everything away for a man that she fears is gone from her life and simultaneously fears might still be there. And this man is still there, in her thoughts and fantasies, which she shares with Bill as a means of demonstrating her own problematic negotiation between her "perfect" life and her lower bodily desires. It is this frightening convergence of reality and fantasy that causes Alice to literally laugh in Bill's face—as she does in her dream the following morning while, as she recounts, "fucking all these men" as Bill watches. She wants "to make fun" of him, to mock him, to laugh in his face, so she laughs as loud as she can. Alice's laughter in her dream echoes her laughter during her argument with Bill. Both incidents of laughter serve a similar function: to mock Bill and undermine his certainty. It is important to recognize the trauma she expresses in retelling the events of this dream; she cries and clings to her husband, revealing that she is not maliciously laughing at Bill, but merely transgressing the boundaries of decorum that he has placed upon her. This is evident even in Bill's fantasies of Alice's imagined sexual encounter, in which she is boxed-off and "enclosed in a room."[68] Through listening to Alice recount both her fantasy of the naval officer and her subsequent dream, Bill's inability to remain oblivious to Alice's grotesque bodily functions and needs bring about his own ongoing crisis as he continues attempting to reconcile his classical sexual fantasies with the grotesque reality of his life.

Carnivalesque Masks and the Double Life: "You will kindly remove your mask"

The most pervasive element of Bill's encounters during the narrative of *Eyes Wide Shut* is that of the carnival or carnivalesque. According to Bakhtin, the carnival is constructed as a "second life" that is "a parody of the extracarnival life, a 'world inside out.'"[69] In other words, the carnivalesque is a turning *inside out* of everyday life, in which prevailing norms and social prohibitions are temporarily suspended and a second life of new possibilities is born.[70] Although we first encounter the tenets of the carnival at the Zieglers' Christmas party, in the sense that everyday life is superficially suspended for the duration of the party—as witnessed in the public intoxication and flirtatious behavior of both Alice and Bill — this suspension does not constitute a second life because all of the norms of society are maintained in an exaggerated form. For example, Bill ceases his flirtation with the two models when Ziegler summons him like a servant; the hierarchical relationship between Bill and Ziegler is not suspended. According to Bakhtin, a "suspension of hierarchical precedence during carnival time was of particular significance ... all were considered equal during carnival," and unlike the Zieglers' party, "a special form of free and familiar contact reigned among people who were usually divided by the barriers of caste, property, profession, and age."[71] It is not until after his argument with Alice that his carnivalesque journey can be said to truly begin, but the carnival that he encounters is one that is minimized through his assertion of rank and status, as well as his inability to participate. Ultimately it is Bill who does not have the ability to enter into the carnival spirit. He is, as Zeigler notes, "way out of" his depth.

Following Alice's confession of her grotesque bodily desires, Bill's world is systematically turned *inside out* or carnivalized through a series of interconnected events, the first of which takes place literally moments after Alice completes her story of sexual wantonness. The phone rings in the background. Although Bill takes time to answer the call, presumably because he is in shock, his professionalism — a term that Alice throws in his face during their dispute — gets the best of him and he leaves without truly responding or answering to her provocation. "Bill is summoned to the home of a patient who has died suddenly. Professional duty displaces a private dispute."[72] Given the subject matter of his private dispute, specifically his misguided belief that women "just don't think like men," Marion's sudden declaration of love and her willingness to throw away her life with Carl just to be near Bill is strikingly uncanny. In her apparent fantastical disregard for her everyday life in favor of the possibility of even a temporary gratification of her grotesque desires, Marion serves as Alice's sexual double. She reenacts the same actions that Alice just told Bill she had fantasized about. This is the second time in the same night that Bill "confronts a woman's confession of illicit sexual desire — for which she is willing to sacrifice her 'whole fucking future' — and once again he struggles unsuccessfully to hold together the structured surfaces of a relationship (husband/wife; doctor/patient) in the presence of a woman's emotional honesty."[73] This uncanny parallel is heightened when, following Marion's open-mouth kiss of Bill — which foreshadows the gaping mouths of the grotesque masks at the orgy — her fiancé Carl arrives. Bill finds himself in the uncomfortable position of bearing witness to his own naive double, one who is guilelessly certain of Marion, just as Bill was equally "sure" of his own wife before Alice's provocative story opened his eyes. Kubrick makes this doubling between Bill and Carl explicit by filming two almost identical scenes, in which a tracking shot follows each of the men as they walk down the hall towards the bedroom containing Marion and her dead father only moments apart. With the knowledge that Marion has just placed Bill in the role of Alice's naval officer, we watch Carl — who from the back looks just like Bill — walking "the same distance that Bill just walked."[74] The fantasy of which Bill previously thought his wife, and all women, incapable has just been brought to life before his very eyes.

This mirroring effect, seeing himself as the man responsible for Marion's irrational bodily desires, causes a stunned Bill to begin aimlessly wandering the streets of New York City. Bill encounters a man and a woman passionately kissing and groping each other on the street, which triggers one of several black and white pornographic imaginings of Alice fucking her naval officer in his head. It is ironic that Bill's imagined fantasies of Alice are the only true scenes of carnivalesque passion that we see in *Eyes Wide Shut*, but they provoke him into a wandering quest for his own carnivalesque adventures to counteract them. Even Bill's initial encounter with Domino, who solicits him on the street, does not live up to his expectations. It seems that he cannot leave behind his "real" life as he embarks on his misadventures; this is made literal through the editing of this sequence, in which scenes of Alice at home are cut into scenes of Bill preparing to have sex with Domino. The carnivalesque qualities of Bill's double life are accentuated by the masks that adorn Domino's walls, which are a key thematic element in the carnival "based on a peculiar interrelation of reality and image, characteristic of the most ancient rituals and spectacles;" the mask, as Bakhtin elaborates, "reveals the essence of the grotesque."[75] Bill's interrelated reality and image of himself are temporarily turned upside down; Domino becomes the professional who gives him advice. When he is with Domino, we witness the "ironic unmasking" of Bill, in which he reverses professional roles and becomes "Domino's patient ... and agrees to follow the 'doctor's' orders."[76] But the carnival that Bill encounters at Domino's is one in which he ironically never fully participates; just as Bill is about to embark on his own carnal adventures, his cell phone rings and he obligingly answers—as he did during his argument with Alice. And it is "Mrs. Dr. Bill" inquiring as to when he will be home. This is the first of many interruptions that prevent Bill from engaging in the carnivalesque possibilities that he encounters during his misadventures in the double life.

From Domino's apartment, Bill returns to the streets. He happens to chance upon the Sonata Café where Nick Nightingale—his old friend from medical school that he met at the Zieglers' party—is playing piano.[77] Not ready to return home to his life and his waiting wife, Bill enters and descends into the bowels of the nightclub. There he encounters Nick, who tells him about his next gig where he plays the piano blindfolded. Intrigued Bill questions him. Nick reveals that the blindfold was not on so well the last time he played, permitting him to peek. He tells Bill that he has "seen one or two things in my life ... but never ... never anything like this ... and never such women." Fascinated by the orgy Nick describes and the secrecy that surrounds it, Bill is determined to go, driven again by the visions of his wife engaged in bodily delights. He discovers the location of this mysterious bacchanal from his friend, along with the necessary password and attire needed to get in—which he acquires at the Rainbow Fashion store.[78] Once at Somerton, hidden beneath his cloak and mask, Bill enters into the spectacle of the "masked party's surreal carnival."[79]

The carnivalesque sequence that we are presented with recalls elements from the opening scenes of the film, specifically the contrast between the classical and the grotesque body. Eleven masked and black-cloaked women kneel in a circle on a red carpet in a vast room with classical white pillars, which recall the pillars that frame our first glimpse of Alice contained within the dressing space of her bedroom. As the camera pans in a mesmerizing circular motion, the women rise in response to the gesture of a masked and red-cloaked man and disrobe, dropping their cloaks to the floor. The women stand like classical statues, much like Alice did at the beginning of the film, semi-nude in black high-heels with their robes discarded on the floor, again reminiscent of Alice's fallen black dress. In an intensely ritualistic scene, the women respond to the rhythmic commands tapped out on the floor by the staff of the red-cloaked "Grand Inquisitor and King of the Carnival," who swings a censer around them in a mockery of a Roman Catholic ceremony.[80] The women kiss each other in pairs, the disembodied lips of their masks making subtle contact, and then each woman departs from the circle to select partners from the surrounding masked spectators. A woman in a feathered mask selects Bill to be her partner and leans forward to kiss him; their masks meet in a disembodied kiss, with no physical contact between their mouths. This is the third extramarital kiss of the evening for Bill, the first kiss given by Marion, who kisses him with her literally gaping mouth—a prominent feature of the grotesque body that can be observed on the masks of several spectators at Somerton—and the second by Domino who kisses him with a closed mouth. As Bill progressively finds himself in ever more sexually charged environments, he ironically becomes increasingly distanced physically from the sexual activities that are unfolding around him. Rather than becoming an active participant in the carnival sexuality that surrounds him, Bill remains a remote spectator. As Bakhtin points out: "Carnival is not a spectacle seen by the people; they live in it, and everyone participates because its very idea embraces all the people. While carnival lasts, there is no other life outside it. During carnival time life is subject only to its laws, that is, the laws of its own freedom," which were most, "clearly expressed and experienced in the Roman Saturnalias."[81] But Bill does not take advantage of his freedom and never engages in anything more than just watching what Nelson terms an, "amalgam of Catholic solemnity, pagan virgin sacrifice, and Saturnalian pornography," all of which is staged in a fake classical environment.[82]

The orgy sequence represents a coming together of the classical and grotesque body, with the classically staged bodies of the nude women engaging in an orgy of grotesque carnality. But Bill is "in danger" within this environment, as he is warned by the woman in a feathered mask — who turns out to be Mandy, the prostitute whose life he saved at the Zieglers' Christmas party. Although he is likely never in any real danger, Ziegler's explanation that the participants of the party staged an exaggerated display to "scare the shit out of" Bill probably being true, the symbolic danger that he was facing at the orgy is extreme. On the most basic level, Bill is immersed in a conflation of fantasy and reality, his problematic inability to balance the two being the reason for his psychological crisis following Alice's grotesque confession. At the orgy Alice's implicit judgment of him through her exaggerated story is turned into a carnivalized judgment, one in which Bill is literally stripped of his mask and almost stripped of his clothing before a tribunal of masked socialites. If it were not for the woman in the feathered mask *redeeming* him, Bill, as a sum of his fears and desires of the grotesque, would have been completely exposed. As Nelson states:

> Because he responds to the events of Somerton through the confusions of his increasingly conscious desires and fears, he does not notice that "Red Cloak," now sitting on a throne, plays the dual roles of Grand Inquisitor and King of Carnival. He does not notice that the mysterious woman in the feathered mask ... who seriocomically appears and announces that she will "redeem" him, noticeably overacts her part. He does not understand what the Venetian masks imply; nor does he notice how most of them gaze at him not only in stern, patriarchal disapproval, but also in grotesque attitudes of laughter and mockery.[83]

Bill misses all of this; he does not understand the meaning of the mask or its relationship to the grotesque body. He again takes the entire situation too seriously and at face value — as he did with Alice's confession — failing to recognize the grotesque qualities of his life. This is a continuing problem for Bill that instigates a rather curious conclusion to his adventures. Bill's carnivalesque double life is systematically revisited the following day as he goes back to the scene of each of his transgressions in an attempt to make sense of the events he experienced, to bring them back into a perspective that would make him "sure" of his life again. But ultimately what he finds is a trail of questions that have no legitimate answer.

Under the Mask: "We're awake now"

The first truly carnivalesque display in which we see Bill engage occurs when he breaks down crying after discovering his lost mask from the Somerton orgy resting in his place on the pillow beside his wife. Alice is asleep in bed, lying on her side facing the mask, which has been placed within a slight indentation on the pillow giving the impression that a head used to be under the mask. This evidence of his double life confronts him on his return to his everyday existence. The carnival life and all its implied dangers have appeared within the confines of his real world. Like Alice's fear and desire for the naval officer, Bill's fears and desires become a palpable presence that he can no longer avoid. As with Alice's laughter during their argument, Bill's tears function as a release, permitting the boundaries "between the body and the world" to be overcome.[84] This is the grotesque release of bodily fluids that Bill has been simultaneously seeking and avoiding throughout his carnivalesque quest.

It is this moment of exaggerated release, when Bill has utterly broken down and collapsed in Alice's arms, that he finally opens up to her and tells her "everything." Ironically this is what Alice was looking for during their argument, not in terms of a confession but an exchange of fears and desires. The disembodied mask to which Bill returns home reminds him of everything that he has gone through, both real and imagined, and embodies all that he has lost. He can no longer engage in his habitual denial of the grotesque realities of both his and Alice's bodily needs and desires, just as he can no longer hide beneath his mask of obliviousness. "As he looks down on his own mask, and gazes into its sightless eyes, Bill relives the shattering experience over Mandy's death mask. But rather than flinch and close his eyes," as was his habit, "at the sight of his now conscious fears and failures" he turns to Alice and shares his bodily weaknesses.[85] More than simply reliving the experience of Mandy's death — a death associated with her voluntary redemption of him — the presence of the mask in place of his own head forces Bill to consider the consequences of his actions during the course of the previous evening; for example, the possibility that he could have contracted HIV from Domino, Nick's welfare after being taken away by two "big guys" for telling Bill about the orgy, Bill's passivity in the face of Milich's prostitution of his young daughter and Mandy's fatal overdose, which might be related to her redemption of him. Ultimately, what is reflected most in the presence of this empty mask on his pillow is Ziegler's comment that "life goes on. It always does. Until it doesn't." The arbitrariness of this perspective in light of his activities, which centered on his grotesque desires and fantasies, is too much for Bill to handle, stripping him of his sureness and leaving him to seek redemption in Alice.

The subsequent scene cuts to a close-up of Alice's red swollen eyes, accentuating the fact that she has been crying, as she sits on the couch smoking, which recalls the close-up of her smoking marijuana just before their argument. Bill is sitting across from her also in tears, apparently having told her "everything"— although we never witness this cathartic event. This exposure of the face behind the mask, the "truth" of Bill's character, is ironically hidden behind Kubrick's filmic image of the narrative, the film functioning as a form of mask presenting a beautiful surface with nothing underneath. According to Chion, *Eyes Wide Shut* confronts "the myth that truth is already close to us, 'under a mask,' such as the mask of the image. We desperately try to remove the mask, certain that the truth lies underneath. The particular relationship the film establishes between what is said and what is shown (the one neither confirming nor denying the other) has the effect of making the image, and particularly the other person's face in the image, appear as a mask behind which a truth is concealed and which the mask hides from others or from itself."[86]

Kubrick strategically reveals and conceals in this scene; the faithfulness of Bill's "straight answer" will never be fully known, as viewers must make assumptions about what Bill has truly seen and what he ultimately says to Alice. The shots that, until this moment, have been used to expose and reveal Bill become discontinuous and function as a mask that hides the extent of his marital honesty with Alice. Just how far Bill lets his social masks drop away can only be guessed at, but if Bill's use of the word "forever?" in the penultimate scene reveals anything, it implies that he has not completely abandoned his earlier façade.

In the final sequence at the toy store, Alice and Bill don their social masks as they engage in a social obligation for their daughter; this is the first time that we witness them in a shared familial activity. Their serious faces and conversation are a marked contrast to the excited expressions of their daughter Helena, who is immersed in the imaginative carnivalesque world of the fanciful toys that surround her. As the Harfords wander through the bustle of the toy store — paralleling Bill's wandering through the streets of New York — the overwhelming colors of Christmas gaiety surround them. This is reflected in the filming with the hand-held camera in a constant state of visual movement, which again implies that the actions of Alice and Bill are not separate from the world, but are part of its unfinished motion, which continually transgresses the limits of their individual lives.[87] Helena is attracted to an ornate baby carriage, which is symbolic of her own possible grotesque outgrowth and the transgression of her bodily limits through the birth of her own child. Alice responds to Helena's interest by saying uninterestedly, "It's old fashioned"— possibly conveying her own lack of interest in being a mother, a role that she took upon herself likely in place of her own career and to support Bill's own professional pursuits. Bill watches and waits for his wife; it is up to Alice in the end to redeem the couple, a task that he is no longer able to claim certainty over. His question, "What do you think we should do?" illustrates the moment of pause or temporary suspension in which they find themselves, the camera itself pausing as Alice repeats his question back to him in consideration. Helena calls their attention to a Barbie doll dressed as a magical fairy — reminiscent of her own costume at the beginning of the film when her parents left for the Zieglers' Christmas party — but both Alice and Bill respond with fake interest, putting on momentary masks of joy for the sake of their daughter.

Near the beginning of the film we witness a marital dispute within the confines of the Harfords' bedroom, one that causes Bill to leave the sheltering microcosm of his world and venture out into the grotesque world without boundaries. Sperb describes this boundless world of *Eyes Wide Shut* as foregrounding. "The absence of narrative meaning as a central subject in the film ... points us to its own story as meaningless *in and of itself*. The event is the event — it cannot be mediated."[88] Bill's continuing attempts to mediate his world and the events that transgress it are symptomatic of his desire to retain and impose a classical ideal upon his life, which ignores the grotesque realities that finally intrude upon his obliviousness; these are attempts by Bill to impose a sense of meaning and truth on a meaningless amalgam of the events he has witnessed. This meaninglessness is articulated when Ziegler says to Bill the previous evening, "Life goes on. It always does. Until it doesn't. But you know that, don't you?" This statement sums up Bill's entire carnivalesque experiences, those known by Ziegler as well as those that are unknown to everyone except Bill — and possibly Alice.

In the final sequence of the film, we witness Bill returning to the safety of this familial microcosm, a shift that is reflected in the filming of the scene. As Alice begins to respond to his questions, the camera tightly focuses on their faces in a series of shot-reverse-shot exchanges that never again reveal the surrounding context. While the world continues on around them as a blur of motion and color in the background, Alice tells Bill that "the important thing is we're awake now and hopefully for a long time to come." Alice is proposing that they simply accept the relative nature of both fantasy and reality, while acknowledging the necessity to be aware of this duality and not get caught up in an effort to avoid this dichotomy. The strength of Alice's character comes from her ability to balance her fantasies and her everyday life; not to reconcile them, but to allow them to exist without trying to impose an artificial sense of meaning or order as Bill continually attempts to do— right up until the very end, as epitomized by his need for this waking state between him and Alice to be "forever." The blank expression on Bill's face for most of this scene is the same one that he has worn like a mask for the duration of the carnivalesque events that take place around him, illustrating his continued obliviousness and his inability to see what is in front of him; the difference in this case is that his certainty in his perspective has been shaken and he now, for the first time, turns to Alice for the sense of surety that he so desperately needs. It is ironically within this carnivalesque environment of playful imagination that Bill must learn to balance the fears and desires that disrupt his perfect vision of the world, and it is ironically Alice — whom he previously failed to take seriously — to whom he finally looks for answers after he discovers that the world he has imagined as real is fake. But Bill's need for his world to be "forever" is the reason we believe that his eyes, to use Kubrick's oxymoron, are still *wide shut.*

Alice counters Bill's absolute need for meaning and truth by again throwing the grotesque body into his perspective when she says that there is something "we need to do as soon as possible." We never see Bill's face respond to Alice, Kubrick does not supply us with a reverse-shot again, but instead we look at the back of his head while we wait for her to enlighten us — because we are just as much in the dark as he is. Her answer, "fuck," represents the complete antithesis of our initial glimpse of the erotic display of her classically framed body in the opening shot. This "fuck" completely counters the idealization of her body with a grotesque image that we never see and are left to imagine as the film abruptly cuts to black. "The film is now closed. It is contained within two borders of time and everything that happens within those borders, between the two cuts of the beginning and the end, now takes on a definitive meaning and can be interpreted."[89] Left in the dark, we must reconcile the meanings and interpretations of the attempt to balance our vision of Alice's classical body and her grotesque body; like the grotesque nature of the body, the film's narrative transgresses its own boundaries and borders, resisting the possibility of a containing meaning.

15 The Phenomenological Quest of Stanley Kubrick: *Eyes Wide Shut*

Phillip Sipiora

The "there" is said to be a wall between us and others, but it is a wall we build together, each putting a stone in the niche left by the other.
— Maurice Merleau-Ponty, *Signs*

To suggest that *Eyes Wide Shut* exemplifies a "rogue" enterprise may strike some readers as a commonplace observation, hardly innovative. Indeed, receptions of the film commonly note familiar Kubrick themes of alienation, isolation, detachment, estrangements, and so forth. These representations, often manifested in a no-man's-land of existential terrain within the unsympathetic boundaries and margins between consciousness and subconsciousness, are a cauldron of erupting emotions.[90] Much of Kubrick's oeuvre is explicitly untraditional in terms of cinematic norms of genre, ranging from camera work to uses of sound and setting, to a continuing engagement with the landscape and inscape of the surreal. *Eyes* is no exception. Indeed, Kubrick's final film is an exclamation point to a four-decade trajectory of ambitious, aggressive, interrogative cinema, driven by a master filmmaker's unquenchable thirst for exploring the unknowable.[91] As Kubrick has said in commenting on the metaphysical significance of *2001*: "It's not a message I ever intended to convey in words. *2001* is a nonverbal experience.... I tried to create a visual experience, one that bypasses verbalized pigeonholing and directly penetrates the subconscious with an emotional and philosophic content."[92] Such a quest is inherently philosophical, particularly within the context of phenomenology.[93] Kubrick, as much as any other contemporary Anglo-American filmmaker, explores in his most powerful films the two dominating metaphysical issues in western civilization over the past twenty-five hundred years: epistemology and ontology.

Eyes reveals a persevering spirit of interrogative phenomenology, one that explores fundamental issues of agency and subjectivity and the ways in which they affect critical realms of human experience: how might one know (epistemology) and how one might/should act (ontology).[94] Through the depictions of characters in action and interaction, and through the use of language, *Eyes* becomes a master metaphor, a synecdoche in the Kubrick corpus depicting a continuing quest for "understanding" and "living" in light of the impossibility of ever arriving at stable codes or processes of knowing and being. The infrastructure of this formidable film represents human existence as an infinite journey of interrogation, a search not for what life "is" or "means," but rather an ongoing, yet unachievable, quest for fragments of suspended knowledge that might function as stepping stones for yet further probing. Bill Harford, scientist and artist, is an example of a distinctive, late-modern yearning for ways of knowing and being. *Eyes* poignantly and dynamically illustrates the desire for the primacy of ontology over epistemology. The painful process of interrogation is one means of determining one's actions (or ontology), which in itself leads not to understanding or explanation, but to yet another round of questions and engagements invigorated by new actions. This cycle characterizes the spirit of the art and act of philosophy, according to Merleau-Ponty: "Philosophy does not raise questions and does not provide answers that would little by little fill in the blanks. The questions are within our life, within our history: they are born there, they die there, if they have found a response, more often than not they are transformed there."[95] Philosophy can never be more than a point of departure in exploring what it means to probe the human experience.

    Eyes, as several critics note, involves a series of dream-like states in which characters, particularly (but not exclusively) Bill and Alice, seem unaware of their "peripheral" status (as if any other condition were possible in Kubrick's calculus of meaning). Kubrick's film is the culmination of a distinguished and stunning career in which he continually treats motifs in ways staggeringly original, especially his emphasis on "unnatural characters" whose presence challenges traditional cinematic notions of subjectivity. As Mario Falsetto argues, *Eyes* "demonstrates that the director maintained and enriched a line of inquiry that ran from his earliest work to the present. More than a line of inquiry, the combination of subjectivity within an objective presentation and objectivity within a subjective presentation ultimately become a necessary component of his vision."[96] *Eyes* opens with three beginnings, each with strategic implications.[97] First, a "portrait" shot of Alice disrobing (disconnected in time or narrative continuity to any other frame in the film).[98] The dress-dropping scene is a disjunction, foreshadowing synecdochically not only a series of ruptures (temporal and thematic), but also emblematizing dislocation and incoherence as crucial motifs. Not coincidentally, Alice reveals only her backside, obscuring and thereby disconnecting her face from her figure.[99] Second, a Manhattan street traffic scene, punctuated with emergency sirens, ever-present horn-blowing, and ubiquitous taxicabs. Third, a scene introducing interrogation as an integral part of Bill's *modus vivendi*. The doctor's first words to his wife, "Honey, have you seen my wallet?" represent the first of many encounters in which Bill and Alice "face off" in engagement; occasionally over trivial matters, but usually over very serious issues. Bill and Alice's interactions with each another are a major component of narrative structure, and these encounters (including self-reflexive mirror images) reveal their attempts to "make sense" out of inter- and intra-personal conflict. In the three-part introduction, Kubrick introduces at least two critical motifs (the body and the face).

Phenomenological Inquiry

    In which ways does Kubrick's complex introduction evoke insights, strategies, and questions of phenomenology? Productive and meaningful perception, according to Maurice Merleau-Ponty (one of the most influential phenomenologists of the last century), depends not upon our translation of an objective world, but rather upon our interpretation of external phenomena, which necessarily includes a conscious acknowledgement of the active role of the subject in confronting objective events. As Merleau-Ponty puts it, "All cognitions are sustained by a 'ground' of postulates and finally by our communication with the world as primary embodiment of rationality."[100] The key term in this premise is "communication." Georges Poulet, literary phenomenologist, emphasizes the correspondence between the text and an author's (filmmaker's) consciousness as a representation of an artist's driving sensibility. Indeed, the aesthetic product can only take shape under the guiding instincts of the creator, and these instincts are informing principles providing a kind of metaphysical, predetermined infrastructure that result in residual key defining qualities of the artist.[101] Merleau-Ponty succinctly characterizes phenomenology as "a matter of describing, not of explaining or analyzing."[102] *Eyes* is a series of scenes of descriptive vignettes that reveal characters seeking shards of meaning. This unsatisfiable quest is not limited to cinematic and literary characters, but extends to viewers and readers as well. The audience is inextricably intertwined with the creative artist in the investigation of subjects and subjectivities. As Howard Pearce suggests, "We connect with other subjectivities; we apprehend structures of relationships that are not simply perceived; we engage in acts of the imagination that interpolate, extrapolate, extend, confirm meaningfulness and purposefulness, in art as in life. As reflectors of the artist, we contribute to his patterning of events and images by seeing meaningfully."[103] Bill and Alice's performances at the Zieglers' party, for example, reveal them to be quite different from one another in their interactions with others. Alice, intoxicated with spirits and the giddy atmosphere of the moment, encourages the advances of the tall, dark stranger, Sandor Szavost. Alice, literally and symbolically, interfaces with him during their dance and her entertainment of his solicitation. Billing and cooing, their faces bob back and forth within an inch or two of one other. This kind of encounter evokes Emmanuel Levinas's illustration of "interfacing." Levinas, a phenomenologist roughly contemporary with Merleau-Ponty, locates ethics in the relationship between the self and the listener, reader, viewer, or collaborator. Levinas's term is *alterite*— otherness, or difference. The act and fact of the encounter, for Levinas, necessarily calls into question self-definition. A collaborator or participant in a discourse exchange necessarily undergoes some level of ethical transaction precisely as a result of the encounter.[104] In the encounter between Alice and Sandor, she renders an explicit ethical judgment in rejecting his offer of a "trip upstairs." In the philosophy of Merleau-Ponty, one must practice the "explication of perceptual relations," as they are revealed in the subject's "opening to the world."[105] Bill and Alice's openings to the world are about to ignite as they struggle with their perceptual relations.

The Good Doctor

Wife and husband engage in comparable encounters at the Zieglers' party as Bill strolls with two models, mirroring Alice's act of flirtation. Yet Bill behaves far more passively than his wife, as he switches identities from model accompanist to medical man when summoned by Victor to rescue comatose Amanda (Mandy) Curran, who has nearly killed herself by "shooting up" a speed ball (heroin plus cocaine).[106] Although Bill's interaction with the models is more subdued and less explicitly sexual than that of Alice and the handsome Hungarian, Bill's face and overall demeanor change dramatically when he dons the mantle of medicine man. Clearly at ease with the protocols of a professional healer upon observing the comatose Mandy, he asks the right medical questions, first of Victor and then of Mandy, takes her pulse, and examines her air passage. Bill is methodically objective and detached, comfortably hidden behind the mask of doctor (not unlike his masked appearance at the masked orgy party, which reveals a far different face from what it becomes and represents when it is unmasked). From near death, Mandy dramatically rouses into full consciousness. Dr. Bill congratulates her on being "a very lucky girl" (although she is 30 years old), cautions her that "you can't keep doing this," and says, "You're going to need some rehab."

Victor thanks Bill profusely, believing that the good doctor brought back Lady Lazarus from the nether world and protected the good host from unfavorable publicity and possible legal liability. Bill emerges from the bathroom triage a hero as Victor gushes, "I can't thank you enough for this. You've saved my ass." It is not clear what the doctor has accomplished beyond determining that Mandy is alive, looking into her mouth, and waiting until she regains consciousness, prompted by his questions: "Mandy, Can you hear me? Move your head if you can hear me. Good, good." This scene, like so many others in Kubrick's cinema, emphasizes the context, the circumstance, the exigencies of the moment of critical time. This kind of special time is *kairos*, a dominant concept from ancient Greece that signifies the strategic importance of timing/timeliness: due measure, harmony, proportionality, opportunity, occasion, convenience, advantage, fitness, propriety, and decorum.[107] Kubrick demonstrates a deft awareness of *kairos* in the scene just described and many of the preceding synonyms describe the context of scenes, dialogue, and interactions in *Eyes*.[108]

From the Mandy scene, Dr. Bill emerges a savior to a deeply relieved Victor, if not also to Mandy (it's hard to tell, she says so little). Yet what does the doctor do beyond simply "being there?" Kubrick's ongoing criticism of western institutions is well known, especially in *A Clockwork Orange* and its ironic depiction of medicine as a "healing art" in the reconstruction of Alex de Large. So, too, Bill Harford, M.D. depicts a subtle questioning of institutional competence, symbolic of Kubrick's lack of belief in human "progress." Bill's medical license and skills are employed primarily to gain credibility with individuals who can benefit him (costume impresario Milich, the hotel desk clerk, a waitress at Gillespie's) and entrance to restricted space, like the hospital morgue. Bill's standard line is, "I'm a doctor. It's OK." Viewers might well surmise that there are multiple Bill Harfords wandering around Manhattan and its environs, each in search of fragments of meaning embedded in the indecipherable tapestry of human conduct. Bill longs for some means of grasping and understanding identity, too, and his reach is not limited to Alice and himself. Such a pursuit is hinted at by the quizzical look Bill gives Mr. Milich once he realizes that the father-pimp is not what he originally takes him to be. Bill is dazzlingly naive with little apparent sense of self-reflection or understanding, a striking portrait compared to the far more sentient Alice.

The phenomenology of interrogation in Kubrick's later films depends upon an ethical context, even when films end in ethical confusion and bewilderment. "Ethics," as Levinas and Merleau-Ponty suggest, reside potentially in relationships and encounters. As Merleau-Ponty says, "We must not, therefore, wonder whether we really perceive a world, we must instead say: the world is what we perceive."[109] Indeed, *Eyes* is concerned with the entropic unfolding not only of Bill and Alice, but their marriage as well. In the scene of Bill and Alice naked following the Zieglers' party, Kubrick brilliantly frames Alice's ethical dilemma (presumptively over her affair with the naval officer) with the pulsating beat and lyrics of Chris Isaak's "Baby Did A Bad Thing."[110] Alice, I suggest, inscribes herself in the questioned persona and this inscription sends her into tears as she breaks away from Bill's advances. Kubrick intertwines lyrics and the music in much the same way by closing *Full Metal Jacket* to the pounding, nihilistic "Paint It Black" by the Rolling Stones. The song's second line is, "I look inside myself and see my heart is black | I see my red door, I *must have it painted black*." These words inscribe the reflecting characters, especially Pvt. Joker. Kubrick employs these kinds of encounters and subsequent ethical reactions to illustrate the belief that stable knowledge, of self or others, is ungraspable.

Ethical Questions

The ethical dimension of the encounter is always a force of positive resistance, according to Levinas, an energy that has potential for productive dialogue, translatable into action. (Productive in Kubrick's art is neither a "positive" nor "affirmative" effect but rather one of "enabling" or facilitating" narrative movement.) Bill and Alice engage in a kind of Levinasian "face making," interacting with each other and in self-reflexive mirrors as they grapple to define themselves through interpersonal and intrapersonal encounters. These transactions, so integral to the mettle of *Eyes*, involve other characters, too, especially through physical masking and role playing. The encounter, says Levinas, necessarily imposes a responsibility on the participants, an obligation that requires a "gift" to the other. Something must be offered to the other and there can be no free interchange without something to give. Alice and Bill, for example, give one another the gift of forgiveness at film's end as they seemingly choose to move on with their lives. Levinas's speculations place him well within the company of other phenomenologists like Maurice Blanchot, whose influential work, *The Writing of the Disaster*,[111] observes the dynamic of the "receding other" as one attempts to embrace the conceptualization of him or her: "In the relationship of *myself* to the *Other*, the Other exceeds my grasp. The Other: The Separate, the Most-High which escapes my power — the powerless, therefore, the stranger, dispossessed."[112] Blanchot observes the dynamic of the "receding other" as an agent/subject attempts to embrace the conceptualization of an objectified (other) him or her. This pursuit of "knowing the other," through language or any other means, can never be fulfilled, of course, as Bill and Alice come to understand all too well. They, like us, can never control the effects of their discourse once unleashed. As Mikhail Bakhtin reminds us, "Language is not a neutral medium that passes freely and easily into the private property of the speaker's intentions; it is populated — overpopulated — with the intentions of others."[113]

Alice's recounting to Bill the details of her fantasy with the naval officer is an example of this phenomenon. Her sex-narrative becomes a dominating obsession for Bill as he continually lives (and relives) her sexual specters, made cinematic in Bill's imagination through his viewing and reviewing the sequences of *his* invented sex acts between wife and lover. Bill's obsessive sexual reenactments of Alice are his way of responding to his forced reexamination of their relationship. One might say that Bill must practice the "explication of perceptual relations," as they are revealed in Alice's "opening to the world."[114] Kubrick depicts these openings through sensory experience. As Vivian Sobchack argues, "Cinema thus transposes, without being completely transforming, those modes of being alive and consciously embodied in the world that count for each of us as *direct* experience: as experience 'centered' in that particular, situated, and solely occupied existence sensed first as 'Here, where the world touches,' and then as 'Here, where the world is sensible, here, where I am.'"[115] Viewers cannot stand outside this process as we are drawn into Bill's voyeuristic re-creation and we voyeuristically partake in the scenes.[116]

The "pot scene" is a strategic phenomenological moment as it sets in motion Bill's nocturnal wandering (not unlike Paul Hackett's all-night meanderings in the labyrinthine, alien underworld of Martin Scorsese's *After Hours*).[117] The heated argument between Bill and Alice over fidelity and the nature of men and women triggers a more powerful reaction in Bill than her telling the story of obsession with and sexual fantasy of the naval officer in Cape Cod. It pains Bill to hear Alice say that she was (and possibly is — even more threatening) ready to give him up, along with Helena, for the officer. The argument neither concludes nor is resolved when a call from Marion Nathanson, the daughter of a dead man, interrupts Alice's monologue. Bill's comment, "I have to go over and show my face," reminds us that so much of his professional life is devoted to registering "face time." Bill rides in a speeding taxi with images of Alice's sexual escapade racing through his mind. Once at the death scene, Bill offers the usual platitudes, cloaking himself in his comforting role of Dr. Bedside: "Your father was a very brave man." After a few moments of inane conversation (Bill: "Michigan is a beautiful state"), Marion informs Bill that her math professor/fiancé Carl Thomas is on his way (to join her grieving). She then suddenly begins to kiss passionately Dr. Bill, who, strangely, does not resist, even after she declares — seven times no less — "I love you." (Perhaps this is not the doctor's first-time experience with grieving daughters.) Marion, like Alice, is ready and willing to throw away her (impending) marriage for an object of desire. After consecutive glimpses into the "nature of women" and their notions of fidelity, Bill's relatively stable life, protected by a superficial sheath of secure knowledge, is strategically called into question, plunging him into a nocturnal world of inquisitive misadventure, unfettered by (shattered) illusions and fueled by sexual cravings.

Nighttown

The night begins as Bill, not unlike Leopold Bloom, wanders through the streets of a city, observing street couples in deep embrace, replaying black and white scenes of Alice's Cape Cod sex throes. Deep in thought, Bill is accosted by several young men, one of whom yells out, "What team's this switch-hitter playing for?" Bill is knocked into a car by the pack, is called "faggot," and stares back in bewilderment at the receding gang, not so much in anger, but more in disbelief that he, a fully-charged straight male, could have been mistaken as gay. This encounter plays no small role in Bill's libidinal wanderlust, leading to his next encounter (to prove his heterosexuality?) with a streetwalker, Domino, whose profession is obvious to any-one except Bill. She stops Bill and asks him for the time, her way of asking for his time. Bill once again reveals his naiveté by actually giving her the time. Once he agrees to stop and talk, Domino, like most experienced prostitutes, realizes that her chances of "scoring a john" have risen dramatically. Domino asks, "How'd you like to have a little fun," to which Bill responds (stuttering), "I'm sorry." What Bill means is, "Excuse me, please explain" or "I don't under-stand," again displaying woefully deficient street smarts. (How has Bill survived in New York as an adult well into his 30s with so little worldly knowledge?) It is almost as if Kubrick has cre-ated an adult child, a professional man no less, in order to dramatize an empty slate undergo-ing basic training, akin to Bloom walking and learning the streets of Dublin, except that Bloom is a far quicker learner than Harford.

Throughout the film Bill acts continually confused when asked questions, and his stum-bling is revealed through reflexive restatement of questions. In response to Domino's playful and punful solicitation, "Would you like to come inside with me," Bill can only respond, child-like, by repeating her question, "Come inside with you?"

Encounters such as these remind us how critical tropes of exaggeration and hyperbole are to Kubrick's depiction of the difficulty, even impossibility, of human communication. At times we are not sure whom to trust. As Falsetto points out: "In *Eyes Wide Shut* we never know who to believe, and the status of the narrative events remains unclear throughout the film. Truth and fiction, objectivity and subjectivity, the public and the private are intermingled to such an extent that the viewer remains in a state of constant uncertainty."[118] Phenomenology is neces-sarily interconnected with perception and the ways subjects react in confrontation with objec-tive experience, including other subjects. Kubrick utilizes Bill's perceptual deficiencies to dramatize and problematize the ubiquity of perceptual challenge. Through the metaphor of hyperbole, wrapped in a synecdoche (Bill), we are confronted by Kubrick's familiar concern with the alien nature of human experience, whether it is in suburban England, America's Pen-tagon, outer space, Vietnam, or the swank and seedy streets of Manhattan flanked by country-side estates. Although Bill is sexually loaded when he meets Domino, he again shows his inexperience in a moment comparable to his insentience upon learning of Alice's sexual desires *and* her infidelity to fidelity. When prostitute and client come down to discussing available services, Domino asks, "What do you want to do?" Bill reveals his inexperience in ordering from a working girl's menu (and respective prices) by responding, "What do you recommend?" Domino laughs and then repeats Bill's repeat of the question. The night worker clearly is not used to transacting business with someone of Bill's innocence. Domino prefers not to discuss the specifics of the potential act, instructing Bill to "leave it up to me." Bill shrugs and says, "I'm in your hands," a nice Kubrickian pun, given the emerging portrait of Bill.[119]

Bill's business with Domino is abruptly cut short (near coitus interruptus?) by Alice's call, reminding us of Marion's interruption of his pot-intensified argument with Alice. The Sonata Café and former college roommate Nick Nightingale are Bill's next stop and it is this connection that triggers the bizarre events that are to follow. Piano man Nick enthralls Bill with teasing hints of the later bacchanalian feast for which he will provide the musical entertainment. "I just play the piano," says Nick, alluding to a brothel keyboardman's usual disclaimer. Once Bill wrenches the password "Fidelio" out of Nick, he is determined to do whatever it takes to participate in the sybaritic soiree. Bill rents a costume from Milich, a corrupt and seemingly unstable proprietor/parent who would be right at home in *After Hours*. His costume shop, Rainbow Fashions, is a play on the models' earlier reference to taking Bill to where "the rainbow ends." Bill mumbles and stumbles in talking to Milich, flashes his medical ID (the words and picture that gives him identity plus entree to all kinds of people and places), but also masks his identity. Once he has identified himself as "doctor," characters seek medical advice (Ziegler and Milich) or smell money (Domino and Milich). Characters are no longer dealing with "plain Bill" but an affluent professional. As Mario Falsetto points out, "*Eyes Wide Shut* is a wonderful illustration of how language can mislead the viewer and is often superfluous to the meaning of a scene." The farcical scene in Milich's store reveals much buffoonery and craziness, but Bill is not about to be deterred from his mission. In full heat and armed for battle with mask and costume, Bill charges forward to the Somerton Ball.

The bacchanalian fest is the grand moment of the film spread over several scenes. For Bill, "the time has come": visions of orgiastic revelry dance in his mind as he approaches the gated mansion, frenzied nerves pulsating in the comforting (and dangerous) realization that the evening is potentially prime. It is getting late but it is also quite early, depending on one's perspective. Masking is the code of the evening and Bill is well equipped, carrying his gear (like a good soldier of the night) that will cover the doctor-mask, that covers the husband-mask, and on and on. As Dennis Bingham explains, "The character of Bill can be seen as split up according to the masks that he wears when he plays his various roles: the face of the hail-fellow (the Zieglers' party), the face of the ardent lover and the trusting husband, the face of the caring doctor, the face of the husband after he has heard of his wife's desire to be unfaithful, the face of the thrill-seeker, the face of the man who has been exposed and humiliated, the desperate face of a man who believes he has caused a woman to be killed, and, finally, the face of a guilty husband."[120] Bill's encounters with nearly everyone confirm an elusive identity behind or beneath the uniforms of doctor and husband. In Kubrick's worldview, such a motif is neither startling nor unexpected if one accepts the premise that much of his art is based on the quest for exposition of the inherently inexplicable. As Kubrick has said, "If a film has any substance or subtlety, whatever you say is never complete, it's usually wrong, and it's necessarily simplistic: truth is too multifaceted to be contained in a five-line summary."[121] The filmmaker's words relate to the suburban orgy as much as to any other scenes in the film. If the preceding scenes are dark, unrealistic, and foreboding, the surreal costuming, masking, rituals, music, chants, tapestries of color, characterizations, and mysteries of the orgy take Kubrick's creative, aggressive impulses to a new level. Upon entering the mansion Bill appears to witness a medieval religious ritual, but a postmodern sensibility infuses the "ceremony." Nick, blindfolded as promised, pounds his fingers to make a funereal dirge while the long-legged, thonged female participants drop their cloaks at the command gesture of the presiding "Red Cloak." The orgy scenes that follow may be the most powerful metaphorical gestures in the Kubrick canon. Particularly stunning are the masks, exemplifying the ancient trope of *prosopopeia*, astonishing in their diversity and representation of caricatures of caricature (created in Venice, the world's capital of mask-making). Kubrick is fond of wielding metaphors and symbols that recede into yet other images, and the colorful, complex quilt of orgy-phenomena, including tantalizing tidbits of sexual variation, makes for a stunning spectacle for Bill and viewer.[122]

The ritual takes a catastrophic turn for Bill once he has been detected as a trespasser and is forced to confront the "court" and unmask himself under penalty of great harm. Bill is "ransomed" by Mandy, who suddenly appears—*Dea ex machina?*—speaking from the balcony. The redeemer's identity is unknown to Bill (and us) at the time of his redemption. Bill, liberated, returns to the presumed security of his Central Park West apartment, yet has unknowingly transported himself from one nightmare to another. After hiding his costume (sans mask?) Bill enters their bedroom to find Alice laughing uncontrollably, locked in deep, dream-laced sleep. Alice is obviously having a nightmare, and Bill responds with a predictable, imperceptive remark: "I thought you were having a nightmare." We are reminded again that Bill struggles to perceive and communicate beyond the banal. The good doctor suffers from much more than simple verbal deficiency. In some ways, he shares similarities with a primitive *2001* HAL with his emphasis on mechanized speech, reactive, repetitive utterances, and a semi-mindless, unself-reflexive mode of perception. Bill is curious, of course, about what has generated his unconscious wife's laughter: "What are you dreaming?" he asks. Alice, now awake and crying, responds, "Just weird things." The dream is about her and Bill. "We were in a deserted city and our clothes were gone. We were naked and I was terrified and felt ashamed. You rushed away.... I felt wonderful and was lying in a beautiful garden, stretched out naked.... There were hundreds of people everywhere and everyone was fucking and then I was fucking other men, so many." Alice's dream (nightmare?) clearly shares some similarity with Bill's fantasy visit to Somerton, but he, like Alice, has yet to have any sexual encounters, imagined or actual, that generate meaningful knowledge. Bill and Alice show scant ability for generative rediscovery of their environment, especially themselves. Such perceptual development is crucial to human understanding. As Merleau-Ponty says: "We find in perception a mode of access to the object which is rediscovered at every level, and in speaking of the perception of the other I insisted that the word 'perception' includes the whole experience which gives the thing itself."[123] Bill and Alice are more alike than they realize in accessing so little of their spousal "Other."

Bill continues to be haunted by Alice's dream and his anguish is exacerbated when he discovers that Nick checked out of his hotel at 5:00 A.M., bruised and muscled away by two big men, "the type you don't want to fool around with," according to the desk clerk. Bill senses a world not right, intensified by Milich's attempt to sell Bill his daughter's favors when Bill returns his rented costume. Bill scurries to work and, once safely back in the sanctuary of his office where he is in absolute control, he drifts back into fantasy clips of Alice's tryst with the naval officer. Trying desperately to make sense of what is happening, Bill jumps in his Land Rover and heads back to Somerton, where he is warned for the second time to stay away. The camera pans in on Bill as he peers through the gated fence, like a prisoner looking at freedom and searching for explanation, so enticeably obtainable on the other side of the bars. Bill returns home, engages in routine husband/daddy talk, yet he can't get Alice's words out of his mind: "I was fucking other men, so many I don't how many I was with." The copulation visions continue. He knows that he is obsessed, not only with the "reality" of Alice's fantasized adultery, but also with the knowledge that he is in the center of a perplexing mystery. The tangle of inexplicable phenomena possesses Bill as he returns to Domino's apartment, only to learn that she is HIV positive and Dr. Bill well understands his brush with danger. The next stop is Sharky's pub, where Bill's newspaper informs him that Mandy died the previous night under mysterious circumstances ("Ex-beauty queen in hotel drug overdose"). Dr. Bill heads to the hospital morgue to see Amanda Curran, his "patient,"[124] showing us that as a man of science he is keenly aware of objective reality and the necessity and importance of scientific confirmation. The doctor stares at the corpse in slot 19 as if in disbelief (similar to his stare at the rowdy youths who attacked his manhood). As he exits the hospital, still in a daze, Bill receives a summons from Victor.

The doctor's avuncular friend (and reality instructor) receives Bill in his garish playroom, furnished with a red-felt pool table under glowing green-shaded high intensity lights. Victor nervously introduces an uncomfortable topic for both men, the Somerton orgy. (Bill naively believes the summons is in regard to a medical problem and still does not realize that Victor is far more interested in the night-man than the day-man behind the license.) Victor delicately probes the subject with Bill, "I think that you just might have the wrong idea about one or two things." Surprisingly, Bill replies, "What in the hell are you talking about?" Why Bill would lie to someone far more knowledgeable about the soiree than he, and clearly more wise in the ways of the world, is not clear. Perhaps Bill reverts to infantile denial. We know that he persistently stalls when asked questions that require momentary times-out and his usual mechanism is to repeat the question, slowly (often very slowly, like a child learning to speak or someone practicing a foreign language for the first time). Victor quickly interrupts Bill's pretense of innocence: "Please Bill. I was there.... I saw everything." Victor is probably feigning innocence, too, when he says, "I couldn't even to begin to imagine how you heard about it, let alone got yourself through the door." Victor subsequently admits connecting Nick Nightingale to "those people," as Victor calls them. Indeed, Victor very well may be Red Cloak himself since he is the only common denominator among Nick, Bill, and Mandy. Victor's admission that he had Bill followed and knew of Mandy's presence at the orgy suggests that he is a far bigger player than he represents in the events of the past 48 hours. As Bill attempts to put together the pieces, he challenges Victor's explanation of the orgy events as a charade: "What kind of fucking charade ends up with someone turning up dead?" Victor summarizes everything with a patronizing platitude: "Nobody killed anybody. Someone died. It happens all the time. Life goes on. It always does. Until it doesn't." Bewitched, bothered, and bewildered, Bill returns home to find Alice sleeping next to his orgy mask, neatly placed in the center of his pillow.

Concluding in Retreat?

Bill is now at the breaking point, utterly exhausted by what he has been through. He has suffered much and apparently learned little (except perhaps having gained the knowledge that explanation is not possible in human interrelations). Standing between Alice and his mask, Bill sobs nearly uncontrollably, waking Alice and tearfully exclaiming, "I'll tell you everything. I'll tell you everything." Presumably he does. The scene jumps to a close-up of Alice, pensive with cigarette in hand, staring at Bill through reddened eyelids. The juxtaposition of these two scenes— with a void between them for our imaginations to fill — reveals Kubrick's brilliant use of *aposiopesis*, an ancient trope signifying "silence" or "pause." Alice's tear-strained eyes, in close-up, tell us much about the confession we did not hear. Alice apparently, has no response, dramatic or otherwise, to Bill's admission of "everything." Is she in a state of denial? Forgiveness? Alice would seem to exemplify Blanchot's "receding other." In a matter-of-fact tone, she moves the topic away from spousal matters to family business: "Helena is going to be up soon. She's expecting us to take her Christmas shopping today." Soon after, Bill, Alice, and Helena embark on a typical upper-class shopping excursion, as if the events of the past couple of days and nights had not occurred. Bill asks Alice a question that is his most philosophical interrogatory in the film: "Alice, what do you think we should do?" Is Bill truly asking Alice to order life for them, to establish a marital ontology they can both live with? Alice, for the first time, begins to sound like Bill as she repeats the question and perhaps she is stalling for time to think. Helena conveniently interrupts her mother's thoughts, thus setting the stage for perhaps the most incisive exchange in the film:

> ALICE: "Maybe, I think, we should be grateful, grateful that we've managed to survive all of our adventures, whether they were real or only a dream."
> BILL: "Are you sure about that?"
> ALICE: "Am I sure? Only, only as sure as I am that the reality of one night, let alone that of a whole lifetime, can ever be the whole truth."
> BILL: "Then no dream is ever just a dream."
> ALICE: "The important thing is we're awake now and, hopefully, for a long time to come."
> BILL: "Forever."
> ALICE: "Forever."
> BILL: "Forever."
> ALICE: "Let's not use that word. It frightens me. But I do love you and you know there is something very important that we need to do as soon as possible."
> BILL: What's that?"
> ALICE: "Fuck."

This essay has suggested that *Eyes* illustrates a desire for ontology over epistemology, which this ending connotes, yet by no means is it an affirmative ending.[125] On the contrary, the final exchange between Bill and Alice reinforces a powerful motif that drives the entire film: depictions of interrogation and encounter that lead not toward understanding and growth (as if possible), but rather toward the only existence possible for Alice and Bill — an ontology of (sexual) escape. Indeed, the limits of discourse, in quintessential Kubrickian irony, are overshadowed by the force of a driving imperative: diversion with all the peripherals. This "resolution" reveals yet another layer of irony in that language is the vehicle for the respite from the terrors of being human. As Dennis Bingham has observed, "The ending of *Eyes Wide Shut* suggests that the world is beyond change and that the only way to deal with the way things are is to create your own world."[126] Indeed, the eyes of Alice and Bill are now fully closed wide shut. They choose not to see, but to live in retreat.

Part III Notes

1. Michel Chion, *Eyes Wide Shut*, trans. Trista Selous (London: BFI Publishing, 2002) 86.

2. *Ibid.*, 84.

3. *Ibid.*, 84.

4. Michel Chion, *Audio-Vision: Sound on Screen*, trans. Claudia Gorbman (New York: Columbia University Press, 1994) 76.

5. R. Murray Schafer, *The Tuning of the World* (Toronto: McLeland and Stewart, 1977) 90.

6. *Ibid.*, 43.

7. *Ibid.*, 91.

8. James Lastra, *Sound Technology and the American Cinema* (New York: Columbia University Press, 2001) 153.

9. Frederic Jameson, *Postmodernism, or, The cultural logic of late capitalism* (Durham: Duke University Press, 1991) 21.

10. Sherry Simon, "Accidental Voices: The Return of the Countertenor," *Aural Cultures*, ed. Jim Drobnick (Toronto: YYZ Books, 2004) 110.

11. *Ibid.*, 112.

12. For detailed accounts of spiritualist beliefs associated with the emergence of reproduction technologies, see: Tom Gunning, "Doing for the Eye What the Phonograph Does for the Ear." *The Sounds of Early Cinema*. Richard Abel and Rick Altman, eds. Bloomington: Indiana University Press, 2001:13–31. And Jeffrey Sconce, *Haunted Media: Electronic Presence from Telegraphy to Television* (Durham: Duke University Press, 2000).

13. Simon "Accidental Voices" 113.

14. Chion, *Audio-Vision* 222.

15. *Ibid.*, 76.

16. Rick Altman, "The Material Heterogeneity of Recorded Sound," *Sound Theory, Sound Practice*, ed. Rick Altman (New York: Routledge, 1992) 29.

17. Chion, *Audio-Vision* 77.

18. Between the Zieglers' party and the fateful conversation between Bill and Alice there are two instances of music which could be considered non-diegetic: Chris Isaak's "Baby did a Bad Bad Thing" and the second instance of the Shostakovich waltz. The Isaak song is heard as Nicole sits naked in front of her mirror as Tom approaches her and they begin to kiss. While the song could be non-diegetic, it also could well be another case of music played from their bedroom stereo. We know they play music in their private space, and Alice seems to be swaying to the beat as she removes her earrings. So the status of the music is inconclusive. As for the return of the waltz, we hear it the second time as we watch Bill and Alice go about their separate daily chores: he at the office, and she

at home with their daughter. Clearly the two of them are not listening to this waltz at the same time in these separate locations. Yet they were listening to this waltz at the beginning of the film, and here it has a similar function: it is the soundtrack associated with the mundane aspects of their lives— getting dressed and going to work. So this could be a case of displaced diegetic sound, a return of this music from its diegetic presence at the beginning of the film to underscore similar activities as were presented there — the theme of life, as Chion suggests (Chion, *Eyes Wide Shut* 33).

19. Chion, *Eyes Wide Shut* 34.

20. *Ibid.*, 84.

21. Robert Kolker, *A Cinema of Loneliness: Penn, Stone, Kubrick, Scorsese, Spielberg, Altman* (Oxford University Press, 2000) 106.

22. *Ibid.*

23. Todd McCarthy, cited in Randy Rasmussen, *Stanley Kubrick: Seven Films Analyzed* (Jefferson, N.C.: McFarland & Company, Inc., 2001) 241.

24. Rasmussen 347.

25. Susan White, "Male Bonding, Hollywood Orientalism, and the Repression of the Feminine in Kubrick's *Full Metal Jacket*" in Michael Anderegg, ed., *Inventing Vietnam: The War Film in Film and Television* (Philadelphia: Temple University Press, 1991) 212–3.

26. Robert Kilker, "All Roads Lead to the Abject: The Monstrous Feminine and Gender Boundaries in Stanley Kubrick's *Shining*." *Literature/Film Quarterly*, vol 34, no. 1 (2006) 56.

27. Kilker 62.

28. White 212.

29. *Ibid.*, 215.

30. Christiane Kubrick, cited in David Hughes, *The Complete Kubrick* (London: Virgin, 2000) 254.

31. Gaylyn Studlar, *In the Realm of Pleasure: Von Sternberg, Dietrich, and the Masochistic Aesthetic* (New York: Columbia University Press, 1988) 3.

32. J.M.Q. Davies, Introduction to *Dream Story* (London: Penguin, 1999) xii.

33. Arthur Schnitzler, *Dream Story* (London: Penguin, 1999) 99.

34. Charles Helmetag, "Dream Odysseys: Schnitzler's *Traumnovelle* and Kubrick's *Eyes Wide Shut*," *Literature/Film Quarterly*, vol. 31, no. 4 (2003) 276–86.

35. Jacques Lacan, "The Mirror Stage" in *Écrits: A Selection*, trans. Alan Sheridan (London: Routledge, 1980) 1–7.

36. Jacques Lacan in Jacques-Alain Miller, ed., *Freud's*

Papers on Technique 1953–1954, trans. John Forrester (New York: Norton, 1991) 142.

37. Jacques Lacan, *Four Fundamental Concepts of Psycho-analysis*, trans. Alan Sheridan (New York: Penguin, 1977):193.

38. *Ibid.*, 75.

39. Laura Mulvey, "Visual Pleasure and Narrative Cinema," in Constance Penley (ed.), *Feminism and Film Theory* (New York: Routledge, 1988) 63.

40. White 222.

41. Mario Falsetto, *Stanley Kubrick: A Narrative and Stylistic Analysis* (London: Greenwood Press, 1994) 32.

42. Larry Gross, cited in Hughes 252.

43. Schnitzler 96.

44. John Baxter cited in Hughes 243.

45. Jacques Lacan, "Of the Gaze as *Objet Petit a*," in *Four Fundamental Concepts of Psycho-analysis*.

46. Lacan, *Four Fundamentals* 92.

47. Mikhail Bakhtin, *Rabelais and His World*, trans. Helene Iswolsky (Bloomington: Indiana University Press, 1984) 25.

48. Kubrick's decision to situate *Eyes Wide Shut* in his hometown of New York City points to the personal relationship that he had with the film and its subject matter, especially considering that only one of his previous movies took place in this setting, which was the 1955 *Killer's Kiss*.

49. Randy Rasmussen, *Stanley Kubrick: Seven Films Analyzed* (Jefferson, N.C.: McFarland & Company, 2001) 334.

50. Tim Kreider, "Eyes Wide Shut," *Film Quarterly*, vol. 53, no. 3 (Spring, 2000) 41–48.

51. Jason Sperb, *The Kubrick Facade: Faces and Voices in the Films of Stanley Kubrick* (Lanham: The Scarecrow Press, 2006) 129.

52. Bakhtin 26.

53. *Ibid.*, 317.

54. Geoffrey Cocks, *The Wolf at the Door: Stanley Kubrick, History, and the Holocaust* (New York: Peter Lang, 2004) 143.

55. Rasmussen 334.

56. Thomas Allen Nelson, *Kubrick: Inside a Film Artist's Maze* (Bloomington: Indiana University Press, 2000) 279.

57. Peter Stallybrass and Allon White, *The Politics and Poetics of Transgression* (Ithaca: Cornell University Press, 1986) 22.

58. Bakhtin 15.

59. Two prominent examples of traditional satires and parodies are Desiderius Erasmus' *Praise of Folly* and François Rabelais' *Gargantua* and *Pantagruel*—the latter works by Rabelais being the basis for Bakhtin's discussion of the grotesque body and the carnivalesque. Both authors use devices such as references to drunkenness and intoxication as a means of indicating that the text is an exaggeration and not to be taken completely seriously.

60. Nelson 268.

61. Bakhtin 303.

62. Nelson 281.

63. *Ibid.*, 281.

64. Michel Chion, *Eyes Wide Shut*, trans. Trista Selous (London: BFI, 2005) 30–31.

65. Stallybrass and White 22.

66. Bakhtin 11–12.

67. Sperb 132.

68. Chion 46.

69. Bakhtin 11.

70. It is important to recognize that for Bakhtin this suspension is temporary and not permanent, and that the carnival could only occur within the bounds of official culture, which this event simultaneously challenges and upholds.

71. Bakhtin 10.

72. Rasmussen 341.

73. Nelson 284.

74. Chion 62.

75. Bakhtin 40.

76. Nelson 285.

77. The name of Nick Nightingale, who plays only at night like a nightingale, recalls the fairytale *The Nightingale* by Hans Christian Andersen, which tells the story of the emperor of China who hears the song of the nightingale and enraptured by its song convinces her to stay as a guest in his court. The emperor is later given a bejeweled robot nightingale that supplants his interest in the natural living nightingale. The emperor's fascination with artifice in the form of artificial beauty, which causes him to lose his connection to the natural beauty of the nightingale, is paralleled in Bill's classical conception of Alice. His artificial notion of Alice's beauty causes him to lose his connection to the natural carnal beauty of his wife.

78. The password *Fidelio* is the name of Beethoven's only opera and it follows the adventures of Leonore, who disguises herself as a prison guard named Fidelio— Italian for *he who is faithful*— in an effort to rescue her husband Florestan from a political prison and his impending execution. The opera has obvious parallels to the end of *Eyes Wide Shut* when Bill depends on Alice to rescue him from the grotesque world that he has found himself caught up in.

79. Nelson 288.

80. *Ibid.*, 289.

81. Bakhtin 7.

82. Nelson 288.

83. *Ibid.*, 289.

84. Bakhtin 317.

85. Nelson 295.

86. Chion 84.

87. Bakhtin 26.

88. Sperb 132.

89. Chion 62.

90. As one critic remarks, "For years, two misleading adjectives have been used to describe Kubrick's work: "cold" and "perfectionist." "Cold" implies unemotional, and it simply isn't true that Kubrick's films lack emotion. They're full of emotions, though most of them are so convoluted and elusive that you have to follow them as if through a maze — perhaps the major reason his films become richer with repeated viewing. He so strongly resists sentimentality that cynicism and derision often seem close at hand" Jonathan Rosenbaum, "In Dreams Begin Responsibilities," *Chicago Reader: On Film* (1999) *www.chicagoreader.com/movies/archives/1999/0799/07239.html*.

91. The "problem" of the U.S. release of *Eyes*, due to Kubrick's sudden death, raises troubling questions about the final cut, especially the outrageous digital editing by Warner Bros. to hide the sexual machinations of orgy participants. However, Kubrick's brother-in-law and producer Jan Harlan has claimed (along with a number of journalists and film historians) that Kubrick did approve of the digital alterations for the sake of obtaining an R rating.

92. Quoted from Allsion Castle, ed., *The Stanley Kubrick Archives* (New York: Taschen Books, 2005) www.taschen.com/pages/en/catalogue/books/film/new/facts/00301.htm.

93. Although phenomenology is generally considered a twentieth-century movement within philosophy (introduced primarily by the work of Edmund Husserl), early strains of phenomenological thinking can be seen as early as the eighteenth-century in the writings of Kant, Hegel, and others. Limitations of space prevent a discussion of the

complications and disagreements of twentieth-century phenomenologists. The intention of this essay is to apply relevant dimensions of phenomenon as they relate to Kubrick's philosophic sensibility in *Eyes*.

94. According to Heidegger, "Phenomenology is not just one philosophical science among others, nor is it the science preparatory to the rest of them; rather, *the expression 'phenomenology' is the name for the method of scientific philosophy in general*." Martin Heidegger, *The Basic Problems of Phenomenology*, trans. Albert Hofstadter, rev. ed. (Bloomington, Ind.: Indiana University Press, 1982) 3.

95. Maurice Merleau-Ponty, *The Visible and the Invisible*, ed. Claude Lefort, trans. Alphonso Lingis (Evanston, Ill.: Northwestern University Press, 1968) 105.

96. Mario Falsetto, *Stanley Kubrick: A Narrative and Stylistic Analysis*, 2nd ed. (Westport, Conn.: Greenwood, 2004) 140.

97. The commencement of any linear work of art is a strategic decision influencing everything that follows. According to Paul De Man, "The point of departure is a 'structural and organizing principle' around which the author's work is centered and which defines the author's individuality. Paul de Man, *Blindness and Insight: Essays in the Rhetoric of Contemporary Criticism* (New York: Oxford, 1971) 82.

98. The opening classical nude shot of Alice would seem not to be a flashforward after the Harfords return from the Zieglers' party as the disrobing dress is clearly not the dress Alice wears to the party.

99. Limits of space prohibit exploring Merleau-Ponty's theory of the body, but such an analysis would be fitting for a film that places so much emphasis on the female figure. Merleau-Ponty's extensive treatment of the body is Part One of *Phenomenology and Perception*, trans. Colin Smith (London: Routledge, 1962) 77–239.

100. Merleau-Ponty, *Phenomenology of Perception* xxiii.

101. See de Man's discussion of Poulet's theory of beginnings in *Blindness and Insight*, 82 ff.

102. Merleau-Ponty, *Phenomenology of Perception*. ix.

103. Pearce, Howard D., "*The Shining* as *Lichtung*: Kubrick's Film, Heidegger's Clearing," *Forms of the Fantastic*, eds. Jan Hokenson and Howard D. Pearce. (Westport, Conn.: Greenwood, 1986) 54–55.

104. Emmanuel Levinas, *Totality and Infinity: An Essay on Exteriority*, trans. Alphonso Lingis (Pittsburgh: Duquesne University Press, 1969).

105. Merleau-Ponty, *Phenomenology of Perception* viii ff.

106. Howard Pearce explores identity in *The Shining*, but his observation has relevance to *Eyes*: "The film is structured, then, on manifold repetitions that involve both discrete images and particular moments in exchange of identities. Those exchanges set in motion transactions that require more than identification of opposites or duplicates. The idea of dualities is temporalized in that our active, interpretive engagement is temporal. We must act among the always—escaping appearances as we inevitably try to place them in a logocentric frame" (84).

107. For a discussion of the historical dimensions of *kairos* in ancient Greece, particularly in the educational program of Isocrates, see Phillip Sipiora, "The Ancient Concept of *Kairos*." *Kairos and Rhetoric: Essays in History, Theory, and Praxis*, eds. Phillip Sipiora and James S. Baumlin (Albany: SUNY University Press, 2002) 1–22.

108. *Kairos* also means relationship between the parts and the whole and is closely related to classical Greek norms of beauty: harmony, symmetry, and proportion. A superficial glance at the female participants in the Somerton orgy (not to mention Alice, too) reveal classic Las Vegas, showgirl aesthetics, all richly illustrative of the adjectives above.

109. Merleau-Ponty, *Phenomenology of Perception* xviii.

110. The title of the song is also the refrain, and the lyrics are structured by a series of interrogatives and responses, which seem to remind Alice of what she has done with the resultant guilt. For example:

> You ever love someone so much you thought your little heart was gonna break in two? I didn't think so. You ever tried with all your heart and soul to get you lover back to you? I wanna hope so.

111. Maurice Blanchot, *The Writing of the Disaster*, trans. Ann Smock (Lincoln: University of Nebraska P, 1986).

112. *Ibid*.

113. Mikhail Bakhtin, *The Dialogic Imagination*, trans. C. Emerson and M. Holmquist (Austin: University of Texas Press, 1981) 294.

114. Language theorist James Kinneavy points out the strategic importance of intersubjectivity in Merleau-Ponty's work, stressing implications of inter- and multidisciplinarily (which would include cinematic art): "Merleau-Ponty maintained that this emphasis on the consideration of the subject and the consideration of the 'other' through intersubjectivity is characteristic not only of philosophy (in phenomenology and existentialism), but has parallel movements in … other disciplines." James L. Kinneavy, *A Theory of Discourse* (New York: W. W. Norton, 1971) 397.

115. Vivian Sobchack, *The Address of the Eye: A Phenomenology of Film Experience*. (Princeton: Princeton University Press, 1992) 4.

116. The replaying of these sexual fantasy scenes intertwines subjectivity and objectivity in that the viewer may share subjective sympathy/identification with Alice and/or Bill, yet can do so only within the context of objectifying either or both of them, engaging then in a second round of objectification of the sexual encounter. Mario Falsetto eloquently articulates the resultant ambiguity: "In *Eyes Wide Shut* we never know who to believe, and the status of the narrative events remains unclear throughout the film. Truth and fiction, objectivity and subjectivity, the public and the private are intermingled to such an extent that the viewer remains in a state of constant uncertainty" (79).

117. Indeed, some of the scenes are set in Soho, such as Sharkey's Café. Bill, like Paul Hackett, is explicitly trailed in this part of Manhattan and it is hard to imagine that Kubrick did not have *After Hours* in mind, especially considering some of the similarities between the two professional-men protagonists trapped in an alien environment and lacking survival skills once out of their protected cocoons.

118. Falsetto 79.

119. Kubrick's playful treatment of sexual conventions is revealed again in the scene in which Bill and Domino gaze lovingly into each other's eyes, like high school sweethearts, followed by a very tender kiss, complete with eyes wide shut (all four). The kiss is not passionate, but rather exceptionally tender. Bill is apparently oblivious to the codes of sex with prostitutes, who often refuse to kiss customers on the lips precisely because it signifies warmth and tenderness and confuses the business end of the transaction with the personal and off-limits arenas of human contact. Further, Domino's apartment has the look of a college student's retreat, replete with old food on the stove, disorganization, and a bookcase prominently revealing a successful college textbook, *Introducing Sociology*. A street

worker studying sociology by day and practicing sociology by night, richly typical Kubrickian irony.

120. Dennis Bingham, "Kidman, Cruise, and Kubrick: A Brechtian Paradise," *More Than a Method: Trends and Traditions in Contemporary Film Performance*, eds. Cynthia Baron, Diane Carson, and Frank Tomasulo (Detroit, Mich.: Wayne State University Press, 2004) 256.

121. Tim Cahill, "The Rolling Stone Interview: Stanley Kubrick." *The Rolling Stone*, (27 Aug. 1987) http://www.archiviokubrick.it/english/content/1987rolling.html.

122. Other illustrations of Kubrick's fondness for light irony: as Bill is escorted to the front of the mansion (on the pretense that his driver wants to see him), the orgy music is "Strangers in the Night." When Bill questions the waitress at Gillespie's about Nick (following Alice's orgy dream), the background music is The Teenagers' 1956 release, "Why Do Fools Fall in Love." Further, the headlines of the newspaper Bill reads at Sharky's scream: LUCKY TO BE ALIVE (reminding Bill that, twice, he may luckily

have escaped death (quickly by Red Cloak's henchmen or slowly from AIDS).

123. Merleau-Ponty, *The Primacy of Perception*, ed. James M. Edie (Evanston, IL: Northwestern University Press) 34.

124. For a discussion of the two performers who play Amanda, see Charlotte O'Sullivan, "Body of Evidence" *The Independent* (27 Aug. 1999) http://www.visual-memory.co.uk/sk/page22.htm.

125. Roger Ebert has suggested such an ending: "The final scene, in the toy store, strikes me as conventional moralizing—an obligatory happy resolution of all problems—but the deep mystery of the film remains. To begin with, can Dr. Bill believe Victor's version of events of the past few days?" Review of *Eyes Wide Shut*, *Chicago Sun Times* (July 16, 1999) http://rogerebert.suntimes.com/apps/pbcs.dll/article?AID=/19990716/REVIEWS/907160302/1023

126. Bingham 273.

16 Mechanical Humanity, or How I Learned to Stop Worrying and Love the Android: The Posthuman Subject in *2001: A Space Odyssey* and *Artificial Intelligence: A.I.*

Scott Loren

In the mid–1990s, Stanley Kubrick contacted Steven Spielberg with an idea for a project he had been working on for several years. The script was based on Brian Aldiss's short story "Supertoys Last All Summer Long," which Kubrick bought the rights to in 1983, three years after the release of *The Shining*, and 15 years after the release of the film it was thematically much closer to: *2001: A Space Odyssey*, based on Arthur C. Clarke's "The Sentinel." "Supertoys" is a story about artificial intelligence and, as in *2001*, about how artificially intelligent machines and humans interact. There were various impediments, though, that kept Kubrick from making this film. For one, the story revolves around an artificial boy, and British law made it prohibitive to work with a child actor for the prolonged periods of time that Kubrick would have required. And he was not willing to make the film elsewhere. After failed attempts to construct a robot that would satisfactorily take the place of the child actor, and although Kubrick had invested years of work in the project, for which he already had a script and hundreds of storyboards, he offered it to Spielberg, and proposed that he produce it while Spielberg directed it. According to Spielberg and longtime Kubrick producer Jan Harlan, Kubrick offered Spielberg the project as opposed to shelving it because he felt that Spielberg had the right sensibilities for this story.

Spielberg was hesitant, though, and it wasn't until after Kubrick's death, when his wife, Christiane, contacted Spielberg and renewed the offer, that Spielberg took over *A.I.* and made it his own. As Harlan has suggested in interviews, *A.I.* is clearly a Spielberg film, and would have been much darker had Kubrick filmed it. Still, we can see traces of Kubrick at work in *A.I.*

A.I. recalls *2001* in various ways: in both films, the plot revolves around an artificially intelligent entity and the question of the role this entity plays within the human community. There are also various overlappings between the cyborgian boy David[1] (Haley Joel Osment) and the

211

super-computer HAL (voice, Douglas Rain) in terms of what they in fact are: machines created for social use/benefit, that are highly intelligent, which develop personalities and human attachments, and so forth. Inevitably, there are also overlappings in terms of what they represent: a fear of technology insofar as it threatens the distinction between the human and the non-human. Of interest to our overall discussion will be to note the structural and thematic similarities between these films, but also to note where *A.I.* departs and clearly becomes a Spielberg project.

From the outset, we can identify departure in the philosophical tradition in which the respective projects are rooted: *2001* is framed within the tradition of Darwinian evolution and survival of the fittest, where *A.I.* is framed within the tradition of the Freudian Oedipus complex. Both, however, are firmly rooted in the more contemporary philosophical framework of the postmodern and the posthuman. They each raise questions of authenticity and subjectivity by juxtaposing the human and the machine. Accompanying these uncanny juxtaposings, and in order to problematize certain notions about subjectivity, there is an elaboration on the human qualities and characteristics of the artificial beings. Both films depict human communities within which AIs—artificially intelligent machines or, in this case, human-like non-humans—have already been integrated to a certain degree. The borders between the human and the non-human are conspicuously ambiguous or even fluid, and in this regard, these are posthuman narratives.

HAL's possession of survival instincts and David's oedipal love for his mother place both narratives in philosophical traditions that attempt to define in what, precisely, the human animal consists. Recognizing that the films share this element, we might ask what the effect of thus portraying the artificial is. As we will see, both films portray the artificial entity as a "subject," in the psychoanalytical or Lacanian sense, and in so doing, they comment on the status of postmodern/posthuman subjectivity, on contemporary notions of subject formation, and on anxieties associated with them. Within these communities, what we witness is the introduction of an AI to a human community, followed by a crisis that is staged in order to give utterance to particular anxieties about humanist notions of autonomy, free will and individuality—anxieties about the very borders between the human and the non-human.

2001: A Human Oddity, Posthuman Normality

In considering the relationship between humans and non-humans within these fictive communities, the first question we want to ask has to do with intent and practice: What are the machines intended for, and how are they, in fact, used? In *2001*, HAL's purpose and his practical application are very utilitarian in nature. He was built as a highly advanced *tool*. This focus on the tool and its relationship to human "advancement" is signaled at the beginning of the film, when we witness what we assume to be a moment critical to the evolutionary development of Homo sapiens. A Neanderthal-like ape-man discovers that it can use a bone to defeat opposing tribes and to kill animals for food, and thus advance along the evolutionary scale within Darwin's logic of the survival of the fittest. The bone as a tool is then equated to the satellite we will see in the following sequence: when the ape-man throws the bone up into the air, we witness it spiraling against the sky, and then there is a jump cut to a satellite platform with a similar form floating through space. What is signaled here is an advance in technology that accompanies an advance in human evolution. This advance, though, is ambiguous, as both images are of tools potentially used for killing (the satellite we see here is intended for carrying nuclear warheads).[2] Also ambiguous is the lack of a subtitle separating "The Dawn of Man" from modern man at the initial cut to the satellite (as we know, subsequent shifts in time are indicated throughout the film).

Regarding HAL's function, we soon find out that he is used for overseeing and attending to the details of a mission to Jupiter. In an earth to spacecraft interview by BBC news, the interviewer (Martin Amor) notes: "HAL, you have an enormous responsibility on the mission, in many ways perhaps the greatest responsibility of any single mission element. You are the brain and central nervous system of the ship. And your responsibilities include watching over the men in hibernation." From this and other comments, we later come to find out that not only is HAL in command of the entire journey, he is also the only "crew member" that knows what the purpose of the mission in fact is. The tone of HAL's "humanness" is already set here by attributing to him anthropomorphic features ("the brain and central nervous system") and is further suggestive of HAL's human-like relation to the other crew members. HAL is clearly an active part of this team. The humans themselves are, by contrast, framed as being "just along for the ride," so to speak. The majority of them are in hibernation for the voyage while HAL navigates the ship. The two crew members who are awake, Dr. Bowman (Keir Dullea) and Dr. Poole (Gary Lockwood), are seen eating, jogging, playing chess, drawing, sunbathing (in a sun bed), and giving interviews. What we do not see them doing is working. This is thrown into even starker contrast when we find out that they don't know what the purpose of the mission is. It is as if the human resources on board are precisely that: resources or tools waiting to be put to use. Thus, we might say that HAL is a *working* machine. He does everything from enabling humans to travel to places they would never reach without such magnificent tools, to keeping a crew psychology report. It's also worth noting that, beyond attending to mission responsibilities, HAL also engages in recreational activities with the crew members. In this sense, his place in this community may be of a utilitarian nature, but he interacts with the other members as an equal (or even a superior), rather than as a tool.

In *A.I.* we might say that David, on the other hand, is really a luxury item. He is intended to replace a lacking real child. As the narrator in the prologue (voice, Ben Kingsley) informs us, "when most governments in the developed world introduced legal sanctions to strictly license pregnancies ... robots, who are never hungry and who did not consume resources beyond those of their first manufacture, were so essential an economic link in the chain mail of society." And as we find out in the beginning of the film, Professor Hobby's (William Hurt) intention is to create an artificially intelligent machine that can love. When we later find out that David is modeled after Hobby's own deceased child, the impulse behind David's creation becomes all too obvious. David is born out of loss and mourning. He is born out of emotional need, and this is precisely the capacity in which he functions in his new home. One of Professor Hobby's employees, whose son has been in a coma for a prolonged period of time, is given the opportunity to take David home as an artificial adoptive son. Obviously, David's purpose and practical application must be less clinical than the application of a common tool. There must be emotional dimensions to the relationships that develop here.

Although David's relation to his "mommy," Monica (Frances O'Connor), is necessarily of a pathetic nature, and HAL's to the rest of the crew isn't, the relationships in both films share a surprisingly similar structure. In each there is a particular dependency in which power relations are formed and which symbolically situates all parties involved. HAL is in charge of ship operations, and the crew depends upon him for the success of the mission. Beyond this, when we take into consideration the crew members who are in hibernation, we realize that their lives depend upon HAL's functioning properly. David returns meaning to his adoptive mother's life, and she becomes emotionally dependant on him as well — as we will see — as he does on her. As to the machines fulfilling their respective roles in these relationships, we might say that they take their tasks "to heart" all too literally. HAL, who has been interpellated as the perfect computer, infallible, superior to humans in efficiency and capacity for learning, retaining, and processing information (his name is an acronym of "heuristic" and "algorithmic"), not only boasts of his capacities when given the opportunity; when he is confronted with the possibility of a malfunction, he doesn't even consider that there might really be something wrong with him. Instead, he suggests that the problem is due to human error. Similarly, David is unable to fathom a change in his (symbolic) function. His interpellation operates as a type of hardwiring that cannot be changed. He has been turned into a "loving machine," and can do nothing other then be precisely that. Interestingly, this exactness of the machine, that they appear to ardently take up the task for which they've been programmed, plays a role in the development of threat, and how all parties will react to it. Before moving on to the element of threat, however, we should consider how the relationships between the humans and the non-humans develop. We will see that the relationships that develop necessarily entail an element of *interpellation*, and that the symbolic function at work here is modeled on postmodern notions of identity building in human communities. Both films are posthuman narratives insofar as they explicitly deal with non-human entities that have human characteristics. In this regard we might say they are approaching the posthuman through the back door: the point is not that humans have integrated the non-human or the external to the extent that the boundaries of the human implode, but rather that the machines have become so humanlike that the boundaries of the non-human, and thus dialectically the human, implode.

The Posthuman Subject: It's Alive!

"Of all the implications that the first wave of cybernetics conveyed, perhaps none was more disturbing than the idea that the boundaries of the human subject are constructed rather than given," writes N. Katherine Hayles.[3] What we recognize as *posthuman* is in many ways an extension of the implications of postmodernism at the location of "the body" *and* the subject. Where postmodernism is based in concepts of fracture, pastiche, "native" instability, and dissemination, posthuman(ism) applies them to bodies as they become increasingly cyborgian, and recognizes the nature of subjectivity and identity as inextricably dependant on a collection of "external" factors, finally making the claim that due to the extimate nature of subjectivity and identity, we are all ultimately cyborgian. In this regard, posthuman ideology is thoroughly, if implicitly, Lacanian: "the subject's 'decentrement' is original and constitutive; 'I' am from the very outset 'outside myself,' a *bricolage* of external components."[4]

In *2001* and *A.I.* the posthuman takes an extreme physical form: HAL and David are entirely composed of/by the external. HAL was built at the H.A.L. laboratory in Urbana, Illinois and "instructed" by Mr. Langley. David was designed by Professor Hobby and manufactured at Cybertronics. We might read these "embodyings" as tropes for what is at stake in postmodern and posthuman notions of subjectivity. It is often the case in cyborgian and posthuman narratives (from *Frankenstein* to the latest adaptation of a Philip K. Dick story) that we, the viewer/reader, are confronted with a human-like artificial entity in a manner likely to align our sympathies, to whatever extent, with the artificial being. This is an essential device in blurring the borders of the human and the artificial, which further works in the service of formulating the skeptic's questions about the nature and origins of identity at the heart of a postmodern/ posthuman view of subjectivity: do we view identity, first of all, as a construct? If so, do we consider the processes involved to be *natural* or *artificial*? If natural, what does this say about the acquisition of identity where the artificial being is concerned? If artificial, what does it say about acquisition of identity concerning "natural" beings? If we are to understand the processes involved in the production of identity in Althusserian terms, then we know that this is an ongoing process that extends beyond the limits of the physical individual in both directions (before birth and after death), and that it is a constructive, constitutive process in the sense that it continually (re)locates the subject. Addressing the question of a difference in the quality of identity between the natural and artificial being, we are on unstable ground from the start. Note that if we replace the word "being" with "subject," the distinction becomes much more problematic. How do we determine what is an artificial subject and what is a natural one? Again following Althusser, identity is a social (or socio-ideological) process, whether public or private, of construction — a social production. In order to discuss how these concepts are manifest in *2001* and *A.I.*, we should briefly outline Althusser's concept of *interpellation*.

In "Ideology and Ideological State Apparatuses," Louis Althusser defines interpellation as a mechanism in which the individual is *hailed* into subjectivity.[5] The locations at which this occurs and the agents involved are always already within ideology: ideological (state) apparatuses such as schools, family, religion, political parties, profession, and so forth, repeatedly hail the individual as a subject. They locate the individual within the ideological (and symbolic) structure in his/her/its symbolic relation to other subjects. As Althusser makes clear, these are inextricable, circular terms: ideology and interpellation consist of and constitute each other. For the sake of clarity, he gives them a "temporal form" in which to discuss them, though admitting that they do not properly exist within a temporal order. We can think of this in terms of the use of names and titles. For example, when one is called by one's name, "Pat," and responds, both actions entail the silent acknowledgement of rich identification and history. The hailing person or structure locates the individual, identifies her/him, as, for example, Pat, son of *w*, works at *x*, believes in *y*, identifies with *z*. The individual hailed acknowledges that s/he is all of these things (or not, that there has been a mistake), all of the things enacted by her/himself in life, and all that s/he "absorbs" from others' projections of her/him, by recognizing the call and responding to it. Thus, a perpetual reestablishing/affirmation of position within the social-symbolic takes place, by which not only is the hailed subject located, but, by being located in relation to all the subtle and not so subtle conditions of the life surrounding — in a word, everything — interpellation functions in an omni-directional manner, situating all subjects. *A.I.* stages a good, if over-simplified, model of interpellation.

IMPRINTING PROTOCAL CAUTION:
Please remember that this Program, once activated, is permanent, indelible, and unalterable.[6]

The cyborg boy is intended as an emotional crutch, so to speak, functioning as an *Ersatzkind* for the mother. We realize by this point that we are dealing with a narrative about the familial symbolic network and positions within it, and in this capacity, with identity. The automaton, David, is not meant to replace the biological child per se, but rather to act as a stand in, to stand in the symbolic position of the absent biological child for the time being. Shortly after Henry (Sam Robards) brings David home to Monica, he tells her about the process of "imprinting"and the magnitude of their responsibility concerning the process. Imprinting irrevocably binds David to the person who imprints him by programming him with "love" for this person.

The italicized text above the preceding paragraph is what is printed on the cover of the protocol pamphlet for David's so-called imprinting. Two days after the husband has *delivered* David, Monica decides to keep him, to go through with the process of imprinting, and grant him the symbolic position that belonged to her biological son. The process entails holding the back of David's neck, and reading the following words: Cyrus, Socrates, particle, decibel, hurricane, dolphin, tulip, Monica, David, Monica. The most important words, according to our purpose, are the names at the end. We might read this scene jointly as a mirror scene, dictating who and what one is by reflecting off of an other, and as a scene of initial interpellation, primarily defining two individuals in their relationship to one another. The result of the imprinting, of this mirror, or initial interpellation, is that it establishes positions, relationships, within a symbolic network, and thus establishes identities. The dialogue that ensues gives emphasis to this point. After Monica imprints David — activating his love for her and thereby defining his symbolic position in relation to her — he mirrors the gesture and does the same in response: he calls her "mommy," after which she asks, "What did you call me," and he repeats it, which prompts her to tellingly ask in response, "Who am I David?" David tells her, "You're my mommy." Monica is immediately returned to the symbolic location of mother, as needed and loved by a son. Through this scene of initial interpellation and subsequent scenes that reinforce their symbolic positions in relation to one another, David has been *irreversibly* called into the position of the son.

In *2001*, HAL may not be "imprinted with love" for another character in the film, but we can see from the scenes concerning his introduction and his relationship to the crew members, that he is in fact "defined" or interpellated via his relationships to the crew members. In this regard, HAL's introduction equally focuses on his symbolic relations, that he in fact occupies a position of subjectivity within a symbolic network, and in so doing, indicates to the viewer that he is interpellated accordingly: "Think of him really just as an other person."[7] HAL takes the role of a formidable though polite chess opponent, engaging in leisure activities with the crew. He shows interest in Dr. Bowman's artistic renditions of the ship's interior and asks "personal questions" based on his sensitivity to Bowman's behavior. Though all of these instances also serve to build HAL into a character that a viewer can potentially identify/sympathize with by giving him human characteristics, the interactivity between the crew and HAL largely to identity/identification: these are illustrations of interpellative (identity building) situations. By situating these artificial entities within human communities and interpellating them, the boundaries between the human and the non-human become less clear. This blurring of boundaries is helped along by giving the machines human characteristics. It's also helped along by "de-humanizing" the humans.

Humanized Machines and Mechanized Humans

2001 introduces supercomputer HAL 9000 directly within the context of his relation to the human crew members, and sets the tone for HAL as a sensitive and sensible entity with human characteristics. In the BBC interview broadcast back to the ship, HAL is questioned as to whether, despite his "enormous intellect," he is ever "frustrated by your dependence on people to carry out actions." To which he responds, "Not in the slightest bit. I *enjoy* working with people. I have a *stimulating relationship* with Doctor Poole and Doctor Bowman. My mission responsibilities range over the entire operation of the ship, so I am constantly occupied. I am putting myself to the fullest possible use, which is all, *I think*, that any *conscious entity* can ever hope to do."[8] HAL's interjection "I think," recalls Descartes' *cogito ergo sum*, immediately situating HAL within the Cartesian tradition as a "thinking thing"—*res cogitans*—which effectually equates HAL with the human: "A thing that doubts, understands, affirms, denies, is willing, is unwilling, and also imagines and has sensory perceptions."[9] We witness HAL do all of these things, from his "doubts" concerning the mission to his being able to imagine the consequences of being shut down. It's worth noting that reference to Descartes' *cogito* becomes more and more the slogan of posthuman, cyborgian self reification within the genre and is always employed to indicate that characteristics elementally human can equally be found within the artificial.[10] Notably, *A.I.*'s Gigolo Joe (Jude Law) will proclaim "I am!" in his last scene, complementing HAL's, "I think." HAL's overall "choice" of words here is telling.

As Randy Rasmussen points out in *Stanley Kubrick: Seven Films Analyzed*, HAL's ability to think is not his only humanizing characteristic: "The words "I enjoy" imply that emotion is indeed a factor in his [HAL's] perceptions."[11] The same can be said of the fact that HAL defines his relationship with the humans as "stimulating." When Dr. Poole is questioned as to what it's like to live and work in such close proximity to HAL, he responds that HAL is "just like a sixth member of the crew," and that you come to "think of him really just as another person." When questioned as to whether he believes that HAL has genuine emotions, Dr. Poole responds that "he acts like he has genuine emotions." Which he then qualifies with, "of course he's programmed that way to make it easier for us to talk to him. But as to whether or not he has real feelings is something I don't think anyone can truthfully answer." The scene ends with this rather pregnant statement, signaling an enigma or an impasse at the heart of the human-machine relationship. This impasse, this diegetic tension, is not resolved in the narrative, but rather takes up a key position vis-à-vis human subjectivity, providing a structure in which "artificial" subjectivity acts as a mirror to human subjectivity.

Where HAL incorporates human characteristics at the site of the artificial, Poole and Bowman do precisely the opposite: they embody an uncanny, machine-like lack of the human. For example, when Dr. Poole receives a video transmission from his parents on earth wishing him a happy birthday, his reaction appears to be restive and he shows no clear signs of emotional response. In fact, Dr. Poole rarely shows signs of emotional response. Upon closing the transmission, HAL also wishes Dr. Poole a happy birthday, "Happy birthday, Frank," to which he responds, "Thank you HAL." HAL's gesture to Dr. Poole mirrors the behavior of Poole's family — human behavior — while Dr. Poole's behavior doesn't seem to distinguish between the human and the artificial. In *Stanley Kubrick und seine Filme*, Georg Seesslen points out that "the human itself has become a mechanical being...."[12] Kubrick further underlines this element in the scene where HAL asks to see Dave's (Bowman's) drawings. All of them are of the crew members within their hibernation units, upon which, as is later made thoroughly explicit, they are entirely dependant for life support. They look like mechanical cocoons (this, like the image we first see of Martin, who is also in an artificial state of suspended animation, visually epitomizes what is at stake in the concept of the cyborgian). Furthermore, we view these images through HAL's perspective. This provides a maximum distance to the human, as there are three "lenses" or windows we are looking through here (four if we count Kubrick's camera): HAL's eye, the drawing itself, and within the drawing, the screen-like window of the hibernation unit where we see the crew member's face. And, moreover, not unlike Magritte's famous *Ceci n'est pas une pipe*— this is not a human, but a representation of a human.

Again, all of this becomes meaningful when placed in contrast to HAL's humanness. Thus we have a juxtapositioning which destabilizes positions of viewer identification and, with it, the borders of the human and the non-human: "If in HAL we see Kubrick's vision of the machine becoming human, in Bowman and Poole we observe how humans are becoming dehumanized and machinelike because of their close association with technological 'offspring.'"[13] Kubrick is, though, somewhat ambiguous here. Although he inverts human and machine characteristics, he is not necessarily moralistic about it.[14] We are not rooting for one over the other from the outset. Rather these "personality" characteristics at the location of the artificial are presented in a manner that encourages us to identify with the machine, while the machine-like behavior of the humans provides a certain distance.[15]

Where Kubrick employs the element of ambiguity, Spielberg is clear about with whom he wants us to identify. In *A.I.*, a young couple must come to terms with the loss of their child. They should be in the process of mourning, we are informed, though the child is still alive. While visiting their son, who is in a coma and being cryogenically kept in a state of suspended animation, a doctor explains that after five years of this condition, the parents' instincts instruct them to mourn. He goes on to explain that, though the child may be lost, there is hope for the well-being of the mother. Shortly after, the husband brings home a "Mecha"-child a mechanical child. The scene opens with the mother waiting at home in front of an elevator, from which the husband emerges. After an awkward exchange in which Monica utters his name, "Henry," and Henry responds, "Don't kill me. I love you. Don't kill me,"[16] David enters the house in an uncannily human manner. He walks in, steps from a carpeted surface onto a wood surface and, noticing the difference, taps his foot. The suggestion or indication here is that he is an aware, sentient being who takes in and processes information based on independent experience. He, like HAL, is also a heuristic algorithmic machine. David then turns to Monica, says, "I like your floor," and we get a close-up of him as he smiles. The possibility of David not being human is imperceptible at this point. In the following scene, in the bedroom now, Monica is crying as she yells at Henry: "I can't accept this! There is no substitute for your own child.... What were you thinking?!" But this is immediately followed by, "I don't know what to do.... Did you see his face? He's so real."

Against David's "realness," and in order to generate viewer sympathy and identification with an android, the humans are portrayed as brutal, unemotional, naïve, self-consumed, immoral, etc. In *A.I.* we are confronted with a stark contrast between humans and androids in which almost every human is in some capacity unappealing: where Kubrick's characters are un-human, Spielberg's are inhumane. The human child Martin (Jake Thomas) is by far the most unappealing: he is malicious, devious, dishonest, selfish, destructive and generally uncongenial. Henry, the father, is an uninteresting, marginally developed character, having no authority and rarely an opinion of his own. He is a virtual void in the narrative. Monica, more tolerable, is also portrayed as immature, insecure, irresponsibly and unreflectively engaging her desires and anxieties. Professor Hobby, despite his benevolent father-like tone and manner, really has to bear the brunt of what goes wrong here between the humans and the machines: he is selfish and self-aggrandized with his fantasies of being a god-like creator, and, most importantly, exhibits a lack of concern for the moral consequences of his work. In contrast to these are all of the "Mechas." Teddy (voice, Jack Angel) the supertoy is reflective, helpful, honest, has a sense of moral integrity and solidarity. Gigolo Joe also has a sense of solidarity, is helpful, resourceful/clever, and charming. David, finally, like Spielberg's E.T., is the innocent child-like other. Frightened, lost, trying to find his way back home, we can't but sympathize with him. Built as a model of Dr. Hobby's own dead child, he cannot be other than an idealized, perfect (dare we say it: "model") child.

Though the human element of the intelligent machine may be framed more blatantly than in *2001*—through David's appearance, but also through identifying him as an emotional, suffering boy—we can see parallels between HAL's and David's introduction insofar as both scenes foreground the machines' human characteristics, focus on their potential role among humans, and, importantly, present the possibility of destabilizing the human community.

Both *A.I.* and *2001* employ various tropes and motifs in order to signal the artificial being's humanness. In *2001*, when Dr. Bowman is removing the memory cards from HAL (a representative central nervous system), HAL pleads with him to stop, saying he's frightened, and then he says, "Dave, my mind is going," which once again brings us back to Descartes and the self-conscious subject. Similarly, in *A.I.* when David returns to Professor Hobby toward the end of the film, hoping to be turned into a real boy, and is informed that neither is he one of a kind nor is there a Blue Fairy who can grant him his wish, he replies, "My brain is falling out." Each moment of the artificial being declaring the status of its *mind*—that it in fact possesses a mind—is accompanied by a high point in the explication of the android's humanness. In *A.I.* it is at this point that we witness the culmination of David's travels, that he indeed has the "determination" and *drive* of a human, and that, at seeing a simulacra of himself, he reacts with a human hysteria and violence that even the android Gigolo Joe cannot fathom. In *2001* it is HAL's pleading for his life, the repetition of the statements, "I'm afraid," and, "I can feel it," and the singing of the song his instructor, Mr. Langley, taught him. Another trope brought into focus here, and used as a motif throughout the film, is HAL's uncanny eye. While HAL is being "disconnected," we get a close-up of his eye, evidence of his "being-ness," which fades away and finally disappears as he sings his last words.[17] The fading of the eye here is used to signal HAL's death, like so many other death scenes in which death is signaled by an inertia and closing of the eyes. The eye as a motif to signal humanness, and particularly uncanny humanness, has a substantial tradition, markedly beginning with Freud's reading of E.T.A. Hoffmann's *The Sandman* and moving onward to contemporary science fiction film.

The Window to the Soul: Uncanny Eyes and Canny Others

Before any narrative information is provided on HAL, our first visual of him is a shot of what would be considered his eye: a type of camera with a red light at the center, like a pupil, not unlike Schwarzenegger's unmasked eye in *The Terminator* (1984). Where Terminator is explicit in framing the uncanniness of the artificial eye, or rather the uncanniness of being able to dress it in an appearance so human-like (the Teminator expels it from its socket, only to illustrate that it is the uncanny other eye doing the real work), *2001* is perhaps somewhat subtler. Nevertheless, the suggestion that this eye marks uncanniness eventually becomes explicit. During the BBC interview mentioned earlier, while presenting HAL, both the BBC camera and the lens through which we, the audience, view the scene are focused on a panel of monitors at the center of which is HAL's eye. When questioned on his confidence in his own abilities, the camera (Kubrick's) moves to a close-up of the eye, where we are confronted by its red pupil as HAL, in a very matter-of-fact tone ("let me put it this way"), explains his reliability. Throughout this segment of the film, Kubrick frames this eye as "watching" the crew members, and when there is interaction with HAL, we are usually shown his eye when he speaks. Later, as we know, it will be strictly through the use of his eye that HAL perceives the threat to his own existence. Although associations between the eye and the human are rather common (with such proverbs as "the eye is the window to the soul"), Kubrick's particular use of the eye as an indication/suggestion of the human and the uncanny effect of its presence in the artificial being left a legacy to filmmaking. It was by no means lost on James Cameron and certainly not on Ridley Scott, where in *Blade Runner* (1982) it becomes a leitmotif.[18]

In *Das Unheimliche*, "The Uncanny," Freud explicates the meaning of the uncanny, in part, through a reading of E.T.A. Hoffmann's *Der Sandmann*, which is about a man who steals little children's eyes and, not incidentally, also about an automaton. In the story, the protagonist Nathaniel thinks back on the death of his father and on his father's associate, Coppelius, who, according to Nathaniel's memory, killed his father and tried to burn Nathaniel's eyes out, equating him with the bedtime story of the Sandman. As the tale goes, the Sandman steals little children's eyes and feeds them to his own bird-like children. Already in the element of anxiety about losing one's eyes, there is the parallel to Oedipus the King, who gouges his own eyes out upon discovering that he has wed his own mother, Jocasta. Later, in his adult life, Nathaniel meets an optician named Coppola, who suspiciously reminds him of Coppelius from his childhood. Shortly after this meeting, Nathaniel discovers that his neighbor has a beautiful daughter and falls in love with her, only to find out that she is an automaton, and that Coppola has supplied her with her human eyes. After being witness to an incident in which Coppola and the neighbor fight over the "daughter," and Coppola runs off with her (Olympia) leaving only her eyes behind (inverting the story of the Sandman who runs off with the eyes, leaving the body behind), Nathaniel falls into a fit of illness similar to the one he had when he was first threatened by Coppelius as a boy. Once he's recovered, he is out for a walk with Clara, his wife-to-be, when they decide to climb the tower at the town hall. From the tower, Nathaniel first notices

Olympia among the crowd below, which provokes the onset of yet another fit, and then he notices Coppelius, at the sight of whom he throws himself from the tower.

As Freud makes clear, moments of trauma in the story are continually related to the eyes and to those interested in obtaining or somehow manipulating them — the threatening, ever-present other: "The end of the story exposes that the optician Coppola is really both the solicitor Coppelius and the Sandman."[19] The motifs at work here — that of not being able to determine the living from the non-living (Olympia), that of ghosts of the past returning (Coppelius/Coppola), and that of disembodied eyes — are bound together in the element of threat. According to Freud's reading, this moment of frightening, uncanny recognition is always accompanied by a threat. The threat at work in *The Sandman* is that Nathaniel will either lose his eyes, or his object of love. Also, as Freud points out, we should recognize that this threat is one particularly associated with castration anxiety, the impetus for which becomes clear upon analysis of the scenes in which the Sandman/Coppelius/Coppola appears. Coppelius — who threateningly appears when Nathaniel is hiding in his father's study, when Nathaniel falls in love with the automaton, and shortly before Nathaniel is to marry Clara — represents the ("evil") father's castrative "No!" This, castration anxiety, is precisely what is at work in Spielberg's oedipal fairy-tale.

Where HAL's uncanniness is signaled through his glowing and all-seeing red eye, David's uncanniness takes shape in his extreme similarity to a human boy. Like the automaton with the real human eyes, he is the automaton we cannot differentiate from the real human. In addition to this, it is precisely his access to his mother and the love he might get from her that is threatened (as Nathaniel's love for a woman is repeatedly threatened by the appearance of Coppola/Coppelius). Here, castration anxiety does not only take place at the location of the human subject, but at the location of the uncanny non-human other, and it is signaled by the return of a "canny" double, Martin.

Miraculously resuscitated, Martin is brought home by Monica and Henry. They enter the house in a manner similar to David's initial entrance, and when they do, roles begin to vacillate and turn over. David, waiting at the elevator on the house's interior, is now situated in the position Monica was upon David's own arrival. With the introduction of an important new element into his family life, it is now his symbolic status that will be altered. Monica, entering the house from the elevator and approaching David, takes the position Henry was in. She is the bearer of some important news about the introduction of a new element into this community, an element that will, once again, disrupt and alter. Martin, replete with synthetic (mechanical) hardware and systems which provide for his mobility, regulate his breathing, monitor his vital signs, and feed him the necessary drugs, has become a proper cyborg, a human mechanized, and is now in the position David, the machine humanized, briefly held. As a dramatic inversion of David's unassisted and uncanny entry into the house, Martin descends the staircase in a wheelchair.

Monica approaches David, takes him by the shoulder and turns him twice: first slightly away from Martin and the nurse, so the frame captures only the two of them against the backdrop of a window, indicating both that we are at a decisive, peripatetic moment in our narrative — a "turning point" made literal — and framing a delineation of the (symbolic) location of this change (the home/family); then, she turns him back toward Martin and the camera pans across the room so they are foregrounded on top of Martin's position as she begins to explain, "the most wonderful thing in the world has happened." Monica backs away from David and, placing her hand now on Martin's shoulder, says, "This is Martin. This is my son." David's position once again becomes unclear. The exclusive access to his mother has suddenly been compromised. The similarities between the scene of David's original entrance into the home and this one clearly offset or encapsulate the narrative of his "being home" in between. We might be inclined to read the span of David's privileged presence in the house as a single chapter: within the diegesis, this is, on one level, David's phantasmatic terrain, the imaging/imagining of the protective family fiction around which the narrative turns and to which in the end it returns. Programmed as he is to unalterably love his mother, he cannot but reject symbolic castration, and thus embarks on an epic journey in search of his originary object of desire — only to return "home," in the end, to the fantasy of the protective family fiction.[20]

The uncanny is inextricably bound to the developing tradition of the posthuman in that central characteristics from the posthuman, particularly human-like machines and the "nonhuman" integrated into the human, have also been central concerns in identifying or defining the uncanny: uncanniness is encountered at locations of confusion concerning the animate and the animated. The three most characteristic manifestations of the uncanny in fiction are present in David. He is at once an automaton, a doppelganger and the dead returned. He can be read as both ghost and fantasy replacement of/for the dead child of Professor Hobby, as well as the ghost and fantasy replacement of/for Martin. In this regard he is a phantasmatic replacement child, a projection. The significance here is the movement from internal wish-fantasy (of Professor Hobby's and of Monica's) to external materialization-phantom: "Some foreign thing projected out of the self."[21] In this regard, we might also read HAL as an externalized fantasy: the dream of creating an infallible being, a perfect intellect with superhuman capacity. This dream is often present in some capacity in narratives on artificial life and intelligence, from stories of immortality and cloning to superior intellect and chess supercomputers. This movement from the internal or familiar, to the external or unfamiliar (or rather the familiar made foreign) is, as Freud makes thoroughly clear, already embodied in the German word *unheimlich*. *Heimlich* is an adjective meaning familiar, home-like, trusted, private, secret; while *unheimlich* is both the negative (unfamiliar, un–home–like) and a conflation or collapse of the negative and positive at an unclear border (also secret or private, but exposed to oneself at a foreign — external — location).

In narratives on subjectivity, which both of these films are to a large extent, this type of

"Orga" mom (Frances O'Connor) and "Mecha" child (Haley Joel Osment) in Steven Spielberg's *A.I.*

structuring of the human self and *unheimlich* reflection has a long tradition, even outside of or prior to the science fiction genre. Within the genre and alongside questions newly posed by technological modernity, these portrayals of the uncanny become central as the rigidity of the borders between what is human and what is not (cyborgs of all capacities, artificial intelligence, clones, the possibility of bioengineered organs and prosthetics, and so forth) become increasingly malleable and fluid. These mirrorings, doublings and externalizations are taken up in locations that point toward this malleability in order to give certain questions utterance. What kind of threat does this uncanny, non-human other pose? And what does this threat represent?

"Chop it Off": Castrative Threat and Other Anxieties

On a rather obvious level, the uncanny non-human other poses a threat to the distinction between human and non-human. This threat, in turn, is symptomatic of anxieties about the nature of subjectivity. If subjectivity is a construct, and is constructed via external agents, what does this say about the nature of one's "self?" How is *one's self* different from the "self" of the artificially intelligent machine? In this regard, what is at stake here is a threat to enlightenment-based, liberal humanist notions of the self, autonomous and in possession of a protected, constitutive inner core. In fiction, and as we've seen in Freud's reading of *Der Sandmann*, this threat is typically represented as a physical threat. But it is sometimes simply framed as a threat to symbolic status.

As noted above, the first element of threat in the narrative is when Martin returns home, which decidedly alters David's status within the family fiction. *A.I.* produces three subsequent scenes that explicitly frame *threat* to the human: the first, when Martin witnesses Monica take David's hand while he's being operated on; the next, when David, under Martin's advice, attempts to cut Monica's hair while she sleeps; and finally when David pulls Martin into the swimming pool. These are all written within the context of oedipal anxieties of castration on various levels, accompanied by various framings of symbolic castration.

We begin with an initial threat to the biological son: after having provoked David into damaging himself (David mimics Martin, gobbling up mouthfuls of spinach at the dinner table), we are presented with a scene in which David's uncanny otherness is explicitly posed. As two technicians operate on David while he lies on a table with his mechanical innards exposed, Monica nervously looks on, holding his hand. David looks up at her and says, "It's okay, Mommy; it doesn't hurt." At this she gasps and falters, then quickly lets go of his hand and walks to a corner of the room, clearly disturbed. By underlining David's otherness, Monica's understanding of her feelings for him becomes destabilized, putting into question certain conditions in relation to their effect. The conditions of David's existence, that he is a machine, essentially, do not correlate to Monica's maternal feelings. At this point, Henry approaches Monica in an attempt to comfort her. "Monica," he says, to which she reacts, "Shh. I just have to...." She doesn't complete the sentence, but rather produces an ellipsis, half turns her head, sighs and half smiles in a gesture indicating that she has now understood something she foolishly hadn't up till that point. The implication is that she understands the significance of her feelings and the symbolic relationship (between her and David) they are bound to; the following scene suggests that she has also understood the insignificance in trying to classify difference at an emotional level.

She walks back to David and securely takes up his hand again, as his mother, as Martin looks on. Martin rightly perceives this as a threat to his enjoyment of his mother. This is our first framing of castration, with the threat directed at Martin. Spielberg brings this into focus by overlapping Martin's voice-track from the following scene onto the image of Martin looking at his mother affectionately grasp David's hand: "Will you do something special for me?" Martin asks David, and then we make the visual shift to the next scene, in which he tricks David into secretly entering the parents' bedroom and approaching the mother with a large pair of shears. He assumes that sending David into the bedroom with this object that is itself a potential threat, meant either to pierce or cut, will result in the actual castration of this object (the removal of the shears), which, as the object stands in metaphorically for a part of David that mustn't enter the bedroom, would by extension be metonymous for the castration of the whole of David (would ultimately result in David's physical removal from the home/parental bedroom).

Here is a second scene of threatening castration: Martin, himself threatened with castration, attempts to precipitate a limit to David's access to the mother (or, in Lacanian terms, the mother being barred). He does this by means of the third castration: fooling David into a position in which he will appear as a castrative threat to the father and to the mother (an inversion of the normal conditions, under which the child's pleasure is curtailed by a symbolic father's castrative forbiddance). David's entering the bedroom with the shears and approaching the bed, makes this gesture a "real" castrative threat to the father and subsequently penetrative threat to the mother. The shears frame a real physical threat of violence, which we also read metaphorically. As if to drive home this element of castration anxiety, David is instructed to cut off a lock of the mother's hair. Martin tells him to "sneak into Mommy's bedroom in the middle of the night and *chop it off*," telling him that, as a result, she will love him more. Notably, the camera shot of the two sons is set against the backdrop of their bedroom wall, on which hangs a painting of a mother holding her child. Also worth noting is that, in the sentence that articulates the command "chop it off," there is no antecedent to *it* (in fact the antecedent is found seven sentences and four "its" earlier), leaving a certain suggestive ambiguity as to what should be lost here, or curtailed, and what gained.

Though Martin, by inference, equates the possession of a lock of hair to the tradition of chivalric romance, we know his intentions follow another tradition: because this lock is not being proffered in a gesture of love or devotion (or at all, for that matter), but rather taken in sleep, *chopped off*, we should read it in the tradition of castrative threat, examples of which we can find in various eras of mythology and literature — Samson and Delilah, *The Rape of the Lock* — and other narrative types such as dream/symbol analysis and psychoanalysis, the hair being another recognized symbol of vitality/potency/fertility.

In the scene following the bedroom incident, the threat enacted against the husband/father in the previous scene is made explicit through his reaction, and then we witness a physical threat toward the biological son. Discussing the event in the bedroom while preparing for Martin's birthday party, Henry is trying to convince Monica that they should get rid of David, claiming that he is a danger to the family. Monica on the other hand refers to David and Martin as brothers ("it's normal for brothers to challenge each other") and says of David, "He's practically human," to which Henry replies, "That's not how he looked holding the knife," meaning the shears, but clearly interpreting them in their penetratory capacity, which would suggests a threat to his symbolic status. Directly following this scene is the birthday party. With the children gathered by the poolside, one malicious boy is explaining David's operational system to the others. He stabs David in the arm to evoke a reaction (repeating Professor Hobby's gesture while giving a lecture at the film's opening), at which point David hides behind Martin, only to drag him into the pool and not let him go until the fathers jump in and release him. Consequently, Henry insists that David be returned to Cybertronics. Thus, this second son, this other son, is jettisoned from the family body, an act justified in the end through a real physical threat, but one we would also interpret as a threat presented to male subjectivity within this familial body, to the stability of these positions within the symbolic family network. As Julia Kristeva notes, it is that which "disturbs identity, system, order ... [and] does not respect borders, positions, rules" that causes abjection.[22] The abandonment scene in *A.I.* and the scene following it at the "flesh fair," which we might refer to as scenes staging abjection, constitute the melodramatic highpoint, and again a turning point, of this film.

The Abject Subject

Abjection works ... as a means of separating out the human from the non-human and the fully constituted subject from the partially constituted subject.[23]

At the "flesh fair," robots and automatons, particularly ones resembling humans, are dramatically slaughtered for human entertainment. They are shot from cannons through rings of fire, mutilated by bladed rotors and chainsaws, bound and splayed and torn limb from limb, and doused with acid or boiling oil as loud music plays in the background and lights flash, the frenzied crowd cheering along. These are grotesquely dramatic enactments of abjection where the non-human is separated from the human. Barbara Creed explains that robots and androids are portrayed as abject because they lack souls, and bodies without souls are equated to corpses, signifying "one of the most basic forms of pollution."[24] By staging what at first appears to be the abjection of abject material — or, by drawing on the idea of the abject — these films do not so much pose the question of "are bodies without souls abject?" as they force us to consider what we think it is that constitutes a soul and how we perceive, as well as conceive, *humanness*.

When it is time for David to be slaughtered, the crowd revolts. The problem is that David resembles a real boy too exactly. Even though the crowd might know he's not human, the symbolic gesture in "killing" him transgresses the bounds of the acceptable because of what he represents. In *Powers of Horror*, Julia Kristeva notes that "the abjection of Nazi crime reaches its apex when death, which, in any case, kills me, interferes with what, in my living universe, is supposed to save me from death: childhood, science, among other things."[25] Thus, there is a conflict or impasse of logics here. In order to maintain the boundaries of the human, we must separate the non-human where it threatens to compromise these borders. On the other hand, David "looks so real" that the idea of killing him goes against our basic assumptions about life: we nurture youth, as opposed to extinguishing it. The impasse that is melodramatically played out in this scene, making explicit what is at stake in David's potential abjection, can be mapped back onto the abandonment scene that directly precedes it.

Monica takes David to a secluded spot in the forest on the pretext of having a picnic, and then, crying, tells him "you won't understand the reasons, but I have to leave you here." David resists, also crying and apologizing for everything he ever did wrong, and begs his mother not to leave him. Like the scene in which Bowman removes HAL's memory cards, this scene has often been described as the most disturbing throughout the entire film. This is due, I would wager, to the ideological mechanisms at work here. They are the same as those in the flesh fair scene, only we are the dissenting audience. What is portrayed in this scene is precisely this equation of Kristeva's, where death interferes with what is "supposed to save me from death"—in this case, childhood. Although Monica does not literally kill David, she enacts a "symbolic murder." By abandoning him, she revokes the very organizing principal upon which he orders meaning in his "life." What constitutes the disturbing quality of this scene is that it is the mother, his primary interpellator and his originary object of desire, who "kills" him. The more humane thing to do would have been to return him to the Cybertronics Corporation and let them deprogram him as a machine, rather than "uninterpellating" him, ideological and identity death, as her human child.

Nevertheless, this is just what the film dare not be too explicit about: death interfering with the child. And thus David is given some money and advice, and the narrative continues. The gesture is thus a turning away from the real horror of the logical consequences to which the abandonment scene gives rise — little children are killed/abandoned by their mothers out in the woods (another fairytale reference in this film — *Hanzel and Gretel*), which we might call an ultimate horror, or the apex of abjection. It turns rather toward another horror, the dream scenario of wish fulfillment that we recognize as the oedipal narrative, though consummate: In the end, David is reunited with his mother, the father and rival brother are not to be found when David returns home, and David beds his blurry-eyed mother. Impossible; we know the kind of tumult this act consequently requires. Though before considering the closing scenes in *A.I.*, we should turn to the element of threat and the subsequent abjection in *2001*.

When HAL predicts that a communications unit will malfunction and there is some speculation as to whether he may have made a mistake, Dr. Bowman and Dr. Poole attempt to privately discuss what the consequences of a mistake on HAL's behalf might be. They go into a pod on the pretext of checking some equipment. After making sure HAL cannot hear them, they determine that any malfunction on HAL's part must result in his disconnection:

> POOLE: "There isn't a single aspect of ship operations that isn't under his control. If he were proven to be malfunctioning I wouldn't see how we'd have any choice but disconnection."
> BOWMAN: "It'd be a bit tricky. We'd have to cut his higher brain functions without disturbing the purely automatic and regulatory systems."
> BOWMAN: "You know another thing just occurred to me. As far as I know, no HAL 9000 computer has ever been disconnected.... I'm not so sure what he'd think about it."

After this exchange we immediately cut to HAL's eye, then to HAL's view of Bowman and Poole speaking. He's reading their lips. Then we cut to *2001*'s famous intermission, which, more than a pause for relaxation, should also be interpreted (in this regard, it's rather a pause for reflection). This "ellipsis" takes the form of a diegetic break in the narrative at a critical, peripatetic moment. What has just been indicated? We might interpret this break in the narrative as signaling the moment when the non-human machine HAL makes an evolutionary step (as we know, the earlier scene dealing with evolution, when the ape-man discovers the tool/weapon, is also marked by a diegetic break).

In the span of this short dialogue between Dr. Poole and Dr. Bowman, a conspiracy is established in that the humans here attempt to cut HAL out of the proverbial loop. Next, the threat of disconnection is determined and couched in language that alludes to HAL's animal biology: Bowman refers to HAL's brain and regulatory systems. Although regulatory systems must not be exclusively biological, they do refer to the evolution of fundamental physiological mechanisms in plants and animals. This biological and evolutionary allusion sets the stage for Bowman's implied suggestion that HAL might revolt, which in turn signals the possibility of HAL's possession of or evolvement of survival "instincts." Also, HAL's "suspicion," signaled by his feat of lip-reading, is equally suggestive, if not merely of curiosity, of the possibility of his possessing survival instincts.

What loads this scene with significance is that with HAL's "animality," with this potential for possessing survival instincts, we are witness to the decisive moment in the evolution of the machine (as we were with the ape-man and the bone/tool), or in the history of evolution in the context of the machine's relation to the human. Just as David's possession of oedipal desire is employed to indicate his evolutionary humanness, HAL's possession of survival instincts indicates a potential evolutionary turning point. Should the machine triumphantly defend itself here against the human, it would represent the machine as the fitter being. At stake would be (by implication) the extinction of the human, or at least its subordination, under the superiority of the thinking machine. Fearing for his "life," HAL triggers a series of events in an attempt at self-preservation. He attempts to kill the entire five-member crew, succeeding with all but one, and a struggle to the death ensues between Dr. Bowman and HAL. As Georg Seesslen suggests, "thus begins the struggle between man and machine, between two thought-systems [Denksystemen], that want nothing else but to survive one another."[26]

Here again we find structural similarity in the two films: there is a potential threat to the human, followed by the rejection or abjection of the non-human, which consequently exposes a human core at the "heart" of the non-human. In *A.I.*, after Monica has "abjected" David, and he makes his journey in search of the Blue Fairy, hoping she can turn him into a real boy so that Monica will love him, the explicit exposure of David's oedipal fantasy (the exposure of his core human quality) is also marked by a diegetic break.

Having journeyed to Manhattan, which has been entirely flooded due to the melted polar caps, David goes to see Professor Hobby. After finding out that not only can he not be made into a real boy, but he is not even one of a kind, David dejectedly throws himself from the Cybertronics building into the water, where, once he has sunk, he sees the Blue Fairy. Gigolo Joe, having watched David fall from the building, follows him in the "amphibicopter" they stole earlier to fly to Manhattan, and brings David back to the surface. As David is explaining that he found the Blue Fairy, Joe is detected by the police and taken away. David then proceeds to dive back down to the Blue Fairy, now with the amphibicopter. Having found her, he is trapped when a large Ferris wheel falls on top of the amphibicopter. He is facing what he believes is the Blue Fairy, who unsurprisingly resembles Monica — and what the viewer recognizes as a statue from the now submerged Coney Island amusement park. He sits there and prays to her to make him a real boy. Here, as with the prologue at beginning of the film, there is an intra-diegetic epilogue (voice, Ben Kingsley): "And David continued to pray to the Blue Fairy.... He prayed as the ocean froze and the ice encased the caged amphibicopter and the Blue Fairy too, locking them together.... Eventually he never moved at all.... Thus, two thousand years passed by."

At this point there is a prolepsis in which we jump forward two thousand years, when humans are extinct and New York is being excavated by some alien-looking beings we assume are an advanced form of the artificially intelligent machine (in fact, they resemble the Cybertronics corporate emblem), technological descendants of David. When they find David, they offer to grant him any wish he has. As we can only anticipate, he wishes to be reunited with Monica. The AIs are willing to comply, but there is, of course, a catch: they can only reproduce a human specimen one time per specimen for a period of one day. David chooses to be with Monica for one more day, and this time when she dies, he will die with her. David and Monica spend an ideal day together at home alone. After he accompanies her to the bedroom at the end of this day, tucks her in, and cries at her unequivocal declaration of love for him, he then gets into bed at her side, and takes her hand, and we are told that "that was the everlasting moment he had been waiting for. And the moment had passed, for Monica was sound asleep — more than merely asleep. Should he shake her, she would never rouse. So David went to sleep too. And for the first time in his life, he went to that place where dreams are born."

Here, at the culmination of David's travels and his return home, we might interpret David as a prepubescent Odysseus: he must undertake this epic journey in order to return home to his object of desire again. As such we find another intertextual reference binding these two films: the epic tradition. Where David might be interpreted as a prepubescent Odysseus, when we take the title of Kubrick's film into consideration, the name *Bowman* immediately recalls Homer's Odysseus, the archetypal *bowman*. The question with *A.I.* is: what to do with this child at the end of his journey? With this prolepsis, we have the introduction of a post-epilogue genie-in-a-bottle-like wish fulfillment narrative, and finally a more decisive entrance into what is clearly an oedipal fantasy.

Though the basis for *A.I.* — that should we replicate humans, we will have a certain responsibility toward these beings — would be the film's legitimate concern, where this narrative potentially

***A.I.* and the oedipal fantasy: David (Haley Joel Osment) and Monica (Frances O'Connor) in bed.**

becomes perverted is when it turns into a consummate oedipal fantasy. The epilogue, though, opens up another possible way of reading the ending.

When David returns to the Cybertronics building in search of Professor Hobby, he encounters another Mecha just like himself. After the Mecha introduces itself also as David, David whispers, "You can't have her.... She's mine. And I'm the only one." He then picks up a lamp, smashes the face of the other David, knocking his head off and across the room, and destroys the room, screaming, "I'm David! I'm David! ... You can't have her!" This scene of mirroring is an initial paraphrasing of what is at stake in *A.I.* On a practical level, David cannot come to terms with what he is: a robot. This very condition of David rejecting his non-humanness signals an ambiguity between the human and the non-human. On a representational level, he is not "willing" to accept symbolic castration (he is not willing to give up Monica). This, in turn, raises the stakes, as his oedipal love acts as a kind of *proof of humanness*. And if we haven't understood what is at stake until now, Professor Hobby enters the scene to offer another paraphrasing:

> Until you were born, robots didn't dream, robots didn't desire, unless we told them what to want.... You found a fairy tale, and inspired by love, driven by desire, you set out on a journey to make her real and, most remarkable of all, no one taught you how.... Our test was a simple one: Where would your self-motivated reasoning take you? To the logical conclusion that Blue Fairy is part of the great human flaw to wish for things that don't exist, or to the greatest single human gift: the ability to chase down our dreams?

David's simple response to this is, "I thought I was one of a kind." When Professor Hobby tells him, "My son was one of a kind. You are the first of a kind," David echoes HAL's "my mind is going" with "my brain is falling out."

After Professor Hobby has gone to fetch his colleagues, David goes outside to the edge of the building, utters, "Mommy," and plunges some fifteen-odd stories into the water (not unlike Hoffmann's Nathaniel, who leaps from the tower upon his final encounter with the "evil" castrative father). This is the first visualization of David's death, and it is accompanied by other indicators suggesting that we might read the ten minutes surrounding this scene as a final death scene. First, there is David knocking his own head off in the mirroring scene. Then, there is his echoing of HAL's "my mind is going." If we read this intertextually, we recall that this is the scene when the artificially intelligent machine dies. David then "commits suicide" by jumping from the Cybertronics building. This is shortly followed by an epilogue, generally indicating the end of the play or story (Spielberg repeatedly gives the viewer indications of this being a "tale," or a fairy tale). Finally, in the epilogue, we are told that David "prayed" until he "never moved at all," which also seems to be another way to say that he "died." If we take these various indications of David's death at face value, we might ask ourselves if it then makes sense to read the epilogue as indicating the proper ending, and the following segment, in which David is exhumed from the ice, as a false ending. To answer this, we can consider what is at stake in the final segment and how it is staged.

"The Play's the Thing!" *Mise en abyme* in *A.I.* and *2001*

As we know, a *mise en abyme* (or a frame story, or a play within a play) is generally employed in the service of exposing or staging a specific knowledge. The point of *A.I.*'s final segment is clearly to stage the reunion between Monica and David: at stake is a visualization of David's desire. A false ending would thus be employed to narrate David's fantasy of his reunion with his mother. The question remains as to how it is staged. There are a couple of elements that would support a reading of the reunion with Monica as strictly a fantasy (and whether we want to interpret this as a false ending or not, this *is* David's fantasy) and clearly as a *mise en abyme*, which in its own right automatically differentiates or splits the segment it stages off from the rest of the diegetic trajectory. When David is approaching the Blue Fairy with the amphibicopter, we get a close-up of a sign that says "once upon a time." In addition to suggesting that the entire filmic diegesis is a fairy tale, a modern Pinocchio, this shot also suggests that we are entering a fairy tale within the fairy tale: this is the entry point to David's fantasy. There are other elements suggesting the use of *mise en abyme* as a dramatic device here. First of all, there is an audience *within* the diegesis watching David's reunion with Monica: The AIs reconstruct the setting of David's home, based on his memories, and observe David as if through a screen from a location above the setting. Thus there is the element of the house being like a stage or a set (David: "Where am I? This looks like my house, but it is different"), and the day being specifically staged, not like the previous days they spent together, but rather an ideal day. As is generally the case with the *mise en abyme*, what is at stake here is the exposure (and at the same time, a concealing, as this is yet another staging presented to the viewer once removed) of a specific knowledge, as well as of desire.[27] In *A.I.* the exposure of desire is mimetic, and through it a specific knowledge is represented: David longs to be loved like a real boy, and the dependency upon this motherly love (or in Lacanian terms, the *lack* at this location) is precisely the register within which he will bring order to his desire; the knowledge represented here—for the inter-diegetic audience and by proxy the extra-diegetic audience — is the knowledge of what it means to be human. As the AIs state earlier, David had direct contact with the humans, and therefore he is an important source for learning about the humans; i.e., he is able to bring them a better understanding of what *the human* consists of (in this regard, it is particularly poignant that what the AIs witness is an enactment of the Oedipal fantasy).

In this case, the device of framing the reception of knowledge within and toward the end of the diegesis— by way of mimetically figuring David's desire — retroactively instructs the extra-diegetic viewer how to process or interpret the knowledge he or she has received (assuming that the *mise en abyme* is not intended to misguide the viewer).

Yet another structural similarity, we equally have a *mise en abyme* in *2001*, in which Bowman acts as his own audience. This sequence ("Beyond Space and Time," untitled in the film) begins with a subjective shot of a predominantly white neo-classical/Victorian-style room, viewed through the oval window of Bowman's pod; thus from Bowman's perspective. Framing this scene through an inter-diegetic "lens" (the pod window) from the perspective of an observer within the narrative signals the very act of viewing itself: this segment is *about* viewing. Notably, this scene is prefaced by a close-up of an eye we assume to be Bowman's, shot in various colors. Moreover, for all the monitors and screens we see throughout the film, it is the first time we see a mirror. Bowman stands in front of it and looks at himself (there are various other elements throughout the film indicating the passive act of viewing: the name of the ape-man from the beginning of the narrative, Moon-Watcher, played by Daniel Richter, for example), also indicating an act of self-reflexive viewing. This self-referentiality not only signals that we are now witness to a *mise en abyme*, as the *mise en abyme* is self-reflexive insofar as it encapsulates the narrative or a part thereof, it finds itself within; it also signals something about what we witness: the "watching" here is explicitly framed as a passive act, and the "action" that is framed tends in any case toward an element of passivity or complacency. We should also note that what takes place in this scene is not so unlike what happens during the mission to Jupiter: Bowman witnesses himself eating and sleeping in a white, sterile environment, again as if there is nothing meaningful for him to do. Thus there is an element of inaction in this scene, which Bowman "doubles" in his passive viewing of himself.

There are various mimetic elements that appear in this segment, including the presence of the pod itself (which further suggests, along with the white sterility, a parallel between the apartment and the ship HAL was navigating). Again, to unravel this play within the play, we might ask what is at stake in this scene and how it is staged.

Bowman sees himself standing in the room wearing a spacesuit; then he is looking at himself, aged, in the mirror; then he sees himself, aged again, feeding himself; then, after inadvertently breaking a glass, he sees himself, aged yet again, lying in bed. A very old man now, Bowman is lying in bed when the black monolith appears before him. He reaches out to touch it (with his index finger extended, the gesture mimics Michelangelo's "Creation of Adam"). This segment constitutes a *mise en abyme* specifically in the mimetic elements of watching (as Moon-Watcher, and, moreover, HAL do), eating (as we saw the ape-men do, as well as Dr. Haywood Floyd, played by William Sylvester, and as we saw Bowman and Poole do) and reaching out to touch the monolith (as, again, we saw the ape-men do, as well as Dr. Floyd). Each one of these elements is the focus of various scenes throughout the film.

Toward the end of this scene, Bowman is suddenly transformed into a fetus in a disembodied womb floating on the bed. Here, panning forward toward the monolith, there is a jump cut to a shot of the earth's moon, which pans down to a shot of the earth, and then the fetus and disembodied womb floating next to it in space with a similar size and shape, the dominant feature clearly the eyes. Here one might observe that a fetus also doesn't undertake any action, but, we can assume, is rather mostly concerned with being nourished. Following this line of logic, that the image of the fetus is also a mimetic device, we will begin to see all kinds of imagery throughout the film suggesting conception, the prenatal stage, birth, death, and rebirth. The life-cycle is also mirrored in the overall diegesis, beginning with the "Dawn of Man" (the first segment, birth), over the journey to the moon ("life," presumably — the central focus here is mobility, along with the ever-present element of eating), onto the "Jupiter Mission" (in which all characters die, Bowman — whose odyssey this is — withholding), and ending with "Beyond the Infinite" (the final segment, rebirth, the Star Child). Considering this framing and reframing of the life-cycle, we might inquire as to where evolution (a "meta-theme" in the film) fits in, and how it relates to the element of inaction or passivity to which we are repeatedly witness.

The evolutionary moments, particularly the ape-man's discovery of the tool and Bowman's defeating HAL, are initiated by an external threat, against which the threatened party advances or evolves by defending itself (signaled by the sudden presence of the monolith). Initially, this happens through the discovery and implementation of the tool/weapon: using a bone, Moon-Watcher defeats his threatening adversaries and is able to supply food for his tribe, securing them a position of dominance among the animals. From this point on in the film, we know, the tool plays a central role (from the bone to the pen, to the various spaceships/shuttles/stations, to HAL, to the spacesuits and the pod), until it is precisely the tool that threatens to make the human obsolete. Notably, Bowman defeats HAL not with the use of any particular tool or with violence, but by outwitting him. Thus, that which enables Bowman to survive HAL/the machine is nothing external to himself, but rather his own sense and his will.[28] In this regard, it is not surprising that the next evolutionary image we get of Bowman is of him (reborn) without tools, a naked fetus. The suggestion is that the next evolutionary step will invert the one we saw at the beginning of the film: it is not the external element that will give rise to survival and evolution, but the internal element — the mind, the will. It is in the form of framing the human's triumph over the very machines humans had become dependant on (and which threatened human obsolescence) that *2001* gives utterance to essentialist anxieties; anxieties over the threatened, compromised or lost human core that are so symptomatic of the postmodern/posthuman era.

Posthuman vs. Oedipal Anxiety

In an interview with Albert Borgmann, N. Katherine Hayles states: "Whereas the human has traditionally been associated with consciousness, rationality, free will, autonomous agency, and the right of the subject to possess himself, the posthuman sees human behavior as the result of a number of ... agents running their programs more or less independently of one another," and that, along with this, recent studies in cognitive science, artificial life, and artificial intelligence "have argued for a view of the human so different from that which emerged from the Enlightenment that it can appropriately be called 'posthuman.'"[29] What is often at stake in narratives such as *2001* and *A.I.* is an opposition between postmodern or posthuman notions of the *constructed* subject and the enlightenment or liberal humanist notion of the self — where the subject is in possession "of a free and autonomous individuality that is unique ... and that develops as part of our spontaneous encounter with the world."[30] As Nick Mansfield notes, from Nietzsche and Freud to Lacan and Foucault, and especially in postmodern and posthuman theory of the last thirty years, there is a widely shared consensus among theorists that "the subject is *constructed*, made within the world, not born into it already formed."[31] Thus, we might argue that the "lost object" of postmodernism/the posthuman is the liberal humanist "self." In this sense, we can see how the rejection of the prosthesis, the tool, the "external" non-human in *2001* might be symptomatic of postmodern/posthuman notions of the self as (in pejorative terms) compromised by the external.

Many posthuman narratives both celebrate the posthuman and expose anxieties about the implications of the postmodern and the posthuman for the individual. We can see how this is true of *2001* and *A.I.*, as they both begin with a potentially utopian vision of technology, only to expose an essential threat to the human at the location of the technological: in *A.I.* differentiation is threatened; in *2001* physical life, or, rather, human autonomy is threatened. These are precisely the elements in question (differentiation, autonomy) in the cyborgian and posthuman era, where the borders between the human and the non-human have become fluid. At stake, essentially, is a fear or rejection of the condition that "the boundaries of the human subject are constructed rather than given."[32] Thus we can see the logic in framing questions about identity and subjectivity through a juxtapositioning of the cyborgian or non-human vis-à-vis the human. Or, to put it another way, we can see the logical progression in which the cultural proliferation of the cyborgian leads to essentialist anxieties over identity and subjectivity. Though as Hayles argues in her discussion of what it means to *be* posthuman, "even a biologically unaltered *Homo Sapiens* counts as posthuman," precisely because "the defining characteristics involve the *construction of subjectivity*," and not necessarily because of "the presence of non-biological components."[33] Or, as Slavoj Žižek suggests, this has long been implicit in psychoanalytical theory: "In short, one should claim that 'humanity' as such ALWAYS-ALREADY was 'posthuman'—therein resides the gist of Lacan's thesis that the symbolic order is a parasitical machine which intrudes into and supplements a human being as its artificial prosthesis."[34]

Thus, if we conclude that the threats posed by the machines in *2001* and *A.I.* act as a trope for the posthuman fear of a lost authentic or essentialist core, then, we might say, they are symptomatic of a nostalgia for something that was never really there to begin with. Where posthuman narratives call up essentialist anxieties, they are drawing from the same well of nostalgia for the always already lost. Curiously, this is where *A.I.* departs from *2001*, and perhaps where it embodies the logical progression of Kubrick's work on the posthuman. *A.I.* moves from the essentialist anxiety at work in *2001*, which we also see at work in *A.I.* through the manner in which humans generally treat the Mechas, and from the *moral ambiguity* accompanying the "killing" of HAL, towards a condition in which the *fact* of the AIs, that they are among us and not going away, must be confronted, and it takes up a position of moral responsibility to the artificial. In this sense, *A.I.* has already integrated or digested the posthuman in the end, recognizing, as Monica does, the futility in differentiation based on the biological, and rather giving importance to the symbolic. In staging the oedipal drama at the location of the non-human, *A.I.* is certainly pointing to a posthuman condition: not only do we live in a cyborgian age where we interact automatically with machines, having integrated them physically, conceptually, and symbolically—the machines have also integrated the human, making one indistinguishable from the other. But A.I. does more than this: it depicts this condition as inevitable, and embraces it as such.

17 Whose Stanley Kubrick? The Myth, Legacy, and Ownership of the Kubrick Image

Robert J.E. Simpson

Despite the increasing public interest in the director as a kind of star, very few film directors would be easily recognized by the average cinemagoer or even ardent cinephile; the Terry Gilliams and Quentin Tarantinos are few and far between. While most film fans could list at least some of Kubrick's output (e.g., *A Clockwork Orange, 2001: A Space Odyssey, Dr. Strangelove, The Shining*), only a small number would have any idea what the director of those films looked like. During his lifetime, Stanley Kubrick remained enigmatic — removed from the public gaze, offering (intentionally or not) a public persona that was often likened in tabloid shorthand to an eccentric reclusive genius. The director with a reputation for absolute control on his film sets apparently attempted to control his public image as well.[35] His few in-depth interviews tended to repeat their content — Kubrick would provide stock answers, elaborating or deviating only slightly each time.[36] He requested (demanded?) final approval before any could be published, a fact that several of the published interviews mention in their text.[37] The interviews themselves are rife with paradoxes of the man who was a mystery.

After Alfred Hitchcock immigrated to the U.S. from Britain, he actively shaped his own very public image — developing an infamous caricature of himself, appearing in cameos in many of his films and cultivating a popular image through his almost comical appearances in the trailers to his films and through the filmed introductions to his TV series *Alfred Hitchcock Presents*. He also contributed to the dissection and analysis of his films by critics the world over, offering much insight into the intentions behind his work.

By comparison Kubrick remained elusive, a name — an ethereal quantity. Like Hitchcock's work, Kubrick's were films that cinemagoers would view based on the director's credit alone (one thinks of the *Eyes Wide Shut* campaign — "Cruise, Kidman, Kubrick" — putting Kubrick on par with the film's stars). And yet, the public had no idea who Kubrick actually was. Aside from a few photographs in unauthorized biographies, Kubrick's face was largely unknown. Released portraits grew even fewer as time went on. In the 1960s, Kubrick moved from the U.S. to England in a reversal of Hitchcock's career path and continued to make all of his films in the U.K. until his death in 1999, just three days after delivering the final cut of *Eyes Wide Shut*. By immigrating to England, it seems that Kubrick was not only seeking more control of his pictures, outside of the influence of the studios, but also looking for security and privacy.

Kubrick moved into a large mansion in the country, complete with a long drive and big fences. He conducted nearly all his business regarding the films by telephone, often late into the night. His colleagues would report having to visit him at his home. By all accounts he was little seen in public, but a vast body of anecdotes about the director's lifestyle and his working methods did appear in print. Kubrick's brother-in-law and long-time producer Jan Harlan makes reference to these stories in his documentary *Stanley Kubrick: A Life In Pictures* (1999), directly engaging with the Kubrick mystique and attempting to counteract it.

The Kubrick image, created during his lifetime, continues to evolve after his death.

Kubrick's working methods were subject to rumor and his private life was subject to much speculation, with Kubrick providing few comments on either. And yet in the years since his death, a wealth of material has emerged analyzing and presenting what we now perceive to be the "real" Stanley Kubrick. This essay is concerned with Stanley Kubrick's public image, engaging with the problem that a man who was intensely private in his lifetime has become increasingly revealed to the world. While the paper will not provide a definitive answer to the questions surrounding the motivations behind this exposure, it is hoped that by voicing them some important debate may be stimulated.

Kubrick's Working Practice

Kubrick not only attempted to control his biographical details in his limited number of interviews, but he also attempted to manage details of his working practices. While Kubrick was alive, only a few accounts of his on-set approaches to filmmaking were available, and they were generally brief. Those that were published raise awareness of the essential problem inherent in all authorized accounts of Kubrick's life and career; Kubrick's established method was to have final approval on all publications that sought his cooperation. As for those texts subjected to his approval, we know that he was in clear control of the image that we received, thus affecting our understanding of the man and his methods.

In his own interviews, Kubrick generally refused to talk about his methodology. He resisted in-depth conversations about his early experiences in film production in the 1950s, and he spurned discussion of the influence of other directors.[38] During his lifetime, he collaborated on only one documentary film about his work, *Making of The Shining* (1980), filmed by his then seventeen-year-old daughter Vivian and broadcast on the BBC as part of the *Arena* documentary strand. This half hour film (edited down from over 40 hours of footage) is vital for its glimpses of Kubrick at work that both support and reject the established myths concerning the director's working practice. Perhaps this is even a further example of Kubrick's control over his own image. In watching *Making of The Shining*, the viewer might assume that the documentary shows a frank and open depiction of the director. Indeed, the involvement of his family in the production might have meant that Kubrick was less guarded than he would normally be. But we must consider the other possibility, that the film was a careful attempt to control and solidify the Kubrick image: we are shown just enough of the control to be humbled by the director's skill, and just enough of a human side to warm to Kubrick as a personality.

In *Making of The Shining*, Kubrick spars with Shelley Duvall, the director growing increasingly frustrated by the actress's complaints and apparent inability to follow simple instruction.[39] By contrast, he is shown working amicably on the set with Jack Nicholson, composing the shots for one scene on an ad hoc basis. The viewer is brought into Kubrick's home, shown sitting around a table with his mother and Nicholson discussing the various colors relating to different drafts of the script, a scene that simultaneously suggests that the script is being repeatedly rewritten.[40]

Is this constant issuing of new script pages a simple case of script changes, or an acute example of Kubrick's ongoing and absolute control over the script itself, even over the entire production? Similarly his desire to visually compose scenes in the moment, such as when Nicholson's character is locked in a storage closet, suggests perhaps a director who is so thoroughly prepared that he is able to consider the alternatives in an instant. How does this sit with most received knowledge of Kubrick's methods, which suggests he is a harsh taskmaster prepared to do fifty takes or more of a scene in order to get a shot right? There is a deliberate contrast in our understanding of Kubrick's methodologies in these juxtaposed sequences, leaving the viewer without a solid definition of Kubrick's directing process. Biographer John Baxter claims that Kubrick provided the final cut on his daughter's film, suggesting that he carefully selected the images of himself for public observation.[41] Presumably footage that did not support the image he wished to be seen was left on the cutting room floor.

Making of The Shining and the small number of authorized Kubrick interviews then attempted to reconcile the few known facts with the public image of Kubrick the enigma. In other words, it is the lack of knowledge about Kubrick that seems to have inspired descriptions like "recluse." The term becomes a shorthand explanation for Kubrick, as exemplified in a montage of various magazine and newspaper clippings at the opening of Jan Harlan's *Stanley Kubrick: A Life in Pictures* documentary. Kubrick's daughter Anya argues: "Recluse is a word that gets thrown at him in practically every article, and as far as I can work out, 'recluse' must be defined as someone who doesn't talk to journalists."[42]

In the early twenty-first century, the cinephiles among us read and write in-depth analysis of even the most mundane and disposable of films. The popularity of home cinema means the ability to view and re-view films; the development of DVD means endless extra features, such as alternate edits of films, deleted scenes, production stills, commentary audio tracks from critics, "making of" featurettes, and the like. There has been criticism amongst Kubrick's fans for the lack of additional representation of his work on the format. During the 1990s, Kubrick chose not to release supplemental features or audio commentaries for the laserdisc issues of his films,[43] and even now Kubrick's earliest films (which he allegedly suppressed from public view) are conspicuous in their absence.[44] His reluctance to discuss his work in more detail, as well as his evident desire to maintain his personal privacy, resulted in the inaccessibility of archival materials. According to Jan Harlan, Kubrick personally supervised the destruction of the outtakes from his films (with the exception of the material from *Eyes Wide Shut*, which will not be released) during the mid–1990s. Harlan added: "Unless some bright spark at the lab or archive duped them before that, they're all gone."[45]

Existing evidence supports the idea of Kubrick's exacting control over his body of work, almost treating each final cut of the film like a final painting, a masterpiece in its own right. We know from contemporary accounts that editing decisions were often made between the previews and first runs of some of his films, even during the run themselves. *2001* was shorn of approximately twenty minutes of material during its opening weeks, for example.[46] Historians and theorists are denied the opportunity to analyze the various footage captured for given films and thus infer something about Kubrick's choices for his final cuts. Instead we can only view what he wanted us to view — the final draft. His attempt at control, exhibited in the "authorized" interviews, had extended to his body of work as well. But like any effort to exert control, it was met with challenges.

Defamation

In August 1998, the English magazine *Punch* published an article in which it employed the services and opinion of a professional psychologist who claimed that Stanley Kubrick was clinically insane. While many bizarre and unfounded stories had circulated concerning Kubrick for years, this marked a change in the Kubrick mythology, directly casting doubts on Kubrick's mental state. In an unprecedented move, Kubrick took *Punch* to court for libel. The exact reasons for the legal action were given as follows:

> The British satirical magazine *Punch* has vowed to defend itself against a libel suit filed by Stanley Kubrick.... The article remarked, "There's a thin line between being an artistic perfectionist and being a barking loon." James Steen, editor of *Punch*, told the London *Independent* on Sunday: "The lawsuit is just laughable, and I'm surprised it started in the first place." The newspaper also quoted a magazine insider as saying, "*Punch* is not *The Lancet* the medical journal. We're not saying he's clinically insane. What it means is he's a well-meaning eccentric."[47]

The *Punch* article moves beyond acceptable boundaries of speculation for Kubrick into the realm of deliberate provocation. It is only when Kubrick's sanity is questioned that he finally speaks out.

Warner Brothers executive Rick Senat was a frequent advisor to the Kubricks and opted to clarify details of the *Punch* case in June 1999.[48] As the proceedings were private, we are dependent on the limited reporting by Senat to reveal the workings of the case. According to his article, the offending phrase printed by *Punch* was: "We're hearing stories that suggest Kubrick is even more insane than psychiatrists have led us to believe." Senat also noted *Punch* filed a defense stating Kubrick: "was autocratic, eccentric and difficult to work with. It based this defense on a hundred or so stories from a variety of newspaper articles and poorly researched books."[49] On March 4, 1999, Kubrick appealed to have the case struck out and "*Punch*'s defenses of justification and fair comment were struck out. Costs were awarded against *Punch*...." Despite the verdict of the courts: "To this day the journalists at *Punch* have treated the whole affair as a trifling matter driven by lawyers, but never once apologized for grossly offensive remarks. On the contrary, in the first issue of *Punch* after Kubrick's death, it misleadingly suggested that it had a defense which would have been heard later this year, failing to mention that its defense had been struck out."[50] Press reports at the time centered on the possible public appearance of Stanley Kubrick. In its obituary, *The Scotsman* claimed "Kubrick's death comes before he was due to make his first public appearance in decades at the High Court in London where he was pursuing a libel action against *Punch* magazine."[51] The idea of the "recluse" entering into the public sphere captured the imagination of journalists, who had so often been denied access to the man himself.

During the trial itself just three weeks earlier, many of the newspapers were already providing obituary-like career summaries in lengthy articles partially concerned with the trial. *The*

Sunday Times dubbed him "a legendary recluse who has not given an interview for more than 25 years," which was very definitely an error.[52] Kubrick had conducted interviews after each and every one of his films including *Full Metal Jacket* in 1987, twelve years before his death. According to his daughter Katharina: "In May, after Stanley died, *Punch* wrote that he went into the garden and shot some picknickers and then gave the picknickers loads of money that he just happened to have around his person so they wouldn't say anything."[53]

Eyes Wide Open

A key turning point in discussions of the "real man" is not Stanley Kubrick's death and the release of *Eyes Wide Shut*, but the publication of a short non-fiction work by Frederic Raphael, the screenwriter of Kubrick's final film, entitled *Eyes Wide Open*.[54] *Eyes Wide Open* recounts Raphael's version of his collaboration with Kubrick; the released book provoked vitriol from many members of the film community.[55] Its form is a peculiar blend of recalled conversations in the style of a film script, juxtaposed with apparent diary entries and prose reminiscence. Some have taken it as a revealing look at the director. Others believe it is a spiteful, warped picture of Kubrick, the author seemingly complaining about the prolonged late-night phone calls and Kubrick's extreme paranoia over Raphael's contract. Kubrick refuses to tell Raphael the name of the source material for the novella on which the film script is to be written (even though Raphael retrospectively claims he recognizes it).[56] His contract stipulates that Raphael must not work on any other writing duties while employed on the film, even down to simple book reviews, and he reacts negatively to Raphael's passing on a copy of his script to his agent for safekeeping before showing it to Kubrick.

That the Kubrick estate should have been so upset by the book and pushed for its withdrawal is interesting. *Eyes Wide Open* was, from the tone of the text, in preparation while Kubrick was still alive; the last two pages of the book read like a rushed update on progress in order to get the book to publication as soon as possible following Kubrick's death, with only the last paragraph his demise. Despite a long-held policy that refrained from commenting on speculations and rumors surrounding Stanley Kubrick, the Kubrick family chose to speak out to the press on publication of the book.

In a statement on her official Web site at the time, Kubrick's widow Christiane rebuked the entirety of Raphael's text in the following statement:

> In violation of that trust and in breach of what would be regarded by many as a normal professional duty of confidence, Mr. Raphael announced the publication of his memoirs within days of Stanley's death.... The timing of the publication of the book was clearly intended to take advantage of the publicity build up immediately prior to the opening of the film *Eyes Wide Shut*.
>
> We believe that Mr. Raphael ... has in fact denigrated Stanley and unjustly caused pain to those who knew him well.
>
> Insofar as this family is concerned, Mr. Raphael's analysis of Stanley's personality bears no relation to the man we knew and loved so well.[57]

When Kubrick died, he in many ways remained a mystery. His survivors clearly did not want Raphael's depiction, coming so soon after his death, to crystallize into the "truth" behind that mystery.

Alexander Walker, a film critic for *The Evening Standard* who had been collaborating with Kubrick on a biography before his death, became one of the first to attack Raphael's tome.[58] Walker likened Raphael's book to a love story, but one of unrequited love; he finds fault with Raphael's inadequate knowledge of French (a knowledge which Raphael boasts of possessing) and his over-analysis of Kubrick's communications. In one paragraph, Walker states:

This is a sad little book, jam-packed with lapidary phrases, but devoted so frequently to embittered stone throwing. What began as a chance to serve genius—better than diving in to that moat in Zenda, eh, Fred? Degenerates into a vulgar dick-measuring contest: show me your genius and I'll show you mine. Only Kubrick won't play. He keeps his zipped up. "I have the whore's consolation," Raphael notes proudly, "whatever I am, he chose me."

Even that may be more curse than favour.

A dim consciousness of this appears: "Pray God my epitaph won't be, 'He worked with Stanley Kubrick. Once.'" But the harm is done.[59]

Harmful or not, Raphael's book was the first key text to emerge after Kubrick's death.

In the weeks and months immediately following Kubrick's death (in particular the interviews with Jan Harlan and Christiane Kubrick in *The Daily Mail*[60] and *Sight and Sound*[61]), the estate raised major objections to Raphael's work. Close reading of the Kubrick estate's *apologias* and Raphael's tome suggests an attempt was made to discredit the screenwriter. But discrepancies emerge between what Raphael is alleged to have said and the actual text of his manuscript. At times Raphael has been misrepresented in reports, even if only in minor ways. For example, much has been made of Raphael's apparent allegation that Kubrick was anti–Semitic. However, *Eyes Wide Open* does not make that direct charge, and it seems that Raphael's thoughts on that subject were exaggerated by a *New York Post* article published days before the release of his book.[62] Regardless, it was perhaps Raphael's own newspaper column and other related publicity that became the source of more ire than the actual contents of his *Eyes Wide Open*.

When asked by Nick James what Kubrick biographies were the most unreliable, Christiane Kubrick named Raphael without further elucidation on the matter.[63] In an interview with *The Mail on Sunday* she details clearly the reasons she finds the book "reprehensible."[64] As her Web site affirms, the family remains outraged that Raphael was "pitching it to publishers not long after Stanley died." She also suggests that Raphael's work incorrectly portrays the family home: "He describes Kubrick as a 'scruffy little man,' and our two rather elegant tiled guest lavatories as a 'row of urinals.'"[65]

In *Eyes Wide Open*, Raphael actually describes the toilet facilities as follows:

I said, "I wouldn't mind a pee myself."

He led me along corridors and down steps and around corners and into the kind of facility you would expect to find in a clubhouse. There were two separate cubicles side by side. As he went to leave, I said, "How do I find my way back?"

"Stick to the left-hand wall," he said, "You'll get back finally."

The house ... It seemed nothing like a *home* whatever. It was a vast shell for the shrewd snail who found protection in it.[66]

While the description of the facilities as urinals doesn't appear in the actual text of the book, the passage itself could well be read as cruel. Elsewhere he describes Kubrick as "vain and self-effacing" and as having blue overalls and frail white hands,[67] both comments being as potentially demeaning as the depiction of a "scruffy little man."

In his original *New York Times* article, Raphael's tone is even more insulting: "He was wearing blue overalls with black buttons, he might have been a minor employee of the French railways. He was a smallish, rounded man.... His hands were curiously delicate and white."[68] Raphael also adds the following anecdote:

Kubrick said, "Do you like New Zealand wine?"

He was already opening a bottle. Again, I was aware of his delicate white hands. As he strained at the cork, I remembered Billy Wilder's doing the same thing and saying, "Forty five years of masturbation, and I still don't have a muscle in my hand."

It should be a witty story, but—in the context of Raphael's article—it seems more like a jibe at Kubrick and his perceived shortcomings.

EYES
WIDE
OPEN

A Memoir of Stanley Kubrick

Frederic Raphael

Award-winning screenwriter of *Eyes Wide Shut*

The cover of Frederic Raphael's 1999 book *Eyes Wide Open.*

Raphael's newspaper article also reveals the source of the "urinal" comment, in which he says:

> [Kubrick] led me along corridors and down steps and around corners and into the kind of facility you would expect to find in a clubhouse. There were two cubicles side by side and a row of urinals. As he went to leave, I said, "How do I get back?"
> "Stick to the left-hand wall," he said. "And keep coming."
> It seemed nothing like a home whatever. It was a vast shell for the shrewd snail who found protection in it. Something about Kubrick's house had the allure of Bluebeard's castle. One did not know, or care to guess, how many screenwriters had died and been buried in its recesses.[69]

In death Kubrick has no control over Raphael or approval over these comments, and so Raphael is free to write as he pleases. That the Kubrick estate conflated what he wrote in his newspaper article and in *Eyes Wide Open* may very well be a minor point, but it might also suggest that negativity towards the article led to Raphael's slightly softer tone in the book.

At first glance, it is possible to argue that Christiane Kubrick and Jan Harlan embarked on a series of interviews after Kubrick's death (which continue to the present) in order to correct the myths of the past and to assert their own impressions, but closer examination shows us that Christiane had been battling the myths for more than 30 years by the time of her husband's death. In a 1973 interview, she said: "Recently the local paper came to see me. It was to do with a fund-raising scheme to help the deaf. Imagine what I felt next day when I saw a headline which said: 'My Husband Is Not A Beast, says Mrs. Kubrick.' It was so funny. Stanley is so gentle, such a shy and sensitive person."[70]

The same article sets up the role that Christiane will play as the guardian of the Kubrick image: "Stanley Kubrick has found a way of protecting himself against intrusion. Christiane is still vulnerable and can be hurt by clumsy nudgings about her German background and worse, the raw curiosity and preconceived ideas about her husband. But, perhaps unconsciously, she has set herself up as his protector."[71] In the aftermath of Kubrick's death and Raphael's writings, the estate's role of protecting Kubrick forged ahead in an active manner very different than in 1973, and their task was made more difficult by other, even more questionable publications.

Imposters: Possessing the Unknown

In 2004, *The Guardian* newspaper printed an investigative report by Kubrick's former assistant Anthony Frewin about Stanley Kubrick's purported final interview.[72] The interview under scrutiny was credited to journalist Adrian Rigelsford, and it was supposedly conducted on the set of *Eyes Wide Shut*. Publication came in the *TV Times* U.K. television listings magazine just a few months after the publication of Raphael's book.[73] *The Guardian* piece revealed a tangled web of intrigue, at the center of which was the strongly supported belief that the interview was a work of fiction and deception; *The Guardian* journalist had spent some months following up the article and investigating Rigelsford in a bid to discredit him.[74]

According to the *Guardian* article, dates and names were verified with the Kubrick estate, but in fact Kubrick had not yet entered into the publicity campaign for *Eyes Wide Shut*. At the time of his death, he had given no interviews for the film.[75] The final conclusion was that Rigelsford had concocted the entire interview from his imagination. Indeed, Kubrick as a rule didn't give interviews during the production process. Does the Rigelsford interview content even sound like Kubrick compared to other authentic interviews? Should we even care, given its apparent fiction?

Rigelsford has received much praise for his research, earning a reputation and certain respect for his encyclopedic knowledge of British film and television, but questions had been

raised regarding the authenticity of a number of his interviews even prior to the Kubrick deba-
cle. *Doctor Who* fans and scholars alike have questioned his involvement in the aborted 30th
anniversary story *The Dark Dimension* (1993),[76] as well as in an article claiming to carry original *Doctor Who* star William Hartnell's last-ever interview. Rigelsford's connection to controversy was compounded in 2004 when he received an 18-month prison term for the theft of over
40,000 photographs from a photo archive in London.[77]

Raphael's texts played with the popular perceptions of Kubrick's image, an image that did
not meet with the family's approval; at the same time, Raphael did certainly know and work
with Kubrick. By contrast, Rigelsford's project was a complete fraud, developed out of the
mythologies that the press had created about Kubrick. The wholly fictitious interview was a
bold attempt at possessing and shaping Kubrick's identity. After Kubrick's death, Rigelsford
apparently believed he was free to offer the creation to the public.

Perhaps Rigelsford was emboldened by the fact that he was not the first person to create a
faux–Kubrick. For at least ten years during the 1980s and 1990s, con man and (apparently)
reformed alcoholic Alan Conway assumed Kubrick's identity in public. Film industry profes-
sionals, rent boys, and a string of other unsuspecting victims were conned out of thousands of
pounds, including a number of men who engaged with Conway in a string of sexual liaisons.
Each of them believed he *was* Kubrick, even though he was a man who bore no physical resemblance to the filmmaker. The con was only possible because Kubrick had been so rarely seen in
public, and so few photographs circulated in the public sphere. Perhaps it is indicative of the
shallow nature of the entertainment business that the name alone was enough to convince people that they were in the presence of the "real" Kubrick.

Who was this man? Conway was a Londoner, complete with an undisguised English speaking voice, as opposed to Kubrick's Brooklyn accent. Physically the two could not have been more
different. Though they were approximately the same age, Conway was clean-shaven, whereas
Kubrick sported a black beard during the time of Conway's scam. It was only following a run
in with an American theatre critic that the fraudulent Kubrick was exposed (though unnamed),
following confirmation from the Kubrick estate that they had already received several reports
about him.[78] Newspapers and magazines repeated the rhetoric of Kubrickian anonymity and
reclusiveness, and certainly Kubrick's lack of visual recognition left the name open to abuse.
Conway would eventually sell his story to several newspapers, confessing his deception.[79] By
the mid–1990s, he was outed on a BBC television program,[80] still attempting to convince minor
celebrities he was Stanley Kubrick.[81]

Why did both Rigelsford and Conway fraudulently attempt to control Kubrick's identity?
What was there to gain from pretending to interview a film director, or pretending to be him?
Journalist Andrew Anthony has written on the need to have a "real" Kubrick by claiming:
"Celebrity abhors a vacuum. If Kubrick did not want to exist in public, then somebody had to
invent him."[82] Both men tapped into the cult of the film director, a phenomenon that extends
the praise, fame and recognition usually reserved for actors and rock stars to the filmmaker,
bringing acclaim to themselves by association with the name of Stanley Kubrick. As John
Malkovich has suggested: "Like many, Conway would have wished to be other than what he
actually was.... Conway wasn't mentally ill, he was just too ordinary for his dreams."[83]

Save for the *Punch* magazine incident, Kubrick generally refused to comment on the various
rumors about him. Conflicting anecdotes circulated, with Kubrick avoiding them. According to
Jan Harlan, Kubrick and his advisors regularly debated about responding to the myths and their
inventors, with Kubrick opting for silence. Hence, friends took it upon themselves to involve *Vanity Fair* in disclosing the truth about Alan Conway. Exposing the con hardly made it disappear, however.

Curiously, Alan Conway has become far better known after Kubrick's death. His story has twice been turned into films, forever granting Conway the fame he desperately sought. The first was Nigel Algar's 1999 short documentary *The Man Who Would Be Kubrick,* in which Conway himself tells the viewer how he came to impersonate the director.[84] Later, a dramatized account of Conway's story became the basis for the little-seen *Colour Me Kubrick* (2004). Directed by Kubrick's longtime collaborator Brian W. Cook and from a script by former Kubrick assistant Anthony Frewin, the film stars John Malkovich as the drunken homosexual Conway, a serial predator whose fiction is brought back to reality when he is tricked over the names of the films he is supposed to have directed.

The Man Who Would Be Kubrick shows a rather quiet, unassuming individual seemingly oblivious to the distress he has caused, even going so far as to suggest he could play Kubrick in a film about the director's life. But in *Colour Me Kubrick,* Malkovich and Cook have given Conway a series of extravagant and garish outfits, more in keeping with the invention of a camp, homosexual predator than with the actual Conway. Cook's film attempts to correct the mistakes of the past, but in the process changes Conway's identity much as Conway affected Kubrick's reputation with his own identity theft. It is as if those who had to be silent during Kubrick's life feel able, even obliged, after his death to be the protectors of his name and image.

The Stanley Kubrick Archive

Since Kubrick's death, the public has become increasingly aware that he maintained a vast personal archive of papers and ephemera collected throughout his lifetime. Elements of it have been released to the public via a series of publications and a touring exhibition.[85] Plans also exist to make the entire Kubrick archive available as an academic resource for film scholars: "The Archives will be secured in a new purpose-built Archives and Special Collections Centre on the campus of London College of Communication."[86]

That the archival material is being released to the public is somewhat in conflict with the private image we have inherited of Kubrick during his own lifetime. Is Kubrick's image changing, and is he moving from the unknown into the known? Or is this an attempt to control the Kubrick image in a manner similar, but far more proactive, than Kubrick attempted in his own lifetime through the "authorized" interviews and the like? Perhaps this is even an attempt to fend off the Raphaels, the Rigelsfords, and the Conways, an attempt to offer the "truth," even if only a controlled truth given the careful selection of materials released to the public.

As Nick James told Christiane and Anya Kubrick in 1999, "Your

John Malkovich as Alan Conway in Brian W. Cook's *Colour Me Kubrick* (2005).

problem now is how to adjust the myth before it sets in concrete," to which Anya responded, "Possibly we're not going to be able to adjust it all that much."[87] Christiane — who has suggested that Kubrick didn't specifically indicate that he wanted the archive released — also told James that she was aware that the family could be stymied in its efforts because the family might be considered "prejudiced."[88]

Jan Harlan has also admitted that Kubrick had never stated that he wanted his archive to be made public, and agrees that the archive's release would probably not have happened during Kubrick's lifetime. But he also adds that Kubrick never directly stated that these materials remain private, a point underscored by the fact that Kubrick did destroy items (such as film outtakes) that he specifically wanted kept from public view.[89] Indeed, perhaps there is something almost inevitable in the archive being made accessible, for it seems that Kubrick was meticulously cataloguing it during his lifetime for some purpose.

In 1997, journalist Nicholas Wapshott wrote: "[Kubrick's] proclivity to stash away favorite props from movies and his belief that he is a master film-maker ensure that there is an extensive archive of material at his home in Childwick Bury. When that is eventually opened, we may get close to understanding the tangled brain which brought to life HAL, the Droogs and Jack Torrance."[90] Some two years before Kubrick's death, we have a press account speaking of the archive being "eventually opened." Perhaps Kubrick *was* cataloguing it for future view, carefully selecting what would and would not be seen. But even if so, the question remains as to why he did not clearly indicate these intentions.

Journalist Jon Ronson picked up on stories about the Kubrick archive in a 2004 article for *The Guardian* in which his recounts his regular visits to the Kubrick estate once a month from the time of his first trip in 2001.[91] He likened his experience to being "in the middle of an estate full of boxes," with multiple electric gates barring entrance to the property. Kubrick's organization of his work and his domestic setting are by implication paralleling Kubrick's persona and mindset, like Russian dolls from which the layers must be stripped in order to reveal something else inside.[92] Materials relating to each film are extensively archived; for example, one entire room is devoted to research for Kubrick's unfulfilled *Napoleon* project, sporting a cabinet full of 25,000 library cards containing information. Ronson also described hundreds and hundreds of boxes devoted to research for *Eyes Wide Shut*.

But at least some of this material will never be made available. According to Jan Harlan, Kubrick's first feature, *Fear and Desire*, will not be legitimately issued on DVD or other formats because of Kubrick's express wishes that it should not be. When asked, Harlan has said that he would be happy to see it released, but that it would be against the wishes of his former friend and employer.[93] In other words, though Kubrick did not specifically suggest what (if any) materials he wanted made public, he did specifically prohibit the release of particular items. Kubrick continues to exert control even after his death; at the same time, the estate exerts its own control in matters Kubrick did not dictate. The archive is putting Kubrick on public display, but in an expurgated manner.[94] Its existence also continues Kubrick's tradition of authorizing projects endorsed for public view, which implicitly makes a comment on unauthorized projects that exist outside the archive.

Regardless, the archive is gradually making its way into the public sphere through a number of different projects. Jan Harlan's documentary *Stanley Kubrick: A Life in Pictures* (2001) provides a 142-minute overview of Kubrick's work, aided by the use of photographs from the Kubrick family and even brief footage from what years earlier would have seemed unimaginable: Kubrick's home movies. Christiane Kubrick's book of the same name, published by Bulfinch Press in 2001, offered dozens of previously-unpublished photos of Kubrick from his childhood to the end of his life. Working with Alison Castle and Taschen, the Kubrick estate has also released a major coffee-table book appropriately titled *The Stanley Kubrick Archive*. Printed in

2005, the weighty tome features page after page of high-quality reproductions of previously unpublished photographs and ephemera from the archive. Accompanying the book is a CD featuring a lengthy audio interview with Kubrick, again offering the previously-unthinkable: audio of the director's voice, discussing his life and career. These releases seemingly pave the way for an announced Taschen book on Kubrick's *Napoleon,*[95] as well as the papers at the London College of Communication.

A portrait of Kubrick included with the presskit for *Eyes Wide Shut* (1999).

The archive is also alive and growing. Since the death of Kubrick, there have been several film projects that can (or at least seek to) claim a Kubrickian authorship. Most famously, Steven Spielberg's *A.I.: Artificial Intelligence* (2001) had originally been a Kubrick project. Even in newspaper articles of the 1990s, the film was still being discussed as Kubrick's film before his notes were passed on to Spielberg.[96] That Spielberg's *A.I.* had Jan Harlan serving as executive producer created yet another important link to Kubrick's estate and archive.

By the end of 2006, a trio of Kubrick's other unproduced film projects were announced as in development: (1) *The Down Slope*, a script written with American Civil War historian Shelby Foote; (2) *God Fearing Man*, a script by Kubrick about a priest who became the biggest bank robber in America, and (3) *Lunatic at Large*, from an 80-page original treatment for Kubrick by Jim Thompson.[97] All three projects originate in texts from the 1950s and are now being put into production, creating the paradox of new Kubrick films without Kubrick at the helm. Again the question of ownership comes to the fore. Producer Philip Hobbs[98] does make the assertion: "I remember Stanley talking about *Lunatic....* He was always saying he wished he knew where it was because it was such a great idea."[99] But considering the precision and time Kubrick spent planning his projects, it seems probable that the projects had been abandoned intentionally.

What we shall learn from Kubrick works revisited and completed some fifty years after their abandonment remains to be seen. Perhaps they will reveal more about the filmmaker, adding new insight to an increasing battery of knowledge that stems from the Stanley Kubrick Archive and other unauthorized sources. Or perhaps they are yet other imperfect pieces in a puzzle that can never be completed. Maybe they are even new creations of a vibrant and growing archive that attempts to own and display the real Kubrick before more Raphaels or Conways have the opportunity to do the same, protecting and serving a man who may or may not have desired to take on these tasks himself.

Conclusions

Kubrick has in death become publicly exposed in a way that in life he never allowed. Discussion of the contradictions between Kubrick's closed possession of everything about him and the posthumous release of so much information poses some difficulties. For example, more than twenty unofficial books on Kubrick and various components of his work have appeared since the director's death in 1999, and bootleg DVDs of *Fear and Desire* and the short films from Kubrick's fledgling moments are regularly traded between fans and admirers. In addition the Kubrick estate has authorized several other pieces, including Harlan's documentary, the traveling exhibition, Castle's *The Stanley Kubrick Archive*, a book of Kubrick's own photography, and another compiling the scientific interviews conducted for *2001*. In an interview, Jan Harlan reiterated that it is unlikely that so much would be available were Kubrick still alive.[100]

Ultimately we must ask ourselves once again, just who really does own Kubrick's image? Is it Kubrick, whose dictates on issues like *Fear and Desire* continue to be followed even after his death? Is it the estate managers, with their intimate knowledge of Kubrick in life and in-depth awareness of the unexpurgated contents of his archive? Is it the critics and historians who have amassed reams of material in an investigation of the man and his methods, and who are perhaps less resolute against voices like Raphael's?

Perhaps in the end the real Kubrick will never be known, and perhaps the owner of the unknown — his image — are the film buffs, the fans, and the collectors. Those persons who track every word printed on Kubrick, and who are thus aware of every resulting contradiction. The myth and legend loom so large after so many years that any new information might in some way be new disinformation. The Kubrick image remains a paradox.

Part IV Notes

1. Though there is some dispute concerning degrees of hybridity in relation to what might be considered "cyborgian," there is general consensus that a cyborg is a hybridization of mechanic and organic; a cybernetic organism is "a mixture of technology and biology," Chela Sandoval, from "New Sciences" in *The Cyborg Handbook*, ed. C.H. Gray (New York: Routledge, 1995). In a strict sense, then, David is an automaton. Though we can reverse N. Katherine Hayles's argument that simply by the "extimate" nature of subjectivity, we are all cyborgs, and say that since the automaton David has so properly integrated human characteristics, he is also a cyborg.

2. According to *The Making of 2001: A Space Odyssey*, Stephanie Schwam (ed.).

3. N. Katherine Hayles, *How We Became Posthuman: Virtual Bodies in Cybernetics, Literature, and Informatics* (Chicago: University of Chicago Press, 1999) 84.

4. Alenka Zupančič, *Ethics of the Real: Kant, Lacan* (London: Verso, 2000) viii.

5. Louis Althusser. "Ideology and Ideological State Apparatuses (Notes towards an Investigation)," *Mapping Ideology*, ed. Slavoj Žižek (London: Verso, 1994).

6. Steven Spielberg, *AI*.

7. Dr. Poole, in an interview.

8. The emphasis is added.

9. Rene Descartes, *Meditations on First Philosophy*, ed. and trans. John Cottingham (United Kingdom: Cambridge University Press, 1996) 19.

10. Take, for example, Ridley Scott's *Blade Runner* (based on the Philip K. Dick novel, *Do Androids Dream of Electric Sheep*), in which Pris, an android or "replicant," directly quotes Descartes. Moreover, the main character's name, Deckard, is a homophone of the American pronunciation of "Descartes."

11. Randy Rasmussen, *Stanley Kubrick: Seven Films Analyzed* (Jefferson, N.C.: McFarland & Company, 2001) 79.

12. Georg Seesslen, S*teven Spielberg und seine Filme* (Marburg: Schüren Presseverlag, 2001) 168. "Der Mensch selber ist ein maschinelles Wesen geworden...." This and all subsequent translations are the author's.

13. Gene D. Phillips and Rodney Hill, *The Encyclopedia of Stanley Kubrick: From Day of the Fight to Eyes Wide Shut* (New York: Facts on File, Inc. 2002) 139.

14. Where he becomes moralistic is in his commentary on how we put our tools to use: for killing. The ape-men use bones to beat each other to death as well as to kill other animals. Similarly, when the shot of the bone-as-tool flying through the air shifts to a shot of a satellite flying through space, the implications are that the use of the tool has not changed drastically, as the satellite we initially see is a model of one that carries nuclear weapons.

15. There is, of course, also more at work here. There is the suggestion that, while the computer is able to integrate human characteristics, the human must forgo the element of passion and emotion in order to evolve, and that this could effectively make the human obsolete, if not simply "non-human." Thus, the suggestion is that, along the chain of evolution, humans will be replaced by intelligent machines. This idea is also explicitly framed at the end of *A.I.* where an advanced form of David's descendants has evolved and humans are extinct.

16. Note this especially here, the first introduction of the cyborg (into a human environment), because this is what the cyborgs often do in these narratives: they return to kill. And if they do not literally return to kill, they always return to metaphorically kill by threatening the defining borders of *human* and *non-human*. Additionally, as the cyborg in this narrative will hold the symbolic position of the son, and being that it is irrefutably an oedipal narrative, the utterance is all the more suggestive: Oedipus is only able to become king and obtain Jocasta as a result of having killed his father, Laius. Thus David must do away with the father, which is in accord with the conditions of his fantasy (if we read the final scene as a fantasy) at the end of the film.

17. Seesslen calls the scene in which Bowman disengages HAL's memory "one of the most horrific and moving scenes in film history" (171). See Georg Seesslen and Fernand Jung, *Stanley Kubrick und seine Filme* (Marburg: Schüren Presseverlag, 1999).

18. In both *The Terminator* and *Blade Runner*, there is a play on the abject *I* and the abject *eye*. In Cameron's film, there is the scene where the Terminator stands at the sink in his hotel room, cuts away the flesh around the eye-socket and expels the artificial human-looking eye. In *Blade Runner*, though, the eye is present in various capacities throughout the film and always alludes to what it means to be alive, what it is to be human, to be able to perceive the world(s) around you. From the opposite end, the gaze of the eye is also a proof to the external world that you are alive. Here we have an explicit visualization of the proverbial window to the soul: The test designed to identify Replicants, the Voigt-Kampff test, is performed using an apparatus that also has a red camera eye, which looks into the eye of the test subject. It measures emotional response through dilation of the iris and pupil. There are various other framings of the eye, including metaphoric

245

ones such as the sun as eye. In its abject capacity, the eye appears in the scene illustrating its mass manufacture for the Tyrell Corporation. Disembodied eyes fill this scene. When questioning the eye engineer, one of the Replicants takes a handful of eyes and places them on the head and shoulders of the engineer. When the engineer realizes that his visitors are Replicants, he says to the Batty (Rutger Hauer) character, "You, Nexus 6. I designed your eyes." To which Batty responds, "If only you could see what I've seen with your eyes." Aside from the cleverness of the response, it is also a commentary on artificial production and genuine experience (authenticity) at the location of the artificial. The irony of this scene is that the eye/I returns in the form of these two Replicants, to its place of manufacture to, once again, destroy its maker. Also, there is the scene of Tyrell's death in which Batty kills him by pushing in his eyes: another scene of abjection doubled by abject eyes. Frank Schnelle also points out that "in order to see better, Tyrell, Chew and the snake-maker Abdul Ben-Hanssan — all three designers of artificial life — wear monserous glasses" ["Um (besser) sehen zu koennen, tragen Tyrell, Chew und der Schlangenmacher Abdul Ben-Hanssan — alle drei Designer kuenstlichen Lebens— monstroese Brillengestelle"]. See Frank Schnelle, *Ridley Scott's Blade Runner* (Stuttgart: Verlag Uwe Wiedleroither, 1994) 83.

19. Freud, Sigmund. *Gesammelte Werke*, vol XII (Frankfurt am Main: Fischer Taschenbuch Verlag, 1999) 242. [This and subsequent translations are the author's.]

20. We might also read this bookended story within the story as the phantasmatic space/narrative of the biological family (particularly of Martin) in the film as well: the child in the coma is representative of a shift to phantasmatic space, in which the suspended child veils castration while traversing the fantasy of wholeness, played out with a representative stand-in, David, only to awake from the fantasy in a brutally altered state, physically debilitated — he emerges from the fantasy properly castrated, which is symbolized in the film by his crippled condition. However we choose to read this scene, we know we are due for a dramatic shift in the course of events and the locations within symbolic relations.

21. Freud 248.

22. Julia Kristeva, "Powers of Horror," *The Portable Kristeva*, ed. Kelly Oliver (New York: Columbia University Press, 1997) 232.

23. Barbara Creed, *The Monstrous-Feminine: Film, Feminism, Psychoanalysis* (London: Routledge, 1993) 8.

24. *Ibid.*, 10.

25. Kristeva 232.

26. Seesslen, *Stanley Kubrick und seine Filme* 171.

27. As in as *The Murder of Gonzago* from *Hamlet*: the "secret" knowledge of Claudius's deed is mimetically exposed, and at the same time Hamlet's latent fantasy of killing the king, and thus vacating the position into which he might enter, is represented.

28. Here (with the will) we might draw a thematic loop back to Nietzsche's *Uebermensch* (super-man or higher being), which is present in the narrative via Richard Strauss's musical interpretation of *Also Sprach Zarathustra*.

29. http://www.press.uchicago.edu/Misc/Chicago/borghayl.html

30. Nick Mansfield, *Subjectivity: Theories of the Self from Freud to Haraway* (New York: New York University Press, 2000) 13.

31. *Ibid.*, 11.

32. Hayles, *How We Became Posthuman* 84.

33. *Ibid.*, 4. [The italics are added.]

34. Slavoj Žižek, *On Belief* (London: Routledge, 2001) 44.

35. In his "At Home With the Kubricks" (*Sight and Sound* 9:9 [1999], 12–19), Nick James poses the question, ""Did he try to use his image for his own purposes? After all, the making of cinema is about the making of myth. Supposing you're saddled with this image and there's a way you can turn it around for your own ends— especially the idea that when Kubrick calls, you do what you're told" (16).

36. Most of these are now gathered together in Gene D. Phillips, ed., *Stanley Kubrick Interviews* (Jackson: University Press of Mississippi, 2001).

37. "In the interest of precision, Kubrick customarily asked an interviewer for the opportunity to read the transcript before it was published. He read the text of an interview with pen in hand, making marginal comments along the way." Phillips, "Introduction," *Stanley Kubrick Interviews*, ix.

38. It is tempting to suggest that Kubrick seldom gave interviews; however, there is a surprisingly large body of contemporary interviews and discussions with the director, most of which were conducted in the aftermath of a film release. A comprehensive list is available at http://www.matthewhunt.com/stanleykubrick/interviews.html. Accessed 2 Jan. 2007.

39. Now available on the Warner Bros. DVD of *The Shining*, complete with a commentary by director Vivian Kubrick.

40. The rhetoric on Kubrick frequently suggests that the director was absolute and unmoving in his vision of the film text, There is, however, a substantial body of evidence to suggest his on-set working practices were more open to improvisation and spontaneous inspiration. According to Brian Cook, assistant director on *Barry Lyndon*, *The Shining* and *Eyes Wide Shut*: "His method didn't vary with the films. First of all, he'd write the scene and adapt it according to the actors." *Colour Me Kubrick Press Kit* (New York: Magnolia Pictures, 2007) 9.

41. John Baxter, *Stanley Kubrick: A Biography* (New York: Carroll and Graf, 1997) 318.

42. James 16.

43. According to Leon Vitali, interviewed in 2001, "Stanley just didn't want much of that to be seen. He wanted the films to really speak for themselves. There was the documentary on *The Shining* that was shot by his daughter. Since that had been done for TV, he felt that it would be good to include — that it was good." Quoted in "Leon Vitali Talks Kubrick on DVD," *The Digital Bits*, http://www.thedigitalbits.com/articles/kubrick/vitali interview.html. Accessed 1 Jan. 2007.

44. In response to questions about Kubrick's early films on DVD, Vitali responded: "Well ... *Fear and Desire*, I have to tell you, Stanley withdrew from circulation and he never wanted it to be seen again. The documentaries, however, he didn't mind. He felt indifferent about them, I suppose ... I guess [Warner] could release them. Certainly, there are no plans right now to do so." Quoted in "Leon Vitali Talks Kubrick on DVD."

45. Jan Harlan, personal interview 2 Mar. 2006.

46. Alexander Walker, *Stanley Kubrick Directs* (London: Davis-Poynter, 1972) 272; Phillips 77; "Shine On ... and Out," *Monthly Film Bulletin* 47 (1980) 562.

47. "Kubrick Sues British Satire Mag Punch," *Movie & TV News @ IMDB.com Studio Briefing* 1 Feb. 1999, http://www.imdb.com/news/sb/1999–02–01#film7. Accessed 1 Mar. 2007.

48. Rick Senat, "Kubrick's KO Punch," *The Times* 8 June 1999.

49. Senat's comments bring up the issue that much of the newspaper reporting on Kubrick is widely inaccurate and of dubious quality. This essay uses such pieces as source material because it is concerned with the widely accepted image of Kubrick, and in a large part this is received through stories in newspapers and the like, inaccurate or not.

50. Senat.

51. Brian Pendreigh and Conal Urquhart, "Stanley Kubrick, The Eccentric and Genius," *The Scotsman* 8 Mar. 1999: 3.

52. "A Recluse Flirts with the Spotlight," *The Sunday Times* 14 Feb. 1999.

53. Quoted in James 15.

54. Frederic Raphael, *Eyes Wide Open: A Memoir of Stanley Kubrick and Eyes Wide Shut* (London: Orion Media, 1999). To call *Eyes Wide Open* a work of non-fiction is heretical in the eyes of some Kubrick followers. Reviews of the book at the time of publication were quite scathing, and members of the Kubrick estate have taken the book to task for the author's invention of factual detail, and a twisted view of Kubrick himself. Questions are asked about the author's motivations and taking liberties that are "offensive." The book itself was published in June 1999, just three months after Kubrick's death.

55. Publication of *Eyes Wide Open* was preceded by an abbreviated account in *The New Yorker* magazine (Frederic Raphael, "A Kubrick Odyssey," *The New Yorker* 14 June 1999), which was itself trailed in newspapers around the world. The uproar surrounding the condensed version of Raphael's complaints overshadowed the book's true scope in providing a complete account of working with Kubrick.

56. It seems odd that Raphael could not have deduced the identity of the work in question, particularly considering Raphael's familiarity with Kubrick's other projects. *Eyes Wide Shut* was first posited in the 1970s, and along with the aborted *Napoleon* was referred to on a fairly regular basis in Kubrick interviews.

57. Christiane Kubrick's Web site, http://eyeswideshut.warnerbros.com/ck/ckenglish.htm. Accessed 1 Jan. 2007. The webpage, as of 1 Jan. 2007, had not been updated since 1999 and still carries the declaration "On this website I intend to take the opportunity to confirm the truths about Stanley and correct the inaccuracies."

58. The eventual text was a slight updating on a well-received earlier biography written with Kubrick's cooperation: Walker's *Stanley Kubrick Directs*.

59. Walker, Alexander, "What Was Kubrick Like?," *The Evening Standard* 19 July 1999: 47.

60. Danae Brook, "I Am Sick Of All These Lies About My Husband. They Wounded Me So Much," *The Mail on Sunday* 12 Sept. 1999: 32.

61. James 12–19.

62. Rod Dreher, "Stanley Kubrick, Self-Hating Jew: The Eccentric Director of *Eyes Wide Shut* as Seen Through 'The Eyes Wide Open' of Screenwriter Frederic Raphael," *New York Post* 16 June 1999: 59.

63. James 15.

64. Brook 32.

65. *Ibid.*, 32.

66. Raphael, *Eyes Wide Open* 36.

67. *Ibid.*, 29, 83.

68. Raphael, "A Kubrick Odyssey."

69. *Ibid.*

70. Ann Morrow, "Christiane Kubrick: Flowers and Violent Images," *The Times* 5 Feb. 1973: 10.

71. Morrow 10.

72. Anthony Frewin, "What Stanley Didn't Say," *The Guardian* 20 Nov. 2004: 50.

73. Adrian Rigelsford and Kim Meffen, "Kubrick: The Last Interview," *TV Times* 4 Sept. 1999. The text of the interview was picked up without question by the AP Newsfeed and passed on to a global audience.

74. Journalist Anthony Frewin actually worked as Stanley Kubrick's assistant for many years. He penned a number of articles relating to Kubrick in recent years, many connected with the theme for his screenplay *Colour Me Kubrick*.

75. According to Jan Harlan, Kubrick was preparing himself for a round of interviews on *Eyes Wide Shut*, but had not begun to do so at the time of his death. Critic and Kubrick biographer Alexander Walker had been shown an early edit of the film and published an advance review which itself prompted a series of angry comments from an unnamed Warner executive: Alexander Walker, "A Sex Odyssey," *The Evening Standard* 22 June 1999: 23; "Standard critic's Kubrick scoop leaves the web world wide-eyed," *The Evening Standard* 24 June 1999: 9.

76. Rigelsford wrote the script for the BBC TV project, which was subsequently aborted late in the day. A number of rumors regarding casting and crew and the production process circulate on the Internet, most casting doubts on many of Rigelsford's claims.

77. The story was covered across most of the UK national papers and the BBC news Web site. "Cunning Photo Thief Is Jailed," BBC News, http://news.bbc.co.uk/1/hi/england/cambridgeshire/3839733.stm. Accessed 2 Jan. 2007; "Author faces jail for stealing pictures," *Guardian Unlimited* 22 May 2004, http://books.guardian.co.uk/news/articles/0,,1227220,00.html. Accessed 2 Jan. 2007.

78. Frank Rich, "Stanley, I Presume," *The New York Times* 15 Aug. 1993: 66.

79. Martin Smith, "Alan Conway Conned Showbusiness Into Believing He Was Famous Director Stanley Kubrick.... But It Was All A Fantasy To Support His Lavish Lifestyle," *The Mail on Sunday* 17 Mar. 17, 1996: 52.

80. *The Lying Game: The Great Pretenders*, broadcast 15 May 1997 on BBC1.

81. Additional information on the Conway story: Frank Rich, "As Queer As A Clockwork Orange," *The Guardian* 20 Aug 1993: 18; Anthony Frewin, "Someone's Pretending to Be Me, Kubrick Told Me. You've Got to Track Him Down And Stop Him," *The Mail On Sunday* 19 Dec. 2004: 47–50.

82. Andrew Anthony, "The Counterfeit Kubrick," *Guardian Unlimited* 14 Mar. 1999, http://film.guardian.co.uk/Feature_Story/Observer/0,,30123,00.html. Accessed 2 Mar. 2007.

83. Malkovich, quoted in *Colour Me Kubrick Press Kit* 5.

84. This wasn't merely a story of complaints about a director who taxed the patience of some but of a lothario who was casting doubts on Kubrick's professional life and sexuality. Conway would die himself, just a few months before Kubrick, and prior to the broadcast of *The Man Who Would Be Kubrick*.

85. Full details of the official Stanley Kubrick exhibition, and the schedule of the tour, which at time of writing has played Frankfurt, Berlin, and Melbourne, and is due to go to Zurich and Rome during 2007/8, can be found at *The Authorized Stanley Kubrick Exhibition Website*, http://www.stanleykubrick.de. Accessed 23 Mar. 2007.

86. "Archives of acclaimed director Stanley Kubrick to be housed at University of the Arts London," http://www.arts.ac.uk/kubrick.htm. Accessed 8 Sept. 2006.

87. James 16.

88. Christiane Kubrick once said, "Perhaps [Stanley] would not have approved of what I am doing now ... but I and the entire family are sick of the lies about my

husband which gathered a sort of dark momentum in the last years of his life." Brook 32.

89. Harlan, personal interview.

90. Nicholas Wapshott, "Stanley on a Knife Edge," *The Times*, November 1, 1997. As referenced in Jon Ronson, "Citizen Kubrick." *The Guardian*, Saturday March 27, 2004, 16, Wapshott is misquoted with "The good news is Kubrick is a hoarder.... There is an extensive archive..." etc.

91. Ronson, "Citizen Kubrick" 16.

92. Ronson describes the sheer volume of material: "There are boxes everywhere — shelves of boxes in the stable block, rooms full of boxes in the main house. In the fields, where racehorses once stood and grazed, are half a dozen portable cabins, each packed with boxes. These are the boxes that contain the legendary Kubrick archive." Quoted in "Citizen Kubrick" 16.

93. Harlan also contradicted the widely discussed belief that Kubrick's documentary shorts *Flying Padre* and *Day of the Fight* would be similarly suppressed. He said the documentaries are owned by Warner and will be released on DVD.

94. In a recent newspaper interview conducted with Christiane Kubrick at the family home, we receive further evidence that the archive has been broken up and not everything will be available to the Kubrick scholar: "past the creepy feathery masks for *Eyes Wide Shut*, and into a blood-red library crammed with art books, Thackery, De Sade and the well-thumbed volumes on witchcraft that Stanley Kubrick collected for *The Shining*." James Christo-

pher, "He Never Stopped Worrying, or Learnt to Love the Bomb," *The Times* 19 Oct. 2006 18.

95. Nick Holdsworth, "Kubrick's Plans for *Napoleon* to be Published," *Hollywood Reporter* 25 June 2002: 12. (Despite this 2002 announcement that a book containing the script and other related research materials was imminent, it has not been published as of December 2007.)

96. Sources disagree about when the project switched from Kubrick to Spielberg, but the two are said to have had a working relationship collaborating on ideas for the project for many years. According to Jan Harlan in the production notes on the film's official Web site: "It simply would have disappeared into the archives if Steven Spielberg had not taken it" http://www.warnerbros.co.uk/video/ai/production.html. Accessed 2 Jan., 2007.

97. Ben Hoyle, "Death is no obstacle to Kubrick's career," *The Times* 2 Nov. 2006: 12.

98. Hobbs is not only producer on the forthcoming projects, but is also Kubrick's son-in-law, apparently uncovering the scripts when going through paperwork following Kubrick's death.

99. Hoyle 12. Curiously, this statement would also suggest that Kubrick's archiving and filing practices weren't as rigorous as others such as Ronson have inferred. Speculatively this may purely be because of the vastness of the archival hoard and a move from the United States to the United Kingdom.

100. Harlan, personal interview.

About the Contributors

Charles Bane has lived in numerous places all over the United States, working as a country music disc jockey, an oil refinery demolition specialist, a movie critic, and an eighth-grade English teacher. He earned his doctorate in twentieth century literature and film from Louisiana State University in 2006. He now lives with his wife, Paulette, and his three children, Ericka, Katherine, and Geoffrey, in Conway, Arkansas, and is an assistant professor of film and literature at the University of Central Arkansas.

Marina Burke studied film at University College, Dublin, where she completed a Ph.D. on editing in Soviet fiction and non-fiction film. She has taught film at University College and Dublin City University, and DCU, Dublin, and is currently lecturing at Queen's University, Belfast, where she teaches courses on documentary film, modernism and film, film and sound, and film and the avant-garde. Her most recent publications include contributions to the Routledge *Encyclopedia of the Documentary Film* (2006), *Film and the Avant-Garde* (Rodopi, 2007), and "Towards a Soviet Cinema," *Bianco e nero*, October 2007. She is currently working on a biography of Soviet documentary filmmaker Esfir Shub.

Lindiwe Dovey is the Mellon postdoctoral research fellow in Anglophone and Francophone film at the University of Cambridge, and a fellow of New Hall. She holds a B.A. Honors in English literature and film (V.E.S.) from Harvard, and a Ph.D. in African film and literature from Cambridge. She has published articles on film adaptation, South African film, and on cinema and exile, and is currently completing a book on contemporary African film adaptation of literature. She is founding director of the Cambridge African Film Festival and has made a number of short films.

Eric Eaton received his Ph.D. (1970) in comparative literature from the University of Michigan and taught at the University of Oklahoma from 1971 to 1978. After completing a fourth degree (in computer science), he worked from 1980 to 2000 as a project leader and senior project manager for NASA and IBM. Currently he is a lecturer in the Film Studies Program at Oklahoma and writing a book in aesthetics and general systems theory.

Julian Jason Haladyn is a doctoral student at the University of Western Ontario. He received an M.F.A. in interdisciplinary art at Goddard College and an M.A. in theory, culture, and politics at Trent University; his principal areas of studies are visual arts and film. He has contributed to such publications as *Entertext, Parachute, C Magazine, On Site Review*, and *International Journal of Baudrillard Studies*. He also has essays in forthcoming anthologies on film.

Reynold Humphries is professor of film studies at the University of Lille 3. He recently published *The Hollywood Horror Film, 1931–1941: Madness in a Social Landscape* (Scarecrow Press, 2006) and is currently working on a volume entitled *Hollywood's Blacklists: Politics and Culture in Context*, which will be published in September 2008 by Edinburgh University Press.

Miriam Jordan is a doctoral student at the University of Western Ontario, where her principal areas of studies are visual arts, video and film. She received an M.F.A. in interdisciplinary art from Goddard College. She has contributed to such publications as *Parachute, C Magazine*, and *On Site Review* and also has essays in forthcoming anthologies on film.

Randolph Jordan is a doctoral candidate in the interdisciplinary Ph.D. humanities program at Concordia University in Montreal, Canada. He is currently researching intersections between the theory and practices of film sound design, electroacoustic music, and acoustic ecology in preparation for his dissertation on sound in film. He also teaches at the Mel Hoppenheim School of Cinema at Concordia.

Homay King is assistant professor of film studies in the Department of History of Art at Bryn Mawr College. Her writings have been published in *Camera Obscura, Discourse, Film Quarterly*, and *Qui Parle*. Her essay "The Long Goodbye: Jeff Wall and Film Theory" appeared in *Jeff Wall: Photographs*, the catalogue for a retrospective exhibition at the Museum of Modern Art, Vienna. Her current book, *Lost in Translation: Orientalism, Projection, and the Enigmatic Signifier*, explores images of East Asia across twentieth-century film and visual culture.

Scott Loren holds a Ph.D. in English and American literature from the University of Zurich, Switzerland, an M.A. from the City University of New York, and a B.A. from San Francisco State University. He is a lecturer in English at the University of St. Gallen, Switzerland, where he also works as a research assistant. His past publications and conference papers have been on contemporary film and literature, with a focus on psychology and theories of identity. Forthcoming in 2007 is "Out of the Past: Freedom, Film Noir and the American Dream's Myth of Reinvention," in *American Dreams: Comparative Dialogues in U.S. Studies*, edited by Ricardo Miguez and published by Cambridge Scholars Press.

Hugh S. Manon holds a Ph.D. from the University of Pittsburgh and is an assistant professor in the Screen Studies Program at Oklahoma State University, where he specializes in Lacanian theory and film noir. He has published on *Double Indemnity* and is currently writing a book that links the rise and decline of classic American film noir with the advent of television. He is interested in Lo-Fi aesthetics, and recently led a graduate seminar entitled "Theorizing Punk," employing the theories of Jacques Lacan, Roland Barthes and others to understand cinema's various representations of Punk music and subculture.

Philippe Mather is an assistant professor of media studies at Campion College, University of Regina. He has degrees in film studies from Concordia University, the University of Iowa and the University of Paris III: Sorbonne Nouvelle. His Ph.D. dissertation is entitled "Cognitive Estrangement: Towards a Semiology of Science Fiction Film." His areas of research include science fiction, film music, authorship and genre theories and the works of Stanley Kubrick.

Kate McQuiston is an assistant professor of musicology at the University of Hawaii at Manoa. She is currently writing a book on contemporary film music co-authored with composer Paul Chihara (Silman-James Press). Her principal research concerns musical topics across films, and music in the films of Stanley Kubrick. She earned her Ph.D. in 2005 at Columbia University.

Gary D. Rhodes is a lecturer at Queen's University in Belfast, Northern Ireland. He is the author of such books as *Lugosi* (McFarland, 1997) and *White Zombie: Anatomy of a Horror Film* (McFarland, 2002), and coeditor of *Alma Rubens, Silent Snowbird* (McFarland, 2006). He is also the writer-director of such films as *Fiddlin' Man: The Life and Times of Bob Wills* (1994), *Chair* (2000), and *Banned in Oklahoma* (2004). He is currently researching the connections between early U.S. cinema and Irish-America, as well as pre–World War II film audiences.

Robert J.E. Simpson holds a masters degree in Film and Visual Studies from Queen's University, Belfast. He is currently researching a history of Hammer Films, which will be published in 2008 by Telos. He also serves on the editorial board for the *Journal of Horror Studies*, published by Intellect Ltd.

Phillip Sipiora is professor of English at the University of South Florida, where he has taught twentieth-century literature and film since arriving from the University of Texas at Austin in 1985. He is the author or editor of three books, two dozen scholarly essays, and has lectured nationally and internationally on literature and film. He has lectured twice at the University of Rome and each summer he teaches a course in Italian cinema in Florence, Italy.

Tony Williams is professor and head of film studies, Department of English, Southern Illinois University at Carbondale. He is author of *The Cinema of George A. Romero: Knight of the Living Dead* (Wallflower Press, 2003), *Body and Soul: The Cinematic Vision of Robert Aldrich* (Scarecrow Press, 2004), and coeditor (with Steven Jay Schneider) of *Horror International* (Wayne State University, 2005).

Jarrell D. Wright is pursuing a Ph.D. in English at the University of Pittsburgh, where his principal interests are seventeenth-century poetry and theories of play in both literature and culture. He earned a B.A. in government with high honors from the College of William and Mary in 1989, and a J.D. from the same institution in 1992. His contribution to this volume — which reflects a long-time interest in *The Shining* and in the works of Stanley Kubrick and Stephen King — was occasioned by a 2005 seminar on film adaptation led by Colin MacCabe, to whom he expresses his gratitude.

Index

Numbers in **bold italics** indicate pages with photographs.

253